PERFORMERS TELL THEIR STORIES:
40 Years inside the Arts

TOM DI NARDO

Dear Aidan,

There are lots of adventures here to help feel closer to musicians — so if you decide to play an instrument — practice!!

Tom DiNardo

Jaygayle Music Books
2016

Copyright © 2016, Tom Di Nardo.

All rights reserved. This book or any portion thereof may not be reproduced or used in any manner whatsoever without the express written permission of the publisher except for the use of brief quotations in a book review or scholarly journal.

First Printing: 2016

ISBN-13: 978-1533356628

Jaygayle Music Books
Post Office Box 8144
La Crescenta, CA 91224-0144 U.S.A

www.jaygaylemusic.com

Dedication

*This book is dedicated to the brilliant and dedicated artists
I've had the honor of meeting, whose willingness to reveal themselves
and generously illuminate the mystery of creativity brings us into their
world and provides constant inspiration.*

*Without the enthusiastic encouragement, constant wisdom,
and infinite patience of Jeannie Gayle Pool,
this book would never have become a reality.*

Contents

Illustrations xi

Preface xv

1. SCRIBE, THROUGH THE BACK DOOR 1
   A Freelance Philosophy 1
   Slight Credentials 1
   Scribe At Last 2
   Writing for Vinyl 3
   How to Get a Newspaper Job 5

2. *BULLETIN* DAYS—AND NIGHTS 7
   Newsroom Noise 7
   Freelance Availability 8
   Ragtime, Grazioso, and Grit 12
   Eroticism and Black Mass 13
   Send the Freelancer 14
   Lots of Exposure 17
   Comedienne and Enigma 18

3. INTERVIEWS OUT OF TOWN 21
   Dell, Mann and Magdalene 25
   Another Inspiration 26
   Piano Legends 27
   Reviewing Notes 28
   Seen In A Different Light 29

4. MORE OPPORTUNITIES 31
   Across The Delaware 31
   Encores and Fatigue 33
   Drawing Room at The Academy 35
   Defining Comedy, Quirkiness, Soul and Noise 36
   Concert Instruments Now 37
   Probable Excess 38

5. SPEAKING TO LEGENDS 41
   South Philly Atmosphere and Velvet Fog 44
   Four Jazz Giants 46
   Variations on Themes 48
   Book Deal—and Book Dealing 49
   The Ring and The Grove 50
   Headlines, Extremes and Finale 51

6. MISSION: IMPROBABLE 53
   On The Job Training 58

  Curtain 62
  Forgotten Values 70

7. BACK ON THE BEAT 73
  Pressroom Personalities 74
  Masters of Song 78
  The Prism of Music 79
  Out of the Park 82
  Computers Decided Value 84

8. INTERVIEW ADVENTURES 87
  Across the Pond 92
  Cartoon Diversion 94
  Motown Jaunts 95
  Grove, Quotes and Elegy 96

9. REVELATIONS 99
  Master and Mentor Mici 100
  More Choral Gems 102
  Up, Up and Away 103
  Four Inspiring Women 103

10. INNOVATORS AND CREATORS 107
  North of Hollywood 108
  Women on Stage—and Staging 109
  Two Brilliant Pianists 112
  Temporarily Bite Size 113
  Music Therapy 114
  Inside Job 116
  Competitions 116

11. COMPETITION, CARMEN AND CREDIT 119
  Carmen, in Person 119
  Grumpy, Doc and Happy 121
  Credit Where It's Due 123
  Three Alumni 124
  Behind the Scenes 124
  A Beacon Extinguished 125
  Grazie, Luciano 128
  Giant-Killer 130
  Debuts, Diva and Curtain 131
  British Imports, Witches and Major Loss 132
  Old Money, A Tradition Lost 134
  Collaboration and *The Amazon* 134

12. CODAS, GLASS, AND DRACULA 137
  Big Space, for a While 141

13. CONFIDENT PERFORMERS, AND VICTORIOUS NUMES 143
Crossover Sells, Pure Has the Last Word 145
Answers by Donizetti 147
Open Door to Music 148
Score! 149
Two Amazing Women 149
It Ain't Heavy, It's My Brother's 151
Three-Quarter Time 152
Terra Ascends 153
Voucher for a Story 153

14. LEGENDS GONE—AND HERE 155
Selling Out Every House 157
Two Philly Institutions 159

15. YOU MUST LOVE WHAT YOU DO 161
Two Fairy Tales 162
Brotherly Love—And Indifference 163
Charmer Charles 164
Passion On and Off the Stage 165
Getting More Serious 166
Yes, Maestro 167
Two Takes, One Dream 168
Never Alive at the Curtain 169
Three-Quarter Time Again 169
Fangs A Lot 170
Twin Talents 171
Two More Operatic Artists 172
Back at the Keyboard 174

16. ON THE COAST WITH EMIL RICHARDS 177
Soundstage Moments 181
Hollywood Insights 185
David Raksin 187
Two Giants Lost 192
Preserving Film Music 192

17. HAPPENINGS IN PHILLY 195
Time for Transition 196
Two Major Voices 196
It's in the Grove 198
Gershwin's Masterpiece 198
Boffo Buffo 201
Be Ready to Go On 202
Good Idea, Bad Business 202
Podium Insights 203
Chamber Interplay 205

Don't Even Ask 205
18. START WITH ACT ONE 207
　More Fun with Denyce 209
　Temporary Loss 209
　Classic Daily News 210
　Two Pairs on Stage 210
　One-Handed Artistry 212
19. HEROES, CARMENS, AND NUTCRACKERS 213
　Two Meaningful Beginnings 214
　Carmens and Tchaikovsky 215
　P.D.Q. Once More 217
　Orchestra 2001—And 2001 217
　Tabloid Opera 217
　Ties with Vienna 218
　Two Asian-Born Superstars 219
　Babes, Possible Maidens 221
　Arts Hotter Than Sports? 222
　Loss and Uplift 223
　Firebird, Denyce and Rorem's 80th 223
　Denyce Back In Philly 225
　A Legend and His Opera 226
20. OUR SOUNDTRACK AND GIFTED WOMEN 229
　Luciano's Farewell 231
　Sopranos Back to Back 233
　Only Play Music You Love 235
　The Reigning Queen 236
21. ABOUT EDITORS 239
　Passion in Music 241
　Booking Dad, and Stepping Aside 242
　Choices Made for Love 243
　Another Italian Maestro 245
　But He Kept Going 245
　Before Superstardom 246
　Buffalo to Carnegie Hall 247
　Misha in Overdrive 247
　Pops on Tour 248
22. OPERATIC ADVENTURES 249
　Playing the Devil 249
　Back to Bergamo 250
　Perfect Casting 251
　Exotic Journey 253
　Singing Insights 255

Collaborative Advantage 256
Mentoring Legend and Dancing Lovers 257
Guests, Genius and Drama 260
The Secret 261
Homage to Genius 262
Drama in Music, and Opera 263

25. PREMIERE, AND PREMIER MUSICIANS 265
Sing What You Love 267
Wind Blowing Good 268
Three Piano Men 270
Imaginative Casting 272
Beast and Dragon 273
Hélène Returns, And Coincidence 273
Steps in Time 274

26. KEEPING A PROMISE 277
Music He Never Heard 280

27. MORE *DAILY NEWS* ADVENTURES 291
Opera's a Bargain 292
Let's Change Things Again 292
Right-Handed Compliment, and Flood 294
"Porgy" Returns 296
Pianist in Transit 298
Collaboration 299

28. GETTNG INTO THE ACT 301
High-Level Hoedown 302
The Diva Returns 303
Bali High 305
Two Great Operas 306
Italian Operatic Legends 309
La Scala 310
Philly Farewell to a Legend 311

29. OLD AND NEW MUSIC 313
Successful Folly 315
Big Ears 317
Basso Profundo 318
Piano Man Finally Solos 319

30. BAD CARTILAGE, BIG HEART 323
Pianos and Pianists 324
Pure Class 327
Astonishing Yuja 329

31. STILL RESOUNDING 70 YEARS LATER 331

New Music from Everywhere 335
All Music Was Once New 337
Latin Mass 340
Legacies, Finale and Champagne 341
Hovering Legacy 342
Scarlet, Completed 344
Champagne Earned 344

37. THE END... SORT OF 347
Head to the Coast 348
A Summer Gig and Connecting Friends 351

40. POST SCRIPTS 353

CODA 368

INDEX 369

Illustrations

Arf 'N' Annie, 1970, by Jessica Stanley.	4
Alec Wilder.	27
Luciano Pavarotti, Moe Septee and Jessica Stanley.	35
Andres Segovia, drawing by Jessica Stanley.	37
Bill Evans, drawing by Jessica Stanley.	42
Dolores Cascarino. Credit: Glamour Photo.	56
Romeo Cascarino in front of poster. Credit: Michael Mercanti/ Philadelphia Daily News.	59
William Penn, first page of score.	64
Penn preaching before his arrest. Credit: Deborah Cascarino.	65
Thomas tells the jailed Penn about America. Credit: Deborah Cascarino.	65
Penn and Gulielma dream of their holy experiment. Credit: Deborah Cascarino.	66
Gulielma singing of staying in London. Credit: Deborah Cascarino.	66
Penn saying goodbye to his family. Credit: Deborah Cascarino.	67
Land Ho!. Credit: Deborah Cascarino.	67
Penn and Taminent exchange gifts. Credit: Deborah Cascarino.	68
Romeo Cascarino. Credit: Edward Carrol.	68
Margaret Garwood.	81
Marc Mostovoy.	90
Denyce Graves.	120
Luciano Pavarotti.	128
Paul Krzywicki. Credit: Jean E. Brubaker.	151
Peter Schickele.	166
Richard Goode.	175
Emil Richards, with his collection of percussion instruments.	176
George Harrison and Emil Richards.	177
David Raksin.	187

Eric Owens.	197
Sarah Chang.	220
Arantxa Ochoa in James Kudella's *The Firebird.* Credit: Paul Kolnik.	224
JoAnn Falletta. Credit: Fred Stucker.	235
Renee Fleming.	237
Keisha Hutchins. Credit: R. Todd Miller.	244
Angela Brown and the author.	252
Mimi Stillman. Credit: Ronni L. Gordon.	268
Joan Myers Brown.	275
Song After Sundown by David Raksin, orchestra score (ASCAP).	278
Song After Sundown by David Raksin, organ part (ASCAP).	279
Hugh Sung.	283
JoAnn Falletta conducting Cascarino session.	285
JoAnn Falletta conducing Cascarino session. Credit: Marc DiNardo.	286
Ignat Solzhenitsyn. Credit: Dario Acosta.	285
Time for Three. Credit: LeAnn Muller.	302
Christofer Macatsoris. Credit: Paul Sirochman.	306
Corrado Rovaris. Credit: Gabello Studios.	308
Kile Smith. Credit: Abu Tilghman.	313
George Crumb and James Freeman.	315
Herbie Hancock, Lang Lang, and the author.	322
Swan Lake, James Ady and Arantxa Ochoa. Credit: Paul Kolnik.	323
André Watts and the author. Credit: Enid Bloch.	328
Jennifer Higdon. Credit: Candace diCarlo.	330
Marian Anderson.	331
Behzad Ranjbaran and the author.	337
Jan Krzywicki. Credit: Boyer College of Music/Temple University.	340
Margaret Garwood, *Scarlet Letter.* Credit: Denise Coffey Stuart.	345
Emil Richards, still playing at his peak. Credit: Rob Shanahan.	348
Ricardo Morales and JoAnn Falletta in Buffalo.	350
Amy Aldridge. Credit: Alexander Izalaev.	352

Preface

There have been forty years of bylines, followed by stories that covered musical entities in every form: symphonies, chamber groups, ballet and dance companies, jazz and pop artists, opera singers, directors and almost any show that requires a ticket. It's now time to take a look in the rear-view mirror, reminiscing over the strange ironies, impromptu situations and conversations with a rainbow of performers.

All four decades have been spent as a freelancer, a category meaning that all insights into the journalistic business came as an outsider. Though the job entails constant reminders of this disadvantage, there's no deliberate intention to flavor these stories with bitterness or a cranky nature. Just telling the stories as truthfully as possible allows the job's quirkiness, and the humorous side of occasionally being stiffed, speak for themselves. The newspaper biz is full of colorful characters, or papers would be boring.

Another factor was the closeness, on my beat, to people of enormous fame. It may seem like a privileged advantage to speak with well-known artists, though I happen to have very little interest in celebrity.

Luciano Pavarotti once laughed at me when I told him the only person I ever wanted to meet—and never did—was Gene Kelly.

"The tap-dance guy?" he roared. "Why him?"

"Because, for a little while after I came out of the movie theatre, I believed I could dance like that."

"Don't you feel that way when you hear me sing?"

"No way!"

"Madonna mia!! He's just a tap-dancer!"

However, I've found through the years that artists who have dedicated their lives to playing an instrument, composing, conducting, singing or dancing simply see the world through a different prism than most of us. My sole fascination in interviewing them has been to discover their completely different—and very possibly inexplicable—points of view. It's an admittedly-impossible attempt to get closer to the creative process by trying to understand why they sacrifice so profoundly to do what they do, why they choose their repertory, how it feels to perform at that level, and how they approach life through a different perspective.

I perceived interviews as a learning experience about entering the edges of their world, and an attempt to communicate it to readers who also craved a window into its infinite mystery. In recognizing my incredible good fortune in being able to meet a wealth of artists whose work I admired, and to try to discover the constants as well as the variables of the creative process, the sole intention is to share any discovered enlightenment.

During this crazy journey, several personalities must occasionally arise in my tale, like friendly ports as a wayward ship follows the coast.

The first connection began, as far as I can remember, while a college senior in November 1957. It wasn't difficult in those days to enter a club if you were under age, and the George Shearing Quintet was playing at George Wein's Storyville Club in Boston's Copley Square. I loved hearing Shearing and everyone in the band—Belgian guitarist and harmonica master Jean (Toots) Thielmans, bassist Al McKibbon, drummer Percy Brice, conga master Armando Peraza and vibraphonist Emil Richards. By chance, Emil and I both came out for a smoke, started a conversation, and have been close friends for the last 57 years. I regularly visited him as he became the king of the Hollywood studio percussionists and, though we're only together once a year or so, it's always like we never left—the truest friendship of all.

Recently Emil asked me to co-write *Wonderful World of Percussion—My Life Behind Bars,* a book about his career which led to many astonishing details. For instance, I was amazed to find that his father came from Pesco Sansonesco—-a tiny village in Abruzzo about 11 miles from the town, Casoli, where my grandmother was born. Maybe ethnicity does mean something. Emil's real name is Emilio Radocchia, necessarily changed to get early work back in Hartford, Connecticut, though he's known everywhere in music as Emil.

Before Emil left the band, I once drove Shearing's bassist Jimmy Bond back home to Irving Street in West Philadelphia. Jimmy also headed to the coast and became a successful producer. Many years later, when doing a story about GAMP (Girard Academic Music Program) and interviewing the young, but now supreme, bassist Christian McBride, I was astonished to find he lived on the exact same block—yet had never heard of Jimmy.

Around 1965, I used to hang around Dirty Frank's at 13th and Pine Streets with a couple of artist friends, and met composer Harold Boatrite and keyboardist Temple Painter. At a concert of Boatrite's chamber music, I became enamored of his concentrated structures and gorgeous harmonies. In time, I studied with them both at their Waverly Street home. Sightreading four-part Bach chorales with Temple and attempting to play Bach, Brahms and Ravel was sheer bliss. Working with Harold was stressful in a different way, and I eventually found myself erasing more measures each week than I was writing. It was obvious that I wasn't a natural talent, and I bless him for the thorough and utterly complete sense of harmony that he gave me.

During years of study with Temple, I had a two-year job assignment a few blocks away from the home of a high school friend, Norm Hinsey, whose mother Dorothy loved to play on a fine upright Steinway. During many lunchtimes for almost two years, I walked over for tea sandwiches and four-hand versions of Ravel's *Mother Goose* Suite and, sometimes, Bizet's *Jeux d'enfants*.

I had a party one New Year's Eve and invited Temple and Harold, who asked if they could bring their friend John Davison, professor of music at Haverford College. At some point, Temple suggested I play the Ravel with Davison, who didn't know the piece at all. Naturally, the thought of doing a piece I had played endlessly with someone who was just sight-reading gave me temporary euphoria.

Davison not only played with brisk, peppy tempos that made me try to keep up, but stopped during the middle movement to kindly mention that I had been playing the tricky rhythm wrong. This provided a major epiphany, forcing one of many realizations that there are those who play the piano—and there are musicians.

In 1978, Davison unveiled his *Mass*, a towering work undeserving of its neglect. The composer was a sincere man with great warmth, and in the 1990s Temple and I helped to get a CD made of his many chamber works on the Albany label.

Around 1971, Harold asked me if I could use my recording equipment to tape an aria for a friend. Of course I said yes, and packed my trusty Ampex reel-to-reel machine and borrowed RCA 44BX microphone and cables over to Powelton Village.

The composer's name was Romeo Cascarino, and his wife Dolores Ferraro and baritone John Darrenkamp sang a haunting love duet from an opera he was writing called *William Penn*. The tape was supposed to be sent to Houston Opera, and I was just happy to have made a tape without hum. I had no way of knowing that their lives would entwine around mine in a way that would enrich us both beyond measure.

There are diversions out of the Philadelphia universe into another fabled one on the West Coast, rich in a different kind of music but no less virtuosity, and a few personal detours as well. In the interest of storytelling, it will become sometimes necessary to diverge from a purely chronological narrative.

Through the pitfalls, joyful rewards and business of writing, the personal expressions of artists emerged much more than mine as time went on. My constant intention was for these deep insights into a performer's creative spirit, whether out of curiosity or human connection, to lure non-concertgoers into the hall to share my passion for the arts.

—*Tom Di Nardo, May 2016*

1. SCRIBE, THROUGH THE BACK DOOR

A Freelance Philosophy

Major insights into the freelance-writing business appeared while laboring on my first review for the *Philadelphia Evening Bulletin* on February 15, 1974. I noticed Max de Schauensee, a short dapper man with an elegant coat, enter the buzzing newsroom, doff his beret, and begin working on his opera critique. De Schauensee, rumored to be a Swiss baron, was the dean of opera reviewers at the time.

The familiarity of his authoritative voice and brilliant elocutions on the Metropolitan Opera's Saturday afternoon *Opera Quiz* made me feel qualified to wander over and humbly introduce myself. Max was very gracious, and took a moment to offer greetings and advice. "Mr. Di Nardo," he confided, "there are only two things you need to know in this business. First, never try to describe what music sounds like. It can't be done. Second, freelancers are always lower than whale poop in the depths of the Pacific Ocean. Always remember, it's nothing personal."

I was stunned by such a remark from this suave gentleman, and could never have imagined that, through all these years, Max's second dictum would occasionally ring in my ears, and to a continually greater degree.

Through these four decades, I've learned that a streak of masochism is a mandatory prerequisite in considering freelance writing. Even those who stick needles into themselves, starve themselves for arcane causes, or walk on smoldering embers find some ultimate rationale to justify the sacrifice. Freelancers must be willing to endure low—or nonexistent—pay, stolen ideas, indifferent treatment, and occasional mangled editing and, since they can rarely count on the eventual checks for bodily nourishment, their individual causes and psychic rewards should be clearly defined.

One example is caring a great deal about your beat, a passion sustaining me throughout a few thousand stories and more editors than I can recall. Therefore I would urge you, dear reader/writer with a dream of freelancing—with an emphasis on the free part—to first measure the depth of your passions, as well as your resilience. If they're both strong—jump in with gusto!

But never let them know you need the bread.

Slight Credentials

I can't claim to have been blessed with an extensive musical background, though classical music, Bessie Smith and Fats Waller were always played in my house. There were horrendous piano lessons in early teens with my Uncle Rod, a church organist who came over after service around 12:30 on Sundays for the likelihood of some vermouth, and taught me the kind of old-fashioned technique that had probably crippled Schumann's hands. If I played well, he threatened Grieg's *March of the Dwarfs* and, since my only real desire was to join my waiting pals and make the 1:05 train to Shibe Park for a baseball doubleheader, I ached to foil his plan. No matter how much I banged and messed up the ending, he called me a good boy and played the Grieg—often causing me to walk the tracks to Shibe Park alone through neighborhoods no reasonable person should have traveled.

At Germantown Friends School, the choir was asked by Elaine Brown of Singing City to join them in Brahms' *German Requiem*, singing with the Philadelphia Orchestra conducted by Eugene Ormandy in April of 1954. Of 62 students, only Skip Barber and myself, who would rather be playing baseball than rehearsing, didn't sing. After college, Skip and I shared my studio, where he prepared exotic cars for many successful races at Watkins Glen, Marlborough and Lime Rock, eventually founded the hugely successful Skip Barber Racing Schools and now owns Lime Rock race track.

My father had taken me to see a lot of operas which, in those days, were put on by the Lyric and the Grand companies. They always had cheap drop backgrounds and ragtag choruses, but they would bring one big star down from New York that day; those audiences only cared about hearing Franco Corelli or Renata Tebaldi anyway. The first I remember was Gounod's *Faust*, seeming endless until the fourth-act *Soldiers' Chorus*. The supers entered stage left, with the first ones stopping halfway across, and when they kept coming the line collapsed and many of them fell forward like dominoes on the stage. It was hilarious, and I remember thinking it was worth it for the comedy portion.

He had followed the funeral processions on South Broad Street with a borrowed violin in his childhood and, and after going to the opera, would fake through them by ear on our Leonard upright piano, getting maybe three-quarters of the notes and singing most of the parts. For years, I attended unfamiliar operas and realized I had heard almost everything before at home—at least partially.

Eventually, he wrote two or three songs, enough to be published and become eligible to become a member of ASCAP. I still have the stub of an ASCAP check, astonishing proof that one of his very elementary songs had become a big hit in Sweden.

In college, there were many evenings in the highest reaches of Boston's Symphony Hall, where Charles Munch led the Boston Symphony in simply spellbinding versions of French masterworks—Ravel, Debussy, Fauré, Franck, Berlioz—including a life-changing complete Ravel *Daphnis and Chloe* with chorus.

Scribe At Last

Philadelphia once had an alternative newspaper called *The Drummer*, a quite irreverent weekly before it morphed into a more mainstream rag. Editor Don DeMaio evidently thought anyone obtaining a library card in the name of Lamont Cranston was daffy enough to fit in. My first experience was writing copy for a political cartoon called *Arf 'N' Annie*, a satire about a dog and a luscious woman drawn by my friend Jessica Stanley. It blasted things in the (Mayor Frank) Rizzo and Vietnam days, when City Councilmen punched each other out and political sleaze was rampant...though little has changed. The editor Don DeMaio let us foment on virtually every subject and, though the pay was meager, Jessica found great drawing experience from making Annie sexy and drawing Philadelphia scenes accurately.

In one panel, Annie was talking about how women should be independent, equal and free of gender stereotyping. The gag was the recent Supreme Court decision that said women could also be drafted, and when they arrive home and she receives a draft notice with a date to appear at boot camp, Annie says, "Don't they know a woman's place is in the home, making pies?!" De Maio was on vacation that week, and his assistant Richard Fisher was there with his wife. "This isn't acceptable," Fisher said, with his wife making faces after reading the cartoon, saying "This is very demeaning to women." I said, "It's a satire, Richard. And who's the editor, you or your wife?" He and his outraged wife had the last word, and in order to save the same drawings we simply pasted on new text balloons and window signs. Instead they talked about the 1970s proliferation of porno shops, with Annie's receiving an ad for racy videos in the mail this time and responding, "Doesn't anybody just DO it?" With strange feminine logic, that substitution was acceptable.

I also had a chance to interview Sam Goody, whose LP store on New York's 49th Street was the first to discount records; this came in an era when stores only ran sales after Christmas. The $3.98 LPs were in bins for $2.89, and people bought stacks of discs in shopping carts. "How can you make a profit selling these LPs at a discount?" I asked Goody, who would soon franchise his name. "I lose money on every record, kid," he confided, "but I make it up in volume."

Writing for Vinyl

My good buddy Bruce Klauber once briefly edited a paper called ELECTRICity, run by the late playboy Harry Jay Katz, a man-about-town who inherited loads of money through his father's patent on seamless panty hose, and had a long string of quite lovely, and often temporary, ladies.

My gig was a jazz review column, emanating from listening to seven or eight LPs on Saturday afternoons at my studio and writing them up. The pay was supposed to be ten dollars, rarely received since Harry felt that getting the free records was sufficient compensation. Fortunately, it was relatively easy to get on the mailing list of some jazz labels, and a few of those discs actually were worth listening to.

Bruce is a drummer and vibist who played Atlantic City casinos in those days, and years later began playing at the 23rd Street Café, a place where talented amateurs could just come in and jam on Tuesday nights. Some

weren't bad, and there were sets when his wife Joy Adams would sing. I remember popping in one night during my later *Bulletin* days, when I was doing occasional jazz reviews, and Bruce stopped playing right in the middle of a tune. "Ladies and gentlemen, the Man is here," he yelled. I looked around to see who had come in, and realized he meant me.

Bruce wrote an excellent book about Gene Krupa, who had inspired his playing, and eventually began making videos for Warners—one on Krupa, a two-tape set on the history of jazz drummers, and another brilliant one on Buddy Rich. They were incredibly well researched, and they taught me more about the art of drumming than in hearing many guys flail away at the skins.

There also was a chance to do long pieces about two idols—pianist Bill Evans and composer Alec Wilder, making all the badgering for small checks worthwhile.

How to Get a Newspaper Job

Most newspaper writers carry their journalism degree through the front door. My entry to the profession resembled breaking though a cellar window in a side alley at midnight, following a series of events much too unlikely for a fiction writer to dream up.

It began when my Baghdad-born piano tuner Alexander Sargis invited me to a séance, supposedly given by a visiting acquaintance from Bali. In a center city apartment fragrant with perfume sticks, I was introduced to James Felton, at that time the classical music reviewer for the now-defunct *Philadelphia Evening Bulletin*. The Balinese gentleman, in full ceremonial regalia, produced a Ouija board, eliciting a heightened sense of skepticism. It brought back memories of my own aunt Julia Abbott, the least mysterious person on the planet, who got away with manipulating the board when I was a kid using candles and a funny hat—until the message transported from the spiritual vortex urged me to consider more broccoli and leafy green vegetables.

Jim Felton and I were talked into going along with the game, placing our middle fingers lightly on the *planchette*. In order to remove the smirks on our faces, our Balinese guru began with some simple questions about Jim's family. To my astonishment, the token was urged to the Yes-or-No edges of the board as if a third hand had forcefully shoved it, and we accused each other of manipulating the token, even though that was physically impossible. Our host continued with questions about his parents, eliciting powerful pressures on the *planchette*, until Jim suddenly howled, stood up and refused to continue. The head-dressed questioner didn't know—and neither did I until much later—that Jim had a history of mental problems, undoubtedly accelerated at age 14 by discovering his father hanging from a noose in a ball park.

Neither of us had any doubt that something besides us had made the token move, though we never spoke about it again. On our ride home, the shaken Jim mentioned that he had been collecting background information for a biography of conductor Leopold Stokowski for many years. He had recently realized that he was simply too emotionally involved with the project to complete it, and had been looking for a ghost writer. I volunteered to do a sample and agreed that the two years Stoky conducted the Cincinnati Symphony, a finite period with specific information, would make a reasonable trial. The chapter went smoothly, and Jim liked it enough to show me an upstairs room piled high with papers, books and notes, some discovered in trips to London and to Poland, demonstrating how fanatical his project had become.

A couple of weeks went by and Jim called with news: my chapter had been stolen from his desk at the *Bulletin*. He felt it was an omen, and soon sold the whole roomful of background material to another writer.

Over a year later, Jim called and asked if I wanted to do a freelance review for *The Bulletin*. And those are the steps I took to be a newspaper journalist.

2. *BULLETIN* DAYS—AND NIGHTS

Newsroom Noise

Frankly, I didn't want to be away from my two children at night, but I had been fortunate enough to attend Germantown Friends School, and since my two were going to go there no matter what was necessary to provide tuition, I said yes. Jim didn't seem to care that I had zero credentials, though it may have helped that he knew I was studying with Temple and Harold.

Since no one had bothered to tell the promoter that a reviewer was coming, I had to pay $10 to attend the first concert I covered, a recital with a violinist and baritone on a bitter February evening. One of the pianists was Cynthia Raim, a great artist who played in my neighbor's church and who would soon reach real renown. At the paper, I fed the five-page colored sheets into an old Royal typewriter and pondered the beginning of a new career before procrastinating in that momentous brief meeting with Max De Schauensee.

For the first few years that packet of pastel sheets was used, each one known as a "book." When you realized that a review would make more sense if some of the paragraphs were rearranged, that meant retyping the whole page. This luxury was rarely feasible, because night editors like Bob Lindsay, sporting a green visor like the tough-talkers in the old movies, would bark for the copy and mark the sheets up with a blue pencil as swiftly as Zorro's blade. If there were other stories to be edited, you just stood around foolishly until he got around to it. How the typesetters in the basement understood the scribble and cryptic arrows on their copy was a mystery. My uncle Charles Mitchell, who went nearly deaf down in the noisy depths of the *Bulletin* composing room, simply said they got used to it; eventually, they actually hired deaf people who found the job easier.

A few years later, a desk editor informed me that I had to use a computer from now on, though no one was willing to provide a logon or a password. I sat there helplessly while the newsroom bustled, until sportswriter Bob Vetrone wandered by. I had read Bob's column, *Buck the Bartender*, for years, and was astonished at his encyclopedic knowledge of sports, even those I didn't care about. Bob, famous for his diet of hoagies and cheesesteaks, was willing to give me his password, BEEF.

The *Bulletin's* fledgling system was a disaster, with lights and sirens that suddenly gave warning of its failing mainframe. At the first blaring alarm, everyone jumped for their SAVE key, though there were many nights when I hit it too late, meaning starting all over again when the system returned and the cursing quieted down.

One night BEEF didn't work, and all I could learn was that passwords had changed. There was no chance of getting help from the desk, and fortunately one of the sportswriters, seeing my panic, gave me Bob Vetrone's home number. Bob somehow had been able to reside at the Palestra, where the Penn team played basketball, and where he had a choice of 40 showers and security. Luckily, he answered and gave me his new login: PORK.

Many years later, to celebrate my friend Bill Rodgers' retirement from the straight job we both worked for, I asked Bob—then writing for the *Daily News*—if he'd have lunch with Bill at the *Bistro St. Tropez* on Market Street. This was a little fancy for Bob's hoagie diet, but he came graciously because I was buying, and he asked Bill when and where he went to high school. When Bill replied Frankford, he was astounded by Bob's recalling the basketball exploits of that period's high school stars from 35 years prior. Bob was a walking encyclopedia, and his son Boop still continues the legacy by doing the arcane statistics and inside sports minutiae for the *Daily News*.

Freelance Availability

To their credit, no one at *The Bulletin* every told me to go harsh or to go easy on anything I was covering. There were lots of other freelancers—Ed Weiner, who always found a fresh slant to write about and eventually became an editor at the *Daily News*, David Thicke and John David Kalodner, who became a famous record producer. After we did a few reasonable pieces without completely embarrassing the paper, we became a reliable cadre for editor Bob Sokolsky—until, for whatever reason, you were not available. Though writing was only a very small, though necessary, supplement to my regular income, people kept telling me that Jim Felton thought I was trying to take his job. I brought this up one evening, and told him that it wasn't true for a host of reasons, including that I couldn't afford it, though I'm certain he didn't believe me.

I evidently was supposed to cover the classical concerts that Jim didn't feel like covering, or those requiring a car, as well as all the pop, rock and jazz that Matt Damsker would prefer not to attend, and anything Sokolsky wanted included that nobody wanted to handle—meaning modern ballet, ethnic traveling dance troupes, or anything out of town. And, especially, weekend concerts, sometimes Sunday matinees and evening shows on the same day.

My first feature article about P. D. Q. Bach (the hilarious spoofer Peter Schickele), only two weeks later, didn't even include interview quotes, just background information about an upcoming concert. It included the sentence "Despite musical and literary discussions about the creative authenticity of certain works by Shakespeare, Mozart, and many others, the academic community has never questioned P. D. Q.'s authorship." Luckily, there were several chances to speak with the droll Schickele in the future.

The magnificent Philadelphia Woodwind Quintet, first-chair players of the Philadelphia Orchestra, gave a program including one of Alec Wilder's woodwind quintets. Wilder attended, and a conversation with the chain-smoking iconoclast was the first of many. I had cherished an old Columbia LP of his lovely works for woodwind solos and strings, conducted by Frank

Sinatra; the crooner had heard some of Wilder's music and had the clout to record them. Several inside musicians have told me that Mitch Miller, the soloist on the oboe and English horn pieces, resented having to play for Sinatra. When Miller became head of artists and repertoire for Columbia Records, he assigned Sinatra junk songs for years while Tony Bennett, Rosemary Clooney and others were launched into major careers. At the end of his recording contract in 1953, with his Gene Kelly movies behind him, Sinatra was virtually forgotten—until *From Here to Eternity* and the legendary Capitol LPs with Nelson Riddle brought him back to enormous fame.

In one chamber concert, piano pieces by Philadelphia composer Joseph Castaldo with the then-hip fiddling inside the piano seemed "derivative in the use of effects without imagination." The next year, his *Lachrymosa* "had layers of long sustained notes, like tuning in slow motion, its themeless construction finally swirling to a frenzy of effect without substance." Years later, interviewing Castaldo about his *Viola Concerto*, commissioned by the Philadelphia Orchestra and to be played by its principal violist Joseph de Pasquale, he brought up both reviews and was gracious enough to say I "had a point." It's an example of the thin skins of creative people whose works are meant to reveal—or to hide.

I really had no idea how to do a substantial interview, or what to ask that someone hadn't been asked a thousand times. After a few baptisms of fire, I eventually realized I cared more about a personal attitude about their art than what they needed to publicize at that specific time.

My first actual interview was a brief, last-minute, hurried one-line phoner with British songstress Cleo Laine, who had performed in *Showboat* in London, done William Walton's *Façade*, settings of Shakespeare by her husband, jazz saxophonist Johnny Dankworth, and an uncanny variation of timbres to shape the vocal line (in English) of Schoenberg's eerie *Pierrot Lunaire*.

In the review of the concert at the Annenberg Center, the headline writer used my last line: "She Came, She Sang, She Conquered." That's a rare occurrence, yet it wasn't the only line I wrote that was used again.

That was the beginning of a long relationship with Cleo and John, two musicians who visited often, as did the Preservation Hall Jazz Band, who first came to Philly in 1974. They were the creation of Philadelphian Allan Jaffe, who had been the window designer at Gimbel's department store at Eighth and Market until he decided to move to New Orleans in the mid-1960s and hear real jazz. To his bitter disappointment, he found that only rock and roll prevailed on Bourbon Street, and that all the Dixieland musicians were working as porters or shoeshine men on the riverboats. He set up a place downstairs from his apartment at 726 St. Peter Street for them to play, passed the hat, and finally charged admission. I remember Sweet Emma Barrett, called the Bell Gal because of the bells wrapped around her calves, the clarinet/trumpet duo of Willie and owlish Percy Humphrey, drummer Cie Frazier and 86-year-old trombonist Big Jim Robinson, who asked my lady friend for a date afterwards. Jaffe played tuba, and his son Ben is still leading and playing bass with the band.

On one New Orleans visit, I sat in the front row with a blond-haired kid who placed a trumpet case under the seat. It turned out he was from Norway, had always loved Dixieland, and dreamed that someday he'd be able to play with his idols. At the first break, I mentioned the kid to Percy Humphrey, and he asked if I knew whether he could play. Of course, I had no idea, and he just shrugged. After the second set, he took the young man into the back corridor, where several scale runs in the distance penetrated the buzz of intermission. In the middle of the third set, Percy said, "Ladies and gentlemen, there's a young man here from…way over there somewhere. Let's see if he can play." The youngster jumped up as if struck by lightning, took out his instrument, and sheepishly stood out front. They played a chorus of "Muskrat Ramble," and eventually Percy simply gave him a grand arm sweep to signal his solo. The audience cheered the boy through three choruses until the band picked up the tail and finished. Those grizzled musicians all patted him on the back, and I'll never forget the thrilled look on that young man's face. It was just one of the many reminders to come of the incredible universality of music's power, even in Dixieland, nothing more than straight four-part counterpoint with syncopation—meaning Bach would have been familiar with the basic materials used by these ancient denizens of St. Peter Street.

The legendary Marlene Dietrich showed up the next summer in a white full-length fur, showing off her shapely gams. "Her voice, sometimes strained and raspy, occasionally holds on to notes or lets them slide into the cracks; throwing away phrases like afterthoughts or rolling them around on her palate with unusual punctuations, she changes the melodies around like silly putty."

I loved the Erlanger Theater at 21st and Market Streets, perhaps because in the early 1960s I had a job as still photographer for tryout Broadway shows, providing black-and-whites in the window cards out front. It had been sheer fun to shoot these shows, and I fondly remember Phil Silvers and Nancy Walker jumping up and down on a bed in a sarcastic number called "It's Legitimate!" from *Do Re Mi*, a Comden and Green classic about the 1970s deejay payola scandal. One night at a break, Silvers wandered into the orchestra pit, and noodled a little on clarinet, violin, piano and trumpet. The surprised musicians asked him what that was all about. I scribbled his answer: "In vaudeville, with five shows a day and two-hour breaks during the movie, there was nothing else to do but hang around with the players and pick up a few tricks."

Yul Brynner came in with *The King And I*, and had insisted that his dressing room and the corridors leading to it be painted a specific color of brown. When he finally arrived in long cape, he took one look and declaimed that it was the wrong shade, turned around and left. The annoyed stage crew spent the next morning repainting all over again.

Another side of show business occurred before the first night of *Little Me*, a hoot about an innocent country girl named Belle Poitrine, who keeps marrying international rich men—who immediately die under weirdly accidental circumstances. There was one show-stopping song, *I've Got Your Number*, by Swen Swenson, a Broadway talent who died way too young. Comden and Green adapted the show into a film called *What a Way to Go* starring Shirley MacLaine which, although not the success they felt it deserved, was their most profitable.

The great Sid Caesar, whose legendary *Your Show Of Shows* was never missed at my house, had the chance to play all these many parts in his famous ability to spoof dialects. Though I had shot the stills at rehearsals, I hung around backstage before the preview when Caesar came in with two huge guys who guarded his dressing room door and chatted with me about baseball. Around seven-thirty, the large-framed Caesar cracked his door open with a look of sheer terror on his face, looked wildly at the corridor toward the street and tried to run out of the house. The guys restrained him and tried to calm him down, but his eyes were wilder than I had ever seen in a human being, and he screamed that he couldn't go on. They locked him in the room, and soon he lost his lunch with a horrible, deafening eruption that sounded like a hippopotamus throwing up. They somehow guarded him in the wings while the overture was going on, while there was a wild look of sheer panic on his face with furtive looks toward the stage door, evidently his exit strategy. He was pushed onto the stage, and was utterly sensational.

I was astonished at such behavior, though the bodyguards said it happened every night, and that after the show Sid would go to Frankie Bradley's for two rare steaks and most of a bottle of bourbon. That's show biz.

Soul singer Linda Hopkins stunned the audience at the Erlanger Theatre. Her piercing interpretations, combined with her relative obscurity, was another recognition that talent and fame need not be on parallel tracks.

Harry Jay Katz eventually bought the Erlanger, brought in Patti LaBelle with the *Voulez-vouz couchez avec moi* tour and a big blockbuster show with Bette Midler, and sold it. The once-thriving house where *West Side Story* and *Gypsy* had passed on their way to Broadway was knocked down and became a parking lot.

Another example of fabulous talent was the stupendous jazz chops of French pianist Bernard Peiffer who, I discovered, lived a few blocks away from me in Germantown. An acquaintance I knew, Nelson Rose, who could eerily duplicate mechanically at the keyboard any piece played for him, studied with Peiffer for a while. In a gig at the Walnut Street Theater, Peiffer's trio performed an arrangement of a Scriabin Etude and his Variations on George Shearing's anthem *Lullaby of Birdland* in a searing blizzard of pianistic miracles reminiscent of Liszt.

Ragtime, Grazioso, and Grit

In 1973, a set of Scott Joplin ragtime arrangements known notoriously in the 1905 New Orleans parlors as *The Red Back Book* was discovered in St. Louis. The brilliant Gunther Schuller, who would also orchestrate Joplin's opera *Treemonisha*, eliminated some of the doubling, made a recording that became a huge seller, and took the concert on the road.

Gunther Schuller:
I essentially subtracted the unison doublings and chose certain instruments to solo, giving changes to the texture. I want to make sure I don't become Mr. Ragtime! Composing is my primary calling as far as I am concerned. (By phone, June 13, 1974)

Schuller, who had played under Arturo Toscanini at age 16, soloed in his Horn Concerto with the Cincinnati Symphony, and had played principal horn in the Metropolitan Opera Orchestra for 19 years, was an astonishingly multi-faceted creator. His huge number of compositions combined with his superb conducting, his publishing empire, his writing of works like the seminal *Early Jazz* and leading the New England Conservatory made this gig just a fun sideline. Schuller even invented the term "third-stream music," though he said later that he wished he hadn't.

Even with all these amazing credits to his name, pigeonholing goes on. Several years ago, at a seminar, a jazzman friend went up to Schuller and said, "I know who you are! You played horn on Miles Davis' *Porgy and Bess* record!" Considering that was in 1958, it must have made Schuller wonder what he had been doing in the last 52 years.

In the 1970s, visiting Boston, I had attended a New England Conservatory concert in Jordan Hall, featuring Strauss' blazing *Ein Heldenleben* in the second half. In the midst of the battle scene, someone signaled Schuller, who was conducting, to stop, and the players and audience were all asked to retreat onto freezing Huntington Avenue.

After about 20 minutes, we went inside to find that someone with German resentment had called in a bomb threat. Schuller said that the arts weren't going to be intimidated by force, and they would start the piece from the beginning—a noble gesture—except for the pained faces of the string players.

Though not much in the way of chamber music was happening in those days, one concert featured my teacher Harold Boatrite's Piano Sonata, played by Cynthia Raim. I still think it's a marvelous work, and it felt good to be able to genuinely sing its praises. Four of the other works were by his students, with the finest a Rhapsody for cello and piano by Sidney Grolnic. Sid and I used to pass on the stairs on Thursday nights, both taking piano lessons with Temple Painter and composition instruction with Boatrite. Our friendship continues, and I was amazed to discover that he has written some highly imaginative plays, and was very impressed by his staging of

Melville's circuitous *The Confidence Man*. I've roared reading his yet-unstaged *Orphans of the Opera*, as the children left over at the curtains of *Pelleas et Melisande*, *Norma*, *Madama Butterfly* and *Wozzeck* bicker about whose tragedy is greater, what would happen to them in a sequel and the meaning of life and art. Sid worked in those days at the famous Fleisher Collection at Philadelphia's Free Library, where the curator was the gifted composer Kile Smith.

At one Curtis Institute concert, the famous soprano Benita Valente found her pianist ill, and was fortunate when Vladimir Sokoloff was able to take over. Sokoloff, who insiders called Billy, was one of the Curtis instructors, as well as the keyboard player with the Philadelphia Orchestra, and was a legendary sight-reader. Though we never met, I heard many stories of his last-minute keyboard prowess, as well as that of composer Vincent Persichetti, who taught in those days at Juilliard on Wednesdays. Because I worked across the bridge from 30th Street train station, I sometimes drove into town and—just accidentally—bumped into him and offered to drive him home in the park near my home. Once he actually asked to see my work, though I wouldn't have dared show it to him; whenever we arrived he would always say, "Don't forget, Tom! Grazioso and grit! Grazioso and grit!"

Miss Valente is married to Anthony Checchia, who heads the Marlboro Festival in Vermont and who, in 1986, founded the Philadelphia Chamber Music Society, a now hugely-successful organization to be mentioned in later pages.

Eroticism and Black Mass

In late 1974, I was introduced to an artist named Frank Root, who specialized in erotic vinyl art. He insisted that his work would be a good story for *Philadelphia Magazine*, and an editor there named Art Spikol told me to go ahead. Since I had a photographic studio, and did album covers, portraits, model's portfolios, magazine layouts and anything someone would pay for, I shot photos of Root and his very suggestive work, wrote the story, and submitted it.

I got a call from Spikol saying that something hot came up at the last minute, and that there would be a kill fee. Somehow, that check must have gotten lost in the mail. Some months later, Frank thanked me for the story, because it evidently ran.

Root introduced me to a filmmaker named Ray Hoersch, who had directed many documentary films, even a *Sesame Street* short, and *The Erotic Memoirs of a Male Chauvinist Pig*, starring two luminaries of the porno genre.

Hoersch was planning a film called *Black Mass*, a portrayal of the Satanic ritual.

Ray Hoersch:
The Satanic Mass is the exact inverse of the Catholic ceremony. Every part is reversed in blasphemy, for its intention is a deliberate corruption, a parody of the Mass.

Starting with the processional, the ritual uses a nude as the alterpiece. The second section is a baptism, when a girl dressed in white renounces her Christianity and seals her pact with the Devil. And the third part is the Invocation to Lust—you'll have to see that. (His home, February 15, 1975)

Frankly, I didn't care about religion or the inverse thereof, though Sokolsky suggested I go ahead and write about it, since it was weird and would be playing in the downtown Arcadia Theater and Germantown's Band Box, two cinema havens both long gone. Hoersch had offered me a goodly sum as the still photographer for the final scenes, and especially wanted large-frame transparencies made with my Hasselblad. In the final scenes, there were many extras dressed in white and black costumes, several nudes walking around, all kinds of fires in tall censers and lots of smoke machines. I took quite a lot of photographs, though the film and processing was expensive, and eventually put the slides in a large bound book for Hoersch to peruse.

Hoersch finished the movie but, after the article came out the following week, the Catholic Church and other organizations picketed the theaters so vehemently that they cancelled showings. When I found out, I drove up to Hoersch's apartment on Winston Road, finding the place empty and Hoersch gone. Somewhere there's a trove of 2-1/4" x 2-1/4" slides, with a bill inside the front cover, and somewhere there's Ray Hoersch. According to IMDB, there was no *Black Mass* (until a Johnny Depp movie with a different plot 40 years later). In 1975 it may have been a shocker, but nothing's off limits these days.

Send the Freelancer

One real trial was the almost-constant summer assignment at the Temple University Music Festival in Ambler, nearly an hour's ride from home. It was possible to drop off the chosen unlucky child en route to the paper; the downside was the 8:30 pm starting time, making it impossible to arrive at the *Bulletin* before 11:30. The editors, who wanted to go home, put hysterical pressure on latecomers to write the story as swiftly as possible. The Pittsburgh Symphony was the resident orchestra, mostly led by Sergiu Comissiona, who led mostly workmanlike performances of standard works.

There was a lot to be learned from these assignments, since the one summertime rehearsal and warhorse repertoire guaranteed that few performances were either stirring or horrible, the two meatiest situations for a reviewer to describe. Ordinary performances test the reviewer, because the most difficult challenge is listening for some moments of inspired playing that allows writing something interesting.

Many of these concerts were also covered by *Philadelphia Inquirer* staffer Samuel Singer, who once asked me if I had a family member named Ann. We discovered that my very modest mother, as an undergraduate, had once written a poetry column for Sam's Temple University magazine under the name Ann Onymous. On one visit she journeyed with me to Ambler, and met Sam for the first time in over 40 years.

Gary Burton's quintet luckily gave the vibist a chance to perform his thrilling four-mallet version of Antonio Carlos Jobim's tune "Chega de Saudade" from his *Alone At Last* album. Anyone with the slightest interest in how virtuosity can assist in making music—in the hands of a master—should get this music immediately.

Another unusual touch was to feature a pop artist with the Pittsburghers in the first half—like Dionne Warwick, Vikki Carr (headline: "Sings Words, Not Musical Phrases") or Glen Campbell in the first half, and even the Buddy Rich band once, followed by Charles Ives, Tchaikovsky, Leroy Anderson and *Carmen* excerpts in the latter. An impressive concert version of *Il Trovatore,* a visit by Beverly Sills and finally organist Virgil Fox with a light show was a typical week.

A wealth of conductors cycled in and out—Sarah Caldwell with opera arias, Leonard Slatkin, Commissiona with Marilyn Horne and a huge Mahler Third, and Julius Rudel. The Temple University Opera Theater performed too, with such obscure gems as Offenbach's *Ba-Ta-Clan* and Weill's *Das Kleine Mahagonny*. Friends still recall the Robert Shaw concerts of *Bach's* B Minor Mass and Beethoven's *Missa Solemnis*, calling them definitive. And one of my last assignments was one with Christoph Eschenbach, who would become the Philadelphia Orchestra's music director 23 years later, playing concertos by Mozart and Bach and conducting Haydn.

At those concerts, I was able to meet the production manager Jerry Grabey, who later on became the general manager of the Mann Center for the Performing Arts. Through the years, Jerry has somehow handled the enormous demands of opera, ballet, pop, rock and every imaginable travelling show, as well as the Orchestra; I have always been amazed at how much madness goes on backstage, and how gracefully and professionally Jerry makes everything go on smoothly.

We were fortunate those summers to get such jazz artists as Sarah Vaughan with the rampaging Buddy Rich band, Lionel Hampton with Illinois Jacquet, Maynard Ferguson's band, Dave Brubeck and George Shearing and the double bill of Ray Charles and Erroll Garner at the Robin Hood Dell. Those days, unfortunately, are long gone.

That Ambler season ended with another visit by Cleo Laine and John Dankworth in a concert I found electrifying. At the end of my first paragraph, I blurted, "The lady is a sorceress; people were burned at the stake for less."

When I went in to the paper the following week, Jim had left me a New York Times ad for the concert Laine had given a few days later in Manhattan. At the bottom, it had my quote, and said "*Philadelphia Evening Bulletin*." I thought at the time it was pretty cool until Max de Schauensee, who happened to be in that night, saw it. "When I say it, I wrote it," he emphasized, sternly. "The *Bulletin* doesn't write anything!"

The Latin Casino in New Jersey was a garish barn, complete with some women hawking giant fuzzy animals and others wandering around with Speed Graphic cameras to capture couples at the event. It was painful to always find a few young men sheepishly holding huge pink rabbits, while girlfriends beamed at this demonstration of evidently serious intentions.

One evening in September 1975 the headliner was Jackie Wilson, one of the seminal figures of rhythm-and-blues in the 1960s and 1970s. His show was powerful and energetic, with much jumping and swiveling, and climaxed with his big hit "Lonely Teardrops." At the last note, Wilson stiffly fell backwards and his head slammed into the floor with two loud crashes, causing the audience to roar at what they considered great showmanship. Wilson just laid there. I had taken a CPR course two weeks before, and ran to the edge of the stage to offer my new expertise to the emcee who was pulling the curtain closed. "Never mind," he said, "we have doctors."

Backstage, there was an ambulance to take Wilson to the Cherry Hill Hospital. In a call to the paper, the night editor insisted I head over there and get the details. Still hanging around the waiting room by 11:30, I realized there would be no further information that night.

It was revealed later that Wilson's fall had caused a massive concussion, and he remained in the hospital for days. Three different women appeared, each claiming to be his wife in case there was an estate, gradually vanishing when Wilson's massive medical bills—and his lack of funds—were made public. The following October, Dick Clark brought a Rock and Roll Revue to the Latin as a benefit, a full house netting proceeds of over $60,000. Lots more was needed, since he eventually was transferred to a hospital in Lawrenceville, New Jersey, where he remained in an eight-year coma until he died in 1984. All in all, it was a horrible event giving me nightmares for years.

Raquel Welch once came and gave a quite endearing song-and-dance show, and I asked readers to "search elsewhere for puns and double-entendres about her construction, even though she uses a few herself, as well as a few gowns quite opposite from Little Bo Peep, because it is the unfamiliar facets we came to see." It made me realize how difficult these personalities must have in convincing people they can be recognized by more than one attribute—or that maybe even a bombshell can actually act, sing or dance.

As the warmup to Manhattan Transfer, comedian Richard Belzer, known more recently as the sarcastic detective John Munch on *Law and Order*, did some phenomenal offbeat impressions of Rod Steiger, Jack Nicholson and even Marcel Marceau with his trademark offhand acidic delivery. And Shirley MacLaine did an energetic rouser, at one point mentioning, "I made 33 films, and I played 14 hookers!"

Another runout was the Valley Forge Music Fair, another 45 minutes out of town, offering many pop acts. The worst of these was the incredibly ungifted Connie Stevens, the opener for Bob Hope, whose act consisted of dragging the unaware onto the stage and humiliating them. Hers was possibly the worst act—other than Ted Nugent—I had the misfortune to catch.

Cyd Charisse and husband Tony Martin did a fine one, with the leggy Charisse utterly captivating. Years later, in a Universal Studios cafeteria, I would see her somewhat closer up.

One night, I was sent to the Robin Hood Dell to cover a gospel concert, a completely unfamiliar genre. It turned out that few concerts could ever achieve that level of intensity on a warm night, considering that the performers were Shirley Caesar, James Cleveland and the Mighty Clouds of Joy. It was an electrifying evening of yelling, clapping, stomping, and electricity. It amply demonstrated something I told many people later: that music from the heart always touches more deeply, and that most people will relate to any performer at the top of their game, regardless of genre.

Lots of Exposure

There was an unusual twist to a *This Was Burlesque* show featuring stripper Ann Corio. The main attraction was a baggy-pants comedian called Slapsy Maxey Furman, whom I had seen during adolescent visits to the lurid Troc burlesque theater. One day I happened to meet Max at an Arch Street bank, and he told me he had bought the Troc and hoped to keep it running. Since the big-name strippers were too expensive, he booked the cycling comedians and simply changed the marquee names of the same three dancers.

Most regulars came for the comics, who did the Doctor sketch, the Traveling Salesman bit and those other long-honed classics of double-entendre ("Don't be afraid, just go up and grab her by the digits") that came just short of justifying arrest. When the girls flounced on and did their disinterested routines to a bored band and pounding drummer, most guys just went outside for a smoke.

One day, Max offered me a few bucks and free tickets for any funny names I could come up with that he could use. Some were not fit for a family paper, though I got away with Ophelia Pulse, Claire Voyant, Lena Genst, Rose Bush, Mercedes Diesel, Ella Vator, Tess Tickle, Rhoda Rooter, Honey Suckle and Crystal Chandelier, with Max putting some kind of tag line above it in the ad.

Just before one Christmas, Max said he needed a little help because, with everyone shopping, the place was usually dead. I pondered it carefully and came up with something in the holiday spirit: "A New Star in The East: Beth Le Hem." I thought it was pretty clever, but it became a classic with Max's added tag: "Be Wise, Men!" Amazingly, the papers ran the ad.

After Max sold the Troc, he was nudged out of retirement to do *Sugar Babies* with Mickey Rooney and Ann Miller on Broadway, and eventually was even the subject of a marvelous 1981 *New Yorker* Profile.

At one show, Paul Anka repeated his contrived story about how Frank Sinatra asked him to write "My Way." Considering that Anka's other famed ditties were "Diana" and "She's Having My Baby," the probability that he had written a much more skillfully-written song seemed unlikely. By chance, I had been poring over a bin of old sheet music some weeks before, and discovered that it was a French song "Comme d'habitude," composed by Jacques Revaux and made famous in 1967 by singer Claude François with lyrics by Gilles Thibault. Anka, a bilingual French Canadian, simply translated the lyrics, and I mentioned these details in my review.

Before I left the Latin, the p.r. contact happened to mention that the *Inquirer's* Bill Thompson had come to the rehearsal the day before and written his review in advance. A few days later, I received a metal Jack Daniels box with very expensive chocolates inside it, along with a message from Anka: "Perhaps next time you can sit next to Bill Thompson and see the same show. Paul." I was very wary of eating the chocolates, and eventually someone put them out at a party without knowing their background. I felt very fortunate that there were no intestinal repercussions.

I later found out that many older West Coast musicians had another reason to dislike Anka, since he had been one of the first guests on the *Tonight Show* with Johnny Carson. His little riff, turning into the show's theme, was detested by many of the band, any of whom could have been asked for a more accomplished tune. As part of the favor Carson was listed as the co-author, meaning a steady stream of huge joint composer royalties for thirty years.

Imagine making a fortune for a riff nobody knew you wrote, and being famous for a song you didn't write.

Comedienne and Enigma

One interview that made me laugh almost too hard to write was with the hilarious Anna Russell, the imposingly-constructed comedienne famous for her classic comic sendup of Wagner's *Ring*. The Australian-born doyenne actually studied with Ralph Vaughan Williams at London's Royal College of Music, and sang in opera until she was bumped into by a tenor in *Cavalleria Rusticana* and knocked over the church set.

Anna Russell:
Well, eventually my vocal acoustic had been bashed with a hockey stick. I was asked to write a comedy bit for conductor Sir Ernest McMillan, for I had an in with him—you see, he and my uncle were in prison camp together.

Once, in San Francisco, Victor Borge and I were doing a two-person radio show, and radio technicians cut off the broadcast when we joked about making the mandatory five union musicians actually appear. I ran into Victor once on 52nd Street, where I was living above a strip joint. Every night they would finish with Ravel's Bolero, *and the tub faucets would fall off from* *the vibration. We went in to complain, and Victor almost got his eyes scratched out by the headliner.* (Philadelphia hotel, February 26, 1976)

Some of Russell's bits were *How to Write Your Own Gilbert and Sullivan*, *Hamletto*, *In Darkest Africa* and *How to Enjoy Your Bagpipe*, a sketch that was paralyzing. Seven years later, the Concerto Soloists premiered a Bagpipe Concerto by John Davison, and I asked for a tape of the performance and sent it to her. I received a lovely thank-you letter from her Toronto home, and wasn't surprised by the address, 7 Anna Russell Way.

In covering all these concerts, I crossed paths with the *Inquirer* reviewers Dan Webster, Sam Singer and John Bull. Dan had his own Max de Schauensee story, from one of his first assignments. He was reviewing Ponchielli's *La Gioconda*, renowned for its amorphous and mystifying plot. After the second act, Dan asked Max, the acknowledged opera expert what the opera was about. Max' response: "There's no way to know."

3. INTERVIEWS OUT OF TOWN

Whenever I traveled to California to visit Emil and accompany him to some film scoring sessions, I asked Sokolsky if I could do an interview while out there. It resulted in one with Gabe Kaplan of the hit TV show *Welcome Back, Kotter*.

Gabriel Kaplan:
I don't consider myself an actor, I'm a standup. As Kotter, I'm really playing myself. In Boston, they didn't play the first few shows, because Kotter confronting the class for the first time seemed too controversial during busing problems. We had to go to New York to get most of the actors for the right speech type, and Vinnie Barbarino (played by John Travolta) gets more fan mail than anyone ever has. (Beverly Hills Hotel, April 1, 1976)

The 1958 album *Legrand Jazz* has absolutely floored me, and it's still my favorite of all jazz records. Michel Legrand had made three "mood music" LPs, the well-known *I Love Paris*, *Holiday in Rome* and *Castles in Spain*, all giving familiar anthems an amazingly novel spin. He was promised a jazz album and, during one week in 1958, had Columbia Records provide three different bands—one with Miles Davis, John Coltrane, Bill Evans, Herbie Mann and more, another a swing band and a trombone juggernaut band with Ben Webster. The musicians soon found out that he had written specifically with knowledge of each individual player, in riffs that were exactly in their style. Bill Evans once told me he went on another day, the only time he ever visited a session when he wasn't playing. The album got a five-star rave in *Down Beat* yet Columbia, for some reason after supplying this amazing A-list of players to a French kid, hardly publicized it at all. In the CD era, they licensed it to Philips Records; this turned out to be an advantage, because the Philips booklets had photos of the sessions, with a priceless one showing Miles and Coltrane with their mouths open at this crazy-looking Frenchman.

Because Michel was close with Emil, we hit it off in a good interview.

Michel Legrand:
I discovered that composition is impossible while traveling—the performance that evening is always on my mind. How I hate to practice—thirds and scales—but I do an hour or two every day. Two months on tour is plenty for me—I have to get back to my home, next to a water mill, outside Paris. The serenity makes me work better. I can't stop, must always be busy. You know, I entered the Paris Conservatoire at age 10—my father was the well-known bandleader Raymond Legrand—and I did nothing but work until I was 20. (By phone, July 25, 1976)

Jessica came along to make sketches on three out-of-town interviews, all resulting in financial losses. One was a trip to Westchester, New York to do an advance for Shirley Bassey, who would not let Jessica, a big fan, draw her during our interview and would not even let her come up from the lobby to say hello. Bassey was, at the time, riding the crest of singing *Goldfinger* in the James Bond movie into stardom.

Shirley Bassey:
I only do concerts now, no clubs, I grew out of being annoyed at drunks and noise, and now only mind people eating steaks when I'm on a diet and starving to death.

I come from the Tiger Bay section of Cardiff, the Harlem of Wales. My father was Nigerian and my mother Welsh, they divorced when I was two and my Welsh mother moved into a white neighborhood, with kids very cruel. Everyone came around when success gave me a break, sheer hypocrisy. If you're famous, no matter what color, you're accepted. If not, forget it. I did a black Jolson-type show, and hated it and became a waitress. I never even wanted to go into show business; if it hadn't been for that break with Goldfinger, I'd be home with eight kids. Some artists are just not happy unless they're performing—offstage they're miserable. I don't live to go on stage, I do my thing and go home. (Westchester, NY hotel, October 1976)

Another journey, to Montclair, New Jersey, was a sheer delight visiting the superb jazz duo Jackie Cain and the late Roy Kral, who were supreme hosts as well as great drawing subjects. Jackie was famous for having such perfect pitch that musicians would tune to her. They had lost their daughter in a car crash only blocks away, and didn't perform for several years, gardening to somehow reconcile the tragedy.

The most memorable was a trip to New York's East Side to interview the brilliant librettists Betty Comden and Adolph Green. The setting was Comden's East Side apartment, where Green arrived from his home across Central Park. With Jessica drawing, Comden sat primly and flung zingers, and Green expressed himself in wild gyrations, trying to explain the theory behind creating a great show. Green, after a rare moment of silence, said, "Look, we don't write this stuff in ink. You first have to have something on paper so you can fix it!" Wise words indeed.

In a television show I had seen, André Previn claimed that Green—who didn't read or write music—could sing every theme from every symphony he ever heard. Of course, I tested Green by throwing symphony movements at him—second movement, Beethoven's Fourth! Third movement, Brahms' Second! First movement—Balakirev! Green sang them all out with gusto, and rewarded us by performing basically the whole first act of their unfinished show *On The Twentieth Century*, their first with composer Cy Coleman. Comden's apartment was a showplace, her walls covered with signed photographs of their pals—Leonard Bernstein, Gene Kelly, Cy Coleman, Cyd Charisse, Fred Astaire and a host of other legends.

Betty Comden and Adolph Green:

Comden: *People seem to be endlessly fascinated by show business, to the yearnings of the theater, to egos trampled on. They can relate to excitement, romance, movement, fun—theater is a metaphor for anyone trying to have fun. If our work doesn't seem dated, it's because these relationships of striving are universal.*

Green: *We meet every day, and work every night when near deadline. We seem to have the same point of view, making it difficult for us, after all these years, to analyze our work patterns. But you mustn't edit yourself out of existence. There must be something to polish and change and, after all, you end up feeling that you've never done enough.*

Comden: *Singin'* in the Rain *came closest to what we had in mind. Gene Kelly and Stanley Donen, both old friends, knew our work. There's an economy to their direction that's rare, never dwelling, avoiding heavy moments, always giving the right value. We saw the picture only after it was completed, and were thrilled. The film* What a Way to Go *had potential, but disappointed us, though it was our biggest financial success. The frustration of the originators is the history of movies. And, in* The Band Wagon, *as the Faust legend becomes a leaden, pretentious flop, it shows how a sweet and charming idea gets heavied up by an 'artist' and the terrible dialogue begins to creep in.*

Green: *By the way, although films are around forever, we did them on salary, before the days of percentage deals. No sacks of gold. We would work six or eight months, come back and say, we've got to get busy on a show. Because of the economics of Broadway, it's a do-or-die affair, not a carefree undertaking.* (Betty Comden's apartment, December 15, 1976)

I asked Green if he had a favorite line. He recalled the scene in *Singin' in the Rain* when Gene Kelly and Donald O'Connor are trying to find a new name for the silent *Dueling Cavalier*, to be made into a talkie as sound arrived in 1929. O'Connor blurts, *The Dueling Mammy!*

The *Bulletin* printed Jessica's drawing, and *A Party with Comden and Green* at another long-forgotten Philadelphia house, the New Locust, was a smash. Afterwards, they seemed surprised at the enthusiastic reception.

Many years later, I saw Green walking along on Broadway above Columbus Circle, and said, "Hello, Mr. Green." "Hey, I know you," he said, and I told him about his wise words about creation from 25 years before. "Did I say that?" he laughed. "That's pretty good advice." Green, who passed on in 2002 at the age of 87, enjoyed every single moment of his exuberant life. He made you wonder what kind of a world it would be if everyone had that much fun doing what they could do, and brilliantly. I've always wished that Leonard Bernstein had been locked in a room with Green and Comden, because their chemistry would have altered the history of musical theatre to an unimaginable degree, and we wouldn't have had to hear the same Andrew Lloyd Webber song regurgitated throughout every one of his shows.

A few years after her controversial Vietnam visit, Jane Fonda was making a film with George Segal called *Fun with Dick and Jane* about an upscale couple who turn to a life of crime when Segal loses his job. While I was in LA, the press rep let me watch some shots, mostly Fonda driving during fake rain in a cutaway car. We went to a makeshift outdoor commissary, where I was offered a roast beef dinner; when I was halfway through, Fonda arrived to find out that mine had been the last meal. This had the makings of a disaster. Luckily, Fonda is a real pro and answered my questions about the sociological message of Dick and Jane's robbery adventures, elusive at best. I learned a bitter lesson that night—never accept!

Jane Fonda:

A strong woman's part throws light on reality. I never accept just because I like a part, always seeming to opt for a more complex role, and a story that penetrates, saying more about where society is going. But in the past, I've had what I felt were good roles in movies that were only fair. You have to avoid getting trapped in role models, in my case the progressive female. (Studio City set, January 31, 1977)

On another trip west, a few years later, I had a chance to interview Western star Sam Elliott, who was appearing in a television miniseries *Wild Times* about sharpshooter Col. Hugh Cardiff. Wearing jeans, denim shirt and bushy mustache, Elliott was candid about being willing to do one show a year for the money, and would much rather be on his farm. During this interview in the lounge of the Beverly Hills Hotel's Polo Lounge, we sat close to the very loud and ostentatious bark of television host Tom Snyder. With an attitude that inferred he didn't know or care who Snyder was, Elliott went over and told him in no uncertain terms to keep his voice down—an entreaty that had its intended effect. Elliott also invited me up to his farm, about 40 miles away, though I figured he really didn't mean it; when I realized later he was married to Katherine Ross, I strongly considered altering a previous rule—always accept!

Sam Elliott:

We had a 20-minute piece of film taken by Thomas Edison, the first ever registered. It was shot in Omaha, 1898, with a camera the size of a piano and was found behind a bank vault in Cody, Wyoming. There's Buffalo Bill doing sign language with the Indian that's on the Buffalo head nickel, and shots of Sitting Bull.

I don't consider myself on a par with East Coast actors, but nobody's more suited for Westerns than I am. My grandfather was shot in the head coming out of a Texas bar in 1903. I loved seeing Gable and Cooper and Wayne, and am still star-struck.

Westerns used to be the backbone of the business, always making money. But costs are very high now for the livestock, wagons, cowboys. The old wranglers and cattle drivers are in the same union as the Teamsters now, driving trucks until there's a movie.

One show a year is enough for me, I didn't get into this business to be a millionaire. I won't do commercials or a series, just fish, ride horses, and wait for a script I can believe in. There's a fascination about the old West, the lone hero, the guy on the rearing white horse, lawless times, man alone against the odds...all universal themes. That's why I'm happy to be thought of as a Western actor. (Beverly Hills Hotel, February 1, 1980)

Dell, Mann and Magdalene

In the summertime, I was able to review the Philadelphia Orchestra at the Robin Hood Dell, including a return by Van Cliburn in the Tchaikovsky Piano Concerto and guitarist Carlos Barbosa-Lima in the famous *Concierto de Aranjuez* by Joaquin Rodrigo. In between those two, there was a gig with the Dizzy Gillespie Band, Earl Hines and Billy Eckstine—glory days.

The Mann Music Center (now Mann Center for the Performing Arts) in West Philadelphia opened in 1977, with colossal concerts by the Philadelphia Orchestra and soprano Leontyne Price, who electrified the mob with Mozart, Verdi, Puccini and a searing "My Man's Gone Now" from *Porgy and Bess*. Tenor Luciano Pavarotti's first appearance in recital came as a benefit for the Marian Anderson Library at Penn, and the grand "Lady from Philadelphia" attended. Pavarotti had come directly from Italy for the occasion, and sang his trademark Verdi and Puccini arias—"Celeste Aida," "Recondita armonia" and "Nessun dorma." Miss Anderson said she wondered why Pavarotti offered to come on her behalf. "Strange things happen," she said, "and I will always send all my love to you." It was a truly magic moment, being close to this frail lady who had more grace, class and sheer heart than any American ever has, before or since.

Yvonne Elliman, a Hawaii-born singer who lucked into the role of Mary Magdalene in *Jesus Christ Superstar*, was disarmingly honest about her credentials.

Yvonne Elliman:

I was playing on Navy bases and thought I was hot, and when an agent listened to my tape and wrote from London I grabbed the opportunity. I would have flunked my senior year anyway, luckily the teachers all gave me Ds and let me pass.

The record paid 100 pounds ($240) instead of a percentage, but I bought a case of wine and had a chance to do backup with Eric Clapton. (Bijou Café, February 9, 1978)

Another Inspiration

Through the years, I had had a few chances to meet with Alec Wilder, the self-professed "president of the derriere-garde," since the Philadelphia Woodwind Quintet, made up of Philadelphia Orchestra principal players, often played his works. He had written an enormous body of sonatas in odd combinations of instruments for his friends and, at that time, he admitted that he could no longer afford to do them gratis; I had no idea that his enormous catalogue consisted mainly of gifts.

His book, *The American Popular Song*, was as much as staple in my house as the Encyclopedia Brittanica, and I spoke to him about it after a performance of his *13th Quintet* and a Sextet with marimbist Gordon Stout.

Afterwards, I sent him a copy of my review and, several weeks later, received this humbling letter:

"I doubt if you can imagine my state of being after reading your review. For 30 years I have sedulously avoided reading the words of any critic. They all seem to despise what I write seemingly because it's not written in this month's fashion or because it makes no attempt to convey aggression, doom, 'relevance,' 'significance,' or 'meaningfulness.'

A friend once saw my name in a review. If she had read it she never would have mailed it to me. I memorized it and have never forgotten a single word. In its entirety it reads: "That anyone in the seventh decade of the 20th Century should have written Alec Wilder's Suite for Horn and String Quartet is unpardonable."

So perhaps you can imagine how I feel/ And considering that I fight hourly to maintain even a modicum of self-respect, you mustn't be embarrassed by my acknowledging that SOMEBODY CARES! (In red ink) And somebody that connects, laughs, and believes in unicorns. Your friend, Alec"

That letter is framed and, if my house is ever on fire, it is one of the few things I would rush through flames to save.

Alec died on December 23, 1980, at 73, a prolific composer whose uncompromising love for beauty and melody when music was in a dissonant cul-de-sac was given a lonely neglect. In 1982, in remembrance of Alec, the Kool Jazz Festival presented an afternoon "Friends of Alec Wilder" program. The bill included Jackie and Roy, Mabel Mercer, Eileen Farrell, Marlene VerPlanck, Stan Getz, Ellis Larkins, Bobby Brookmeyer, Joe Wilder, Gerry Mulligan, Marian McPartland, and many others—all friends who cared deeply about this neglected legend. To this day, there is an annual April concert in New York celebrating his legacy.

Incidentally, that same evening Kool presented a Buddy Rich retrospective with Mel Tormé, Zoot Sims, Jo Jones, Dizzy Gillespie, John Bunch, Harry (Sweets) Edison, Phil Woods and tapdancer Honi Coles—they don't do stuff like this anymore, folks.

Alec Wilder.

Piano Legends

In one memorable Curtis Symphony concert at Drexel University, the piano soloist was the 82-year-old Mieczyslaw Horszowski, playing an unpublished concerto written by the 13-year-old Mendelssohn. Horszowski, who had played the Beethoven First Piano Concerto in Vienna at ten and performed for the Pope Pius X at fourteen, soon demonstrated his artistry personally to Fauré and Saint-Saens. Years later, he made some stunning recordings at Curtis for Nonesuch records that catapulted him into a late fame. His unshowy, pearly touch and his interpretations of Mozart, Chopin and Schumann had an inevitability earned over a lifetime of love.

One night, Jim Felton and I were invited to a post-concert party in which John Ogdon, whose recording of the two Rachmaninoff Piano Sonatas were a staple of my LP collection, was a guest. After a while, Ogdon—obviously one of the great sight-readers on the planet—started just playing anything placed in front of him.

Ogdon asked Felton if he had anything to play, and Jim went out to my car and brought back his notebook. He had been working on a gnarly twelve-tone piece, and the pages were filled with scribble, with three measures crossed out for every remaining half-measure. When Ogdon opened the notebook with this dog's breakfast, Jim tried to refuse before Ogdon placed it on the music stand and blasted through the dense rambling with some semblance of style. When it suddenly ended, out of notes and inspiration, he just handed it back to Jim and played something else. Nothing was said on the way home, though we were both thinking the same humbling truth: there are people who try to play and compose, and then there are people with real talent.

Reviewing Notes

That brings up an attitude regarding reviewers, some of whom are failed musicians and some others who simply delight in blasting performers. It's true that when there's a terrible act or concert, artists deserve to be savaged. In place of any specific background in reviewing, though, my criterion was solely intuitive rather than specific, whether right or wrong, especially with contemporary chamber music. Is the composer really trying to tell us something from the heart, even though it may not be easy to grasp, or just note-spinning? Are the performers really trying their best to connect to us, or just phoning it in? Often the answer is obvious. My reviews were a lot about intention, not just talent, with the implicit awareness that everyone else in the hall actually had to pay for their tickets.

Because reviewing was truly a vocation without guidelines, the only thing I could go on was honest reactions. If a performer wasn't note-perfect, obviously trying to create an experience, that person got the benefit of the doubt; a composer who was obviously not even trying to connect with an audience—especially in those days of dissonant, sterile academic drivel—received a deserved lack of respect. That era meant lots of extended development of non-existent themes and, in pop shows, often little attempt to demonstrate some measure of talent. I found early on that whenever a performer says "Put your hands together" or brings people up from the audience, you can guarantee that the muse didn't offer anything to the perpetrator.

In one week, for instance, there were four pop disasters: Sonny Bono ("His is the longest act since *Die Gotterdamerung*"); Billy Paul's pandering medley of his hit "Me And Mrs. Jones;" Kate Smith, whose folksy, sour belting would have been booed if she hadn't been famed for singing *God Bless America* for our hockey team the Flyers; and Tom Jones, trying to keep a straight face while dodging thrown underwear and accepting booze, fruit and phone numbers. James Durante surely was right: everyone wants to get into the act.

I surely wasn't perceptive enough when Frank Zappa arrived with his Mothers of Invention band at the Spectrum arena, saying it was "a frontal assault of frantic excess." His albums *Freak Out, Weasels Ripped My Flesh* and *Burnt Weeny Sandwich* were known quantities, though that night's solos were interminable. Emil and some other Hollywood friends later told me about his scoring gifts that, despite his wildman persona, he hid with modesty. Years later, when his music was performed by no less than Pierre Boulez, Zappa had the last laugh. One son Dweezil still tours and holds Dweezilla seminars, Ahmet is a writer, daughter Moon Unit is an actress and author and Diva Muffin is an artist.

Emil, who played on Zappa's early *Lumpy Gravy* album, recounted that when Zappa performed his *200 Motels* with the Los Angeles Philharmonic in the mid-1970s, conductor Zubin Mehta came out first to warn the staid audience that what they were going to hear was a little different than usual, continuing with other platitudes. An annoyed Zappa walked on stage, took the microphone from Mehta and began, "I wrote this one night in a motel while I was masturbating," causing Mehta to exit stage left. The show went on anyway, despite the fact that the beats were meant to be on 2 and 4, while Mehta beat his usual 1 and 3, confounding Zappa's percussionists and making the piece incomprehensible.

Seen In A Different Light

I have a warm spot in my heart for an evening at West Philadelphia's Tower Theater, when I was assigned to review a poignant concert by David Crosby and Graham Nash. By chance Margie, a lovely young lady I had hoped to spend more time with, was excited to hear them. She insisted afterwards on coming back to the paper, waiting patiently until I finished the story and could drive her back home, before announcing that she had decided to be with me. Certainly David and Graham played with more juice than they realized.

Though she knew little about jazz, Margie was willing to come along to the Atlantic City Jazz Festival. During the ride, she offhandedly mentioned that she had gone that afternoon to visit her sister Ruby Veney, who was busy talking to a lawyer; while waiting, she chatted with the man who was tuning Ruby's old upright piano with a pair of pliers.

A young, talented acquaintance had heard Stan Getz' new recording of pianist Jimmy Rowles' tune "The Peacocks," and wondered if he could offer the lyrics. Jimmy was playing for Ella Fitzgerald at that concert, and Emil suggested I use his name and introduce myself afterwards. Dizzy Gillespie's band was on the bill too, as was the Modern Jazz Quartet.

When the MJQ began their first tune, Margie pointed at vibraphonist Milt Jackson and blurted out, "That's Ruby's piano tuner!" The adjacent folks shushed her emphatically, and I cringed with embarrassment.

Afterwards, I went to talk to Jimmy Rowles, who gave me his card and said he'd be happy to entertain the young man's lyrics (he eventually used someone else's). While Margie was waiting, Dizzy put his hand up her dress, to her surprise and displeasure. Ella, standing right there, deadpanned "That's why they call him Dizzy!"

It turned out that Bags actually was a friend of Ruby's lawyer and, while he was waiting, had used the pliers to fix the most out-of-tune keys. You can't make stuff like this up.

I once took my son Marc to hear Bags at a West Philly club and, afterwards, he said, "That was just wonderful, Mr. Jackson." He said, "Thank you, but nobody has called me Mr. Jackson in 30 years."

It's disappointing to realize how many venues are gone, recalling such perfect sites as the New Locust Theater for chanteur Charles Aznavour with his haunting anthem *La Bohème*, or the Bijou Café for the stunning Helen Schneider.

There was a jarring evening at the Bijou, when Otis Blackwell performed a set that made the audience's mouth drop. At first, this black composer of such early rock anthems as "All Shook Up," "Return to Sender," "Love Me Tender," "Don't Be Cruel," "Great Balls Of Fire" and "Whole Lotta Shakin' Goin' On" at first seemed to be an Elvis impersonator. It became quite evident that this man with the emotion, rhythm and gyrating moves was the source, having done his act long before Elvis, without the advantage of being white. Though he must have done well with the song royalties, his own superstition prevented him from ever meeting Elvis. "Blackwell is a true innovator with no regrets, a neglected giant of rock who watched through the race curtain as the bubble-gum and three-chord millionaires passed him by." It was only the beginning of all those "cover" hits by white artists, a bitter reality that this forgotten creator stunned us into—through simply performing.

4. MORE OPPORTUNITIES

Across The Delaware

During May 1975, I received a call from the *Camden Courier-Post's* features editor Stan Goldstein, asking if I wanted to do some reviews for them. In order to avoid conflict with the *Bulletin*, I used the *nom de plume* Tom Draper, the middle name of a beautiful girl I once fumblingly pursued as a teenager.

The first review was of an opera called *The Nightingale and the Rose* by Margaret Garwood, coupled with Leonard Bernstein's *Trouble in Tahiti*. Garwood's work struck me as lovely and intensely melodic, with the lead role sung by soprano Dolores Ferraro Cascarino, who I had recorded in her husband's aria four years before. It turned out that Garwood had been married to Romeo Cascarino before Dolores, and surely had shared with him his love for tonality, melody and lush harmony.

One interview involved a new anchor for KYW-3 television, a woman named Beverly Williams. She had come from Portland, Oregon, where my sister lives, and I was given a clue that she could be a tough cookie. We met in a restaurant, and I simply asked her how she liked Philadelphia. "I didn't come here for chit-chat," she said, urging me to turn on the tape recorder and ask, "What makes you think you can handle the fourth largest national market?" She suddenly got very friendly, without saying anything unusual worth mentioning.

There was a chance to hear Cleo Laine again, and by that time I was receiving her annual Christmas cards, picturing she and John, plus their children Alec and Jacqui, on their farm in Milton Keynes, England. They ran a summer program called the Wavendon Allmusic Plan, bringing students and famous musicians together.

Cleo Laine:

In August, we have small children in and they camp out on the grounds. They create their own play, write the music and words with the help of teachers and friends, and finally perform it for their parents when they come to collect them.

We're fortunate to have friends who come down—André Previn, (guitarist) John Williams, John Ogdon, Vladimir Ashkenazy, Janet Baker—because they believe in what we're trying to do. It's really satisfying, and I get down and wield a paint pot too. (By telephone, July 10, 1975)

Some years ago, on a London visit, these two invited me to the taping of a show showcasing Dankworth's band with both swing, jazz and rock drummers at the remote Elstree TV studios. They offered me a ride back to London after the session, on their way to a gala record-biz award ceremony. Dankworth (in trademark floppy hat) had forgotten his tuxedo, and asked the limo driver to stop at a suburban mall while Laine polished her nails. Eighteen minutes later (the astonished chauffeur, used to such capers, timed him), he ambled out in full tuxedo regalia. As he got in the car, she extended her wet nails and said, "How do they look?" Except for the driver's do-you-believe-this look, his transformation seemed too unsurprising for comment. Twenty minutes later, they exited to flashbulbs and fans at the Hotel Dorchester. That's life in the music biz.

Carlos Montoya came to the Academy, his flamenco style a counterpoint to Segovia's classical edge. Afterwards, he also signed one of Jessica's great drawings, which is mounted with Segovia's.

Carlos Montoya:

Flamenco music is all from the heart. As you explore and live life, it goes into your music, and your personal style is part of it. Many younger players try their hand at flamenco, and have good technique, but lack heart. That must be there. An artist can fool an audience one year, but not for 25. (Philadelphia hotel, October 15, 1975)

Another program I was fortunate to attend for the Courier-Post was another recital with Luciano Pavarotti. And the Chicago Symphony, under Carlo Maria Giulini, came to town and performed Persichetti's Symphony (the 5th) for Strings.

All in all, these were great opportunities, including some time with Arthur Rubinstein in advance of his 89th birthday concert, complete with a 359-pound cake shaped like a piano to be shared with the audience.

I asked Rubinstein before the concert how he kept his playing as fresh, considering that he was playing the pieces frequently on tour. His response was that, in the case of the Saint-Saens Piano Concerto No. 2 played with orchestras, he simply didn't practice in order to keep his intensity up at the concert. In the case of recitals, he mentioned the fiendishly difficult three-part piano reduction of fragments from Stravinsky's *Petrouchka*. He said that, once in a while, he would simply switch hands in the second movement to keep himself on his toes. For all I know he was pulling my leg, if not my toes; besides being an astonishing man, he was a charmer who relished having audience members share a gigantic cake.

Emil told me recently that Rubinstein's son John, an acclaimed actor and accomplished composer, went to Paris to visit his father on his 90th birthday in 1977. When asked how it went, the son said he really didn't have a chance to see his father very much. Because his eyesight was starting to fail, he was trying to learn as much unfamiliar music as he could, and played all day long. That's something to think about whenever you don't feel like practicing.

Some of these pieces allowed a little more space, yet it took a lot of badgering and phone calls to get paid. I remember calling Stan to ask about a check for my last six pieces, finding he was no longer at the paper and no one knew anything about it. I'm still waiting for that check.

Encores and Fatigue

It seemed evident that a responsible part of the job was to stay for the encores. When they were unfamiliar, that meant either guessing or going backstage and fighting the artist's fans to find out. The latter entailed a delay of at least 45 minutes, resulting in yelling by the desk editor and a scramble to finish, especially annoying because anything that seemed arcane would probably be cut for length anyway.

In those days, all reviews were 'overnights,' since the *Bulletin* first hit the streets around 10:30 in the morning. There was also an afternoon edition for the homebound commuters, complete with partial baseball scores on the front page. Now, of course, reviews appear several days after the performance, with writers avoiding a mad rush and simply e-mailing it the next day after reflection.

In an orchestral concert, the concerto or new piece was usually in the first half of the program, and the staff reviewers of both the *Bulletin* and the *Inquirer* would regularly leave at intermission. One usher later confided in me that he called the reviewer after the concert, just to reassure him that the conductor hadn't fallen ill or that the chandelier hadn't fallen on the audience. These reviews usually ended with a single sentence, such as "The orchestra also played Beethoven's *Eroica* Symphony." One impetus to this insurance was the firing of San Francisco Chronicle reviewer Heuwell Tircuit, whose Percussion Concerto was once played by the Philadelphia Orchestra. Tircuit had not noticed a program insert mentioning a substitute ballerina so, when he waxed rhapsodically about the wrong dancer, word spread—unfairly—that he had not actually attended or just made it up.

Many pieces were written under the weight of sheer fatigue, since my regular employment began at 7:45 a.m., in a building across the bridge from the *Bulletin* Building. To get home at 1:30 or 2 o'clock in the morning, wake and make sure my two children were dressed and on their way to school, and arrive at work that early may not be as difficult for a youngish person, but doing it two or three nights a week became rough. I can honestly remember being at work and not being able to remember one word of what I had written the night before, terrified that I had somehow slid some nonsense past the editor, and being immensely relieved upon sneaking out to the newsstand around 11 to find that it was at least somewhat relevant to the performance. Looking at some of those late-night pieces 35 years later, I'm convinced that exhaustion, coupled with a looming deadline and an insistent editor who also wants to go home, is a real advantage in organizing and focusing your thoughts.

Most of my reviews were classical, though there were occasional pop, rock, dance and jazz shows that the staffers didn't feel like covering. Since Jim didn't drive, that meant all shows out of center city were mine as well. Of course, any Sunday concerts were freelancer fodder, sometimes a matinee as well as an evening show to shoot a whole day. And I covered probably every ethnic dance troupe on the planet, or anything else that seemed socially worthy—yet not enough for a staffer to interrupt a weekend.

Considering the door-to-door time involved in a review, each one worked out to something just less than minimum wage, even less for shows out of the city. After six years of doing two or three reviews a week, I asked if there could be some compensation for the gasoline, bridge tolls and time involved in traveling twenty or thirty miles to venues. Don Harrison, who later joined the editorial board of the *Daily News*, eventually relented and bumped those reviews up a hefty five dollars, from $20 to $25. A few years ago, when I bumped into Don and told him I intended to include reference to his enormous generosity in this book, he frowned and insisted that mentioning this could completely destroy his skinflint image.

One night an envelope was left for me with a 3x5 card inside; someone had written "No man but a blockhead writes except for money."—Samuel Johnson. At first, my naiveté felt that this was a cynical attitude, though Johnson knew what he was talking about.

The truth of Max's second tip rang true on a weekly basis. Jim Felton would type up the next week's suggested reviews on Monday, and give it to Bob Sokolsky. The call from Bob never came until around 4:50 on Friday afternoon, meaning a suspension of all plans or family outings until the last minute—after my 4:45 commuter train had left 30th Street Station.

After a positive review of a Lola Falana concert at the Latin Casino on a Friday night, Falana actually sent flowers to the paper on Monday. I didn't hear about it until my usual Friday afternoon assignment call and, choosing to pick them up rather than make my usual train home, found a bouquet of dead, discolored, pitiful-looking straggly flowers on Bob's desk. I salvaged the card—"Thank you! Love, Lola."

Yet Bob was a quite friendly person, and did a column every week about the vagaries of television or show business. Behind his back, everyone kidded about his inability to take a stand, always starting a column with the Columbia University-mantra of a hot lead meant to keep people reading, then taking the other side. One reporter kept a list posted of openers—"Well, you had to be there," "Someone was bound to do it," "It was only a matter of time," or "No one thought of it before." There were a whole host of qualifiers—""But then there were those who would say..," "Looking at it from another perspective," "It would also be legitimate to say…" and the constant "On the other hand…"

Bob was very amenable to my suggesting feature stories, especially for the Sunday section; he rarely gave me a green light until the last minute, making every one a scramble under great time pressure. At one point, I was told that Nessa Forman, the art critic, would now be my editor, and to pitch stories to her. About once a month I would stand in her doorway, give about five ideas, each in one sentence, until she waved a "next" and gave a response: no, no, yes, no, yes. No second chances allowed, actual definite answers at last.

Drawing Room at The Academy

For years, I wrote the jokes for cartoonist Jessica Stanley, who occasionally came to concerts with me. She began bringing a sketch book, soon noticed by head Academy usher Marc Scuncio, quite enamored of the new tenor Luciano Pavarotti. I had no idea at the time that Scuncio, who held the post for over 40 years, also taught Spanish, French and Italian at Lincoln High School. Marc asked if Jessica would make a drawing for him, and he placed her in the proscenium box to provide a great profile. After she finished, she only had time for a quick sketch for me, with the experience enough to cement our relationship with Scuncio and his assistant, Andy Pantano, who succeeded him.

She made booklets full of drawings whenever I took her along and, despite the pressure of the late hour, the ushers insisted on our going to the Ormandy Room and showing the sketches to the artists. On Pavarotti's second visit, there was a huge line waiting to see him after the concert. Andy saw us in the corridor and motioned me past the line by saying, "Please come this way, Dr. Di Nardo," and many people probably thought he was ill; it was amusing to have this honorary title bestowed on me—at least temporarily. As soon as Pavarotti saw the drawing, he grabbed her hand and wouldn't let go for about four minutes, a moment captured in a photograph with astonished impresario Moe Septee.

Moe Septee, Luciano Pavarotti and Jessica Stanley.

Virtually every artist liked them, and even signed them—Andrés Segovia, André Watts, Riccardo Muti, and many more. Vladimir Horowitz complimented her profusely, though he was the only artist who ever refused to sign. Spanish pianist Alicia DeLarrocha held her drawing up to show a roomful of friends, taking about five minutes to write an exuberant message under her likeness. Years later, when Jessica gave up cartooning and moved, she made me a present of these priceless drawings.

Defining Comedy, Quirkiness, Soul and Noise

After a Bijou gig with Henny Youngman, at whose classic one-liners I thought I would never stop laughing, I went up to the green room to ask his advice to help me as Jessica's cartoon joke writer. "What's the essence of comedy, Henny?" I asked. "You won't like it, kid," was his response. "Don't ask." After clumsily persisting, he removed that big smile and gave me his answer.

"If I get a paper cut, it's tragedy. If a piano falls on you, that's comedy."

I found it hard to believe that all humor is based on someone else's misfortune. Still, if you consider the Chaplin agonies, the Keaton pratfalls, the pies in the face, the Marx Brothers insults, all the way to the wildly popular current television shows where people fall down and get hit by inanimate objects, Henny was right. "Doc, people don't like talking to me." "Next!"

Out on the Main Line, the Main Point brought in the fledgling country-rock stars about to hit the big labels. One December night, I took my son to hear the iconoclastic Mose Allison, who regaled the crowd with some of his quirky signature tunes like "Your Molecular Structure" and "Meet Me In No Special Place, and I'll Be There At No Particular Time." My son loved the lyric "Got No House In West Chester/Got No Chris-Craft to Cruise/Sold All My Basie With Lester/Ain't Got Nothin' But The Blues." Even a 15-year-old would understand that tragedy.

One night, at a Melba Moore concert at the Shubert (now the Merriam) Theater, everyone was standing outside on Broad Street. It turned out that Moore had brought her own band, and the promoter didn't want to pay the five musicians required by the union at that house. Evidently the five guys got another gig, and someone was sent to the club to find them, for they were to show up and sit around if they were going to be paid. And, a few nights later at the Academy of Music, Joan Baez ended her marathon show with impressions and a barefoot disco number with camera flashes going off like an air raid.

One week I was less than enthusiastic about Aretha Franklin's harsh screaming into a high-pitched mike, and the recalling of Melba Moore's shrieking that pierced like daggers. You call it soul, I call it commercially successful device.

As a single parent, doing a review meant missing my two children for a whole evening, and I tried to take one of them when possible. One night the assignment was Ted Nugent, the Motor City Madman (and now armament fanatic), and I thought my daughter Lisa would enjoy the rock instead of a constant diet of classical music. The Spectrum press box was located high up in the center of the stadium to better view the basketball and hockey games, and the rock stage was all the way at one end of the floor. Despite the enormous distance, the physical impact of every one of Nugent's chords was like a sickening punch. Lisa found cotton for her ears, wrapped a scarf around her head, cowered in the alcove between the press box and the food oval, and still heard ringing for days. Unfortunately, I had to stay for the whole assault, and could only wonder about the brain damage occurring to those sitting on the main floor a few feet away from those gigantic monitors.

Concert Instruments Now

Another attraction was country singer John Sebastian, who I called a gutsy John Denver. It recalled a couple of visits with my father to meet John Sebastian Sr., originally Sebastiani, a virtuoso who had invented the chromatic harmonica, allowing playing with enormous flexibility. He not only performed all over the world as soloist and with the Philadelphia Orchestra, and had concertos written for him by Alexander Tcherepnin and, my favorite, a sprawling four-movement concerto by Heitor Villa-Lobos. I still have three of his LPs—two on the prestigious DG label and a Columbia of three *Bach Flute Sonatas* transcribed for harmonica.

Andres Segovia. Drawing by Jessica Stanley.

Before the third Andrés Segovia concert I was to review, I went to a New York hotel to interview the great man in the lobby. He was pleasant, and asked me for my favorite guitar music. My answer was the Villa-Lobos Preludes and Etudes and, when pressed, revealed that the recording I played, the only LP of that music at the time, was by Narciso Yepes. "That peasant!" fumed Segovia, who said nothing I could use after that and cut the interview short. However, upon seeing Jessica's drawing after the concert, he did sign his name in a marvelous guitar design.

A few days later, on my regular job, I received a call summoning me to the huge corner office of Dale Davis, the *Bulletin*'s publisher. He was livid, raved a bit about the madness of hiring stupid freelancers, and eventually got to the crux of his rant. His neighbor had attended the Segovia concert, and complained that he couldn't hear the music clearly. Davis' objected to my review because it didn't mention the lack of amplification. I blurted that Segovia's guitar had never been amplified in all the many years he had been playing. Eventually Davis admitted that his neighbor was elderly, had sat in the amphitheater (the fourth and top level in the acoustically-deficient Academy of Music), and used a hearing aid—turned all the way up. He still ended our meeting with the order, "For Chrissakes, don't do THAT again!" Whatever THAT was.

Probable Excess

Conductor Marc Mostovoy's preference was solely Baroque repertoire, with concertos played by his string players in smallish halls. When his concerts moved to the much larger Academy of Music, noted guest artists were essential. He brought in recorder player Michala Petri, and even took my advice to book soprano Marni Nixon, Hollywood's "Ghostest with the Mostest," who sang *Red, White and Cole*, a Cole Porter medley, and Rachmaninoff's magnificent wordless *Vocalise*.

Despite some apprehension, I convinced Mostovoy to also book Brazilian guitarist Laurindo Almeida, more familiar through his work in bossa nova than the classical idiom. The week before his appearance, a Philadelphia judge, Richard Klein, had caused a media furor by asking the victim in a rape case whether she had been a virgin, which he felt would give the police an easier method to determine proof of the crime. The judge also happened to be the president of Mostovoy's board, and played drums in a jazz band called The Fifth Amendment.

Almeida played Bach, Fauré and Ibert and, for an encore, played several bossa nova tunes with a bassist from the orchestra and Judge Klein, who beat the drums with a "relentlessly mechanical, unyielding tattoo." The review may have gone a little too far by saying, "Someone should tell Hizzoner that bossa nova is sexy, not virginal." I hope he took it in good humor, though I'm glad I didn't have to come before him in court. Over 25 years later, I heard him playing a lunchtime concert at Reading Terminal Market with the late ex-City Councilman and pianist Ed Schwartz, and was pleased to hear him play with a slightly more varied beat.

Jazz reviews were much less frequent, though I learned a serious lesson when covering legendary jazz alto saxophonist Lee Konitz at a South Street club called Grendel's Lair. My drummer pal Bruce Klauber's band was its opener, though the sets never went off on time because they always took a break to go into the back room and watch *Benny Hill* on television. I hadn't realized my low tolerance for coherence when spirits were involved, and a few beers while waiting were my first and only instance of alcohol before a review. Konitz' florid lines somehow spun my addled brain to write several preposterous sentences. Three months later Nels Nelson, the *Daily News'* esteemed jazz writer, chided me—fortunately unnamed—on my sudsy indulgence.

Nels: "By far the most severe case of Konitzophrenia I have encountered struck a local fellow—again, a sensitive and altogether agreeable scribe—who, on the occasion of a Konitz appearance last October, was entranced by Lee's 'arched stanzas that modulated subtly from the clutches of blind alleys, the breathy warm sound searing and liquid.' He also applauded Konitz for his 'arabesques of near-baroque filigree.'

"There, for the grace of God and a decision by wiser heads to eschew musical reviewage in these pages, go I." Bless you, Nels, wherever you are.

5. SPEAKING TO LEGENDS

Because of deadlines, most interviews were done by phone. It's fairly easy when you've met the artist before, but a cold connection can be daunting. My goal was often to infer that the assignment was voluntary, not assigned. Years before, I had read an interview with violinist Itzhak Perlman, speaking about an unprepared reporter, who asked, "So you're a fiddle player, right?" That nudged me to carefully consider the questions I would ask in the few granted minutes—and never anything already published about their career or their accomplishments. I found that artists were rarely asked about those other aspects I found most fascinating: why they chose their difficult life, what the music meant to them, how they saw the world outside their art, how does it feel to perform at that level, and why they felt they needed to communicate through the talent they were given.

Considering I was just another voice on the phone, this turned out to be very wise, because most seemed to have a good time talking about things close to their heart, and they usually welcomed me when we actually met. Jazz violin legend Stephane Grappelly, guitarist Tal Farlow, Michel Legrand and drum master Max Roach were examples of artists spoken to by phone who were incredibly gracious in person after their set.

I was very fortunate to have a long chat with jazz legend Bill Evans, who agreed to meet at the now-defunct Bijou café, once the legendary Show Boat, after a long advance phone interview, in exchange for a corned beef special. His albums were revered at my house, and the classical background he had covered at Mannes College of Music showed me how much serious background meant in any playing. He had just made a recording with the great harmonica player Jean ("Toots") Thielmans, who I had met often when he played with Emil in Shearing's quintet.

It was a treat to show him a table card from Birdland that he had signed a few years before, with "$5 cover charge" on one side and his "real" chord changes to "Green Dolphin Street" on the other. Evans was brilliant, succinct, friendly, with a wistful sadness, and came about as close as an artist can to expressing his art.

Bill Evans:
My influences? I would have to say Nat Cole, George Shearing, Bud Powell and Erroll Garner as inspirations, as well as lots of horn players. In the beginning, it was a hard-driving, straight-ahead thing, but in feeling my identity I came around to a more basic form for me. I'm a quite simple per son who loves down-to-earth music that moves me, whether it be Brahms,

Bill Evans. Drawing by Jessica Stanley.

Stravinsky, Bartok or jazz. If I can feel something for the material that I can respect, and it has meaning for me, I have to hope that audiences will feel the same.

I tend to re-record tunes that I like very much, sometimes dropping them out of the repertory for a while. If you play a song a lot it becomes a challenge to find something fresh to say. It tests your resourcefulness, forcing you to dig deeper. This is a marvelous discipline.

In record sessions, like that recent one with Toots, there's not much rehearsal time possible. You have to rely on chemistry and mutual respect and, usually, the spark happens. I used to be more aware of harmonic structure in a song, not always keeping the melody line in mind. (By phone, January 10, 1979)

Bill mentioned in passing that he had written the chart of "Blue in Green," a magical tune on the famous Miles Davis album *Kind of Blue* with harmonic invention far above the other great riff tunes. Everybody except Miles just got paid for the gig, though the album soon became the best-selling jazz record in history.

In those LP days, record stores had a huge book of yellow pages with details on available songs called *PhonoLog*, with new releases and deletions each month for employees to update. I called *PhonoLog* and told them that the writing credit on the label, —M. Davis— was wrong, and wrote a letter to ASCAP and BMI. I don't know whether someone asked Miles, and surely others became involved; after a while the tune began to be recorded by other musicians, and the writing credits began to list Evans as the composer. Bill died tragically early, in 1980 at only 51, and I hope his family gets some of the royalties from his great tune.

In my carriage house studio, I had a vibraphone and, after a long day at work, I relaxed by playing along with the seminal Miles Davis-Gil Evans *Miles Ahead* album from 1957. It was the first CD I bought, for $18.95, and was astonished to find that those 33 minutes did not include what I had played along with for years on the LP. I called Columbia, before it became Sony, and bounced around until I reached a person in the jazz department who knew what I was talking about. Someone called back weeks later, and said that somehow the outtakes had been used, and it would be fixed. Sure enough, out came *Miles Ahead*, 33 minutes, without even including those outtakes, another $18.95 for a 23-year-old recording. On the album cover, Sony had the nerve to say, *Miles Ahead* is back by popular demand. For the first time, this album can be enjoyed exactly as it was intended 36 years ago."

In the 1990s, Jimmy Cobb was interviewed, being the last survivor of the classic 1959 *Kind Of Blue* recording everyone had purchased on LP, stereo LP, cassette, CD and gold CD, all at full price. He said he never listened to it, because it didn't sound at the right speed, and an article produced a flurry of investigation. It finally turned out that that the first three tracks had been recorded on an Ampex machine that was a quarter tone slow and, when played back on a Studer deck, was slightly sharp. Once again, Sony finally released it with the admonition, "Here, for the first time, is *Kind Of Blue* complete." With record companies, as in politics, there is utterly no shame.

On the original LP, the second side featured an undulating piano figure by Evans entitled "Flamenco Sketches," and a late-night, almost Styx-like dirge called "All Blues." The CD reversed the names, and many jazz writers justified the name changes through interpretation of Bill Evans' liner notes, though I'm still partial to the titles from the LP.

South Philly Atmosphere and Velvet Fog

Another local venue was the famous supper club Palumbo's, a South Philadelphia oasis featuring performers loyal to the owner Frank Palumbo. It was a legend that immigrant Italians, who landed on the dock, would know nothing about America except that they should immediately locate Palumbo's to find a job. Kippie Palumbo, Frank's wife, was an effervescent spirit who exuded graciousness to everyone who came, especially the press, while her husband was rarely seen. I was astonished when, one evening, Palumbo came over to the table and expressed condolences about the death of my father, who had passed on a few weeks before in Florida. Kippie and I were even more surprised another time when he gave my daughter Lisa, my 11-year-old guest to the club, a beautifully wrapped bottle of perfume.

Sometimes, though, the entertainers were long past their prime, and were simply nostalgia acts. Eddie Fisher appeared, his voice loaded with pounds of vibrato, no intonation, and the bad choice of a Jolson medley.

The poorest was an interminable evening with 79-year-old Rudy Vallee, who went through his long career with the aid of poorly-synchronized slides, taped accompaniment, and distorted singing. His theme *My Time Is Your Time* was certainly prophetic, since we were stuck for almost three hours of indulgence. He may have been a one-time bandleader, crooner and radio personality of the 20s and 30s, yet it was astonishing that the obvious essentials of his past image—the raccoon coat, megaphone, and even his unearthed late success in *How to Succeed in Business Without Really Trying* were omitted. No wonder they sent out the freelancer.

Mel Tormé had a huge success there in my early days, and I promised myself to try to tie in with him the next time he cycled through Philly—one that was kept in spades. In 1979, we had a chance to talk as he played the Fairmont Hotel, soon to revert back to the Bellevue Stratford.

I knew Mel had begun performing in a sailor suit at age four, was a drummer, singer and arranger for Chico Marx's band at 17, and had written several TV episodes of *The Virginian,* several novels and *The Other Side of The Rainbow*, the controversial, drug-ridden dark side of being the musical director for Judy Garland's television show. Nicknamed *The Velvet Fog* for his smooth delivery, his autobiography *It Wasn't All Velvet* added another bittersweet chapter to his legend. And, maybe most impressively, I knew he wrote all his own arrangements.

Mel Tormé:
I'm lucky that people let me do my thing, allowing me to stay passionate about the things I do. Symphony dates have become a big thing for me, and I get a chance to conduct Percy Grainger and Frederick Delius with the Pittsburgh Symphony soon. And Mel Tormé and Friends *will come to Carnegie Hall in February—I'll have Gerry Mulligan, George Shearing, Teddy Wilson, Woody Herman, Zoot Sims, Dizzy Gillespie, Carmen McRae, and Bill Evans. Imagine working with a genius like Bill Evans! There's nothing as wonderful in this business as being admired by people you admire.*

I don't always play drums in my act now, but I use Gene Krupa's original set. I wanted to have the drum head exactly like it was when Krupa was with Benny Goodman, and found a clip of the band from the film Hollywood Hotel *and had it hand-painted—G.K. on the shield with heraldic script and the B.G. art deco insignia. It must have gotten to Benny, because the next day he said, "Hey, you weren't bad." You have to know Benny to know what a compliment that is.* (Fairmont Hotel, Philadelphia, November 16, 1979)

Goodman's coldness was legendary, with the pinnacle his firing of pianist Jess Stacy after playing a magnificent extra chorus in the legendary "Sing, Sing, Sing" 1938 jazz concert at Carnegie Hall. One pianist told me he was rehearsing at Goodman's apartment with singer Ernestine Anderson, who complained that it was quite chilly. Benny went into a closet and put a sweater on.

Anyway, my conversation with Tormé turned to Delius, and I told him that I had a bunch of LPs that I had brought from England. Along with his drummer Donny Osborne, we made our way up to my Mount Airy studio, where he 'borrowed' seven of the British-pressed LPs. On my piano stand was the reduction of Delius' magical miniature *Upon Hearing the Cuckoo in Spring*, and Mel played it flawlessly. It was quite a joy to host Mel, who was always quite friendly after that, and once got us a table at the Fairmont in San Francisco in a gig with George Shearing.

On the ride back to town, he talked about how he looked forward to Christmas. "In August of 1944, we wrote a song in about an hour based on some lines my friend Bobby Wells had written to cool off. Nat Cole recorded it with his Trio, though he messed up a couple of words and did it again the next year, and once again with strings in the version everyone knows. "The Christmas Song" paid for three divorces, and when people sing it they probably don't realize that it was written by two Jewish guys with their feet in a Beverly Hills pool.

"But, after all," Mel said, "Irving Berlin gets you at Easter with "Easter Parade," the fourth of July and ballgames with "God Bless America" and "White Christmas," and he's not worried about it either!"

After the death of Hollywood studio percussionist Lou Singer, Emil made an arrangement of Delius' *Cuckoo* for six marimbas to be played at the memorial service. Even though Delius hadn't made the published piano reduction of the piece, the Delius Trust wouldn't let Emil publish his arrangement. Since Mel, who had worked with Emil, was a member of the Delius Society, I asked him to intercede, without success; John Dankworth gave it a try too, and the answer was still no. One day, Emil learned that the copyright had run out, and that put an end to all the shenanigans.

A venue called Café Society operated briefly, and brought in a nostalgia act called "The Incomparable Hildegarde." Celebrating 50 years in show biz and once a big international personality, she did the too-too-divine bit without anyone telling her that her slip was showing. Some attendees made the mistake of speaking during her act, and were admonished by "The show is on, and I am it!" Another time people clapped feebly at the end of a number, and were chided by a scornful "Don't clap now, it's only a segue!"

Fortunately, Sylvia Sims played the hall a few later, showing the subtlety characteristic of the truly great saloon singers.

Four Jazz Giants

Blind pianist George Shearing came to town to play with Peter Nero's Philly Pops and, after telling Emil stories, we settled down to talk.

George Shearing:
I'm always ready to play the Bach D Minor or several Mozart concertos, but since it's a pops concert about love, I'll have some arrangements ready. Peter wants to try some of my old things on two pianos, like "Brain Waves" from around 1949, meaning I'll have to practice up.

As one gets older, new approaches and explorations become stimulating. I love Delius and Debussy for their subtlety and shading, and would like to do some Alec Wilder-type chamber things with bass and percussion, no drums. With my (second) wife Ellie, we take a tandem bike ride in Central Park every chance we get! (Philadelphia hotel, January 30, 1981)

In a West Philadelphia club called Dino's, the famed drummer from the early bebop days Max Roach was scheduled to play, and I asked for the assignment.

Max Roach:
It's flattering to see kids working to get my old style down pat, but change is the only constant in music.

A creative musician should surround himself with new music, and play with the finest talent available. Charlie Parker, Bud Powell, these were ex-

emplary individual thinkers. That's what I look for, individuality, though it goes without saying that a high level of musicianship is required. (By phone, February 26, 1981)

Ripley's was another place to play concerts, named after a clothing store on South Street whose sign was too big to remove. (Years later, it was converted into a Tower Records shop, now a shoe store.) In June 1981, 73-year-old violinist Stephane Grappelly performed in the hall, still playing brilliantly since his early-1930s work with Django Reinhardt in the Quintette of the Hot Club of Paris. His sound is unmistakable, and the joy that flows from his instrument on his many recordings was a sure cure for any blues.

Grappelly was as sweet a man as his playing, and was riding the crest of several albums, including one with Yehudi Menuhin. A British interviewer had mistakenly booked them both for one show, and asked if they would play together. On a Grappelly video, he says he was completely in awe of the fabled Menuhin, and Menuhin says he was terrified to play with such a giant since he had never improvised one note in his life. In a tense rehearsal room, Grappelly asked Menuhin what song he wanted to play, though Menuhin simply didn't know any...except "Jalousie," a tune he had played with his sister Hepzibah as a kid. Menuhin wrote out the whole part and simply read it on the show, while Grappelly improvised all over the place. The show was an immense success, leading to an album of duets that has made me smile for years—-and three follow-up albums as well.

Grappelly had just played with Pink Floyd, David Grisman and Paul Simon, and traveled with a bunch of very young-looking players.

Stephane Grappelly:
That's how I keep young! I taught myself how to play, learning to listen very well. I'll be playing only acoustic violin here, although sometimes I like to experiment with electric ones.

Philadelphia was the birthplace of Joe Venuti, my old friend (Venuti died in 1978), and we toured Italy together around 1965. My father was Italian, my mother French. But because of our names, they thought we were natives—maybe that's why were well-received! (Philadelphia hotel, June 19, 1981)

Before Grappelly's concert, I drove to West Philadelphia to pick up Margie in a house where a party was going on. Though in a hurry, I was inveigled into buying a lottery ticket for a late-night drawing. Returning after a blissful evening with Grappelly's soaring music, I found I had won a 21" television set, and considered it an encore from the great Frenchman.

A few weeks later, master vibraphonist Red Norvo dazzled the Ripley playing his the xylophone ("wood voice"), originally a vaudeville instrument. In Paul Whiteman's orchestra, the vibraphone was played for effects and the marimba was for solos. After a 1944 rehearsal with Benny Goodman, Norvo turned the rotating vibraphone paddles off to make his notes more precise, eventually placing tiny microphones under all the metal bars.

Red Norvo:
There's a clearer sound without the motor—for instance, with guitar, bass and flute, the vibrato would sound like Bert Lahr singing with the Mills Brothers.

I really can't describe what happens when musicians with different viewpoints play together. In the studio with (bassist) Slam Stewart and Dizzy Gillespie, we didn't have one note worked out, but something happened. Regardless of style or age, something jells if the attitude is there.

I don't like the pressure of having to work constantly. I turned down a tour of 61 straight one-nighters recently, and it made me remember the old days. Five shows a day, seven days, a Sunday matinee, plus 24 to 30 hours broadcasting on the radio every week. But I wish I had composed more—I guess I'm a frustrated writer! (By phone, July 2, 1981)

Variations on Themes

On a Hollywood trip, I had a chance to meet the team of Jack Elliott and Allyn Ferguson, two composers who had written the theme music to a wealth of television shows like *Charlie's Angels*, *Barney Miller*, and so many more. Elliott, who had studied with no less than Bohuslav Martinů and Lukas Foss, and Ferguson, who had worked with Ernst Toch and Aaron Copland, clearly knew what they were about. They had begun the Foundation for New Music in 1978, attracting contemporary music and taking music into the Los Angeles area schools and public places. At that time, commissioning was relatively dead, with few opportunities for new music to be performed.

While I was out there, their performing organization The Orchestra (changed later to the New American Orchestra) played a concert at the Music Center, with its roster filled with the cream of the crack studio players. It was a thrill to see bassist Ray Brown, reedman Bud Shank, the magnificent hornist Vincent De Rosa and many more, plus Emil, in a concert of electrifying music by Dick Grove, Lalo Schifrin and many more great composers.

In April 1981, The Orchestra came to New York for a live two-hour televised concert from NBC's famed Studio 8-H, sharing the spotlight with Sarah Vaughan, Steve Lawrence and Eydie Gorme, Henry Mancini and dancer Gregory Hines. It was an opportunity to hang out and watch the complex sets revolve from behind a bass case in back of the band.

Jack Elliott:
Go down the list of the movie and TV producers, studios, independents. They won't give something back into the industry, but they receive, boy, do they receive. Maybe we'll commission the next Rhapsody in Blue—*or green, or purple.*

We can't play Strauss waltzes like the Vienna Philharmonic under Willi Boskovsky, but nobody can play American music like us. When Bartók and Liszt and Brahms and Mozart wrote from nationalistic melodies, it was art; we have different sources, but Americans don't yet see them as legitimate. (By phone, April 24, 1981)

Book Deal—and Book Dealing

My straight job had a bi-weekly newsletter, giving me a chance to write a column of theatre, music and film attractions. It finally morphed into a movie review column, whose rating system of zero to four tried—and sometimes succeeded—in having a clever tag line befitting the film. It couldn't be forced, and sometimes it wasn't ideal, though it was fun to try to make it work out.

A few years later, about 1979, the first VCRs arrived and video stores sprang up in every neighborhood. Since I had accumulated quite a few reviews by that time, I asked some of the staff people who dealt in printed material and advertising in local papers for advice. After printing the pages on a primitive Epson computer and printer, and receiving a cover drawing from my artist friend Jessica Stanley, I soon found myself with 1,000 copies of *On the Set*, a title we thought appropriate and clever. With batch ads in local weeklies and a post office box at the main Post Office, I was ready to roll—selling them for a steal price of three dollars. I also took some to B. Dalton books at 15th and Chestnut Street in Philadelphia, and happened to chat with the manager and buyer John Pawley, who agreed to put some on the checkout counter.

During those years a local house, Running Press, was doing very well with reprints and with the Trivial Pursuit game, and someone suggested I contact them. It turned out that the owners, Larry and Buzz Teacher, seemed very impressed that I had sold as many copies of *On the Set* by myself, and offered to put out a much slicker edition. In time I received the marked-up galleys from an editor named Deidre, who sported Goth black lipstick and a haughty attitude. I was to receive a $500 advance, and royalties dependent on sales. Things looked pretty rosy.

The title was changed to *Movies on Tape*, and sported a book in the shape of a VHS tape, quite superior to my more simple design. I found later that my review of *Terms of Endearment*, calling it manipulative and phony, had been rewritten and given three-and-a-half stars instead of two. (In a phone call about this alteration of my opinion, Diedre's curt response was, "You were wrong.")

I mentioned John Pawley in the dedication, and he was gracious enough to suggest a book signing. It turned out to be a double signing, with my $3.95 paperback sitting next to the opulent $35 art book *Art Nouveau Jewelry* by the famous doctor Joseph Sataloff, father of my friend Dr. Robert Sataloff. You often hear people say "he wrote the book on that," but this father-son team of ear-nose-throat doctors actually wrote the book on Otorhinolaryngology.

There were 500 reviews in the book, and after a few years we spoke about a new edition. Though I hadn't a thousand reviews yet, I went back and rented some that had fallen through the cracks and soon padded the total list to reach that grand number. The galleys were edited, and the second edition was ready to go when Larry called to say there would be no advance, only money on the back end.

Around that time, there was a highly-publicized law suit by columnist Art Buchwald, who proved in court that he had written the idea behind the Paramount film *Coming To America*, a hit starring Eddie Murphy and James Earl Jones. Though the picture hadn't cost much to make and grossed over $100 million, the studio accountants testified that the movie lost money and, after a lot of media attention and scandal, Buchwald settled for an undisclosed amount. That led me to believe that there were layers of accountants with canny skill in fudging numbers guaranteeing that there would never be a back end. Since the new reviews had already been published in the small paper, I declined. It's one thing to work for a small amount, but working for free for others to profit is bad luck.

Around that time, the famous *Chicago Sun-Times* critic Roger Ebert had mentioned his favorite 10 movies on his popular Siskel and Ebert television show. I sent him a copy of my book with my 10 favorites, nine legitimate ones with, thrown in as a gag, the film *Beneath the Valley of the Dolls*, knowing that he had co-written the script with bosom maven Russ Meyer. Unfortunately, I mixed it up with another Meyer film, the much raunchier *Beneath the Valley of the Ultra-Vixens*. Ebert's friendly response:

"Thanks for your encouraging letter and for being the only person I know who includes *Beneath the Valley of the Ultra-Vixens* on the same list, for whatever reason, as *Alexander Nevsky*. Not everybody picks up on the montage."

The Ring and The Grove

Applause, the house organ for the local PBS radio/television station, was another outlet for a monthly classical piece. The most fun, in retrospect, was a long interview with Otto Schenk, the famous German director who had designed the huge—and now, foolishly scrapped—Metropolitan Opera production of Wagner's gigantic *Ring* cycle, conducted by James Levine.

Otto Schenk:
I took an oath in heaven that I would never direct Wagner's Ring *or Goethe's play* Faust, *because I felt my talent was not up to my wishes. But it has been a luxurious thing not to do it, just to love it and imagine how it could be. Levine had the right words to approach me, to seduce me, to make me hungry to do it, after long discussions. He would not accept my "no."*

In Germany right now there is an illness—I call it 'interpretitis'—in which the stager shows his own political, 'nowadays' approach by applying it to The Ring. When working on it, you can feel the passion continuously, like hypnosis. There was no way for him not to write The Ring, and in working on it you must feel that there is no way not to do it.

These characters are very human, they are not gods. There's greed, promises, children disobeying, a brother loving a sister, not enough love, too much love. These traits are human, not god-like—no one knows how a god behaves. God's great trick was to make Jesus like a man, allowing us to understand his actions.

Nothing bothers me while doing this work but my lack of talent. It's a child living for itself, I'm only the mother. (At Metropolitan Opera, April 10, 1990)

The magazine had sent a photographer separately to photograph Schenk and, at his request, I sent him a copy of the magazine. The photographer must have pleased him because, in June of 1990, I received the following formal letter from Vienna:

Dear Mr. Di Nardo:
This is the best story that was ever written about me! And on the pictures I look like I would love to look like.
Yours,
Otto Schenk

I was also contacted to update the Philadelphia section of the *Grove Dictionary of Music*, which involved receiving a complimentary copy of the 29 volumes.

Freelancers need to take every opportunity they can, and the message of this section is to negotiate the eventual regularity of articles and the pay schedule up front, always asking for a bit more, without any inference that you really need the money. The publication must have the outlook that they need you more than you need them, even if that's far from the case.

Headlines, Extremes and Finale

Newspaper readers may not realize that reporters do not write their headlines, subheads or photo captions. (Sometimes editors will also change the lead line (or "lede"—spelled this way to distinguish it from the word lead, the kind used in old typesetting machines.)

This stark lesson was learned in a December 1981 concert by the Concerto Soloists of Philadelphia (now the Chamber Orchestra of Philadelphia) led by Marc Mostovoy and featuring the famous German hornist Hermann Baumann. After brilliantly soloing in the Mozart Rondo and Concerto No. 2, plus the Haydn D Major played on a valveless Baroque horn, Baumann asked the enthusiastic audience if they would like to hear examples of other ancient instruments. He performed melodies on another ancient horn, a hunting horn, and even one made out of kelp used to signal Norwegian sailors. The next morning, my review's headline summed up the whole brilliant concert: "GERMAN HORN PLAYER MAKES MUSIC ON SEAWEED TUBE."

One dark day soul singer Millie Jackson, known for her raunchy persona, appeared at the staid Academy of Music. Jackson began by stunning the audience by singing the whole first movement of Beethoven's Fifth Symphony with "Fuck You" as the sole lyric. (Fortunately, she didn't take the repeats.) I wrote, "profanity needs the strategy of a bunt—once in a while, when unexpected, it has great impact; when every other word, it's just a flaunt."

Of course, I could only refer to it obliquely. In my story I wrote the phrase, "a singer that took liberties," and an editor corrected me by insisting on "a singer who took liberties." At the time I thought this ridiculous, considering the context, though she was absolutely grammatically correct. And, besides such basic rules of grammar, every newspaper also has its style guidelines; for instance, the New York Times still refers to rocker Meat Loaf as "Mr. Loaf."

But, while driving home, I wished I had said, "Quick, somebody call Ira Gershwin, and have him change his song title to "The Girl WHO Got Away!"

In the last days of 1981, the utter opposite of the artistic spectrum brought in Barbara Cook, Marian the Librarian from *The Music Man* in the flesh. This pinnacle of cabaret singers asked for the lights to be turned on to admire the details of the Academy's elegant interior, and made the house into a large living room.

During the period when commissions were given to the most abstruse atonal music, every composer was learning to write in this dodecaphonic style. Harold Boatrite referred to this as bloop-bleep music; it continued until the audiences only consisted of the composer's friends, the commissions dried up, and composers suddenly discovered tonality. This music was difficult to comprehend, but less boring than the ensuing onslaught of minimalism, long stretches of repetition in faint hope of a key change.

In the last days of 1981, there were shifts in publishers and much talk of cutbacks. At that time, the *Bulletin*'s circulation was over 400,000, more than the *Philadelphia Inquirer* and the *Philadelphia Daily News* combined. Nevertheless, with more upstairs suits on the payroll than the advertising would support, things became grim. On January 29, 1982, the *Bulletin* published its last edition, with the January paycheck never to be seen. That's it, I thought, the end of that road.

All I remember now of that bustling newsroom was a notice plastered on a column:

"If your mother says she loves you, check it out."

6. MISSION: IMPROBABLE

Here the story necessarily rewinds a few years.

When Romeo Cascarino was a boy, he passed through Philadelphia's City Hall and noticed William Penn's *Prayer for Philadelphia*, mounted on a plaque in the North access. The words moved him deeply, and when he received a commission in 1950 from Singing City to write a choral work, he used the text of the *Prayer*. He became fascinated by Penn's life and legacy and, when another commission came up three years later, he used the text of the famous Indian Treaty with the Lenni-Lenape tribe, one of the few that was never broken.

The idea of using these choruses as the finale of an opera came to mind, and he asked his friend Peggy Gwynn to begin work on a libretto.

William Penn begins with a London scene, with three people bragging about informing on the Quakers for money; Penn assembles his people to demonstrate that their faith is no threat, and is arrested. While in jail, a friend who has visited America tells of its opportunities, and Penn and his wife Gulielma envision a new world of religious freedom.

The second act features a heartfelt farewell scene, since Gulielma could not travel (and would die while he was in America); the words come from Penn's emotional letters to her. Cascarino said he was too emotionally drained for over a year before starting on the shipboard scene, depicting the journey with constant deaths and an urging by Penn for the remaining travelers to keep believing in their cause. In further conversations, I discovered the reason for his slow progress, his instinctive and patient search for each *note choisi*—the already-chosen, or perfect note for that moment. For this reason, the work's completion occurred 25 years after that first chorus.

The opera's finale is set in the new town of Philadelphia, through the eyes of a stranger seeing its progress, and ends with the procession, the *Prayer*, and the final tableau of the Treaty Scene, familiar from the famous Benjamin West tableau painted 89 years later.

I was assigned to review performances of *William Penn* in 1975 and 1977, both in the cavernous hall at Drexel University. At these readings, I recalled having made the recording of the farewell duet years before. As I wrote in my review, it deserved much, much more rehearsal time, as well as a staging to bring it completely to life. Romeo gave me a recording of that second performance on two cassettes, though I didn't listen to it for several months. One night, driving back from Boston in the wee hours, I played the cassettes and somehow heard through the mistakes, the tentativeness of the orchestra and the echo of the hall; I could hardly concentrate on the road, because I absolutely heard the utter spirit of his intention.

The next day I called and told him that he had written a masterpiece. In his gracious way, he thanked me and said, "Well, at least it was heard."

It bothered me tremendously that a man could work on something that close to his heart, for a quarter of a century, and receive only a performance far from ideal, without even the theatrical aspect to emphasize the pageantry of his vision. I suppose that conversation made it my mission, although it was clearly represented an impossible project. Several acquaintances—I suppose they weren't really friends—assured me that with a responsible straight job, two teenagers, reviewing for the *Bulletin*, and portraits and models' portfolios to shoot whenever possible, getting involved was a noble, yet foolish endeavor.

Yet I couldn't stop thinking about it, and requested a meeting with the director of the Opera Company of Philadelphia, Margaret Anne Everitt. She had developed some imaginative ideas, including bringing in a fabulous New York City Opera production of Janacek's *The Cunning Little Vixen*, and sponsoring the first Pavarotti Competitions—though her imagination would soon mean leaving the company with a huge deficit.

We met in her office, and I boldly suggested that if I somehow raised the money, she could add it to her schedule; that way, as a co-production, I'd be able to use her resources of professionals who knew how to stage, contract and promote the opera. She mentioned that opera productions cost more than I probably could guess, that she doubted that such a joint project was in her interest, and that it was extremely unlikely that such an opera could—or would—be staged in the Academy of Music. It was actually a very severe brushoff, though in the descending elevator I was struck by an unfamiliar sensation—that nothing could possibly stop me.

Full of inflated certainty, I called her the next morning to ask her assistance with some details and left a message, something I repeated every business day for the next month. None of the messages were ever returned, though I developed a very friendly relationship with her secretary.

Having basically no clue about how to proceed, I asked Marc Mostovoy for some advice. He suggested having some influential people hear some of the music, and arranged for Romeo, Dolores, and baritone Edward Bogusz to perform several arias and play a recording of the final choruses. At a small center city apartment, they performed for Otto and Dorothy Haas, William Kohler (who handled the Haas affairs), Todd Cooke (president of the Philadelphia Savings Fund Society) and Mrs. Peggy Cooke. Kohler thought the singing was too loud, though Marc thought Mrs. Haas was impressed.

One day, on my job, I received a call from Michael Korn, the founder of the Philadelphia Singers, who also led them as Opera Company's chorus. To my astonishment, Michael wanted a contract for his chorus to perform in *William Penn*. "Michael," I said, "I have no money yet, it's just an idea." "I don't care," he insisted. "I was just told that if we sing in your opera we're all fired, and nobody's going to treat me like that!" He said that the musicians were given the same ultimatum, though none of the opera's players I asked recalled such an edict.

Though it was still about 1979, I found that the City was planning an event called Century Four in 1982, celebrating the 300th anniversary of the founding of the city by William Penn, an event captured in the opera's final act. Though I spoke to some of the promoters, no one was very interested in the opera.

Marc Mostovoy came through again. Evidently he had been talking to Mrs. Haas, who liked the idea and the music, and to Richard Doran, the managing director to Mayor Bill Green. He said that Doran had promised to match any contribution by Mrs. Haas, and that a meeting was set up to discuss the project. I was elated, thinking that maybe she would offer a few hundred dollars to start the ball rolling.

I found that she was the embodiment of old money: she had revamped the historic Walnut Street Theater, the panorama of Philadelphia's early street layout at Welcome Park, the Morris Arboretum and many other noble projects, all without her name on them. She was a dear woman who came in on the train to the Reading Terminal, looked not at all like a wealthy person and was remarkably kind. On several occasions when I had to visit her at her home in Ambler, she was on her knees gardening.

The meeting was attended by Mrs. Haas, Doran, assistant managing director William McLaughlin, myself and Marc, who made sure to mention the matching offer. I described the opera and its relevance to the upcoming celebration, and Mrs. Haas reiterated her thought that it would be a worthy and important event.

Finally, Doran asked how much she was willing to invest in the project, and Mrs. Haas calmly looked at me and said, "Well, Tom has assured me that it's a very worthy project, and I'm willing to contribute $50,000." Doran and McLaughlin reacted as if they were punched, squinting at me as a flimflammer supreme. At that moment, I had no idea that Mrs. Haas was going to be asked to contribute substantially to the Century IV celebration in the future, and that she would be treated with kid gloves—meaning no possibility of reneging on this deal.

After that, a committee was hastily assembled including Marc, Mrs. Haas and Mr. Kohler, Sol Schoenbach, who had been Romeo's friend since Army days, Academy of Vocal Arts artistic director Dino Yannopoulos, David Crownover and Henry Gerstley, who offered his lovely home on Panama Street for meetings. I wanted to come up with an interesting name for our odd group and suggested William Penn Alliance, a title that Crownover felt sounded like ships in the North Atlantic, so we settled for the generic William Penn Opera Committee.

I mentioned that having Dolores, a trained soprano who had studied with legendary soprano Licia Albanese and taught voice at Combs College of Music, in the role of Penn's wife Gulielma, was part of the deal, and fortunately no one objected.

Dolores Cascarino. Credit: Glamour Photo.

Marc had also suggested that I approach Glenmede, a wing of the prestigious Pew Foundation, now that Mrs. Haas' name could be used. Requirements for proposals in 1980 were nowhere near as rigorous as they are now, and I put together a package, asking for $10,000, and dropped it off on Rittenhouse Square.

A few days later I received a call from a lady named Ruth Parker from Glenmede, who wanted to meet with me. She was very gracious, and thought that the opera was an excellent idea; she kept pushing the proposal back toward me and, when I asked what she didn't like, she said several times, "There's zero wrong with it, just think it over again."

I mulled it over all weekend, and mentioned it to Margie. She said, "If she kept saying there's zero wrong with it, maybe she meant the amount." "Do you think I should have asked for $1,000?" I asked. "Well, one thousand won't really help you that much. Why not add a zero and make it a hundred thousand? What do you have to lose?" Somehow, her clarity made a lot of sense. I dropped it off on Monday at lunchtime with great hesitation, just before one of our committee meetings.

When I mentioned it, some of the members treated me with sheer disdain. "Well, you've just scuttled your project," Crownover said. "You should have asked us for advice before doing something that foolhardy." I felt completely silly, though Mrs. Haas and Marc were kind enough not to comment.

A few days later I received a call from Ruth Parker. "Hello, Tom," she said, "every thing is approved. All we need is your bank account number to transfer the funds."

I was stunned. Two weeks ago I had nothing but a goofy idea and, assuming the City would come through, I suddenly had two hundred grand—and not even a bank account! It simply doesn't happen like this anymore.

It was decided that the tax-exempt status of Combs College of Music, where Romeo and Dolores taught, would handle the funds, and its president, Helen Braun, agreed not to tell Romeo—just in case the whole project fell through.

I thought this vast amount of money was sufficient, and realized I'd have to learn how to produce an opera. The first step was to ask Doran to produce a letter from Mayor Green written to the president of my company, requesting some kind of leave to be able to work on the opera for the civic good. My president agreed—as long as I was able to complete my regular work.

My most important meeting was with John Callahan, the head of the stagehands and also the head of the union, an Irish stronghold. He agreed to head up the job for $1200 weekly, when the time came, and suggested John Breen for prop man at the same rate.

I began dealing with the Academy of Music manager Hugh Walsh, first through his assistant Maureen Lynch, who took my enthusiasm for this project with an unsurprising skepticism. Before long, though, my dealings with Maureen, Hugh and his assistant John Schmidt became enormously helpful, and they guided me through some technical details I never could have discovered elsewhere. Maureen is still the engine behind the Academy's operation, a dear friend to me and everyone who works in the house.

The committee assumed that Yannopolous would direct, and he suggested his Swiss friend Toni Businger to design sets and costumes. Little did I know that Swiss opera houses were subsidized by the government, meaning that Businger had no concerns about cost. He sent sketches to Adirondack Scenic, who would begin to warn me about the colossal scope of his designs.

As far as casting the title role, I asked James Morris (an Academy of Vocal Arts alumnus), John Shirley-Quirk and even Sherrill Milnes—though Milnes was willing to be on our board if only to make our stationery more impressive.

Marc's orchestra was booked by agent Thea Dispeker, who suggested her artist John Cheek, a bass-baritone who regularly sang at the Met, and fortunately he was available. Yannopoulos saw a great opportunity for the Academy of Vocal Arts, because there were eight small roles to give their artists experience at the Academy of Music. It also meant the baton of Christofer Macatsoris, for whom I had enormous respect, as conductor.

I wanted to wait until all the contracts were signed before telling Romeo of the plan; the fear of my inexperience scuttling the project was never far from my mind. On December 20, 1980, my children and I visited Romeo and

Dolores and, after dinner, someone turned on the television to a live opera from the Met. They were presenting the first performance of Alban Berg's *Lulu* with the restored third act, and there was an announcement that the indisposed soprano Teresa Stratas was being replaced by Julia Migenes-Johnson. We watched this work, about as far from Romeo's lyrical music as one could imagine, out of amazement at an understudy stepping in to this fearsomely difficult vocal challenge.

The plan was to tell him about the project, though we were captivated by the opera until it was over. I had to wake up my children before making the announcement, showing Romeo and Dolores the contracts and scheduling for his opera. It was truly a night to remember, certainly no less emotional than it was for Migenes-Johnson.

On The Job Training

Lots of details went unattended due to my lack of experience, and the unwillingness of the Opera Company to offer assistance with such details. I once was in a meeting with my vice-president when his thoughtful secretary put a call through on the speakerphone; Hugh Walsh at the Academy of Music needed the insurance certificates for the sewing machines. What sewing machines? For the seamstresses. What seamstresses? Well, though you've sent the singers' measurements to Malabar in Toronto, they always need adjustment when they arrive. Whoops! Find some sewing machines and seamstresses.

Another time, someone from the wigmaker's union left a message at my job to mention that wig forms now must be wooden, not foamcore. What? Wigs? Wigmakers?

Except for Marc and Mrs. Haas, the committee offered no real assistance, only constant skepticism that this could be a successful venture; regardless of the reports, they had no awareness of the complexity involved. Every week I constantly discovered more of the hundred basic production essentials, usually handled by opera staff people. The usefulness of the meetings was often wasted by Yannopoulos' insistence on long examples of what he must have considered his skill as a raconteur. Another time Schoenbach came and took up 40 minutes of our hour with Mrs. Haas telling funny stories without relevance. After each instance I asked them not to attend and, in Schoenbach's case, with more annoyance than he was used to hearing—"Sol, are you Romeo's friend or his enemy?"

Every week I became aware of innumerable details and basic production essentials, as well as advertising, promotion, costuming, equipment, legalities and many other aspects. Through suggestions made by Walsh, Callahan and others who were used to chores executed by skilled professionals, it became a crash course in what opera staffs do, though usually too late. I made up posters and flyers, and tried to do the basic publicity;

Romeo Cascarino in front of poster.
Credit: Michael Mercanti/*Philadelphia Daily News.*

each day meant running around the city, working at my office until late, finally driving up to see Combs president Helen Braun late at night to explain why I needed certain checks. She also had begun a fund-raising project, though at the time I thought $200,000 enough to cover anything.

While at the *Bulletin*, I had been contacted by Ruthanne Gage, who had handled the public relations for the Opera Ebony company. Since their performance went on in April, I thought her skills would be most helpful after her show was over. Fortunately, she was indispensable and willing to do a thousand detail chores with energy and commitment, as did my daughter Lisa, a theater major who acted as assistant stage manager.

Toni Businger came to Philadelphia a month before the premiere, and he and Yannopoulos were highly annoyed when John Callahan wasn't available. It wasn't a matter of pique—he just happened to be running the now-defunct 100,000-seat JFK Stadium for The Who's farewell tour, with opening acts Santana and The Clash; 91,451 showed up for one of the largest ticketed single-show, non-festival stadium concerts ever held in the United States.

Callahan actually visited Adirondack Scenic, and returned to say that the five sets were enormous. He had a great suggestion—there were some huge boxes at the Academy, four by four by six feet, and he asked them to save wood by building some of the sets to fit over those boxes. It was obvious that he had a certain amount of contempt for Businger, who had designed without any consideration of practicality. Academy manager Hugh Walsh told me it was one of the largest, if not the largest, sets that had ever been in the Academy of Music.

At the first rehearsal, John Cheek stunned most of the choristers when they saw that he had memorized his huge part. At one point there was a reception at Henry Gerstley's house, where the host showed John his collection of rare original Donizetti scores. John was amazed, though he declined when Gerstley offered to loan him the score for a Donizetti opera he was rehearsing.

Macatsoris wanted as many orchestral rehearsals as possible, and I scheduled seven—lots more than for any other project. There were six choral rehearsals as well, all attended by Romeo and myself. Mostovoy contracted the orchestra, including many musicians who were friends. I told trumpeter John Thyhsen he would have a big solo in the second-act intermezzo; we still kid that, although it was memorable, it wasn't actually as long as I had claimed.

Besides the chorus, consisting mainly of the superb Philadelphia Singers, there was a need for an amateur chorus to portray the dissenters in the first act and the Indians in the finale. I had spoken with Sean Deibler, who was creating the Choral Arts Society (with whom my son Marc would eventually sing), which couldn't be formed soon enough.

In another stroke of good fortune, Dr. Robert Sataloff was able to involve his Thomas Jefferson Chorus. They were excellent, and it was fascinating that their day jobs ranged from nursing and maintenance to world-famous surgeons.

Sataloff, who had received his Masters from Cascarino at Combs College, founded and led Jefferson's orchestra and chorus, presenting some of the greatest choral music and masses at Jefferson's main hall, eventually expanding to First Baptist Church. It was an ideal way to foster morale and mutual respect across the myriad professions, a human relations coup.

Over 25 years later, Sataloff became profoundly disappointed when Jefferson decided not to fund the $40,000 annual stipend necessary to secure the venues for its annual concerts. This was even more troubling because, around that time, Jefferson was secretly negotiating to sell Thomas Eakins' iconic painting *The Gross Clinic* to the Crystal Bridges Museum of American Art, under construction in Bentonville, Arkansas by the Walton (Walmart) family, for $68 million. Eventually, money was raised through donations and the selling of paintings by the Philadelphia Museum of Art and the Academy of Fine Arts to keep the painting in Philadelphia.

During our planning, the Opera Company had a show at the Academy. Our advertisement for *William Penn*, paid for in advance, was mysteriously absent from their program. We printed leaflets for the ushers to stuff into the programs, infuriating Everett, who insisted that it be stopped. Luckily, the ushers paid no attention.

Yannopoulos was an excellent director infected with a huge amount of insecurity, thrust into working on the premiere of an opera. He acted with petulance during the rehearsals, insisting on calling his co-star Dolores Cascarino instead of her professional name, Dolores Ferraro, just to needle her. She actually was asked to audition in the empty Academy, singing quite well—though I told Yannopoulos, Korn and conductor Macatsoris that they were hired to do their job, not to choose the lead singers.

I was Dino's whipping boy for virtually everything that occurred to him, with lots of constant yelling and screaming, for he evidently needed someone to punish. This went on publicly until about three days before the premiere, when I lost my temper, brought him a copy of his contract, and told him that I always wanted Kay Walker to direct, and if he wanted to tear the contract up, I'd gladly accept. Curiously, he acted with civility from that time on. I continually insisted that he didn't need to create stage busyness at every moment, just have some trust in the music, the ultimate guide to the action; no visuals can disguise a lack of musical merit.

Nevertheless, when he found out one of the singers' partners was a choreographer, he had him work out a dance for the shipboard scene. I told Yannopoulos that, if he had Quakers dance, he would guarantee a roar of laughter from the audience. We tried to have just the sailors dance, but only a few of the choristers who could dance were dressed in sailors' costumes. He did it anyway, his only big mistake.

At one rehearsal of Act II, doing the change between the farewell and the shipboard scene, Yannopoulos asked if it could be done faster than the eight estimated minutes when the hall's lights would be lowered and the curtain drawn. Callahan simply left the curtain up and, when the first scene ended, an army of men ran onto the stage, disassembled the set, furiously brought in the new set and put it up in almost exactly eight minutes. "Think we could do it any faster, Dino?" yelled Callahan, with all the stagehands looking at Yannopoulos.

His idea for the end of the shipboard scene, though, was brilliant, though it may now seem obvious. The call from the crow's nest comes in two "Land Ho!" declamations (with, in between them, the chorus singing 16 separate lines), suddenly turning toward the audience as the curtain falls. The cheering attendees got it completely—they were US.

Though Callahan needed to hire a huge staff to run the show, they did everything possible to keep costs down. In those days, because the Orchestra didn't allow spotlights in the Academy to be permanently mounted, lights were rented for each opera from a company in Newark. John sent one of his men to pick up the lights, and the driver called me one afternoon. He was taking the lights home, because if he brought them for load-in to the Academy that evening it would cost double time, and the next day after the

Orchestra's morning rehearsal they could come in on the Orchestra's eight-hour dime.

Hugh Walsh, the friendly manager of the Academy, needed insurance for the lights before they could be brought into the house. I asked Marc Mostovoy for the name of his personal insurance man, who found it hard to believe a stranger was asking him to insure $180,000 worth of lights, currently stored in someone's garage. By some miracle, he was willing to fax a certificate to the Academy office, and received a couple of comp tickets. Afterwards, I called to thank him, and he reiterated that he simply couldn't believe that he had done anything that crazy.

Curtain

The week before the performance, I arranged for a deli lunch in the Academy lobby to thank the stagehands, light personnel, flymen, and all the people behind the scenes that the public never sees. Romeo shook hands and thanked every one of them. They knew that Romeo wasn't personally responsible for it turning out to be a monster project, and were grateful for the recognition because no one had ever done anything like that before. A few weeks after the show, a few stagehands took me down into the bowels of the Academy and showed me a signed photo of Romeo posted on their Wall of Fame.

At the dress rehearsal, I brought in my Hasselblad to take some photographs. Romeo's niece Deborah Cascarino took some too, as well as someone from the Port of History Museum, who was putting together a show of photographs about Philadelphia's history.

The backstage guys told me that, at intermission of that final dress rehearsal, someone took the fuses from the speaker monitors, preventing the chorus from hearing themselves. The late Jim Gilroy, known by everyone as Rainbow, told me that he followed the person, who he claimed was from the Opera Company, into the Locust Rendezvous across the street to get the fuses back.

Luckily, I was able to find three seamstresses, because the costumes needed lots of alterations. The sets finally arrived in five enormous vans, with the crew showing amazement at their size and insisting that they could only fit one at a time into the Academy.

We had also arranged that, after the performances, the sets could be stored in the basement of the rarely-used Philadelphia Civic Center at 34th and Spruce Streets.

The performances were originally scheduled for Sunday, October 24, the final day of the year-long Century Four celebration with a large ecumenical council in the morning, Tuesday the 26th and Friday the 29th. It was disappointing that the Tuesday performance was cancelled due to poor ticket sales, meaning that only two shows would be performed.

Recordings of the Orchestra during an interim year were made by an engineer named Ed Kelly, who placed a few microphones on the stage and taped both performances for us. Jessica made some beautiful signs with the names of the performers for their dressing rooms, and it became apparent that the opera might actually happen.

I asked everyone to sign three posters—one for Romeo, one for Mrs. Haas, and one for me. John Callahan signed, and made sure his name went just above Toni Businger's.

I had taken some tickets to give away, and distributed a few through the board members, the insurance guy, the people on my job who had put up with two years of my task, Jessica, Ruthanne and her parents, and Mrs. Haas—who insisted on paying for a box. Todd Cooke left a message asking for comps, and I left a message saying sorry, he'd have to buy them. Sol Schoenbach wanted 16 tickets for his friend Mr. Segal from Detroit.

Since I was writing for the *Daily News*, I couldn't write about my own project; the paper sent Nels Nelson, the jazz writer who had also done theater reviews, to the show. Dan Webster wrote a Sunday *Inquirer* interview with Romeo, and said he attended that night though that his editor nixed a review. It seemed a little bizarre—here was an opera written by a Philadelphian, about the founding of the city and performed on its 300th anniversary, performed by the (expanded to 60) Chamber Orchestra of Philadelphia, the Philadelphia Singers, and our Academy of Vocal Arts, with a Met star in the lead, and it wasn't worthy of a review. Fortunately, many others wrote about it, including Variety, and seven regional papers, all enthusiastically.

I had written the late Andrew Porter of *The New Yorker*, who chose the cancelled performance and couldn't attend the last show, never responding to a request to return the vocal score.

That weekend was a whirlwind. My mother flew in from Florida, my sister from Oregon and my son from Boston. I knew my daughter Lisa was running around backstage doing a thousand chores I couldn't even imagine. Sitting in a box next to Romeo's, I felt in his hand squeezing mine in the exhilaration of his vision, finally happening on the Academy of Music stage. When he finally went to take his bows, the audience went completely crazy, one of those moments you can never forget.

After the opera, we held a reception in the Academy ballroom for the performers and invited guests. The mayor had evidently had a few drinks before the opera and sat through it while completely bored. He was standing with assistant managing director Bill McLaughlin when a lady came up and said, "That was the most beautiful thing I've ever seen. How about if I have the second performance filmed for video?" Mayor Green said, "Never mind, we took some pictures for our exhibit, that's enough."

Out of utter exhaustion and pure astonishment, I just stood there. I found out later that the lady was Mrs. Ethel Wister, who everyone called Peppi, part of the Pew family and eminently able to bring in a video compliment the next Friday. Why I didn't go up to her and say, "Forget what the mayor said, lady, please go ahead while you remember what you heard!" I'll never know, though I've kidded good pal Bill through the years about my stunned paralysis.

First page of "William Penn" orchestral score.

Penn preaching before his arrest. Credit: Deborah Cascarino.

Thomas tells the jailed Penn about their holy experiment. Credit: Deborah Cascarino.

Penn and Gulielma dream of their holy experiment.
Credit: Deborah Cascarino.

Gulielma singing of staying in London. Credit: Deborah Cascarino.

Penn saying goodbye to his family. Credit: Deborah Cascarino.

Land Ho!. Credit: Deborah Cascarino.

Penn and Taminent exchange gifts. Credit: Deborah Cascarino.

Romeo Cascarino. Credit: Edward Carroll.

Years later, at a reception, I met Mrs. Wister and blurted that she had been in my nightmares for 15 years. She graciously wanted to know why and, after I told her, said that she remembered her feelings about the opera well and wished I had spoken to her about it.

Since the Academy of Music stage had a slight rake, Callahan actually cut the angle from all the sets, in case it would be performed in another theater without a rake. I found this quite amazing, considering what they had gone through; ironically, when the Academy was later refurbished, the rake was removed.

I wrote a list I intended to pass on to anyone crazy enough to produce an opera:

—Love the work passionately.
—Begin with plenty of naiveté, time, money and energy, otherwise your balloon will often be popped.
—Get lots of help.
—Don't expect anyone to care how tough it is.
—Don't be discouraged by your board, just don't expect them to help you.
—Support artists, they are not paid enough.
—The crew won't chisel you, you'll be treated fairly.
—Be honest, even though some will think you simple-minded.
—Don't be surprised if the director wants everything—he's just afraid.
—If the composer is alive, don't expect ready agreements to changes.
—Designers expect others to execute, even the impossible.
—Expect covenants, betrayals, just go on.
—Musicians will do their job, with a camaraderie no one else can understand.
—Don't expect to sleep well.
—Dream.
—Love the work passionately—or don't attempt it.

After a week, I headed to Aruba to wind down, and after six days of writing notes to myself about details of wrapping up, I finally went onto the beach after Margie extended our stay for two days.

On the beach, I kept flashing back to the first rehearsal of the final act, when Adirondack Scenic set up their version of the Treaty Elm, famous from the Benjamin West painting. Above the trunk was an exactly-shaped replica of the branches, with leaves blown onto a glue-covered mesh.

Early on, I had found a shipbuilding expert, who had provided detailed sketches to Toni Businger about the construction of Penn's ship, the Welcome. He attended the rehearsal and cried out, "They're maple leaves!" Adirondack Scenic actually took it back to their shop, blew elm leaves onto it, and brought it back two days later.

Considering the soaring music and passion of that final scene, I'm sure no one in the audience perceived this astounding level of detail.

The sets went into the Civic Center museum, and the bills arrived from the Academy. It was not a surprise at that stage that we didn't have quite enough; the sets had cost $145,000, and the final total ended up to be $424,240, more than $40,000 in excess of our funds. Somehow it was paid for by Combs' plea for help, and possibly Mrs. Haas had a role in it as well.

I was given the few leftover tickets by the box office personnel, including an envelope with 16 tickets for Mr. Segal. Months later, I absent-mindedly picked them up before heading through Rittenhouse Square for lunch, and happened to bump into Sol. "By the way, Sol," I couldn't help saying, "here are the tickets for your friend Mr. Segal from Detroit." He bought me lunch.

Forgotten Values

Another remarkable event occurred in 1982, the resurrection of an architectural wonder. I had heard that Mrs. Haas was also involved in restoring the magnificent wood paneling by Alexander Calder in City Hall's Conversation Hall. Intended for ceremonial use, it had been used to store trash (thrown out the window to the street below) and, in 1955, as a warren of offices.

The architect at that time, horrified that the carving would be damaged or removed, secretly built a wall five inches thick, with added insulation padding, before installing the office walls. The chandelier was covered and the office ceiling was built below it. Few people realized the treasure that lay behind those panels until 1982, when the city's 300th anniversary was the impetus to restore the room. While visiting the press office in the Hall, I happened upon this revelation when the office walls began to be removed; I called a *Daily News* reporter to jump on the story, and he found the son and grandson of the Italian contractor who had cared enough to protect this stunning room, used now for important receptions. There's a guard on duty at Room 200 but, if you claim you've come thousands of miles to see the room, you'll usually be escorted in to see its wonders.

About fifteen years later, Marc Mostovoy was informed that the Civic Center Museum was going to be permanently closed, and the sets would have to be moved. Since the cost for transporting and storage would be staggering, we tried to get some support for leaving them in the shuttered building. I asked Robert Driver, who headed the Opera Company, to write a letter saying that the sets were too valuable not to keep, though he perceived it as a scheme to get him to perform the opera. He never wrote the letter, but did say that their $145,000 cost in 1982 would translate into half a million dollars to construct in 1998.

Somehow, I requested a meeting with Midge Rendell, the wife of the Mayor (and eventual Governor) Ed Rendell, who was really the engine behind the concept of the Kimmel Center. Her secretary granted the meeting without knowing who I was or what I wanted, and she mentioned that it was

Mrs. Rendell's last day at the firm, because the next day she was to be confirmed as a Federal judge.

She was very sympathetic to the possible loss of the sets, and gave me some numbers of people who might be able to help, and agreed to let me use her name. While leaving, I said I hoped I would see her again, and she cheerily said, "Sure, as long as it's not in an official capacity!"

Finally, Marc and I met with the Director of Arts and Culture, Diane Dalto, who agreed to let them stay in the Museum, though the building would be uninsured.

Ten years in the future, I ran into Stephanie Naidoff, who had been an early president of the Kimmel Center; she had been asked by Mayor John Street to be Director of Commerce, including arts and culture, since he had fired the city's excellent deputy city representative in the Office of Arts and Culture, Carol Lawrence. We talked about the opera, and she said that Penn was in the process of buying the building. She said she would call and give me the name of the person at Penn handling the transaction, and when I didn't hear from her I left three messages with the receptionist, with none returned. Since she had a lot on her plate, this must not have seemed very important at the time.

While doing a number of radio pieces for Jim Cotter's "Creatively Speaking" show on WRTI-FM, I suggested a piece on Peter Nero, who ran the popular Philly Pops. The interview was done at the office of Senator Vincent Fumo, who had rescued the Pops from bankruptcy by soliciting fiscal aid from some high rollers. After the interviews, I mentioned to Fumo about the opera and the sets, and he said he thought he knew someone who could move and store the sets, promising to get back to me.

I had my doubts but, true to his word, one of his representatives called a few days later. It seems that the sets had still been in the Museum, and the building had been razed to the ground the preceding week. At least I had to give major credit to Fumo, who stepped forward to help, though he would soon be spending a term in Federal prison for a whole host of corruption charges.

So much for concern for the city's arts and culture, a half-million dollars of the city's legacy discarded for lack of interest. Such was the sad end of one long journey. And it wasn't over yet.

In what I saw as a necessary act of masochism, my daughter Lisa began working at AVA that fall to learn stage management, once again under the heels of Yannopoulos. She worked on *The Barber of Seville*—the one by Giovanni Paisiello, hugely famous at the time the young Rossini dared to write another version. Another was Puccini's *Il Trittico*, vividly remembered because the front of the set at the Walnut Street Theater collapsed during the opening *Il Tabarro,* and the audience could clearly hear Dino's backstage cursing.

She also played Paulette the bear in Seymour Barab's delightful *The Toy Shop*, presented by AVA at the large theater in the now-closed Strawbridge and Clothier department store. The kids loved the cavorting bear and, after the show, they ran down the aisle to hug Lisa in the bear costume; this often caused a delay for the people waiting in line for the next show.

7. BACK ON THE BEAT

In those next few months of learning the hard way about producing an opera, doing a movie column and a monthly piece for the PBS magazine Applause, besides a highly stressful real job, not having to do reviews was a relief. In March of 1982, plans began for a special concert to commemorate Harold Boatrite's 50th birthday. Six conductors had signed on to lead the half-dozen pieces with the Concerto Soloists, and the program began to take on the makings of an event. Temple asked me if there was anything I could do for the concert.

One night, at the Pen and Pencil writers' club, I saw Ron Goldwyn, an ex-*Bulletin* political reporter, one of a number of staffers like Jack Morrison, Kevin Bevan and many more who switched to the *Daily News*—and to the *Inquirer* as well. Ron suggested talking to the features editor, Carol Towarnicky, who would be there for an affair the next evening, and gave me Carol's description.

His highly candid description was perfect, and I asked Carol if she would go for the story. She agreed, and I went ahead with Boatrite's interview for that Friday's paper, April 2, 1982. Early the next week, she called and asked me if I had something for the next Friday. I did, and had something for the next 24 years of Fridays. It doesn't work like this anymore.

Harold Boatrite:
Composing is a lonely profession—you go along writing for two years until you feel you don't exist. I don't buy the common notion that an artist has no responsibility except to himself. By writing in a language that is understood, I've been accused of writing down to an audience. My constant worry is whether my music will communicate with people.

For years, foundations gave grants for avant-garde music that drew tiny audiences. They finally gave up on serialism, only after setting the harmonic tradition back 25 years. The blight has finally reached the Midwest—one promising young student, now at Michigan, was told his music was too lyrical. That's like saying the Bible talks too much about God.

The general public is so intimidated by all the intellectual hocus-pocus in the arts that it refuses to make critical judgments. This to me is a very unhealthy situation, since it allows anything imaginable to pose as art. After all, if you think something you've heard is ugly, it just may be that it is.

The sorry scandal of musical composition is that many teachers don't know any more than their students, since both repudiate every aesthetic canon or standard associated with past tradition. Colleges and universities seem to be in business to prevent education. For 12 years as a college professor, I watched the cynical manipulation of young people's opinions to suit the purposes of self- justifying academic committees.

Composition is simply my best aptitude—I can't think of anything else to do. Creation comes at random moments. On album covers you read about Brahms walking in the quiet woods for inspiration. Sometimes it comes for me at the kitchen table, with distractions all around. I can understand why teenagers do homework with the TV on, it takes the tension out of it.

Both a professional and an amateur can write a theme, but the pro knows what to do with it. Experience has taught me that the use of repetition allows change to come out of necessity, from a feeling of inevitability. That selectivity is as mysterious as free choice.

The artist deals in deception, creating an illusion. Bach's music gives a feeling of spontaneous inspiration, for instance. You can take all the time you want with a passage from a book or painting, but in music only the chord that's being played exists at that moment. Everything else comes from memory and repetition. That's why tradition is important, for only by the past and future can the present be understood. (His home, March 25, 1982)

Months later, I was talking to Carol at the office, and Goldwyn came into the room. "Do you know my husband Ron?" she asked. Ron hadn't mentioned this little detail, teaching me a little more about how real reporters operate. He eventually switched from political reporter to a kind of post you'd only find at the *Daily News*—religion and Mummers reporter; he was featured for years on television as the well-informed color man at the New Year's Day parade. For years, Ron and Carol headed to New Mexico for native Indian causes.

Fortunately, Carol wasn't interested in reviews, leading to a lot more interviews and the end of late nights. *Daily News* pay was triple the *Bulletin*'s, and Carol was open to almost any good story, allowing pieces about artists at the Mann Music Center and disc reviews during the slow times of July and August—great days.

Pressroom Personalities

The *Daily News* had a history of colorful characters, and prided itself on its "People Paper" sense of fun—compared to the staid and more formal *Inquirer*, both with the same owners and in the same building.

After Carol came Barbara Beck, who had lunch sent in on Wednesdays and invited everyone—even me—to brainstorming sessions. Beck was smart and tough, and suggestions were either received with "Great! Do it!" Or "That's dumb!" I still have a memo stating, "I have lost my mind, and I'm declaring Friday as Hawaiian shirt day. All those entering the office must wear a Hawaiian/Polynesian shirt of reasonable facsimile. I will provide the Hawaiian food."

This was typical of the zany eighth-floor atmosphere, with iconic jazz writer Nels Nelson, pop writer Jonathan Takiff (who had started with the Drummer), and lots of colorful characters wandering around. Going into the office was like walking into a Damon Runyon story. One example was Rick Selvin, who also did a grab-bag of delightful morsels of fascinating, though probably unnecessary, information called *Brain Candy*.

When Rick died in 2008, Jack Morrison started his obituary with a classic Selvin story.

"Rick Selvin arrived at the *Daily News* in 1980 to apply for a job. When he got to managing editor Zack Stalberg's office, he hesitated at the door.

"I'm really sorry," Rick said.

"What are you sorry about?" Zack inquired.

"Well, I usually wear a necktie to these interviews," he said, "but my tie was frozen in the trunk of my car after it got wet, and when I tried to put it on, it broke."

"Zack, recognizing a guy who would surely become a true *Daily News* character, hired him on the spot."

That was the kind of spirit that infested the paper in those days before the internet, when money and practicality didn't dictate its spirit.

In later years, I tried to avoid going into the office except to pick up mail, because a freelancer is an expense on two legs, easy to be cut when visible. On several visits, I recall hearing the remark, "Here he comes again with another inspirational story!" I always took that as a compliment.

The year 1982 brought lots of great visitors, some without a warm welcome. In July: "Last night's Mann concert had to cope with a chilly breeze, police sirens, backfires, planes, firecrackers, and a sputtering, buzzy motorbike circling the parking lots. Yet the music defeated the racket as conductor Charles Dutoit led the Philadelphia Orchestra with grace and control."

Soprano Wilhelmenia Fernandez, famed from the French film *Diva*, finally sang with our Opera Company in Purcell's *Dido and Aeneas*, also singing Gershwin with the Philadelphia Orchestra and judging the Academy of Vocal Arts' fledgling Giargiari Voice Competition.

For Concerto Soloists founder and conductor Marc Mostovoy's 40th birthday that December, the company's lawyer—who also happened to manage the rock group Robert Hazard and the Heroes—thought a joint concert would be a great gag gift. That was okay with Mostovoy—as long as his strings played the synthesizer parts.

One day around 1984, staffer Joey O'Dowd put up a sign on the bulletin board.

We need players for the *Daily News* softball team.
If you can't catch, we don't care!
If you can't hit, we don't care!
If you can't field, we don't care!
If you don't want to chip in for the beer, THEN WE CARE!

Despite the ominous nature of this entreaty, I actually signed up and played with this colorful crew through many raucous seasons, and a few championships, though decorum and an intention of articulating good taste prevents me from describing most of the details.

Our coach and domineering pitcher Jack McKinney, who became a columnist heavily into the strife in Belfast, began at the *Daily News* in the 1950s as a writer on music and opera. He swore that, after more than a month, he wondered when he was going to actually get paid. He knocked on the door of the editor, J. Ray Hunt, to inquire, without hearing an answer. Walking into his office, he heard snoring from inside a large roll-top desk and said, loudly, "Mr. Hunt?" The door slid open and a sleepy Hunt asked what he wanted. After McKinney explained that he had been reviewing the Orchestra and opera, Hunt said, "Get THEM to pay you!" and rolled the desktop down.

Occasionally the actual possibility of playing softball games was a nail-biting occurrence, because big stories prevented writers from making it to the field on time; eventually the team became the Pen and Pencil crew, meaning 18 or 20 players instead of the bare nine. I'm proud to say I have played with that crew intermittently, though with ever-declining skills.

Back in those primitive computer days, I had to write my Friday story at home, rushing over from my straight job at lunch time on Mondays to type it in all over again. This went on for some time, though I asked the paper's computer expert if there was any truth to the rumor that it was technologically possible to actually transmit to the paper from home. He gave me all kinds of codes and network parameters, without my being able to make it work.

One day I mentioned my frustration to Rose De Wolf, one of the funniest and most professional writers at the paper. Rose could make an interesting story out of almost anything, and was brilliant at coming up with pieces no one else would ever have imagined. It was a curious thing to bring up because Rose was known to be baffled by the slightest technology, and had tried for months to figure out how to make her alarm clock and VCR work.

One day Rose called me at work, and said to try it again from home. Through some miracle my story had transmitted, and Rick Selvin called to say it had arrived safely. It turned out that Rose had gone up to the cramped 14th floor storeroom where the huge modems were stored, and read the instruction manuals that were packed inside the original boxes. She finally deduced that the dip-switches were set wrong, and she clambered behind them and took care of the resetting. All I could say once again was, Now, THERE was a real reporter.

Many years later, when the Philadelphia Orchestra was playing a concert at the Mann, a car hit a pole on Parkside Avenue and knocked out all the lights, except for a few emergency ones. Fortunately, there were three people playing that night, violinist Zachary DePue and two Curtis-trained subs—violinist Nicolas Kendall and bassist Ranaan Meyer. These three had been playing bluegrass and funky rhythmic music in a now-famous group entitled Time for Three, and they came out and thrilled the crowd until the lights came on much later.

Rose happened to be there, and asked would I mind if she wrote about it, though it was my beat. This was one of the only times anyone ever had the courtesy to ask such a question, and of course I was happy for her to do it. It was a good article and brought them a lot of recognition, and they have been riding high ever since. Zachary, whose brother Jason was also in the Philadelphia Orchestra, quit to become concertmaster of the Indianapolis Symphony, allowing half the year to travel with the trio. The gifted Philadelphia composer Jennifer Higdon even wrote *Concerto 4-3* for the trio and orchestra, and they have played it all over the country to deserved renown.

Don Russell was another creative reporter who discovered that the Public Utility Commission in Harrisburg had granted a six-year life to city cabs, meaning that cab companies could buy the beat-up New York City cabs after they came to the end of their pulverized three-year life. That caused question into the state capital's reputation for being open to greasing, and actually allowing cab companies to inspect their own vehicles. Don followed up by acting as a cab driver and having the (now-defunct) AAA Diagnostic Clinic in Broomall discover that all five of his assigned cabs would cost more to inspect than they were worth. He also found that the drivers got about 30 minutes instruction, and to test them he would ask to go to Betsy Ross House or City Hall, and chronicled being driven all over the city by drivers who had no idea where they were.

Once, at the old Veterans Stadium ballpark, he bought an 18-ounce beer, took the cup home, and found it was less than 16 ounces. His front page story, showing that the missing two ounces of the 750,000 $5 beers ripped off imbibers for half a million dollars each season, and with a 1,364 percent markup as well, caused a furor. The next day, vendor Ogden taped over the word "ounce" on every sign in the ballpark.

In a classic *Daily News* circus moment, Don testified at a City Council meeting investigating the vendor, whose representative said they had made no claims about ounces—until a huge blowup of the original front page was produced. Russell poured an exact measurement of 18 ounces into his original cup, causing a probably-anticipated spill onto an outraged councilwoman's desk. It's unlikely this kind of fanaticism toward moral right could have happened at any other paper than the *Daily News*.

Don's column Joe Sixpack, both before and after his retirement from the paper, has built Philadelphia into the land's unquestioned top beer town. He launched the now-packed Philly Beer Week, with a huge hammer making its way to all the major pubs in the region and, finally, into the hands of Mayor Nutter, who hammered the opening tap. The event eventually grew to the point where other organizers became involved and who made the unexpected decision that guiding spirit Don, and his slice of the pie, could be eliminated. Since that major slight, Don's scope of activities have blossomed even more into an highly-enjoyable suds empire.

Because of longtime publicity guru Sam Bushman's drag with editors, I was given an assignment to interview the Clancy Brothers and Tommy Makem for their annual St. Patrick's Day concert—-something Sam managed to pull off for four straight years. (Sam used the *Daily News'* printers to make his press release copies). These rambunctious guys were fun to hang with in the Irish Pub, and Bobby Clancy insisted that if I could get to Shannon Airport, I could spend a week at their seaside pub/hotel and wouldn't spend another dime. This was another sincere offer that, sadly, expired with Bobby's death in 2002, teaching me once again: always accept.

Masters of Song

Since the Academy of Vocal Arts' artistic director Christofer Macatsoris was going to conduct *William Penn* that October, my involvement with the paper would prevent my interviewing him about it. But we spoke in May before the AVA presentation of Giuseppe Verdi's *Un Giorno di Regno* (*King for a Day*)—his second opera, his first comedy and the last until his final *Falstaff* 53 years later. Both Verdi's wife and two children had died during the composing of this light-hearted work, an eerie statement about the unpredictability of genius—even early genius.

Christofer Macatsoris:
*This work was once compared unfairly to Rossini, but it's a delightful, charming opera closer to Donizetti. It's fun to conduct, because there are passages foretelling the Verdi to come—*Aida, Falstaff, *and* La Forza del Destino, *as if looking into the future.*

When performers give something they know is their best, it cleanses away the troubles of the past and redeems the spirit of the struggles that went into it. Certain works, certain performances jell and you always remember them, although you can never tell exactly why. There's a vibration that can't be analyzed. To try to feel what Verdi was feeling and putting into the music, despite the tragedy of his personal life, shows how amazing the human spirit is. (AVA studio, May 10, 1982)

The Singing Simpson Family performed all over the Philadelphia region, especially in churches every weekend, and their father, a postal worker, insisted that most of the proceeds go to charitable causes. Soprano Joy Simpson had attended AVA, Temple, Juilliard and the Curtis Institute of Music, toured internationally including a tense tour or Russia, and sang with Billy Graham's crusades.

Simpson was to play Leonora in a production of another Verdi opera, *Il Trovatore*, presented by the African-American company Opera Ebony, her first operatic venture.

Joy Simpson:
Our family sang all religious music, nothing classical. Gospel, hymns, anthems, spirituals—we sang everything we knew. I was the youngest student ever to be admitted to the Academy of Vocal Arts, and eventually studied with (director) Tito Capobianco, who scared me a little since I hadn't sung much opera.

The Russians cry, they moan, in their liturgical music, with an effect very similar to what you hear in black churches. Pressure was everywhere in the air, and everyone said waiters and cab drivers were KGB.

I believe the spiritual source of my music has been my greatest asset. Certainly, there are stylistic inflections, but both styles show off the voice—gospel singing or bel canto, one enhances the other. A singer needs a variety of experiences—when my friends came to hear me sing Schubert in Alice Tully Hall, some were surprised it wasn't a church. (Her home, May 16, 1982)

In a horrible March 1987 postscript to this interview, Joy was singing "Sometimes I Feel Like a Motherless Child" in a Cape Town, Africa concert when she collapsed from a brain hemorrhage. This event caused a great controversy after reports claimed that the musicians kept playing, thinking that her falling was in some way part of the performance. Her death a few days later brought back those haunting memories of Jackie Wilson's collapse at the Latin Casino.

The only possible good thing that can be said about this huge loss that her sister, Marietta Simpson, is still performing as one of the most acclaimed mezzo-sopranos on the international scene.

The Prism of Music

During this transitional era from LPs to CDs, an esoteric struggle began that continues to this day. Joshua Rifkin's famous 1982 recording of Bach's B Minor Mass featured one singer per vocal part—instead of multiple choral singers; sometimes there was just one instrumentalist, instead of a section. Claiming that Bach wanted it that way, the sonic result was either icy clarity offering new insights or a feeble watered-down prissiness—take your pick. Critics have become highly polarized about this period-instrument clash, many claiming that Bach would want as many singers as he could get and that the whole choral aspect is destroyed using this method. It's almost, though not quite, the same unprovable argument suggesting that if Bach had a modern piano instead of a harpsichord he would have used it, or if Beethoven had been able to hire a 80-piece orchestra instead of a 32-piece band, he would have preferred it.

The late Michael Korn, who founded the Philadelphia Singers (and who was about to lead and play in all six Brandenburg Concertos in his Bach Festival) had a definite opinion about this controversy.

Michael Korn:

This whole premise is nonsense. Many things may be inferred from cryptic notes on original scores that were hurriedly prepared for performance, but Bach's letters clearly indicate a desire for several singers to a part, preferably as many as four. Some thorough research has been done on Bach's music, and this whole question has become more controversy than scholarship. (Chestnut Hill Church, November 2, 1982)

Korn would have broken-hearted to realize that, after 43 years, the lack of funding sources caused his professional chorus' final concert in the spring of 2015.

Peter Nero was building the Philly Pops back thirty years ago, while also leading pops orchestras in other cities as well. He had shown off his famous chops the season before by playing duets with George Shearing. But, this time, he was quick to extol the local band and chat for the first of many interviews.

Peter Nero:
I think it's the best orchestra of its kind in the country, period. We're developing an orchestra that can play anything, like the studio orchestras in Hollywood but with more day-to-day feel for the standard orchestral repertoire.

Labeling in music is ludicrous—like the word 'serious'—it just has to have content and quality, without regard to who wrote it. When there's an 'anything can happen' feeling that brings excitement and an audience can feel it.

I remember watching Art Tatum on Steve Allen's Tonight Show *before Tatum died in '56. My jaw dropped when I heard him play, tears came to my eyes.* (By phone, March 15, 1983)

A few months after his passionate comments about Bach's choral intentions, there was another chance to speak with Michael Korn, whose Philadelphia Singers functioned as the Opera Company of Philadelphia's chorus. Although he had prepared the chorus for 22 company productions, he was surprised to be offered his debut in conducting the upcoming *Carmen*.

Michael Korn:
I would never have accepted if I wasn't ready. It's like a dream world, the biggest, most expensive production yet. In our production, Franco Corsaro has moved the setting up to the Spanish Civil War of the 1930's, portraying Carmen as a revolutionary who uses the soldier Don Jose for her cause. It's easy to relate to the character of a Carmen, or any exotic compulsion, in a passionate way. (His home, April 10, 1983)

Way back in *Bulletin* days, I had reviewed an opera entitled *The Nightingale and The Rose* by Margaret Garwood. There was an expectation of lush orchestration and soaring melody when Pennsylvania Opera Theater, performing works only in English translation, presented Garwood's newest opera *Rappaccini's Daughter*. Though Nathaniel Hawthorne's haunting short story had been set by many others, Garwood's personal connection with the

Margaret Garwood.

author's works must have made it worth its nine-year gestation process—and perhaps planted the idea for another opera based on Hawthorne—appearing 28 long years later.

Margaret Garwood:
If you give your music enough time, it will come out the way it wants to and say just what you want it to say. At the time I began, the concept of a woman composer was outlandish, but composition is a self-taught art.

You just can't tamper with the subconscious. In a way, I don't ever want to know what I'm doing—I don't want to get to the point where devices are used consciously. Stravinsky called it the intuitive grasp of an unknown entity. There are no formulas, for any creator the blank sheet of paper is frightening. But there was never an instant's doubt from the start that what I wanted to do was worth doing. Rappaccini is me, I'm all the characters. (Rehearsal hall, May 15, 1983)

Guitarist Andrés Segovia returned to play a concert in the round at the Valley Forge Music Fair. Luckily, he had evidently forgotten my slip of the tongue years ago, though it was hard to forget that he had been asked every question imaginable for 60 years. He had given his first Parisian concert in 1924 and made his New York debut in 1928, and was responsible for hundreds of careers, as well as music by Villa-Lobos, Turina, Ibert, Roussel, Ponce, Torroba, de Falla, Castelnuovo-Tedesco and many others.

The column read, "His recitals are events bringing music to life, as the magic of Bach and the Spanish tradition pours from his fingers almost undaunted by time. For most of us, it's an annual visit with a supreme musician; for guitarists, it's a master class with a Legend.

"The Legend is Spaniard Andrés Segovia, now 90 plus five months, with a 41-year-old wife back in Granada, sons aged 62 and 13, and a heart full of music. His eyes sparkle when he talks about the source of his inspiration, raised double-handedly from obscurity to a concert instrument. He wears a beret and string tie and carries a silver-tipped cane; when he hums a theme to demonstrate a point, his eyes narrow slightly like a drowsy cat, and the room turns into the gardens of the Alhambra."

Andrés Segovia:

Playing in the round will be fine, with everyone equidistant. You know, Pascal defined God as 'a circumference, the center point of which is everywhere.' I succeeded where others failed, because I realized that the sound of the guitar would carry to every seat in a large hall. The penetration of waves from the guitar is mysterious. I have never used amplification, because it modifies the poetry, and the guitar is the most poetic of instruments.

My family objected to the guitar as a career, and I am a self-made man because I had to be. But that is a bad term, because once I heard a person call himself a self-made man, and someone asked, "Who interrupted you?" But I never commissioned any music. Composers came to me. I always had to modify, to transcribe, to adapt the music for proper guitar writing.

Guitarists have never been good composers, therefore there was little music for guitarists to play—a vicious cycle. Remember, instruments are like islands. Some have beautiful flowers, some have exotic vegetation, some are arid. But music is the ocean. (Philadelphia hotel, July 1983)

Out of the Park

The aforementioned Bob Vetrone, famous for his "Buck The Bartender" column, was one of the colorful reporters who segued to the *Daily News*, and in June 1983 he discovered a poem I had written about Shibe Park, the abandoned, decrepit shell that had been the home of the Phillies and Athletics.

"A youngster of yesteryear, Tom Di Nardo, visited Shibe Park one April day in 1975, opening day at Veterans Stadium. If this brings a smile to your face, that's fine. If it brings a tear to your eyes, that's fine too. It'll make at least two of us. Here it is:"

Today, opening day, the crowd
Miles from these empty bleachers
Cheer, the legacy of the park's birthday,
Sixty-six years ago, forgotten.
On October 1, 1970, in the last of the tenth,
Oscar Gamble singled home Tim McCarver,
Mobs fought over base bags, carried home

Broken souvenir seats and infield dirt
And the stadium died.

Lou Gehrig hit four homers here one day,
As did Pat Seerey, remembered only in records.
For fifty years, Connie Mack managed
In straw skimmer and starched collar;
With the Million-Dollar Infield, and Cochrane, Foxx, Simmons, Grove,
He maneuvered he A's into pennants,
Blessed unerasable World Series,
Then sold greats, one by one, for cash.
(In '54, a year after the stadium
Received his name, he sold the team;
For every fan, it remained Shibe Park.)

Jackals bunted on badleg Brissie here,
Konstanty a surprise starter in Series opener,
Roberts fogged the fastball and Ennis
Shouldered boos and clubbed in runs.
Fain, foolishly anticipating a bunt,
Charged Ted Williams, ducking just in time.

Trash cans sprouted in parking places
And Sunday innings, mysteriously sacrosanct,
Could not begin after 6:59.
Entering now through a locker room window
Through the dark halls where giants stalked,
Ruth and Williams and Musial and Mays,
Only echoes of names and bodies remain.

Through the pillaged dugout, the first shock
Is high weeds and barrels, mosquitoes,
An occasional derelict,
Trash and a square jungle.
The tree in left field, barren,
Searches in vain for the baselines.
Pirates long ago exhausted the treasures.
In seats blackened with soot, girders
Twisted obscenely from vandals' fires,
Roars are now silence's whispers.

In deep right field, through muffled time delay,
Scoreboard flaps bang indignantly in the wind,
The ghosts of pinch doubles, parabolas of hope
Buoyed in air by the crowd's expectancy.
Light towers loom like blind monsters.

*No sound, no plate remain, a cadaver
Without the vendors' cries.
The precarious roof moves, creaking,
An ominous, unrequired guard.*

*I came here prepared, like all the others,
Walking the tracks, carrying a worn glove
For that ever-possible foul ball,
Statistics proudly recall-ready
For the benefit of the adjacent.
Set to drift into closer seats,
Autograph book ready for post-game tribute.
"Did'ja get Richie's? Did'ja?"*

*Standing at second base, or where it might have been,
Without a marker to Cobb or Wills or Ashburn or Brock,
My childhood shrieks before me.
No pennant had graced Philadelphia for twenty-five years
And the pained park felt the blame.
The corpse now weeps, begging for euthanasia
To end its shame.
It ached for pennants, not squalor.
Denuded and disgraced,
The ruin of so many hopeless dreams
Sees my tears of pity, and even yet
Wishes I had not come.*

Eventually the park was demolished and, on its site, rose the Deliverance Baptist Church. Seventeen years later, on the same block where Roberto Clemente, Joe Di Maggio and Henry Aaron roamed, the Philadelphia Orchestra would play a neighborhood concert.

Computers Decided Value

In the years when Muti was recording for EMI, a period that produced the Beethoven Symphonies (and later a shift to Philips for the Brahms Symphonies), the dapper Tony Caronia, at that time president of EMI records, came to town for the sessions. In those days, when I could get away with some record reviews and CDs came in the mail as frequently as bills, EMI put out a monthly catalog showing the new releases and those on the deletion list—in other words, order while you can.

One month, I noticed that three of my absolute favorite desert-island CDs were about to be deleted: Walter Gieseking's definitive disc of Debussy's complete Preludes, pianist Arturo Benedetti Michelangeli playing sublime renditions of the Ravel and Rachmanoff Fourth Piano Concerto, and the Thomas Beecham-conducted *La Bohème*, made in New York hurriedly after a contract dispute with Jussi Bjorling, Victoria de los Angeles, Robert Merrill and Lucine Amara. I showed this to Tony, and he said that that was the way EMI did it: if a record fell below a certain sales level, it was automatically deleted. He was at least gracious about it, emphasizing that it was a business, not a perpetual archive, and that everybody had their own idea of a classic recording. He said he'd see about it, though I don't think anything could really be done.

Fortunately, as years have gone by, orchestras have gotten too expensive to record, especially in standard works with dozens of recordings; this is why many orchestras now issue their own CDs. In the past, a label wouldn't issue the same work with a different artist, a principle long abandoned. Major labels like EMI now see the economic value in reissuing material from their vast vaults, though most are now available through streaming services, and those three have been available again for some time. If somehow, for whatever reason, they are not on your shelves, rectify that immediately, and that urging comes with a money-back guarantee.

8. INTERVIEW ADVENTURES

Someone introduced me to Irwin Yeaworth, a large, tall man who, naturally, was called Shorty. He had directed *The Blob* with unknown actor Steve McQueen, shot on his Paoli farm, a Phoenixville diner, and easy-access locations in the Philadelphia suburbs, and sold his interest before it became a cult favorite. He was very active with the Church of the Savior in Wayne, and envisioned launching an arts program.

One of my suggestions was to present the King's Singers, since a small contingent of the group were doing a 15th anniversary American tour, and he enthusiastically booked them for a Sunday evening concert, along with the Concerto Soloists. I had their 1967 recording of Fauré's celestial Requiem, an LP Temple and I loved in part because of the boy soprano's celestial singing in the *Pie Jesu* section.

By coincidence, the Swingle Singers—with the incredible soprano Christiane Legrand, sister of Michel on those stratospheric high runs—were appearing with Peter Nero and the Philly Pops that same Sunday in the afternoon. Though completely different in aspect, they had more in common than differences; in voice blending, pitch accuracy, rhythmic emphasis, instinct, and phrasing worked out over the years, each ensemble sings as if one instrument.

Through some slippery conniving, I somehow convinced six of the King's Singers to come down to the Academy the day before, where the Swingles were rehearsing. I took a photograph of them all facing each other and singing with arms outstretched, somehow got the photograph made by the next day, and they all proudly signed it for me on Sunday, with Ward Swingle's notation at the bottom, The Swingle Singers v. the King's Singers!

After the Wayne concert, there was a party at Yeaworth's home where the Brits were invited. I had brought my LP of the Fauré, with a cover portrait of the whole serious-looking ensemble—except for one round-faced kid sporting a big smile in the center. I asked the guys if that was the person who sang the beautiful solo. "Yea, that's Bobby Chilcott!" they all yelled, and it's no wonder he was smiling. He joined the group the next year and, in the last 15 years, has become an acclaimed choral composer.

After a few accidental-on-purpose meetings, leading to rides home and conversations with Vincent Persichetti, there was a chance to actually visit him and chat about a new work *Flower Songs*, written for Michael Korn's Philadelphia Singers and the Concerto Soloists. Though he had written 70 commissioned pieces by that time, there were conditions to each one.

Vincent Persichetti:
I never write a piece unless it coincides with my development at the time. Michael asked me for a piece years ago, but one just wasn't ready.

This setting of e. e. cummings' poems emerged recently, and the premiere with him luckily worked out. Poetry distills and avoids reactions. cummings heard some of my settings years ago, and I'm proud that he gave me carte blanche to use any of his works.

I still consider myself a student, because composers are not in competition with each other, or shouldn't be. Philip Glass, Steve Reich and Peter Schickele all studied with me, and each one is special, each statement of theirs valid. Who can foretell a piece for the next century? I just gather up what my century has offered, and some from the past. There hasn't been a problem with writer's block because there are overlapping works going on all the time. (His home, April 17, 1984)

Of course, he remembered to remind me: "Don't forget, Tom, Grazioso and Grit!"

The ever-enterprising Michael Korn heard about the first performance of the newly-discovered *Roman Vespers* by Handel, and somehow convinced RCA to record it. The Mabel Pew Myrin Trust offered a grant of $175,000 to underwrite the project, to be recorded at Swarthmore College's Lang Concert Hall.

Korn assembled his Philadelphia Singers, the Concerto Soloists and five famed vocal soloists—contralto Maureen Forrester, sopranos Judith Blegen and Benita Valente, tenor John Garrison and baritone John Cheek, returning to work with Korn after *William Penn* in 1982. My teacher, harpsichordist Temple Painter, and organist Michael Stairs improvised the continuo parts of the work's 31 sections.

The interview below was done at the sessions, not running until a year later when the RCA box set was issued.

Michael Korn:
Handel was 22 when he went to Rome as a student, and these pieces were first played in 1707. Bach didn't need to go! But Handel was already a consummate musician, polishing his craft, brashly learning every effect of 18th-century style. Art is born, not made . . .

I heard about the Vespers *through the musicological circuit, a hot item, and someone else was sure to do it. We were fortunate to raise the money locally. B-Flat to Handel meant war, and there's plenty of ferocity in those movements. He wrote string music for the voice then, pulling out all the stops. Some of it is impractical Handel, unwieldy at times, but we think it's a masterpiece.* (Lang Concert Hall at Swarthmore College, April 16, 1986)

RCA's Big Red, a large, battered, faded-red truck looking like something you'd expect to see abandoned under a railroad bridge, sat outside, leaking cables like electronic entrails. Inside the nondescript exterior of this mobile recording unit were two huge tape machines, Soundstream equipment, digital amplifiers, TV monitors and a haven of other recording equipment.

The eventual 2-LP set was lavishly illustrated, with background and historical notes are by the eminent H. C. Robbins Landon. I took my Hasselblad to the session, and the paper used some photographs of the performing forces to run with the story.

When the 72-year-old Anna Russell returned with her one-woman-show zaniness, I wondered whether she had any more stories that would crack me up. Interviewing her meant playing straight man, because her responses to ordinary things were filtered through a hilarious lack of pretense. Besides her classic *Ring*, *How to Write Your Own Gilbert and Sullivan Opera* and bagpipe bits, she had a few other gems up her sleeve, like recalling her satirical operetta, *The Prince of Philadelphia*.

Anna Russell:
I can't find anyone to sing that one and, heaven knows, there's no operetta without a prince. It comes from a long time ago...way back then, in London, I remember Stokowski—he was Leo Stokes then, playing organ in a Piccadilly church.

You know, all classical music starts as popular music. After the composers are dead, then it becomes classical music and the mink coat and tiara set come to get culture. The veddy, veddy dignified Sir Malcolm Sargent was conducting once at an Albert Hall concert for the Queen, and I shot him and started leading the orchestra. He lay there, part of the act, but when he got up for the bows he had added a fake bloodstain on his shirt. Maybe we all should take this thing called music a bit less seriously. (Walnut Street Theater, January 12, 1984)

Tenor man Stan Getz was born in Philly, and baritone man Gerry Mulligan grew up here. They both showed up at the Academy of Music for the Kool Jazz Festival, with Getz playing "Lush Life" for his Aunt Silvia and Mulligan mentioning the musicians he had heard in that hall—Charlie Parker, Glenn Miller's Air Force Band, Frank Sinatra singing "Ol' Man River" and Stravinsky conducting the Philadelphia Orchestra in his own music.

Three nights later, James Levine conducted, with the legendary soprano Birgit Nilsson singing Wagner at the Mann. Legends galore, like a musical All-Star game.

That September marked the 20th anniversary of Marc Mostovoy's Concerto Soloists of Philadelphia, finally reaching the level of full-time contracted chamber orchestra (the only other American one at the time was the St. Paul Chamber Orchestra.) The ensemble had migrated from a Wynnefield church to center city churches and the Walnut Street Theater, finally making the huge step to the Academy, a venue they couldn't possibly fill.

Mostovoy came to Philadelphia from Atlantic City for study at both Temple and Penn, also privately at Settlement School and the New School. Three summers in Nice, France, were a chance to study musicianship from the legendary oboist Marcel Tabuteau, who had retired from the Philadelphia Orchestra, and Viennese-school conductor Hans Swarowsky.

Marc Mostovoy:
Conducting a chamber orchestra is vastly different from conducting a symphony. We play mostly works from the Baroque and classical periods, where the (written) music has only notes, without specific indications of tempo, dynamics or ornaments. Each work must be analyzed to specify note lengths, fingerings and other small details to give the orchestra a unity.

Of course, a symphony conductor who must play 35 series of concerts a year could not possibly do take the time to do this, but he has a different kind of discipline. His concept is like a huge oil painting, a big mural, while ours is a small etching.

There's a lot of talk about period or ancient instruments these days, but when we began 20 years ago, few people were playing them and it was impossible to get musicians of a high caliber. The only thing I object to is playing old music without the proper style, making Mozart sound like Sibelius. To know what the composer wanted, that's what we're all about. You just have to feel it. (His home, September 20, 1984)

Marc Mostovoy.

The keyboard part of the Mozart Ninth Piano Concerto (which would soon be played with the Concerto Soloists) stopped when I rang the Delancey Street doorbell, and soon Viennese pianist Paul Badura-Skoda was pouring us some strong tea and asking where in the paper he could find the chess news. He had been a strong enough player to have challenged the great Anatoly Karpov (though he lost after a daring gambit), and even a mountain climber (another strange bent for a pianist). I had seen a photograph of the 12 antique pianos in the living room of his Vienna Woods home, and had heard about his donning overalls during a concert intermission to adjust his piano, making it evident that this charming and funny man could get very serious on the subject of pianos and piano music, as well as his unique feel for the great Austrian tradition.

Paul Badura-Skoda:
Not every Viennese is a musician. But it must mean something to breathe the air that Beethoven, Mozart, Schubert breathed. You must know Vienna to play a Schubert waltz, to get the rhythmic stress just right. My students can deal with a difficult Beethoven sonata, but Strauss and Schubert waltzes are hardest to play. They defy notation.

Playing old and new pianos is more a question of approach than of instrument. Once I played five different pianos in public the same day. Some are more sensitive than others, just like lifting a heavy weight and then being thrown ping-pong balls—it's a surprise. It used to take me days to adjust, then hours, then minutes.

In Papua, New Guinea, I was practicing the Beethoven Fourth Concerto among the fruit, wild scenery and coral, playing one of the few pianos on the island. My host raised wild ducks, and while I practiced they assembled every time at the window. That was a tribute I still remember. (Guest residence, February 7, 1985)

What Jean-Pierre Rampal and, later, James Galway did for the flute, Andrés Segovia did for the guitar, and Maurice André did for the Baroque trumpet, Richard Stoltzman did to elevate the clarinet out of the ranks. He was booked to play both a classical work and jazz with the Philly Pops.

Richard Stolzman:
I used to go to the park (in Cincinnati) in the summertime, seeing the musicians get out of the band buses—Les Brown, Stan Kenton, Woody Herman. It seemed like a dream to be able to do that, a thrill to play with that sound force and the special band feeling.

Orchestral players are heroes. I admire them very much, and realize how they must somehow mute their personality for the good of the music or because the conductor wants it.

Inspiring composers to write music for my instrument—that's what my life is for, to inspire a piece that wouldn't have been written. No matter how well you play, only the music lasts. What good would the clarinet be if (Anton) Stadler hadn't commissioned Mozart to write his concerto, or it (Richard) Mühlfeld hadn't asked Brahms to write the Clarinet Quintet? (By phone, March 10, 1985)

In May 1985, Marc Mostovoy was convinced to play the music from Bernard Herrmann's score to the thriller *Psycho*, scored for strings. (It received another performance by the Chamber Orchestra in February 2016). The score was rented from John Waxman, who I had met at the Society for the Preservation of Film Music conventions. He asked if I could ask Marc to play (and record) some music by his father, the famous film composer Franz Waxman, who had written string arrangements of 12 sonatas by the Italian Baroque composer Benedetto Marcello, and Marc scheduled six of them during that season.

Across the Pond

Serendipity always seems to change the flavor during travels. Three different trips to Amsterdam's magnificent Concertgebouw, for instance, remain embedded in memory, though my first visit was a sellout. Three minutes before the lights dimmed, the box office agent relented and sold me a ticket for eight guilders, a measly sum. An usher escorted me down the aisle—that is, way, way down the aisle—and into the back of the orchestra pit, where there was one wooden chair behind the trombones. The musician in front of me made a gesture with his slide, warning me not to be in line with it while he played. Eugen Jochum conducted, with the last work the Brahms First Symphony. The trombones have nothing to play until the fanfare in the final movement, and the player directly in front of me read a comic book in French—*Woody, le Pec-Bois*. The last movement finally began, and at their cue Jochum suddenly turned and pointed ferociously at the trombones. I could feel their bodies stiffen, and their sound drowned out the rest of the orchestra. It was the first time I realized that orchestral players simply cannot hear the whole orchestral sound like those seated in the audience.

Another year there was an awards concert, and since the winners were Neville Marriner and the Academy of St. Martin-in-the-Fields, flutist Jean-Pierre Rampal and the late harpsichordist Gustav Leonhardt, it was natural to perform Bach's Brandenburg Concerto No. 5. In the Concertgebouw, the audience is wrapped around the orchestra, and soloists leave by going up the stairs and return to take a bow. Soprano Edith Mathis had also won, and realized that climbing up and down those steps must be a nightmare to those in high heels and long skirts.

The most marvelous experience in that hall, with the names of composers emblazoned on the facades—-Meyerbeer and Sweelinck too—came at the first of two concerts on the same day. In the evening, Jean Fournet led a French orchestra in a concert performance of Ravel's magical, virtually unstageable *L'Enfant et les Sortilèges* and Roussel's explosive *Evocations*, a lovely work with choral finale I've never heard since. But, in the afternoon, the Netherlands Bach Ensemble performed Johann Sebastian's B Minor Mass, the pinnacle of Western music; Bach never heard his masterpiece, having dared to use Latin in a German Lutheran church work. I am always sent into a rapturous world while hearing this piece, stirred into an emotional and spiritual state of bliss. In the midst of being carried away by the sheer beauty, I noticed a flicker of radiance around Bach's name on the façade, and imagined that some angelic or magical signal was being sent by the heavens. While joining in the standing ovation, I happened to look back into the rear corner of the balcony and notice a small spotlight with a rosy gel.

I wish I hadn't seen it.

In 1984, on tour with Riccardo Muti and the Philadelphia Orchestra, a whirlwind tour through Italy clearly demonstrated the fatigue of traveling, as well as having to play at an exalted level. At one point, Muti's wife Cristina asked Margie if she thought she should allow her daughter Chiara to go to Paris and see Madonna in concert. Margie replied that, if she were a good girl that, yes, she should let her go. Evidently that happened, with Chiara crashing at the George V, although Margie always wondered why hers was considered a valuable opinion on the subject. (Chiara has become very famous on the Italian stage).

On my first visit to Paris, I had seen the madhouse of Les Halles, the so-called Stomach of Paris, later moved from that maze of medieval streets, food purveyors, cacophony and luridly partially-dressed ladies of the early morning right out of *Irma La Douce,* to distant Rungis. Someone had taken me to a restaurant called *Au chien qui fume,* whose walls were covered with imaginative paintings of dogs smoking cigarettes, pipes and hookahs, traded for meals to struggling painters by the proprietor in long decades past.

When the area was demolished to make room for the Pompidou Centre in 1977, the restaurant was the end building to survive. On two Philadelphia Orchestra tours, we had met David Stevens of the International Tribune and, on one later trip to Paris, talked him into trying this quirky place. The food wasn't that remarkable, but there still was a dog, this time just lying on the floor by the juke box. Suddenly, when one song played, the dog stood up and made weird crooning sounds that made everyone in the place stop talking and listen. As soon as the song was over, the dog laid down as if nothing had happened. When the waiter came over, we asked what that was all about. "Oh, that dog," he said, "he loves Pink Floyd."

When conductor Neville Marriner guest-conducted the Philadelphia Orchestra in October 1984, we did a phone interview, and he graciously suggested that we meet in person and have coffee together after the first concert. I happened to mention to him that, in those days, I bought LPs of English music by mail from a little record shop called Crotchet & Co. in Shropshire, England, whose proprietor and I always traded friendly correspondence. A few days later, I received a packet with the book *88 Charing Cross Road*, the Hélène Hanff story about the Manhattan woman who corresponded for years with a British bookseller. (The story was made into a 1987 film with Anne Bancroft and Anthony Hopkins). Inside was a handwritten note:

Dear Mr. Di Nardo,
We thought you might soon be able to write a musical version of this, after some more dealings with Crotchet & Co.—
Yours sincerely,
Molly Marriner

How sweet those British!

Cartoon Diversion

Through my cartoonist friend Jessica Stanley, I became involved in an organization called the Cartoonists Guild in the 1970s. Their mission was to galvanize all the artists together, establish rates for cartoonists depending on the circulation of magazines and stick to it. It worked quite well for a while, until a few artists made side deals at a discount and the experiment crumbled. However, the Guild was one of the many entities involved in helping to write the current copyright laws.

Though *New Yorker* cartoon editor Lee Lorenz sometimes laughed at her cartoons, and many of the staff artists begged to make copies of her drawings on the primitive copy machines, Jessica never sold him one. One of the cartoonists said he had heard the remark, "Women aren't funny," even though they were my jokes. In those days, they bought ideas to give to other artists—the word was that Charles Addams had run dry and hadn't done an original cartoon in years. Even if asked, I wasn't about to sell Jessica out, putting an end to that episode.

The Guild published two books with our cartoons, though, one called *The Art In Cartooning* and another called *Animals Animals Animals*. At one of the book launches, I had about 20 artists do animal drawings inside the front covers that still crack me up. Cartoonists don't necessarily draw funny things—they draw things funny. At the annual conferences, I realized how these humorists saw the world completely differently than we civilians, and represented a true parallel with the insights I had tried to invoke from the musicians and singers I had met.

One, Gahan Wilson, always made a big deal out of Jessica's drawings, and when he was making a book tour to hype his *Gahan Wilson's America*, in January of 1986, Rick Selvin gave me the okay to interview him. Gahan came to the paper, and made a huge drawing in crayon on a wall to accompany my article.

Wilson wrote the text for this book as well, though he was mostly famous for his weird Gahan-green monsters, haunted visions and diabolical creatures which appeared in many magazines. Maybe I was less surprised that this Midwesterner was famous for his flamboyant depiction of the macabre when I discovered he was a descendant of P. T. Barnum.

Gahan Wilson:
If you're going to do something fantastic, it's important that the strange things take place in a realistic setting. If you have a ghost in a haunted house, the house must be believable or it won't be shocking.

I did one for Playboy that showed workmen cleaning a farmhouse chimney. In the middle of a tarpaulin is a horrible, dried-up corpse dressed as Santa. One workman says, "Guess we found what's been cloggin' up your chimney since last December, Miss Emma." They got a flood of angry letters, but what could be in worse taste than some of these real religious entertainment parks that make theology into a sideshow?

I'm in debt to Goya, especially the way he draws hands, to W.C. Fields, even to the Victorian cartoonists like Tenniel (who illustrated Alice in Wonderland*). But we're all midgets standing on the shoulders of giants.*

P.T. Barnum certainly understood America, he was the opposite pole from Lincoln. He wasn't above making use of people's stupidity if it would pay off, but if you went to Barnum's Museum, you'd see the best show he could get. He'd scout the world for the best acts, the most monstrous monsters, the most bizarre things. I'm very proud of P.T. He was a swell ancestor. (*Daily News* offices, January 6, 1986)

Motown Jaunts

In January of 1987, when the *Daily News* was still owned by Knight-Ridder, someone from the Detroit Free Press called the *Daily News* to see if a reporter would like to do an assignment in Detroit. It seems that the verdict was still out on their new conductor Gunther Herbig, and they wanted some independent opinions.

Since they were paying air and hotel, plus a fee, I thought it could be a fun job. My colleagues were the quite esteemed Robert Marsh from the *Chicago Sun-Times*, Robert Finn from the *Cleveland Plain Dealer* and John Guinn from the *Detroit Free Press*. I went back two weekends, the first for a concert in the old, drafty Symphony Hall (the cabbie knew it only as the old Paradise Theater), and one in the newer Ford Theater downtown.

It wasn't an easy assignment, coming from the electricity of many Muti concerts, because Herbig's performances had little personality and anything resembling confident playing. I'd never heard the bursting Dvořák Eighth Symphony in such an earthbound way, or seen musicians play the work with such gloomy faces.

We were asked to grade the Orchestra, sections, Herbig and general experience with the A to F designations, an exercise we all did—except for Finn, who gave an incomplete to the four sections, saying "no self-respecting teacher would issue grades after only two classes." In fairness, Finn probably was the only one of us who was right.

Grove, Quotes and Elegy

By some twist of good fortune, I was given the assignment to update the Philadelphia entry in the newest production of the famed Grove Dictionary of Music—-this time, the 5,000-article *Grove Dictionary of American Music.*

When published in the early days of 1987, I was even given copies of that four-volume *American Grove,* with my *Daily News* review finishing this way:

"This exhaustive and reference for schools, libraries, serious music lovers, and musicologists from the huge range of American sounds is a triumphant effort. And how often can a reviewer state he hasn't finished the whole book, admit he's fallen asleep reading it a dozen times, and still recommend it as a bargain for $495?"

I even had a luncheon interview with Stanley Sadie, the erudite and scholarly editor who turned out to be a delightful man with a twinkle in his eye and a boisterous laugh.

Rick Selvin called one day, mentioning some funny recent negative reviews to classical pieces, and suggested I put some together for a *Brain Candy* column:

—Composer Max Reger: "I am sitting in the smallest room in the house. I have your review in front of me. Soon it will be behind me."

—Aging violinist Mischa Elman: "You know, the critics never change; I'm still getting the same notices I got as a child. They now tell me I play well for my age . . ."

—Composer Jan Sibelius: "Pay no attention to what the critics say; no statue has ever been put up to a critic."

—President Harry S. Truman to the *Washington Post* after 1950 concert by daughter Margaret: "I have read your lousy review of Margaret's concert. I've come to the conclusion that you are an eight-ulcer man on four-ulcer pay . . . Some day I hope to meet you. When that happens you'll need a new nose, a lot of beefsteak for black eyes, and perhaps a supporter below."

—Composer Richard Wagner: "The immoral profession of musical criticism must be abolished."

—George Bernard Shaw: "There are some experiences in life which should not be demanded twice from any man, and one of them is listening to the Brahms Requiem."

—Liberace: "What you said hurt me very much. I cried all the way to the bank."

—Bennett Cerf: "The Detroit String Quartet played Brahms last night. Brahms lost."

—Composer Ned Rorem: "To the social-minded, a definition of concert is: that which surrounds an intermission."

—Violinist Isaac Stern: "If nobody wants to go to your concert, nothing will stop them."

—Jazz guitarist Eddie Condon about comments by French jazz critic Hugues Panassié: "Who does that Frog think he is to come over here and try to tell us how to play? We don't go over there and tell them how to jump on a grape."

—Composer Arthur Honegger: "They don't want new music; the main thing demanded of a composer is that he be dead."

—Trumpeter Miles Davis: "It took me 20 years' study and practice to work up to what I wanted to play in this performance. How can she listen five minutes and understand it?"

—Frank McKinney: "Classical music is the kind we keep thinking will turn into a tune."

—Alexandre Dumas: "Music is the only noise for which one is obliged to pay."

—Act of Parliament, England, 1642: "If any person or persons . . . commonly called Fiddlers or Minstrels shall be taken playing, fiddling, or making music, in any Inn, Alehouse, or Tavern, or shall be taken entreating any person to hear them play . . . that every such person shall be judged rogues, vagabonds, and sturdy beggars . . . and be punished as such."

—Claude Debussy: "Music is the expression of the inexpressible."

Besides such bagatelles, I was allowed to write about the Biltmore Estate in Asheville, North Carolina, fashion designer Maria Hart and the lyrics of Cole Porter—who, by the way, had studied in Paris with Vincent D'Indy and composed a jazz score for the Swedish Ballet pre-dating Gershwin's *Rhapsody in Blue*.

The saddest assignments, though, were the obituaries of those I greatly admired, and that included Vincent Persichetti, who died at the age of 72 on August 14, 1987. The Philadelphia composer, who had created a huge catalog of works, and had taught at the Juilliard School since 1947, had touched the lives of many composers whose names became even more famous than his.

9. REVELATIONS

Emil had often told me about his work with unique composer Harry Partch, and all the recordings and instruments they had made together. When the American Music Theater Festival announced a presentation of his *Revelation in The Courthouse Park*, it was obvious that this was a once-in-a-lifetime event. Harry Partch's singular, sometimes bewildering vision is a Pandora's box of dramatic unanswered questions, buoyed by his idiosyncratic, supremely confident music.

The Greek tale of sensual Dionysius, returning to Thebes to convince King Pentheus of his godliness but inflaming the king's mother instead, alternates four times with the parallel pageant of modern rock singer Dion, revered by the mob and his fanatical Mom—though not her weak Sonny.

The perfect setting for this parallel of Greek myth in a small-town setting was the large Great Hall of the Hellenic-styled Philadelphia College of Art (now the University of the Arts) at Broad and Pine Streets. Since *Revelation* had only been performed once before, by students at the University of Illinois in 1961, this program had the feel of a real event.

Partch, who wrote the work in 1960, saw Dion (really Elvis Presley) as both the symbol of sensuality and mediocrity, and perceived audience fanaticism as becoming close to a religious experience. Partch meant to have fun opening the doors of controversy, not closing them.

While in his twenties, Partch decided that the notes in the standard diatonic scale weren't capable of expressing his musical ideas. His invention of a 43-note (instead of the usual eight) scale required instruments that he (and Emil) would have to construct. Mostly made of glass or redwood, the 26 one-of-a-kind instruments include Chromelodeons, stringed Kitharas, marimbas and cloud chamber bowls made from gigantic chemical bottles.

This unique vision began an odyssey for Partch of creation, construction, hard times, rejection, moderate acceptance, eviction along with his bulky instruments and general controversy until his death in 1974. Some of his quirky, humorous music—often with a mystical or theatrical connotation—was recorded by Partch's own Gate 5 label and eventually by Columbia.

Partch's instruments were then housed at the University of California, San Diego, curated by Danlee Mitchell, for 22 years a professor of traditional theory and percussion. Emil considered him an expert on Partch's music and curator of the unique instruments, since he was another of the musicians who had performed most of Partch's works while the composer was alive and has continued to encourage performance since.

Because of this connection, I tied in with Mitchell, who had carefully packed and loaded 18 of the precious instruments into a rented truck and driven them to Philadelphia during the summer. Since none of the local musicians (local freelancers recruited though the music departments of area colleges) performing these works had even seen these bizarre instruments before, Mitchell spent two months rehearsing each of them individually for the series of concerts.

Danlee Mitchell:
There are many messages in Revelation *portraying the modern rock audience frenzy as a religious/ fertility rite . . . as well as a satirization of the transference of sexual energy to religious zeal.*

The modern sections revolve around Dion, a popular singer who is a vessel of unsophisticated sensuality and the leader of blind followers inspired by heightened sensory awareness. Partch, a very literary man who considered this his musical extravaganza, was underlining the need for balance in the human psyche. (Philadelphia College of Art, October 1, 1987)

The Great Hall's Greek architecture framed the mythological scenes as well as a courthouse park setting in Midwestern America. The exploding opening scene, with baton-twirlers, tumblers, marching band and lusty followers of Dion was an outrageously surrealistic piece of pop-art Americana. Partch alternated between singing, chanting and spoken utterances, between traditional and his own scales, with staging including eerie lighting, striking masks and swirling animation.

The excellent local musicians, expertly coached by Mitchell on the 18 unique instruments, were visible behind a scrim. His understanding of Eastern and Indian music was evident in lute-like smears of color, deeply throbbing percussive sounds like the inside of a Javanese clock shop at midnight, and a underwater-like tapestry of seemingly random, mystically sophisticated textures over simple rhythms that eventually compel the listener. It was a fabulous enterprise, an insight into the mind of one of the most completely original composers in musical history, and was fortunately recorded on the Tomato label.

Master and Mentor Mici

Pianist Mieczyslaw Horszowski had been a legend to many for 85 years but, to the general public, the three CDs he made for Nonesuch in his mid-90s were the rocket to legendary status. The first disc of Mozart, Chopin, Beethoven and Debussy garnered several best-of-the-year awards; he included Mozart, Schumann and Chopin in the second and Bach, Chopin and Beethoven in the third. In clarity, conception, and freshness, the performances were a revelation. Horszowski has considered every note over the years, playing with the freedom of deep understanding and sympathy with the music.

His career was simply astonishing. His first Viennese recital took place in the year 1902, when he was 10; his teacher, Theodor Leschetitzky, had studied with Beethoven's pupil, Carl Czerny; he played for Fauré, Ravel,

Saint-Saëns, and his friend Villa-Lobos; and his performing associates through the years have included cellist Pablo Casals, violinist Joseph Szigeti and conductor Arturo Toscanini.

Horszowski's career took him around the world at an early age, and he lived in Milan until 1940; after a period in Brazil during World War II, he came to Curtis Institute, where he had taught since 1942. He first married at 89 in 1981, speaking mostly Italian with his gracious wife, Bice. They have no CD player or television, and Bice confided that her husband rarely listens to his records anyway. "When he heard the first Nonesuch record," he exclaimed, "I wouldn't buy this record!"

His pupils at Curtis are a list of some of the greatest modern masters: Murray Perehia, Peter Serkin, Eugene Istomin, Cecile Licad, Richard Goode, Cynthia Raim, Anton Kuerti and Seymour Lipkin, among others.

In mid-December 1988, I had the opportunity to visit Horszowski's apartment near Rittenhouse Square and, in his study, were pictures of him with Pope Pius X at age 14, with Albert Roussel and, as a youngster, sitting on the knee of Arrigo Boito (librettist for Verdi's final *Otello* and *Falstaff*). There was a photo of an Italian composer named Zanetti and, when I asked who that was, he immediately sat at one of the apartment's three pianos and began a waltz Zanetti had written for him. "You see, *tempo di valse* has two meanings—not just the speed, but the time a waltz should have."

I mentioned that my father loved some obscure operas by Italian composers, and when I mentioned Ildebrando Pizzetti, he jumped on a stool and pulled one of many green leather-bound scores, all without names on their spines. Inside was the inscription, "To my great friend Mici, Love, Ildebrando." He clambered to return it, next to Verdi, remarking, "He's in good company." Bice came in, saw him up on the stool and said, "Don't get excited, Mici!"

I could have spent a day just admiring the accolades and the remnants of those great musicians with whom he rubbed elbows, and I indulged myself in his memorabilia before his student came—suddenly realizing that had gotten few quotes. I knew that his failing eyesight meant that he was limited to the works he had already memorized and, fortunately, we finally have those magnificent recordings. It's not often you meet an authentic, flaming legend.

Almost two years later, on October 1, 1990, we found ourselves in Paris walking past the Theatre de Champs-Élysées on Avenue Montaigne, the notorious theatre where Stravinsky's *The Rite Of Spring* had caused a riot in May 1913—and seven years after Horszowski had played that command performance for Pope Pius X! I was stunned to see that he was scheduled to play that night, bought tickets and waited anxiously. He toddled out onto the stage, a frail figure who played with utter gusto in a complete program. At the end, he simply walked off without even acknowledging the audience, ignoring the tumultuous ovation. Two seats over, someone was howling and cheering at the top of his voice, and I noticed it was flutist Jean-Pierre Rampal. Finally, Horszowski returned, played the fiendish Chopin B-Flat Minor Scherzo, waved sheepishly, and disappeared.

I've always felt only some kind of strange fate could have brought me to that place on that day. Those late discs have a truth, an insight and a flaming immersion into that music that approach bliss. He played his last concert in Philadelphia one year later on October 31, 1991, and died in 1993, a month shy of his 101st birthday. Playing great music is surely the finest therapy.

More Choral Gems

Howard Haines had been the head of choral music at Drexel University for 18 years and, upon his retirement, a 110-member chorus and orchestra of 53 was assembled for the occasion. Dolores Cascarino, who had known Haines from his days at Combs College, was asked to be one of the 16 solo singers in Ralph Vaughan Williams' sublime yet impractical *Serenade to Music*, set to text from Shakespeare's *The Merchant of Venice*, before the second half with the Brahms Requiem.

Howard Haines:
I'll miss working with the students, for we've been doing some pretty impressive stuff for a school having no music majors until last September. People have told me that the students won't be able to do this or that. But notes are notes—if they can hear it, they can sing it. I don't believe in putting limitations on anyone because they happen to be engineers or science majors. I started playing in church at 16, and 49 years later I have never had to call off a performance because singers couldn't sing the music. (Drexel University, March 2, 1989)

Whenever there was an opportunity to speak with Margaret Garwood, who took years to complete works, it always yielded remarkable insights into the creative process. Her *Tombsongs*, written for Sean Deibler's Choral Arts Society, were to be performed before Stravinsky's *Symphony of Psalms*.

The Philadelphia native taught piano for years before deciding to devote her energies to composing, a traditionally male-dominated pursuit in Philadelphia—and everywhere else. In her home was a chest-high pile of boxes, manuscript sketches of her opera *Rappaccini's Daughter*, an endeavor taking nine years to complete.

Margaret Garwood:
I probably shouldn't have accepted writing a piece to be played on the same program as the Symphony of Psalms*! Stravinsky's piece has a very odd instrumentation—no violins, violas, or clarinets, no upper middle register sounds to plug the hole, but still a big orchestra.*

The creative process keeps going on in my head even if I'm not composing. When you're writing, you imagine this perfect work, but years later you hear many things in it that you would like to change.

A composer doesn't pick influences, they pick you. (Her home, March 20, 1989)

Up, Up and Away

On April Fool's Day 1989, engineers discovered two widening cracks in a wooden ceiling truss high above the Academy of Music's auditorium. The Opera Company was scheduled to perform *L'Elisir d'Amore* and *Luisa Miller* with Luciano Pavarotti, and the Philadelphia Orchestra had concerts scheduled, but safety was the most urgent factor.

The Orchestra under Wolfgang Sawallisch moved to the 1,850 seat Forrest Theater, with the maestro also performing chamber concerts there and at the Church of the Holy Trinity. *L'Elisir* was performed, without staging, at the Cathedral of Sts. Peter and Paul, and the *Luisa Miller*, originally planned to be televised, was moved to the 1,790 seat Shubert (now Merriam) Theater, bumping some University of the Arts student productions.

Four Inspiring Women

One major international artist who rarely performed at home was the marvelous soprano Benita Valente, a familiar face at the Metropolitan Opera who hadn't sung opera in Philadelphia for a decade.

In February 1990, the Opera Company of Philadelphia strayed from the standard repertory to present Valente in Handel's 1734 *Ariodante*, with the late mezzo Tatiana Troyanos singing the title role originally written for a male castrato. Michael Korn directed from the harpsichord, with sets from the Spoleto Festival and costumes from a Santa Fe Opera production featuring Valente.

The gracious soprano, who is married to Anthony Checchia, founder of the enormously successful Philadelphia Chamber Music Society and head of the Marlboro Festival in Vermont, spoke about the show, singing at home and singing love duets to another woman.

Benita Valente:

There are good and bad things about working at home, because you feel demands of house, home and family that are absent on the road. I probably know more people in the Met audience than I will here at home. And singing to a woman isn't really distracting, since you learn to relate to the role. There's great drama in this music, with very strong emotions. (Her home, February 13, 1990)

Michael Tilson Thomas is well-known these days as the gifted conductor of the San Francisco Symphony. I recall being impressed with his many talents through a recording of the two-piano *Rite of Spring* with Ralph Grierson, the only complete recording of Carl Ruggles' orchestral works with the Buffalo Philharmonic and his interplay with Ira Gershwin when he was still a youngster.

In March 1990 he conducted the world premiere of his own *From the Diary of Anne Frank*, narrated by no less than Audrey Hepburn, at that time UNICEF's goodwill ambassador. His orchestra was the New World Symphony, founded by the conductor in Miami the year before, and still going strong.

Michael Tilson Thomas:

The concept of the work was Audrey's, but it's special to my heart, and led me in some inventive directions as a composer. My aim was to make it expressive and hopeful, allowing the bright, shining spirit of the innocence of Anne Frank to come through.

To hear Audrey reciting these words with her fine, delicate phrasing, with the music providing the fabric—it's as if you were listening in to Anne Frank herself. (By phone, March 16, 1990)

The tiny violinist Midori always brought huge excitement to her appearances. Born in Osaka, Japan, she dropped her last name (Goto) when her parents were divorced, moving to New York's Juilliard School at age 10 with her mother, a professional violinist and teacher. Performing with Zubin Mehta at a New York Philharmonic New Year's Eve concert, appearing in *Life* magazine with her Snoopy doll, playing on the Tonight Show, soloing with Leonard Bernstein at Tanglewood and playing in concert at the White House were early milestones which allowed her, at 15, to leave Juilliard and concentrate on concertizing.

She seemed too frail to have such a powerful, muscular tone, and her phenomenal technical virtuosity and enormous assurance seemed impossible to pour from such a tiny woman. When she came to Philadelphia as a veteran, playing a recital at the ripe age of 18, Sony had just released her performance of the complete 24 Paganini Caprices, with the two Bartok Concertos in the can.

Midori:

It's fun to travel, especially because of the many different foods. At home, I have a specialty—fried chicken.

I never even thought about success, because I just love to play any time and want to practice. CBS (now Sony) suggests things to record and I say what I want, but nobody can push me to do anything I don't want to do. (Academy of Music, March 26, 1990)

Another remarkable woman is the Philadelphia-born Ann Hobson Pilot, the harpist in the Boston Symphony since 1969 (first-chair since 1980) until her retirement 40 years later in 2009. In addition, she bore the brunt of being the first African-American woman to hold a principal position in any major American orchestra.

Pilot grew up in Germantown where her mother, Grace Smith, taught piano in Philadelphia schools until 1972. All other instruments except the harp were taken when Pilot got to Girls High; her mother was skeptical until her teacher was impressed by the girl's speedy progress and a rental harp found its way into their living room.

Lessons with Philadelphia Orchestra harpist Marilyn Costello at Philadelphia Musical Academy followed, and Pilot found another encouraging mentor in the orchestra's retired harpist, Edna Phillips, who arranged a stint at the Cleveland Institute of Music with Alice Chalifoux and enrollment at the Marlboro Festival in Vermont. When the National Symphony's regular harpist injured a finger, Chalifoux and Phillips recommended Pilot for the post, and she eventually transferred to the Boston Symphony.

Pilot was asked to solo with Orchestra 2001, playing Ravel's incandescent *Introduction and Allegro*, Walter Piston's *Fantasy* and *Ennenga* by the shamefully underperformed William Grant Still. She was staying with her mother, who lived within walking distance of my house, allowing me to hear her mother's reminiscences about accompanying alumna Marian Anderson in the song "Murmuring Zephyr" as a sophomore at South Philadelphia High School for Girls, and playing Beethoven concertos with German orchestras during her overseas years.

Ann Hobson Pilot:

When I was 16 or 17, Edna (Phillips) told me I was going to have to be twice as good as anyone else. It didn't dawn on me then what she meant, but being a black musician really did mean proving myself all the time and being looked on as a curiosity. There weren't any role models for me, no black players to look up to. No one I knew played the harp. But if it had not been for the free Board of Education programs, it would not have happened. I know that there's a budget crunch for arts programs in Philadelphia, but the Boston school district also canceled a program taught by my husband. (Home of Grace Smith, January 22, 1992)

After Pilot retired from the Boston Symphony, she received an enormous demonstration of respect: the world premiere *On Willows and Birches*, written for her by John Williams to play the season *after* her retirement—and conducted by James Levine.

10. INNOVATORS AND CREATORS

By 1991, composer John Duffy had won two Emmys, including one for the 12-hour PBS series *Heritage: Civilization for the Jews*. His 50th anniversary tribute to the troops lost in Pearl Harbor was to be performed at the USS Arizona Memorial that December 7, and was working on a music-theater piece based on the life of Joe DiMaggio.

Duffy had come up with a brilliant idea 16 years before that—of supporting American composers and American music. Starting with $54,000 from the New York State Council on the Arts, he created a new organization called Meet the Composer. Soon funded by the Philadelphia Music Project, the Pew Foundation and the Laila Wallace-Reader's Digest Foundation, it funded 33 composer-in-residence posts with 21 orchestras; post-concert composer Encounters with orchestra audiences; a $4.5 million consortium commissioning program by several performing or presenting groups; a new composer/choreographer project awarding $400,000 to 20 choreographers and 19 composers for new dance works; an educational program that provides school residencies and music composed for student players; and a residency program for small orchestras as well as opera, dance and music-theater companies, allowing them to expand in scope, ensuring multiple performances of each work.

More than $2.5 million is involved in all programs annually, with about 43 percent going to women and minorities and about a third to jazz composers.

I had a chance to speak with Duffy, mentioning how Riccardo Muti urged more performances of contemporary music, often insisting that 100 works had to be played to discover one masterpiece.

John Duffy:
Muti is absolutely right, though it may be more like 1,000 to one. Most classical premieres get only one hearing, like raising a dying grape arbor. We must create a situation where these works are nourished and composers can tinker, have workshop sessions with musicians in advance of the premieres. After all, Aida *had 400 rehearsals for Verdi to make changes . . .*

I agree with those composers who resist discussing their music, and insist everything they have to say is in the notes. They shouldn't have to justify their music, because no words will make bad music good. But their availability for discussion makes the creative process more comprehensible, more humanizing to lay people. Audiences are interested in how music is created, how melodies are written.

People once were afraid that audiences would walk out on contemporary works, but it's no big deal. I was at a Mets game last night and half the crowd walked out in the fourth inning. (By phone, July 21, 1991)

It was a fabulous idea, and created many, many new works. But, like many noble ideas, it eventually became an inside job.

North of Hollywood

I missed out on meeting the great film composer Alex North, who was always out of town when I was out in California with Emil. Because Alex' late brother Harry had become a good friend, it was doubly hard to write Alex North's obituary, though Emil was willing to give me a quote.

North never had a contract with a studio, ferociously insisting on only scoring films with pertinent social value, including many versions of Broadway plays like his classic *A Streetcar Named Desire* (the first to use jazz throughout), *The Rose Tattoo* and *Who's Afraid Of Virginia Woolf*, among many others.

Few people knew that North had been hired to write the score for Stanley Kubrick's iconic *2001: A Space Odyssey*, which was recorded in Hollywood. While shooting in England, the obsessive Kubrick matched his scenes with the now-famed excerpts of Richard Strauss' *Also Sprach Zarathustra*, Johann Strauss' *On the Beautiful Blue Danube* and *Lux Aeterna* by György Ligeti. Basically, he did what is known as a temp track, music used during filming and initial exhibitor screenings before the score is completed. When North traveled to New York for the premiere, he heard not one note of his music. After his death, Jerry Goldsmith re-recorded the score, which demonstrated just how brilliant North's instincts were.

North, who died at 81, was one of the last giants in the neglected art of film music. He created brilliant and imaginative scores for more than 70 films, including epics such as *Cleopatra* and *Spartacus* and character dramas such as *Cheyenne Autumn*, *The Misfits* and *Prizzi's Honor*. For that last film, he used a snippet from Puccini's *Gianni Schicchi*, a one-act opera about a schemer whose sarcastic music makes it clear that deception is afoot. It was the perfect choice for the titles, yet those few non-original measures made him ineligible for an Oscar, a decision many composers protested.

North was always searching for a film's underlying motivation or implied truth. "I find it practically impossible to score anything that does not move me emotionally," he insisted, "and I attempt to convey the internal, rather than the external, aspects of a film. By this I mean the music should be related to the characters at all times, not the action." For this reason, North said, he found grand epics the most difficult films to score.

Emil voiced immense respect for North as creator of unique effects. "Alex would call me about unusual instruments, hoping to find sounds as authentic as possible to match the locale of the picture. When the music was composed, it always showed he had done plenty of homework. For one main title, he called for striking a whiskey bottle filled with water to get just the right sound."

He avoided producers who feared input from musicians, once recalling one who said, "I don't like your music, it sounds like that guy Barstop." When North realized that the producer meant Bartók, he decided to wait for another film.

In 1986, after 15 nominations, he received an honorary Oscar for his "brilliant artistry." When receiving that honorary Oscar in 1986, North said, "Let me make a humble plea to those in our industry to encourage and convey hope, humor, compassion, adventure and love, as opposed to despair, synthetic theatrics, and blatant bloody violence. Sex, sex, sex by all means, but with a bit of mystery, charm and elegance—and lots of imagination."

Amen.

Though in poor health for a few years, North's spirits were lifted when a producer of the hit film *Ghost* insisted on using North's 1955 "Unchained Melody" as the movie's key song. That resulted in a generous royalty, another meaning for a term that described Alex North's reputation perfectly.

After this was published, Harry, who made wedding rings for my son and his wife, thanked me for his brother's obit with a sterling silver key ring, about one by three inches, with a miraculously-etched *Guernica* of Picasso. He later wondered why I didn't use it every day, but it's safely wrapped in felt and stored in a special drawer.

Women on Stage—and Staging

Mozart's enigmatic opera *The Magic Flute*, premiered only 66 days before his tragic death at 35, presents an immense challenge to stage directors. Originally created for a theatrical troupe in what we would call an entertainment, it's crammed with mystical Masonic clues, childlike behavior and shrouded meaning, an outpouring of ravishing, light-hearted genius.

Pennsylvania Opera Theater, offering operas sung in English conducted by founder Barbara Silverstein, went outside of the usual directorial suspects and investigated a fresh theatrical approach: she chose Maggie Harrer, who had danced with Martha Graham and Merce Cunningham before setting up her own dance theater company in New York. Harrer was well known for stressing the necessity of having theatrical ideas completely worked out in every detail, allowing them to fully convey their meaning.

Maggie Harrer:

Theater should enlighten us, not confuse us. This story had never made sense to me, but after studying the historical aspects, I realized that 1791 audiences would see the many subtle political subtexts of their day in a Monty Python-esque way. Deeper down, it's about the balance of right for the world between its extremes—man and woman, sun and moon, earth and sky, spirituality and carnality.

Fairy tales always have a serious side under the fun. Finding that deeper aspect, without the advantage of the lost historical references, is essential to translate it to 1991 audiences. (Schubert Theater, November 5, 1991)

For a *Don Giovanni*, presented by the Academy of Vocal Arts, director Mirciam Bazell also saw the essence of the opera's theatricality in a new way. She was using the Prague version, with a much darker conclusion than the happier ending attached for the more conservative Viennese audience.

Marciam Bazell:
Though the production looks traditional, the characters conduct themselves in a much darker way. A director could do a lot of stagey/blocky stuff, but this piece is too important—this is about life and death.

I think of Giovanni not just as a seducer of women, but as a man who traps everyone in the story in some way, and only through his death can they be freed. He constantly turns from an instinctive animal into a thinking person, charming but schizophrenic, destructive yet always believing in what he says—for him, it's always the truth.

Like a drug addict, he's never satisfied but is compelled to search without self-pity for the next conquest. (Academy of Vocal Arts, March 3, 1992)

The premiere of Giacomo Puccini's final opera *Turandot* at Milan's La Scala in 1926 has achieved the stuff of legend, mostly because of the few pages uncompleted at the time of his death seventeen months before.

Since the work really doesn't have a convincing ending, Puccini may have painted himself into corner without certainty about how to complete it. His publisher Giulio Ricordi chose composer Franco Alfano to work from Puccini's drafts and sketches and complete the work, and Alfano composed two settings: one of 377 bars, and a shorter one, usually performed today.

Conductor Arturo Toscanini insisted that the original ending setting be reduced, and later chopped again, with Alfano sarcastically responding that perhaps he should resign his post as director of the Turin Conservatory and take composition lessons from Toscanini. As might be expected, Toscanini was not pleased. On opening night at Milan's La Scala, just after the work reached the death of Liu and ensuing chorus (known to have been written by Puccini), Toscanini stopped and laid down his baton. He turned to the audience and announced: *Qui finisce l'opera, perché a questo punto il maestro è morto (Here the opera ends, because at this point the maestro died).* One can only imagine how Alfano felt! However, Toscanini led Alfano's completion at the second and third performances.

The Opera Company of Philadelphia used *Turandot* as its season closer, knowing that by that time, thanks to Luciano Pavarotti, the tenor aria "Nessun dorma" had become a familiar anthem. The fearsome Chinese princess Turandot doesn't sing until the second act with a gigantic headdress and a scorching aria, "In questa reggia," vowing eternal revenge on men. Turandot has asked three riddles of all prospective suitors hopeful of winning her frigid hand; the many losers have found themselves detached from their head, yet the tenor wants to try.

In this performance, Turandot was sung by Alessandra Marc, a Berlin-born soprano whose real name is Judy Borden.

Alessandra Marc:

In 1987 (the legendary Turandot) Birgit Nilsson coached me in the role, and she told me I sang it better than anyone—but not to sing it for four or five years. She wore an enormous headpiece—mine is on a platform constructed to sit on my shoulders. Sometimes I feel like I'm in Star Trek! *And my gown has a 30-foot train carried by servants.*

After I sang at the Metropolitan Opera auditions, I was backstage listening to the applause for my aria, when someone asked me for my name. Since my name was similar to many other singers, I just said, "Alessandra Marc," and that was it. It's strong, feminine, different. And no matter what country I'm in, Marc is easy to remember. (Academy of Music, April 16, 1992)

Another unique thing about *Turandot* is its history. Though its origin may come from Persian tales a thousand years old, Italian *commedia dell'arte* master Carlo Gozzi wrote the original play *Turandot, Princess of China* in 1762; Friedrich von Schiller, the German poet, philosopher, historian and dramatist followed with *Turandot, Prinzessin von China* in 1801. Where Gozzi's focus is comical, satirical and cruel, Schiller's princess struggles with emotions stifled by pride (Puccini was familiar with the Schiller version).

Karl Vollmoller wrote a translation of Gozzi's play for actor-director Max Reinhart in 1911, eventually given with incidental music by Ferruccio Busoni, who had his own ideas about the answers to the riddles. Many composers have written works based on this story, though it's fascinating that, in each case, the answers to the riddles are different.

The riddles (sometimes slightly changed) are:

"What is born each night and dies each dawn?"
"What flickers red and warm like a flame, but is not fire?"
"What is like ice, but burns like fire?"

The answers were:
Gozzi:
Sun
Year
The Lion of Venice

Schiller:
Year
Eye

Plough

Vollmoeller:
Hope and faith
Knowledge and power
Love

Busoni:
Human mind
Custom
Art

Puccini:
Hope
Blood
Turandot!

Two Brilliant Pianists

Russian pianist Vladimir Feltsman's artistry had become a legend, even during the eight years of cancelled concerts and non-person status in Russia—due to his request to emigrate to Israel and eventually to the United States. Though he claimed to have 30 concertos in his repertoire, he played no more than 70 concerts a year, enjoying his teaching post at the State University of New York in New Paltz.

He had already finally played in recital, and with the Philadelphia Orchestra, before he returned to play a recital of Bach, Schumann and Prokofiev, and we had a chance to chat about his repertoire and living outside of Manhattan.

Vladimir Feltsman:

I don't see any problem playing Bach on a modern piano, for it enables you to achieve any results or impressions you want to express. You can play Bach on a balalaika or pieces of glass, but you must play with spiritual loyalty to Bach.

Years ago, I once visited (the legendary, always-nervous Russian pianist Sviatoslav) Richter at his home. In his studio, he had about forty chairs, all full of large stuffed animals. When I asked why, he said, "So I can practice playing in front of people." (Coffee shop, March 24, 1991)

The annual visit by pianist Richard Goode is always an inspiring season highlight, bringing transcendent interpretations that always seem ideal. He had just recorded all 32 Beethoven piano sonatas, and was including an early one, plus one each by Mozart and Schubert and some Debussy preludes, in an upcoming recital. It was a homecoming in a way, considering that the Bronx-born Goode had studied at Curtis Institute with two giants—Rudolf Serkin and Miecyslaw Horszowski.

Goode invited me to interview him at his large apartment in New York, close to the Metropolitan Museum of Art. Every room was graced with walls of books, and our extramusical conversations made it clear that Goode had one of the most brilliant literary minds that I was likely to ever meet.

On the piano were piles of different editions of the Beethoven sonatas, many with slightly different notations by annotators through the decades. He had gone through every one before his recording marathon, choosing the editions he felt most likely to mirror Beethoven's original intentions.

Richard Goode:

Fifty years ago, before there were recordings of most music, a performance of a work was magnified by its scarcity. Today, life is conducted to a soundtrack of musical wallpaper—I mean involuntary music. People are beginning to feel it's natural to always have music going. This for me is very pernicious and degrading.

Yet those old records of Alfred Cortot, Edwin Fischer and Artur Schnabel were a tremendous part of my musical education. I could hear a wonderful shadow of their art, their huge musical personalities. There are mistakes and flaws, but they're like blemishes in a face you love. I like to do recordings in one complete take, and though you sometimes can fix mistakes, you only do it if everything else is right. There are good wrong notes and bad wrong notes, and I think many recordings today have an obsessive emphasis on cleanliness and perfection of a narrow kind.

This may sound piano-chauvinistic, but a piano is more an instrument of the imagination than any other, it depends on illusion. The nature of being a pianist means being able to make this illusion work on many different kinds of instruments. Once in a while you meet one so harsh and unfeeling—like a pit bull—that you must cancel, but usually you can do what Mr. Horszowski called "making friends with it." (His New York apartment, December 9, 1991)

Temporarily Bite Size

One thing certain about the features section of a newspaper—especially the *Daily News*—is that there will always be format changes. If you're a freelancer, you will just find about it after all the meetings have been held and the staffers have all adjusted.

Once in a great while, the change is actually good. That September, I was given a chance to write a weekly column called *The Score*—actually a way to combine various weekly morsels without important time factors into one column.

So, for a while anyway, items were presented in freestyle bite sizes.

For the first column, I thought I'd take a shot and keep it offbeat in typical *Daily News* style.

ACT I: WHY CLASSICAL? Few genres are burdened by such a clumsy term. Strictly speaking, it denotes music composed between about 1750 and 1830 (mainly Haydn, Mozart, Beethoven and Schubert), the bridge between Baroque and romantic styles.

We really need another term. Serious? Hey—rappers and country singers don't take their music lightly. Enlightening? Too cosmic—besides, some music is meant to be just pretty, not deep. Lasting? The music of Scott Joplin, Irving Berlin and Jerome Kern has more longevity and receives more performances than most Arnold Schoenberg and Anton Webern. Orchestral or chamber? They also define the London Symphony playing the sound track of *Star Wars* and many jazz ensembles. Notated? Lots of pop and big band jazz arrangements are written out, and Baroque music is sketched out in the same improvisational style as jazz chord changes.

Until somebody comes up with an alternative, using the term "classical" is like perpetually walking around with an ugly tie.

LENNY BERNSTINI? I heard last week that the final corrected proofs of the upcoming Grove Dictionary of Opera, sitting directly under a water pipe that burst about 3 one morning in the London editorial offices, were saved only because two editors were working a rare night shift. It jogged me to pull down a random volume of the New Grove Dictionary of Music and Musicians, the musical bible, and happen to turn to Creston (a CD of his music was reviewed in a recent column). Guess what—he was born Giuseppe Guttoveggio. Take his five symphonies, nine by Peter Mennin (born Mennini), eight by Walter Piston (Pistone) and nine by the late Philadelphian Vincent Persichetti, and you find that the American symphonic tradition has an Italian heart.

(Received a bunch of letters over that last remark, several of them in the same handwriting, saying "Why do you have to get ethnic about it, goombah?")

In his new CD, Czech-born Canadian pianist Antonin Kubalek, postulates a fascinating theory: that Brahms' earlier piano style, full of "extroverted bravado," shifted to deeper, more intimate expression after he grew his famous beard at age 43. "Was the beard responsible for the music," asks Kubalek, "or the music for the beard?"

Actually, the column seemed like it would work out—allowing some inside information, mixed in with a little irreverence. Plus, I was honored to go to a downtown club, sit at a piano, and do a publicity photo with Nels Nelson and Jon Takiff, a proud moment indeed.

Music Therapy

In working with two community programs, I discovered more ways that proved music to be an inspiring and positive force.

Philadelphia Orchestra violinist Robert de Pasquale and his wife Ellen Fisher founded The Academy of Community Music, the only Suzuki school in the region, in 1983, after de Pasquale saw a Japanese Suzuki tour at the

Academy of Music. By 1992, the school was giving nearly 1,300 students with lessons on violin, viola, cello, piano, flute and guitar with a faculty of 30.

Suzuki method stresses learning music early, as a natural language. It emphasizes hearing, repeating and playing sounds and songs even before being able to read music.

Specially-challenged children were accepted at the Academy from the start, and it became immediately apparent that Suzuki methods worked for them, too. The formal creation of Crescendo Music Program followed in 1985, and seven years later more than 450 children—from 18 months to five years—discovered the gift of music at 12 neighborhood centers with group instruction of a more specialized nature.

Some of those fund-raising concerts were startling, as these little tykes with every conceivable malady trooped onto stages and played tunes with incredible intent and their last shred of energy; event the flintiest souls could be seen wiping tears from their faces.

Later on, we had an opportunity to host one of these affairs, one of the most fulfilling days I can remember.

Many now-famous artists studied at Philadelphia's Settlement Music School, begun in 1908 by Jeanette Selig Frank and Blanche Wolf Kohn, who began giving piano lessons for a nickel in the Southwark section. Now spread to six venues, it has been copied by many cities, though nowhere equaled in scope and support by the community.

Its Kardon Insititute provides individual instruction, where Crescendo Music Program necessarily offered primarily group sessions. Terminology was also different: Crescendo children were referred to as "specially challenged," yet Kardon Institute of Music for the Handicapped uses the term "disability."

I discovered that the difference between music education and music therapy, according to Kardon's director Tamara Zavislan, is merely a matter of emphasis.

Tamara Zavislan:

The goal of music education is to play an instrument and learn music theory. In music therapy, music is secondary to other attainments—like independence, self-esteem, accepting direction, interaction, motor development.

Parents say it's one of the few places their child is treated with respect. You can be yourself here, free to be creative and expressive, with no judging. One parent insists that music therapy turned a D student into a B student—there's great power in accomplishment. We can't fix a disability, but we can fix the environment to remove a handicap. (Kardon Institute, September 27, 1992)

Invited to one of the sessions, I saw 23-year-old Sue Smith, in her wheelchair, play keyboard under the guidance of Zavislan. Smith, a bright, articulate Widener Memorial School graduate, was paralyzed—except for her right hand and arm—as the result of an auto accident 18 years before. Despite her disability, this session of playing, composing and singing is a joyful time, punctuated with hugs and squeals of laughter.

"It has taken three years for Sue to play 'Three Blind Mice,'" said her mother, Ellen Smith, "but she did it. These young people are totally accepted and uplifted, surrounded by teachers, parents and others who understand them."

These two centers made me return home with a renewed sense of the human spirit's power and the magic of life.

And, for a long, long while, a new and huge appreciation for the ability to practice the piano.

Inside Job

When *Daily News* reporter Joseph Blake wrote a play for the African-American Bushfire Theater, no staffer was willing to review a play by a colleague. The solution: put the freelancer in that awkward position.

A final paragraph: "The play's title, *The Courage of Flies*, was a metaphor for the perseverance of a group of black neighbors, some of whom lived on the crumbs of society for years yet somehow survived. In a world of crooked politicians, cruel urban development, fragility of neighborhood ties, and shifting values, it offered an often-wise relevance to take home."

The play, given in an old West Philadelphia movie theater, had its moments and was quite well portrayed, though it could have used some tightening. You're always obligated to tell the truth, no matter what and, luckily for me, it was worth experiencing.

Competitions

In May of 1992, Taiwan-born pianist Jenny C. C. (Chia Ching) Lin played a Beethoven sonata at the Mozart on the Square competition preliminaries—and made the competition unnecessary. Lin became was the only unanimous choice in the now-defunct festival's 12-year history and, the following October, played the Mozart Piano Concerto No. 15 with the Concerto Soloists of Philadelphia under Marc Mostovoy.

Though she had been working on Beethoven's *Emperor* Concerto and Rachmaninoff's enormously difficult Third Piano Concerto, she found Mozart a different kind of challenge.

Jenny Lin:

The difficulty of Mozart is the clarity, for you must emphasize every note, every voice. You need ten ears to hear all the voices, and you must be conscious of everything. In something like the Rachmaninoff, there are lots of automatic things, but in Mozart everything must be thought through. I try to hear the orchestra sing inside me, and treat the solo voice as part of the ensemble. (Walnut Street Theater, October 16, 1992)

Lin has made many albums in recent years, some sponsored by Steinway, and has become even more popular through her YouTube videos.

American composer John Cage's usually far-out compositions, which flitered originality, Zen, literature, cacophony, humor and silence through an unfettered artistic spirit, came to an end with his death in fall 1992. To honor his imagination, the Philadelphia Museum of Art filled up a small gallery in the 20th-Century wing with his manuscripts, relevant photographs and artworks by his friends Marcel Duchamp and Jasper Johns. Cage shook up the pomposity and dicacticism of the musical establishment, and thereby changed the ground rules forever.

Around this time, besides doing occasional disc reviews, I was allowed to do a column called *Take The Music Home*, recommending CDs of pieces that were played live by the various ensembles that week. Messages from patrons showed that they appreciated suggestions on buying discs of music they particularly enjoyed in concert. It gave an opportunity to play and choose from discs languishing on my shelves, some review copies provided by the major labels. Sadly, the column didn't last long, and neither did the generosity of the labels.

11. COMPETITION, CARMEN AND CREDIT

In the fourth—and last—Luciano Pavarotti International Voice Competition, held in November 1992 under the auspices of the Opera Company of Philadelphia, there were plenty of tense dramatic moments.

More than 1,500 candidates had been judged in preliminaries lasting three years, and 117 singers from 25 countries had come to Philadelphia to audition in two marathon gala concerts. Arranging the largest operatic competition of its kind in the world was an expensive proposition for the Opera Company, with its payoff the casting of the winners in upcoming Opera Company productions, either singing with Pavarotti or working under his direction. The judging chores were shared by OCP director Robert Driver and its artistic administrator, Danielle Orlando, plus conductor Edoardo Muller. Piano accompaniment was handled brilliantly by the indefatigable Leone Magiera, Pavarotti's friend and conductor.

Acting as emcee from the judging table in the back of the Academy, the supertenor—draped in his trademark king-sized scarf—often made conducting gestures and once sang the male part in a soprano's aria. To the 56 hopeful finalists who walked out onto the lonely stage on the second and last day, Pavarotti was a distant voice who suggested arias, interrupted to give suggestions, and sometimes even sang softly to illustrate. His instructions were sometimes cryptic, though more detailed to those fortunate enough to speak Italian.

To a sight-reading young singer who made a mistake, he laughed, "Don't worry, I make that same mistake myself!" And later, when a young man wiped his brow: "If you don't sweat, you don't achieve anything."

The audience had been instructed not to clap or cheer at the auditions, though that meant an awkward silence after each dramatic aria; when one fan yelled "Brava!" after a young woman's effort, Pavarotti broke up the house by seriously saying, "The husband should not clap."

In another comic moment, he requested a specific number by saying, "Everybody knows that aria—la la la, da da—something like that."

One young singer was asked, "If you were asked to perform in New York next month, what aria would you sing?" he replied, "In that case, I would work very hard on (Donizetti's) "Una furtiva lagrima," a work the super tenor had sung a thousand times." All right," said Pavarotti, "do that one for me now!"

After five and a half hours of operatic arias, plus 90 minutes of backstage deliberation, Pavarotti finally named 37 lucky—or maybe unlucky—competition winners.

Carmen, in Person

With the kind of dramatic strokes found in operatic plots, sultry mezzo-soprano Denyce Graves suddenly became the American incarnation of Bizet's *Carmen*. Taking over for Marilyn Horne in San Francisco in 1991, Graves caught her shoe in the set at the final dress rehearsal and snapped a bone in her foot. Good fortune returned a few months later when Agnes Baltsa cancelled in Los Angeles, and Graves found herself singing to famed tenor Placido Domingo.

Denyce Graves.

When Graves came to sing *Carmen* in Philadelphia, we set up an interview. She said she had some good stories for me—and she surely did.

Denise Graves:
That night in San Francisco, I was rushed to the hospital still wearing my mantilla and full costume, and did opening night wearing a cast.

I got lucky with Carmen, *but I was good at it. Our profession has become more visually oriented, and in this very physical part, with lots of dancing, I can look the part. I could never get bored in the role, and with each director, I discover new approaches and continually develop my grab bag of Carmen tricks.*

She's close to my own personality, I can feel her soul, it's not a big jump. She's complex, and she constantly reminds me that I could be living better if I were more like her in many ways. No one can get to her, to who she is. She's very discriminating, and sees in Don Jose a man very different than what she's known. He wants her soul, and she wants her freedom—like two fires, very strong personalities. She's the most honest woman. She says what she means, has strict rules, pays her debts. She will be furious, then it's over—just as when love is over, that's it.

Though Carmen *has opened the doors for me, my only concern is not to be pigeonholed or typecast. I've turned down more Carmens than I've accepted, only taking the choice engagements—San Francisco, Vienna. But they must offer me another role as well, for there are many I'm itching to do.*

Those stories...well, when I first did Carmen *in Vienna, there were cancellations, and I was told Luis Lima would eventually sing Don Jose, and we rehearsed with a sub. Since he didn't come to say hello, even on the day of the opera, and I didn't know him or what he looked like, I was getting pretty apprehensive right up until closing time.*

The curtain went up, and as I walked among the soldiers I kept whispering, "Are you Don Jose?" "Are you Don Jose?" Finally Luis said "Yes," and I began singing to him. It was the most exciting Carmen, *for there was an immediate, unbelievable awareness of the part. I still get excited when I think about it.*

When I did my first Carmen *with Placido, I was wildly excited to be singing with him. In the second act I was eating slices of an orange and, when he was singing to me, I impulsively stuck an orange slice in his mouth, and the juice dribbled down his face. His eyes were furious and I thought, there goes my career! As soon as the act was over I ran back and said to him, "Placido, I'm so sorry! Please forgive me, I got carried away!" He said, "It's all right, that's what Carmen might have done. If you feel it, leave it in!" I said, thank you, God. That kind of artistic generosity is another reason why he is such a legend.* (Warwick Hotel, November 12, 1992)

Grumpy, Doc and Happy

At holiday time in 1992, I just had to insert a bit called *The Grinch Lives*:

I don't get grumpy about audiences standing for the *Hallelujah* chorus, just amused. It all started when George II stood up at the 1743 London premiere of *Messiah*, though he may have been getting up to go to the bar, the loo or beat the traffic back to the palace. After all these years, we continue a practice begun by the father of the guy who sent British troops to shoot at our frozen, shoeless men at Germantown and Valley Forge. Traditions long outlive their sources.

Because of his weight problems, Luciano Pavarotti's doctor suggested cancelling out on the Opera Company productions of *La Bohème* and *La Favorita* (which he was going to direct). The 5-foot-9 tenor was thought to weigh more than 280 pounds. It was a shock to the company, with plans to use some of the last Competition winners in major roles.

Pavarotti's cancellation, naturally, left a wealth of disappointed patrons. Reports came out that some had cursed and even physically threatened Opera Company personnel—about the casting of an opera about struggling young lovers, no less. It turned out that most of the outraged noise came from a Wilmington ticket scalper who had bought up over a thousand bucks of cheap seats hoping to make a last-minute killing from Pavarotti fans.

My take: "One sure bet is that he'll be healthy before April, when he's scheduled to sing *Pagliacci* with Riccardo Muti in Milan. Even Pavarotti is not going to stiff Muti at La Scala—that is, if he ever wants to work in Italy again."

Pavarotti's dining habits during his frequent visits to Philadelphia didn't paint a picture of the gregarious eater the public imagines him to be.

"He had a lot of self-discipline," said Carla Fusaro, who owned *Il Gallo Nero* near the Academy of Music. (This extraordinary restaurant, also a favorite of Riccardo Muti, closed soon after). He liked fish a lot, and he tried to stay away from salad and desserts, especially gelato."

Another favorite was *Girasole*, a restaurant now in a different location and still close to the halls. "Actually, most of our diners ate more than Luciano," said owner Franco Iovino. He loves a small dish of pappardelle (a flat, long noodle) with fresh tomato sauce. No heavy cream sauces. He'll have a small filet of veal, grilled, with a touch of olive oil. It's not very much, and he usually wants it very fast, right away. We serve Pavarotti our best Abruzzese red wine, Caroso. For dessert, he loves Haagen-Daz French vanilla. And an espresso."

Angelo Marabella of Marabella's said he had sent meals over during rehearsals. "He was very strict about avoiding anything fattening," Marabella said. "I never saw him eat dessert."

Several weeks after Luciano Pavarotti cancelled, 36-year-old Martin Thompson, one of the winners of the 1988 Pavarotti/Opera Company of Philadelphia Competition, stepped in to sing Rudolfo in *La Bohème*.

Though Thompson had sung the role over a hundred times in many opera houses, he didn't take the usual route to the operatic stage. He had never taken a lesson, except from his father, who sang at home in Portland, Oregon with Thompson accompanying him on the piano. He made four albums of classical-based gospel music until seeing a newspaper ad seeking voices for the Portland Opera chorus. He showed up in a wool shirt, sang the "Flower Song" from *Carmen* ("in the world's worst French," he said), and they put him in a small role in *Tales of Hoffman*. He studied opera, not voice, at Yale, but his plans for a career as a voice teacher changed when Thompson sang his first lead role—as Rodolfo in *Bohème*.

When Pavarotti cancelled, the production's director Beppe de Tomasi remembered Thompson from their collaboration the previous season in the company's *The Pearl Fishers*.

I wondered how much pressure he felt filling the giant shoes of Luciano Pavarotti.

Martin Thompson:

Honestly, I feel no pressure at all. I revere Pavarotti, and it's a great honor to be asked to step in.

The Pavarotti Competition came after singing my first La Bohème *in front of 8,000 people in Central Park. You get the ear and perspective of a great master like him, then make the connection to the company to take on* a small or large role. It's a real advantage over the usual competitions. We're talking here about a career, not a short-term splash.

The character of Rodolfo, a striving young poet, parallels the careers of many singers who attempt it. Those who sing this role find that at some point, and not just musically, the light goes on. You think, am I going to make it or not? Am I a bohemian who's not a great poet or painter? Is this all I'm going to be, will I amount to something? Those things have to come up in a young singer's mind. (Academy of Music, February 1, 1993)

Seen in the audience at those performances was legendary mezzo-soprano Rose Bampton, whose voice bewitched even the uncompromising maestro Arturo Toscanini—who cast her in Beethoven's *Fidelio* in his first live radio broadcast of a complete opera. Bampton once sang the soprano title role in *Aida*, as well as the mezzo role of Amneris, a week apart at the Met. Still sharp at 84, this Bryn Mawr resident provided a vivid example of why love of the arts keeps the spirit forever young.

Credit Where It's Due

In December 1992 Marc Mostovoy had called with exciting news. His board chairman Kenneth Jarin, a close friend of Al and Tipper Gore who had worked on the Clinton/Gore campaign, had snagged the Concerto Soloists of Philadelphia (eventually to be called Chamber Orchestra of Philadelphia) to play at the Inaugural affair. It was an invitation-only bash for 1,400 at the National Building Museum in the Pension Building on Judiciary Square. Also scheduled were cellist Yo-Yo Ma, Take Six, Nanci Griffith and the Peter Duchin dance orchestra.

Since Marc admits to little awareness of popular music, I told him that he had to play the traditional "Arkansas Traveler" for Clinton and the "Tennessee Waltz" *for* Gore, and found he hadn't heard of either one.

Marc asked David Saturen to quickly make an arrangement of both works. During the rehearsal of these two pieces and some short Baroque and classical background music, I noticed he was playing the Waltz at about twice the proper tempo. Though the event was a joyful affair, it's a terribly sad song and I suggested a slower, though non-largo, speed for the tune. He adjusted his tempo with the musicians until I was satisfied and, afterwards, asked how he could thank me for my suggestions. That was easy: I wanted the composers to be properly credited in the Inaugural booklet. Though probably no one in the world except me noticed, that elaborate Inaugural program booklet listed the performed composers: Mozart, Handel, Pachelbel, Vivaldi and Pee Wee King.

"After we played, the Secret Service immediately cleared the musicians, music stands, and chairs from the stage," said Mostovoy later. "After his address, Bill and Mrs. Clinton left on the side of the stage where I was standing. He saw my baton and shook hands, and I congratulated him. I thought Hillary looked stunning in her black dress."

Three Alumni

André Previn returned to conduct the Curtis Symphony Orchestra, leading the world premiere of alumnus Ned Rorem's Fourth Piano Concerto, for the left hand. Of course, it was written for Curtis president Gary Graffman, who had tragically lost the use of his right hand.

Previn had come from London where, in two concerts of standard works, he kiddingly said that few musicians even looked at him and that it was a real switch to have a hundred sets of eyes watching both his stick and his expressions.

Rorem and Graffman first crossed paths fifty years before, when the brilliant young composer was touched by the eight-year-old phenom's interpretation of a Chopin Ballade. Since those early years, Rorem has become America's finest composer of art songs, a controversial diarist and writer of 10 books and the creator of an enormously diverse catalog of instrumental music—many with a small-scaled French sensibility.

Ned Rorem:

Their aesthetic is to say what you have to say, then shut up. The French are profoundly superficial—you have water lilies, La Mer, *then the sun shifts and it's different. By comparison, the Germans are superficially profound.*

I feel that the Curtis Orchestra is as good as any professional orchestra around. They're young and not jaded, they have pride in their music. (By phone, January 30, 1993)

Behind the Scenes

In recent years, I've been fortunate to become close friends with Kile Smith and his incredible musical family. I had never met him before I wrote this in March of 1993:

"Local composer Kile Smith gets to hear the premiere of his piano trio, Hymn and Fugue No. 2, at 3 p.m. Sunday, played by the Davidsbund Chamber Players.

"Smith gets double kudos for launching the impressive newsletter of the Pennsylvania Composers Forum. It's packed with interviews, editorials and articles, plus practical information about copyrights, getting pieces performed and who's doing what in the state.

"Curator of the Free Library's Fleisher Collection (the world's largest repository of circulating orchestral music), Smith and his colleagues first produced a directory of all pieces written by Pennsylvanians since colonial times. It's another effort to elevate composers from their endangered-species status; in recent years, audience willingness in a conservative town to hear new music has spawned many contemporary groups eager to play it.

"Smith's tastes are eclectic. He once put a Led Zeppelin guitar riff in the cello part of a chamber work. "We keep trying to write the piece we always wanted to hear," he said, "but naturally, we keep working and never succeed. The problem with listening to music is that we ask the wrong questions, like "Do we like it?" One night after hearing Mahler's Sixth Symphony I realized that such questions were as ridiculous as asking that about the Grand Canyon. Just listen!""

A Beacon Extinguished

On April 8, 1993, the world heard that the 96-year-old "Lady from Philadelphia," Marian Anderson, had passed on. Her legacy was vast and, through her rich, soaring voice, she had become one of this century's most inspiring and powerful symbols of the struggle for equality for African-Americans.

Here in Philadelphia, her name is on the Marian Anderson Sickle Cell Anemia Care and Research Center at St. Christopher's Hospital for Children, on a bronze plaque on the Philadelphia Music Alliance's Walk of Fame on South Broad Street and other sites. She was presented numerous awards, including the Presidential Medal of Freedom (1963), the Congressional Gold Medal (1978), and the first Eleanor Roosevelt Human Rights Award of the City of New York in 1984.

Her greatest tribute rests in the opportunities she created for other black singers, opportunities that often are taken for granted today. Her determination and the sheer musical and emotional power of her talent overcame the barriers of discrimination and forever shattered the myth that blacks could not excel in classical music and in opera.

She rarely talked about prejudice, saying in a 1960 interview: "Sometimes it's like a hair across your cheek. You can't see it. You can't find it with your fingers but you keep brushing at it because the feel of it is irritating."

The deeply religious Anderson was the first black singer to perform at the White House, the first to sing at the Metropolitan Opera and the first to perform for Japan's Imperial Court. And she did it by raising her voice in song, not in anger. Her choice of Negro spirituals was a protest in song. The spiritual power of the words in tandem with the sheer emotional force of her voice often moved many in her audiences to tears and to examine their own consciences.

"She was grateful that she was able to make a difference, but her goal in life was really to make music, and when that opportunity was denied, there was the outrage of a nation, rather than her outrage," her nephew James DePreist said the day afterwards.

Nowhere was a nation's outrage expressed more fully than at Anderson's 1939 electrifying concert at the Lincoln Memorial, an event attended by more than 75,000 people now regarded as a pivotal moment in American Civil Rights history.

That concert was a stunning symbol of her long struggle against racial discrimination, and it happened because the Daughters of the American Revolution refused to rent Constitution Hall in Washington to Anderson for a concert. DAR officials said the date was already taken, spurring first lady Eleanor Roosevelt to believe Anderson was a victim of discrimination and resign from the organization. Mrs. Roosevelt made the arrangements for the Lincoln Memorial on Easter Sunday. It was the largest public tribute since Charles Lindbergh returned from France a decade earlier.

Her program included *America*, Schubert's "Ave Maria" and the spirituals "Gospel Train," "Trampin'" and "My Soul Is Anchored in the Lord," a program which would be recreated 70 years after the legendary event.

The singer's unwillingness to criticize the DAR made her accomplishment even more powerful to oppressed people of all persuasions. She told the racially mixed audience: "I am so overwhelmed, I just can't talk. I can't tell you what you have done for me today. I thank you from the bottom of my heart, again and again."

Later, she said: "If you've ever been tremendously excited about something or frightened—have you ever heard your heart beat heavily enough so that you almost lose your breath, so that you can't hear much else that's in your ears? Well, this was the sort of thing that happened for me at the Lincoln Memorial."

As a girl, the Philadelphia native scrubbed steps near her Webster Street family home to earn $4 to buy a violin. She was one of three daughters born to a coal and ice dealer who died when she was 12. Her mother, Anna, had been a Virginia schoolteacher, and since her certificate had been lost in a fire, she had to take in washing. Anderson started singing at age three and joined her church's junior choir at six. She earned her first pay as a singer—fifty cents—two years later. She would become the prime breadwinner for the family while attending South Philadelphia High School for Girls.

Anderson's vocal talent was nurtured at the huge Union Baptist Church on Fitzwater Street, where she learned to sing all the parts from soprano to bass. Her first duet was with legendary black tenor Roland Hayes, who took an interest in her growth. By age 15 she had not had formal instruction, and her parishioners created a fund to pay for her lessons with coach Giuseppe Boghetti.

As a youngster, she was refused admittance to a Philadelphia school of music because she was black. Years later, in Atlantic City, she was given the keys to the city without being allowed to stay in any of the city's hotels.

Anderson won first prize over 300 others in a 1925 New York Philharmonic competition, earning a summer concert in New York at Manhattan's Town Hall. She realized that her lack of familiarity with foreign languages kept her from the top echelon of singers. With financial support from fellowships, Anderson studied art songs, or lieder, throughout Europe, eventually singing more than 200 songs in nine languages, some for the kings of Sweden and Denmark.

"You are the greatest singer alive," famed conductor Arturo Toscanini said after hearing her sing in Salzburg. "A voice like yours is heard only once in a hundred years." And Finnish composer Jan Sibelius hailed her as "the perfect interpreter of my songs."

She became the first African-American artist to appear at the Metropolitan Opera, singing the role of Ulrica in Verdi's *The Masked Ball*. Although her voice was no longer at its best, the audience cheered her with such a roar that the orchestra came to a halt.

"The only color that mattered was the color of her voice, one of the richest and most moving of her generation," Associated Press writer W.P. Rogers noted.

As was her custom, Anderson described her reaction in the third person: "Ever since one was in high school in Philadelphia, one wanted to sing opera—at the Metropolitan Opera, if that could be. Now one is speechless."

The Masked Ball was the only opera role she ever sang on stage, opening the door for a new generation of black singers. The next to sing at the Met was baritone Robert McFerrin, father of jazzman Bobby McFerrin, who had already been contracted.

Anderson's final tour, in 1965, included a huge success at Carnegie Hall and an outdoor concert at Robin Hood Dell in Philadelphia's Fairmount Park, drawing more than 35,000 people. Her 75th birthday was celebrated at Carnegie Hall with a star-filled roster. And, in August 1979, the Mann Music Center opened with that special Marian Anderson Day concert sung by tenor Luciano Pavarotti, who flew in from Italy just to honor her.

She regretted all doors had not been open to her during her prime. "If I only could give what I had to offer then. But they wouldn't accept it, or me," she said. "Other Negroes will have the career I dreamed of."

Anderson's nephew and conductor James DePreist attended as well. When I next saw DePreist, I told him a story close to my family. My mother had gone to South Philadelphia High School for Girls a few years after Miss Anderson, and it was announced that the top students would have the opportunity to introduce this distinguished alumna as the graduation speaker (another student introduced Margaret Sullivan). At that time, Anderson was very well-known in Philadelphia, though not yet famous on a national—and eventually international—reputation.

My mother was barely able to distinguish one note from another, leading to her only non-excellent grade, in music. Yet this very shy girl worked tirelessly for the chance to introduce Miss Anderson and, when trembling in the wings before the introduction, was given a warm handshake and told that she'd be great, and to just have fun. Afterwards, she was given a hug and thanked for her inspiring words. It was a moment my mother never forgot and, later in life, spoke about it to us with misty eyes.

Recounting this to DePreist made him chuckle, and I asked him why he though it funny. His response moved me deeply: "No matter where I go, I hear stories like that about my aunt a couple of times a day!"

We should all leave such a legacy of gracefulness and all-encompassing love.

Grazie, Luciano

In the 1980s, the Opera Company of Philadelphia had held the Luciano Pavarotti International Vocal Competition, bringing singers from all over the world to audition in public concerts at the Academy of Music. Winners would get to sing for free in future Opera Company shows, the only apparent perk besides the identification with the tenor, considering the cost of putting on the Competition. One—Leila Guimarães—actually sang *Bohème* with him. Several times, though, he boiled it down to 30 or 40 singers and said, "They all win!" This wasn't very helpful to a singer, because when they said they were a winner on their resume, bookers said, "Who wasn't?"

The Opera Company realized after the fourth Pavarotti Competition that it was a huge investment with little payoff. And the tenor's cancellation of his involvement in their *La Bohème* and *La Favorita* productions probably didn't help in their decision.

Later, the company's general director Robert Driver said, "Producing operas has to be our primary focus. We must bring a balanced season of operas that we can do well, without limitations or constraints. Our season should be driven by the repertory, not by the singers."

The Competition's chairman Jane Nemeth, who had left the Opera Company after the last event, attempted to keep it in Philadelphia under different auspices. She received verbal support from Mayor Ed Rendell and the current Senator Vincent Fumo, who said they would talk to Pavarotti when he appeared at his concert at the Spectrum arena later in May. Yet there had been rumors that he might take it elsewhere.

I didn't know anything about this until I happened to be at the paper one day, and editor Zack Stalberg mentioned that the Competition might be leaving Philadelphia. We had spoken about three times in ten years, making me surprised when he shrugged, said, "Find out," and walked away. To Zack, my work at the *Daily News* had not essentially been what could be considered tough reporting.

I discovered that Pavarotti's manager was Herbert Breslin, known in the trade by everyone I asked as "Horrible Herbert." He happened to answer the phone, and when I told him who I was and that I wanted to contact Pavarotti, he yelled, "I don't know where he is, and if I did know, I wouldn't tell you!" and hung up.

So I called a buddy at *Variety*, asking (in those not-yet-internet days) if he knew Pavarotti's schedule. In a few minutes, he called back, saying the tenor was giving a concert that night in Dortmund, Germany. Are there five-star hotels in Dortmund? Yes, the Hilton, here's the number.

Luciano Pavarotti.

So I called the Hilton, assuming they'd never put me through, but hoping I could at least leave a message. "Guten Tag. Mister Pavarotti's room, please?" "Just one moment." Silence. More silence. Then—-

"Pronto!"

"Luciano, it's Tom Di Nardo in Philadelphia."

"Tommaso! Come state?"

I was astonished to have reached him, and asked him if rumors were true about the Competition leaving Philadelphia.

Luciano Pavarotti:

You must be joking! Other cities in America and Europe have approached me to bring the competition there. But for me, it deserves to be always in Philadelphia, because there was an involvement of the entire city. I live for this competition and the chance to work with these young singers.

My idea is that the Opera Company should have nothing to do with the competition. Of course I will sing and work with the winners in one or two operas, but we should produce them ourselves, not with the Company. It should not be too hard to get the Academy of Music for two weeks every four years. But if we're going to do it for '95 or '96, we need to begin immediately.

Tommaso, thanks for calling me, mille grazie. But I have to go now, and sing a concert. Ciao, ciao. (By phone from Germany, May 2, 1993)

When I hung up, I was stunned that I had actually gotten the interview, contacting him by a crazy fluke to get the scoop of the century. I took the story in to the day editor, and said I had a fabulous interview with Luciano Pavarotti about the Competition. He asked me how long it was, and I said twelve inches.

"Hey Charlie," he yelled, "I got something for that hole on page 14."

That's the newspaper biz.

A week later, he appeared at the huge Spectrum, where he had sung in 1985 and 1986. He knew reporters would ask him about his cancellation here and at La Scala because of weight problems and knee pain. And they would surely bring up the *Don Carlo* he had sung at La Scala, a long and difficult Verdi role he was singing for the first time, when a couple of errant high notes caused the notoriously critical premiere crowd to boo.

Beforehand, I had had a chance to speak to him for a few minutes by phone and thank him for speaking to me in Dortmund, and he brought up his problems himself.

"Certainly, these things were embarrassing. It's been a very emotional year, and I hope to return to Philadelphia in good form. I get tired now only when I stand a lot, and feel stronger each day. I'm not sure yet what I will sing, because we must check not to do the same arias as the last Spectrum concerts."

I asked whether the Italian press was critical when he had to cancel at La Scala. "No, they were very kind about it. But they treated me badly when I sang!"

Giant-Killer

By 1993, the budget label Naxos had begun to threaten the major labels, thanks to the persistence of German entrepreneur Klaus Heymann. He was shrewd enough to know the excellence of the Eastern European orchestras that had been invisible before the collapse of the Iron Curtain, and that they would be overjoyed to record the standard repertoire for small fees without royalties.

Naxos undercut what many buyers think are inflated CD prices, although American disc costs at that time were only about half those in European shops, with major labels selling for $34.

It was the first of several contacts with Heymann who, at that time, had 800 discs on the market, selling at $5 or $6 instead of the $15-$18 of the major labels. In just a few years, he had captured five percent of the American and eight percent of the international market, though he now oversees a gigantic empire, a vast catalog of every imaginable subset of music, and a colossus now defining the industry in both CDs and streaming audio.

Klaus Heymann:
We're about selling music, not names. At five or six bucks, listeners are more adventurous, willing to take a chance on music or artists they never heard of. This kind of buying enlarges the repertory, because people will walk out of the shop with three Naxos discs instead of one full-priced disc.

I never expected this to be as big. But I will always win a price struggle, because it only costs about $1.25 to produce a CD. My overhead is 2 percent, compared to 20 percent for the majors; that's 12 cents for me, $3 for them. And I don't pay royalties, only a flat fee per minute of time on the final release. We'll spend however long it takes in the studio until everyone is satisfied with the performances.

Nor do I duplicate repertoire like the majors do—one label may have four complete Beethoven cycles, competing against themselves. Our CDs have been proven to be quality products. I never said we would achieve 100 percent, but I'll put our recordings against any on the market. (By phone from Hong Kong, May 20, 1993)

Of course, Naxos now dominates the market, having recorded relative obscure, though worthy, works that the major labels would never touch, and distributes a long list of other labels.

There would be more dealings with Heymann 13 years later.

Debuts, Diva and Curtain

In the Opera Company's production of Tchaikovsky's *Eugene Onegin*, based on the Pushkin play, Bulgarian soprano Elena Filipova made her debut appearance as the central character of Tatiana. After the first performance, we accidentally met and she recounted some amazing stories about being called in the afternoon to perform an opera—which she didn't know—at the Sofia theater that very evening.

Elena Filipova:
There are very young characters in this true story, and it needs good-looking people. It's a big risk to play Tatiana, because she is first innocent and naive, then a more experienced woman who must reject the man she still loves. The singing voice is almost the last thing you need, because you must concentrate much more on this character's soul. (Academy of Music, April 15, 1993)

That August, two pieces in the British magazine *Gramophone* seemed relevant enough to repeat.

One was a 1962 comment by the last conductor Sir John Barbirolli, who was annoyed at the way musical experts scared away potential listeners.

"The highbrow should not be confused with the true music-lover, broadminded in tastes and outlook alike," Barbirolli wrote. "On the contrary, the highbrow is a self-opinionated, disgruntled individual who adopts a patronizingly possessive attitude about music, musicians and the public that might be considered amusing if it were not deliberately harmful." Amen, Sir John.

The other story was about prima donna and famed soprano Kathleen Battle, whose diva antics forced her firing from the Met. The article said that Battle was driving around New York in a chauffeur-driven limo. Seems she called her agent on her hardwired car phone, telling him to call the limo service to phone the driver—on his car phone—and say he was driving too fast.

After that publicized expulsion form the Met, Battle's career went swiftly downward, and I once received a letter from her promoter, offering to fly me to Jamaica and put me up if I would do a review of her recital there. But she gained a reprieve 22 years later for a fall 2016 recital of spirituals.

Barbara Silverstein's visionary Pennsylvania Opera Theater announced its demise that August after 18 seasons. They were left with a deficit of $250,000, with longtime head of the Met Rudolf Bing's remark, "Opera has no business making money," little comfort.

The company had presented spirited productions of Dominick Argento's imaginative *Postcard from Morocco* (1977), local composer Margaret Garwood's *Rappaccini's Daughter* (both with piano in 1980 and fully scored at the *Troc* in 1983), David Amram's *Twelfth Night* (1981), Bernstein's *Candide* (1982 and 1989), the world premiere of local composer Vincent Persichetti's *The Sibyl* (1984) and Robert Ward's *The Crucible* (1988).

Others, myself included, always felt the indefatigable Silverstein's insistence on English translations, often her own, was a misguided mission. In familiar evergreens like *Rigoletto*, Tosca and *La Traviata*, for instance, the English words sounded, at worst, like ludicrous parody. "Women are devious" in place of "La Donna é mobile" could have come from *Saturday Night Live's* Operaman. Frankly, it's difficult to understand most English words when they're sung. Many may have found opera in English more accessible, but the now-common device of projected supertitles made those translations unnecessary.

Nevertheless, it was a sad day for local operalovers. The company was slain by a modern Sparafucile (the assassin of *Rigoletto*), whose knife was a looming deficit. It was a tragic curtain, with no applause.

British Imports, Witches and Major Loss

From the earliest days of the LP, the most recorded orchestra was the Academy of St. Martin-in-the-Fields, begun in the Trafalgar Square church in London and led by the ubiquitous Neville Marriner. They performed with modern instruments, while the vibrato-less period-instrument movement began to pick up steam in England.

Marriner's concertmaster for many years was violinist Iona Brown, a student of Henryk Szeryng, who took over the conducting post in 1975. She made her first Philadelphia appearance by leading the Concerto Soloists

Chamber Orchestra, teaming with two members in double concertos by Vivaldi and Bach.

Iona Brown:

We became very aware of the period-instrument movement, and—for about five minutes—some thought we might have to stop playing. To me, the method isn't as important as the architecture, the long line, the arch of the musical phrase. We were confident enough in our approach to stick to it, and the Academy is still going strong.

For someone who does as much traveling, I really have a problem flying. In fact, being on the road can get to you, it's a dog's life, but the music is worth it. It's a delight, for there's no time for egos these days. I like Americans, and the way they express themselves and want everything to be right for you. I honestly believe music is the most powerful of the arts. Our business is emotion. (Walnut Street Theater, December 11, 1993)

Though we've had several long conversations, I've never had the opportunity to do a formal interview with Simon Rattle, though I had a chance to see him work his magic with young people. He was in town to lead the Philadelphia Orchestra in Mahler's Ninth Symphony, stopping in at the Girard Academic Music Program (GAMP) at 22nd and Ritner streets to work with the chorus.

Watching the curly-haired Briton coach a religious work by Mendelssohn, who considered Rattle's musical base of Birmingham, England, his second home, was remarkable.

Working in a bright windbreaker, Rattle emphasized that he was looking for feeling, not perfection. "Some people object to emotion," he insisted. "But you have to ask, "Why are we singing this? What's the message?" He implored the singers, "Forget embarrassment, don't be shy. You have to sell this!"

The animated conductor asked the students to examine the texts and sing just the vowels, making their facial expressions mirror the joy or sorrow in the words.

At several points he urged, "Don't give me froth, give me fist," "Give it some calories," and later, "Make this like a secret instead of a challenge." After 45 minutes, the chorus sounded quite unified.

"When you're singing about joy," Rattle said with a laugh, "imagine something wonderful, something surprising—like a good cup of coffee in England."

Just before Christmas, the Academy of Vocal Arts presented Humperdinck's *Hansel and Gretel*. The role of the threatening witch was portrayed in campy style by AVA's Roy Wilbur, whose hilarious stage makeup was applied just below his three hats: performer, director and publicist. Wilbur had portrayed one of the characters in *William Penn*, and for me that meant a lifelong interest in his work.

Wilbur had coached 51 dedicated students from Shawmont Middle School, the Shipley School in Bryn Mawr and Conrad Middle School near Wilmington, chosen from 400 who had auditioned.

"For most of these kids, it's their only opportunity to be involved in the artistic process," Wilbur said. "And when I stand offstage in my witch costume and watch the teen-age dancers go on, see the chorus go on stage in the dark after the witch's house explodes, it moves me—every time."

Another enormous AVA asset for years has been the remarkable Val Starr, who somehow designs, fashions, makes or somehow appropriates costumes, acts as mentor to the young students and handles innumerable chores behind the scenes. Val is one of those rare people who are truly irreplaceable.

Old Money, A Tradition Lost

The arts community lost a vital champion in January 1994 with the death of Dr. F. Otto Haas. His efforts on behalf of the Walnut Street Theater, Morris Aboretum, Welcome Park and many arts groups were generous and heartfelt.

Concerto Soloists Chamber Orchestra music director Marc Mostovoy said the ensemble would have folded without the interest and dedication of Haas, a longtime board chairman.

Haas' late first wife, Dorothy, had the same concern for the city in such projects as Welcome Park and City Hall's magnificent Conversation Hall, and had selflessly aided me in getting *William Penn* produced. Haas' widow Carole has spearheaded many important efforts as well, and I hoped to become lucky enough to be involved in her future projects.

In an age of self-promotion, they shunned the limelight and preferred near-anonymity while enriching the city's cultural and civic life. This kind of old-money civic concern and dedication is their magnificent legacy.

Collaboration and *The Amazon*

Soprano Diana Soviero and Montreal Opera head and director Bernard Uzan, a famous husband-and-wife team, brought the Opera Company a sizzling version of *Tosca*.

Diana Soviero and Bernard Uzan:

Uzan: *Puccini boiled down a five-hour play to less than two hours, and every single detail has meaning. You have to begin with establishing Cavaradossi and Tosca as passionate young lovers in the first act, because the audience must believe in them and care about them from the beginning. Some singers, very big names, see their opening scene together as solo opportunities. Sometimes they don't even touch! Diana doesn't work that way. She gets into the characters more deeply each time.*

Soviero: *In some productions, Tosca just barges into the church yelling. She wouldn't do that, nor would Cavaradossi just keep on painting as is sometimes done—Tosca would just walk out.*

In the second act, Tosca often enters with a very belligerent attitude toward Scarpia, sometimes even slapping him, but that's not believable. She knows that, with one flick of the wrist, this madman could order her lover killed, and we see her personality change through this confrontation. It's interesting that Puccini heroines always develop during the operas, though the males never seem to.

Uzan: *Don't forget that Tosca kills Scarpia not just out of vindictiveness, but out of despair because he is coming between her and her lover.* (Academy of Music, February 11, 1994)

Mozart's *The Magic Flute* marked an Opera Company milestone, the first time their company designed the sets, scenery and costumes. In addition, general director Robert Driver—who had directed the lion's share of productions in his previous posts—would take over as stage director.

Driver, born in Sao Paolo, Brazil, moved the timeless tale to the Amazon jungle, setting the tone with palms, tropical flowers and bird calls in the Academy lobby. The stage was filled with animals, from alligators to beautiful birds, deer and other creatures. There was humor, along with the heroic, noble moments, and rear projection was used to ease the cost of the nearly 30 scenes.

Few operatic projects are as hard to get right as *The Magic Flute*. The work's symbolism, Masonic references, magical as well as naive characters and universal message of humanity make just the proper balance elusive. Audiences must revel in the spirituality of the fable, its humor and delicate artificiality.

Robert Driver:
I feel Flute *is Mozart at his best, showing his innate sense of music and theater. It has been done as a serious Masonic piece with Egyptian overtones, or as a fantasy. It must be a transporting, elevating experience, bringing you to a higher level of awareness. Finally, all evil intentions have been overcome, the good guys win, and there's order in the world.*

This production begins with Tamino being chased by a large serpent, almost like an Indiana Jones opening. When the Queen finally appears to Tamino, she's almost like a calculating Mrs. Robinson. And later, when she argues with her daughter, she flies into a tantrum. I thought we could use rear projection for this, going from a green forest to red and yellow fire and finally a charred jungle during her aria.

On various productions of this work, I've been stage manager and assistant stage director and business manager, plus rolling out the Queen, cueing the lights, and doing the thunder backstage. Believe me, I know how difficult it is to put on a show. (Academy of Music, March 3, 1994)

12. CODAS, GLASS, AND DRACULA

Well, I had the Monday column gig for two years. Some folks in a meeting decided on a new format beginning in April 1994, one that would push me into a topic-by-topic (their description) situation. I'll complete that trek by inserting a leftover dessert from that 24-month residue: some of the musical quotes that finished each column under the heading CODA.

Out of hundreds, here are the ones readers responded to most:

"Music is what awakes from you when you are reminded by the instruments."—Walt Whitman.

"It is not hard to compose, but it is terribly hard to let the superfluous notes fall under the table."—Johannes Brahms.

"It is only that which cannot be expressed otherwise that is worth expressing in music."—Frederick Delius.

"The task for the performer consists in establishing an equilibrium between the composition and his own conscience."—Yehudi Menuhin.

"I believe that the use of noise to make music will continue and increase until we reach a music produced through the aid of electrical instruments"—John Cage.

"Music is the electrical soil in which the spirit lives, thinks and invents."—Ludwig von Beethoven.

"Opera is when a guy is stabbed in the back and instead of bleeding, he sings."—Ed Gardner on radio's *Duffy's Tavern*.

"If someone doesn't understand what invention means, they should stop violin playing—you can't explain everything!"—Nathan Milstein.

"As a musician I tell you that if you were to suppress adultery, fanaticism, crime, evil, the supernatural, there would no longer be the means for writing one note."—Georges Bizet.

"If, as is nearly always the case, music appears to express something, this is only an illusion and not a reality."—Igor Stravinsky.

To a temperamental singer who had threatened to jump on his harpsichord: "Let me know when you will do that and I will advertise it. For I am sure more people would come to see you jump than to hear you sing."—George Frideric Handel.

"No good opera plot can be sensible, for people do not sing when they are feeling sensible."—W. H. Auden.

"The British may not like music, but they absolutely love the noise it makes."— Conductor Sir Thomas Beecham.

"Opera—an exotic and irrational entertainment."—-Samuel Johnson, "Dictionary of the English Language," 1755.

"A composer's first responsibility is, and always will be, to write music that will reach and move the hearts of his listeners in his own day."—Randall Thompson.

"It sometimes seems to me as if I did not belong to this world at all."—Franz Schubert.

"My aim is to warn the age in which I am living of the simultaneous beauty and danger of its unconscious mechanistic philosophy."—George Antheil.

"They make it sound authentically Hungarian—which was, and always has been, my intention in all my music."—- Miklós Rósza.

"It was a pity I wrote *Cavalleria* first. I was crowned before I was king."—Pietro Mascagni.

"My dear Cherubini, you are certainly an excellent musician; but really, your music is so noisy and complicated, that I can make nothing of it."—Napoleon.

"My dear general, you are certainly an excellent soldier; but in regard to music, you must excuse me if I don't think it necessary to adapt my compositions to your comprehension."—Luigi Cherubini.

"Gershwin is the prince who has taken Cinderella (jazz) by the hand and openly proclaimed her a princess to the astonished world."—Conductor Walter Damrosch at the first performance of Gershwin's Concerto in F.

"Composition is notation of distortion of what composers think they've heard before. Masterpieces are marvelous misquotations."—Ned Rorem.

"The trouble with music appreciation in general is that people are taught to have too much respect for music; they should be taught to love it instead."—Igor Stravinsky.

"Music is the inarticulate speech of the heart, which cannot be compressed into words, because it is infinite."—Richard Wagner.

"The first act of the three in *Parsifal* occupied three hours, and I enjoyed that in spite of the singing."—Mark Twain, "A Tramp Abroad").

"I have never encountered anything more false and foolish than the effort to get truth into opera. In opera everything is based upon the not-true."—Peter Ilyich Tchaikovsky, diary.

"I write for today. I don't care about posterity."—Kurt Weill.

"It is not easy to determine the nature of music, or why anyone should have a knowledge of it"—Aristotle, "Politics" (c. 340 B.C.).

"You must have the score in your head, not your head in the score."—Conductor Hans von Bulow, talking to Richard Strauss.

"Opera in English is, in the main, just about as sensible as baseball in Italian."—H. L. Mencken.

"Last year, more Americans went to symphony concerts than to baseball games. This may be viewed as an alarming statistic, but I think both baseball and the country will survive."—John F. Kennedy, after a White House concert, 1962.

"A symphony is a stage play with the parts written for instruments instead of for actors."—- Colin Wilson.

"In the end, it all depends on a libretto. A libretto, a libretto, and the opera is made!"—Giuseppe Verdi.

"Music is the sole art which evokes nostalgia for the future."—Ned Rorem.

"To write a symphony is, for me, to construct a world."—Gustav Mahler.

"Melody is a form of remembrance . . .It must have a quality of inevitability in our ears."—Gian-Carlo Menotti.

"The hardest of all the arts to speak of is music, because music has no meaning to speak of."—Ned Rorem.

"No man is complete without a feeling for music and an understanding of what it can do for him."—Zoltan Kodaly.

"If you would know if a people are well governed, and if its laws are good, examine the music it practices."—Confucius.

"Chamber music conceives itself as a world of sound that has external boundaries but no internal ones." —Hans Werner Henze.

"I go to concerts of new music in New York, and I say to myself: 'What's the fuss about? The fellows in Hollywood do this every day in the week and think nothing of it!. "—Aaron Copland.

"The best music always results from ecstasies of logic."—Alban Berg.

"The stick is never wrong."—Traditional musicians' jibe.

Joseph Franklin, the founder of the contemporary-music ensemble Relaché, met composer Philip Glass while producing a concert series at the Annenberg Center and suggested a commission years ago. Glass' acceptance made fund-raising easier, and half of the commission fee for the piece *T. S. E.*, was raised from John Duffy's Meet the Composer Foundation.

Glass was also going to present his rewritten music to the classic 1946 Jean Cocteau film *Beauty and the Beast* in a few months. It had seemed to me, after seeing the film *Koyaanisquatsi*, that his music was best as accompaniment to visuals, and later to tremendously successful operas, rather than as concert works, though *Gramophone* magazine had recently named Glass the world's best-known serious composer. His work usually consists of many chords repeating over and over, and many assume he just bops it out at a computer. I had been pretty negative about his music in a few disc reviews and, though he admitted to having read them, he was completely amiable in a brief interview.

Philip Glass:

I recomposed the music for the film in the form of an opera. It's really a new art form, a music theater piece. It's different than a silent movie, not as much a 'talkie' as a 'singie.'

I know you think I do it by computer or something, but I write in ink. I'm 57 now, and came up too late to realize this recording technology and sound sampling. I even use human copyists for the individual performers' parts.

That Gramophone business doesn't bother me because I don't think it's true. Composers my age seem to feel threatened more, but those in their

20s and 30s don't. I don't ever bother to be insulted by anything. (By phone, September 18, 1994)

Besides Glass, lots of composers suddenly got on the repetitive bandwagon, known as minimalism. One of Harold Boatrite's students, who had sat through a whole concert of this music, said, "Well, it wasn't minimal enough for me!"

Studying with Harold was an enriching experience, and he always had comments about blatantly audience-indifferent atonal music, and the musical cognoscenti who could feel superior by praising it.

Harold was once visited several times by someone asking about the possibility of his writing a score to a documentary film. He tried without success to find what kind of music the man wanted, until eventually he admitted, "Kind of like Norman Dello Joio's *Air Power* (the stirring 1956 television series about military aviation)." Harold asked him why he just didn't get Dello Joio. "Oh, we can't afford him!" was the rejoinder.

Another of Harold's students gave me a cassette of a Roy Harris lecture, in which he spoke about accepting a student interested in writing a symphony. He would say, "Do you think you have anything to say that Mozart, Beethoven, Haydn, Schubert, Mahler, Prokofiev or Shostakovich haven't already said?" If the student said, "Well, if you put it that way.....," it was unlikely, because he was looking for the person who would say, "Yes, I do!"

Composing is such a difficult art, in which your skill is at the mercy only of your taste. If you're successful enough to be commissioned, you're wildly fortunate, though most composers have little possibility of performance, lacking the sales and schmoozing techniques to sell their works.

I wrote a few times (and no one challenged it) that, until recent years, Mendelssohn was the only major composer in history who didn't have to write music to put food on the table.

Plus, it's a dangerous business. Consider the odds of all these unfortunate deaths:

—Anton Webern, shot by a GI the day after the WWII armistice.

—Jean-Baptiste Lully, gangrene from hitting his foot with a stick used to conduct.

—Mieczyslaw Karlowicz, killed in an avalanche at 33 while skiing.

—Ernest Chausson, in a bicycle accident.

—Enrique Granados—drowned while trying to save his wife after his English Channel boat was torpedoed by the German Navy.

—Johann Baptist Krumpholtz—when his wife ran off with Jan Dussek, he threw himself into the Seine and drowned.

—Guillaume Lekeu—got typhus from eating contaminated sorbet.

—Arnold Schoenberg, who was a triskaidekaphobe (fear of the number 13), died on Friday the 13th at 13 minutes to midnight.

—Franz Schubert, of syphilis at only 31.

—Wolfgang Mozart, of still-unknown malady, at 35.

—George Gershwin, of brain tumor at 38.

It's a tough racket.

The first operatic commission ever given by a record label was *The Dracula Diary*, composed by Philadelphia composer Robert Moran. The opera was performed in March 1994 at the Houston Grand Opera, about the time the Mendelssohn Club and Concerto Soloists were recording Moran's Requiem for RCA Records at Girard College.

Robert Moran:

I realized that opera usually comes down to sex and murder, but—except for Marschner's obscure Der Vampyr—no one had ever written an opera about vampires.

It's daunting to do something new that has become hackneyed. What would happen if a baroque operatic troupe was full of vampires, and suppose someone actually got Dracula's diary but used it the wrong way? It's amazing how many people are fascinated with the legends of vampires, sexual, mysterious, taking by force. Every country has some kind of undead. In India they appear as butterflies. All we know about is Hollywood cliché. But what they all possess is a horror story beyond hell—the curse of eternal life. (By phone, November 6, 1994)

Big Space, for a While

In Philadelphia, as in many other cities, huge old-time bank edifices have been turned into hotels and restaurants. The Packard Building at 15th and Chestnut Streets once housed, as its first-floor occupant, the now-defunct First Pennsylvania Bank; it boasts an enormous 80-by-200-foot space, with carved arches, looming Ionic columns, ornate carved ceiling and 16-foot-high windows. In its basement, an eight-foot-diameter vault door yawns open, a circular portal to hundreds of partitions and metal drawers in a seemingly endless maze of abandoned rooms.

After being absorbed by CoreStates Bank, whose main office at that time was a block away, the space became deserted for years. When a foreign investor was negotiating to buy the building, the City referred to a five-year easement that mandated that some space be available to the public. Since the main attraction was the availability of many office floors above, the deal went through.

While this process was going on, attorney David Segal, at that time president of the Philadelphia Youth Orchestra, negotiated an exclusive lease for the magnificent space to be used for the PYO's rehearsals and performances. He envisioned the space—listed on the National Register of Historic Places—as home for a consortium of musical organizations.

"I grew up in a house where at least two people were always practicing," said Segal, "and envisioned this space as a cultural beehive, with practice rooms for many performing organizations, with the PYO as host of the space. The only criteria are that the groups be nonprofit and play free concerts. It's part of an unutilized infrastructure, and each city is rich in it. We're just recycling."

Joseph Primavera, a former Philadelphia Orchestra violinist and demanding taskmaster, had conducted without a contract since 1954. Segal became involved with the PYO in 1988 as the proud parent of a gifted musical child. His daughter Rachel, a former concertmaster for both the PYO and then Colorado's Central City Opera Orchestra, recently returned to found the Primavera Fund in Philadelphia to assist young musicians achieve their career dreams.

Though this was a temporary godsend and an imaginative use of a great building for a few years, the lease eventually expired and the grand space is now a steak house.

13. CONFIDENT PERFORMERS, AND VICTORIOUS NUMES

For the first time in 30 years, the Opera Company offered the wildly dramatic *Salome* of Richard Strauss, an opera that has challenges not found in operas three times longer.

Fortunately, the company cast soprano Cynthia Makris in the lead role. Salome had become a signature role for her, though it represents an enormous double challenge—penetrating through Strauss' enormously complex and huge orchestrations and gracefully portraying Salome's famed, seductive 15-minute "Dance of the Seven Veils." Strauss assumed the beefy soprani of his era would be temporarily replaced by ballerinas, but a singer as shapely and attractive as Makris must be asked to do her own dance.

Cynthia Makris:
I turned down Salome *for a long time, and was eventually talked into a splashy, scandalous production. I had trouble sleeping while learning the part. Strauss is one composer who lets the audience know how difficult his roles are.*

I've never studied as a dancer, and in all the productions, haven't ever done it the same way twice. And I've never found an audience that was unkind about my dancing. To me, Salome is an anti-heroine, an innocent. I love fragile, troubled characters who have inner strength and use it with complexity.

I wouldn't recommend to American singers that they work here first. There's no security, not enough rehearsal time. In Freiburg, for instance, where I held a house contract, you have six weeks of rehearsal, a single cast, a 10-month season, and 35 performances. The American way means very little rehearsal time, hard work and driving ambition, fast learning. But you can be all dressed up with no place to go. (Academy of Music, March 3, 1995)

Another of the city's many unique treasures is the Academy of Vocal Arts, in many ways an unheralded one. From its elegant Spruce Street address and Victorian theater, the country's only tuition-free conservatory exclusively devoted to operatic training, the Academy of Vocal Arts, has poured talent onto the world's major stages for 60 years.

Every five years, there's a gala event called "BrAVA Philadelphia!" led by music director Christofer Macatsoris, full of arias by all the noted alumni who could make it. In the 60th anniversary gala, ten 10 operatic legends including Licia Albanese, Rose Bampton, Robert Merrill, Sherrill Milnes and Patrice Munsel even attended in non-singing appearances.

AVA represented more than just a school to tenor Stuart Neill, a 1992 Pavarotti competition winner with a huge, sumptuous voice, who appeared prominently in the gala concert. Neill was officially in his third year, though he had already launched an enormously international career. He studied with two legendary teachers, Richard Raub, pianist and vocal coach, along with David Antony Lofton, two of the best in the business.

By that time, Neill was singing all over the world, and actually had to decline offers by Riccardo Muti three separate times.

Stuart Neill:
I was working at a paint store in Atlanta, and on my 26th birthday (in 1991) decided to try music. AVA's enrollment was full, but I begged for an audition anyway. With a three-day notice, I came and sang two and a half arias. Luckily, two tenors dropped out and I was accepted.

AVA has nearly one faculty member for each student, and nowhere in America is there such attention to detail. Chris (artistic director Macatsoris) brings enormous personal experience to the preparation of any role. He will say, "I remember Corelli did it like this," and we'll try it that way—25 times.

When I sang La Bohème at the school Chris asked, even before I sang, "Does Mimi live on the same floor? If she lives upstairs, has Rudolfo met her before, because he would recognize her voice when she knocks on the door. Has she really been flirting? When Musetta says in the last act that she's left the viscount, does it change your perception of Mimi?"

I'll come back to sing at AVA, do a recital every year, as long as I'm breathing. That's how I feel about the school.

Maestro Muti was very understanding each time. He faxed me a friendly message, saying he would like to know "who is this tenor who has turned me down twice for La Scala! But we'll work it out soon." (Academy of Vocal Arts, March 26, 1995)

Another AVA alumnus who came back after making it big was Lando Bartolini, who had spent five years at the school, to portray Giordano's *Andréa Chenier*.

Lando Bartolini:
Q: How important was your AVA training?

A: My career has the school to thank, for I could not have afforded training in Italy. I first came here—on my honeymoon—to enter Settlement School's Mario Lanza competition. Winning it helped me to enter AVA, where I spent five years. The final year was extra, and during it they even helped me get European bookings.

Q: What advice would you give young singers?

A: Use your voice properly—don't make it do roles that don't suit it. And don't make my mistake, of not having a publicist and not being more of a businessman. (Academy of Vocal Arts, October 13, 1997)

Crossover Sells, Pure Has the Last Word

When Claude Bolling's 1975 recording *Suite for Flute and Jazz Piano*, with classical flutist Jean-Pierre Rampal, hit the top of the classical chart for more than a year, every label jumped at crossover.

In one long column, crossover CDs went from the sublime—famous operatic soprano Sylvia McNair singing a gorgeous Jerome Kern songbook with pianist André Previn and bassist David Finck—to piles of junk.

Flutist James Galway tried lamely to play pop, violinist Itzhak Perlman played with Oscar Peterson in case nobody would notice he wasn't swinging and soprano Kiri te Kanawa even sounded stiff with André Previn. Individually, even the Three Tenors didn't impress when off their turf. The worst was the usually-impressive tenor José Carreras, about whom I reluctantly wrote:

"How did Atlantic get him to disgrace himself on *Hollywood Golden Classics*? It's painful to listen to this great voice sound ridiculous on "Born Free." Say it ain't so, José."

In 1994, EMI released a CD of music recorded by 20 now-famous Spanish monks in a remote Castilian cloister between 1973 and 1982, fancying it up with Magritte-style packaging and calling it *Chant*. This disc of obscure medieval *a cappella* music made its debut on the Billboard classical charts at No. 1. (Naturally, Angel/EMI neglected to spend a few pennies on texts and translations for American release, essential for those few listeners not fluent in Latin.)

EMI could hardly wait to scour the landscape for anything that could also take advantage of this medieval boomlet; as Jimmy Durante used to say, everybody wants to get into the act. They turned to the hypnotic vocal music of Hildegard von Bingen (1098-1179), some of the earliest known notated music unless Fred Flintstone wrote some tunes, for a CD called *Vision*, complete with rhythm tracks.

The 850-year-old settings of Hildegard's inspired revelations have an otherworldly, mystical quality that immediately grips the emotions and causes an exhilarating connection. Angel felt that her soaring, celestial vocal lines wouldn't appeal without a contemporary hook, and hired arranger/ "interpreter" David Souther. His previous credits, which the label somehow saw as ideal for medieval music, included non-monastic work for Frank Zappa's *Mothers of Invention*, as well as for Pat and Debby Boone.

He also threw in added synthesized Middle-Eastern rhythm and instrumental effects, male voices and other "sonic enhancements" to the vocal strands. (Hildegard, who called herself "God's little trumpet," actually sanctioned instrumental accompaniments: the strings to denote the soul, the harp for blessedness and the flute for the presence of God.)

EMI spokesman Tony McAnany said they were also going to issue dance mixes based on the record, and assigned a team whose credits included mixes for Janet Jackson, Madonna and Chaka Khan.

"We wanted to do dance mixes for *Chant* too," said McAnany, "but the monks wouldn't allow it." Who could have guessed?

Hildegard had one of the most fascinating lives in recorded history. As her family's 10th child, she was offered to a monastery and eventually started her own order. Educated (in itself a rarity for an 11th-century woman) and multi-talented, she wrote books on politics, diplomacy, natural history and medicine, though she was plagued with debilitating headaches. Four popes recommended her for canonization, and her sainthood is celebrated in Germany, if not officially by the Catholic Church.

Her divine perceptions of humanity, eventually collected in a book called *Scivias (Know the Ways)*, were clairvoyant revelations that appealed to popes, kings and emperors. Yet not even this visionary, called the "Sybil of the Rhine," could have predicted that her vocal settings of ecclesiastical verses, with added synthesized rhythm tracks, would be touted as the next blockbuster CD 850 years later.

"All of creation is a symphony of joy and jubilation," Hildegard proclaimed, and no one knew it better than Angel's accountants.

Hildegard's music in more respectful interpretation was soon issued by the early music group Sequentia, by the Gothic Voices on a CD entitled *A Feather on the Breath of God*, and medieval chants followed by the female quartet Anonymous 4.

Yet the late Wynnewood pianist/teacher/composer Sylvia Glickman had been on the case for years, as founder of the Hildegard Publishing Co., issuing 70 of Hildegard's songs and commissioning 35 more, the only ones then available in modern notation.

Glickman had enthusiastically promoted and published music by women composers through her Hildegard Chamber Players. She also published a timeline and calendar of 391 women composers (of the 6,000 she claimed), with an even earlier one than Hildegard— a nun named Kassia, who was born in Thessalonika (Greece) in 801 A.D.

"You know, Queen Victoria invited Felix Mendelssohn to court," said Glickman, "and sang his songs with Prince Albert. She indicated her favorite, actually written by his sister Fanny. His name was on it because Fanny would not have been taken seriously—their father insisted that her musicianship just wasn't ladylike.

"Perhaps this new CD will help bring Hildegard to the public's awareness," said Glickman. "Remember that it was originally sung by untrained nuns, and it's hypnotic but not because it's repetitious. After all, Hildegard was a renaissance man before the Renaissance."

Now the story becomes an adventure.

Hildegard of Bingen wrote down her florid melodies in what is known as "neumes," or neumatic notation. Conceived centuries before development of the five-line staff, bar lines and key signatures familiar today, this series of complex squiggles, dots and markings merely implied the shapes of one or more notes set to a single syllable. Scholars have uncovered hundreds of different neumes, varying widely in regions throughout Europe, Turkey, Russia and Tibet.

Transcribing texts from neumatic notation is an exercise in interpretation, made by a musical scholar who has insight into the composer's intentions. Since many interpretations are possible, any published version of such music begins a copyright of its own, since no one else could have made the same unique musical choices.

In other words, every melody is necessarily an arrangement—and therefore, eligible for compensation under the copyright laws.

Five of the *Vision* CD's 17 tracks used versions of the medieval manuscripts transcribed into modern performing notation by Glickman's Hildegard Publishing Co. and, Glickman said, Angel Records/Capitol Music failed to recognize the company or pay royalties for use of the music.

"Angel purchased 16 works from our editions for consideration, and signed licenses for the use of five," said Glickman." The licenses are standard for establishing rates on each CD sold, and for credit on liner notes. Each page of the music mentions the copyright, yet to date Angel has failed to pay royalties under federal copyright laws. However, they made a verbal offer for use of the music that was inadequate and even insulting."

Rates for copyrighted—not public domain—"classical" pieces earned the same as for any pop song: at that time 2.2 cents per minute or 6.6 cents per track, whichever is greater. Since one of the artists from the *Vision* discs has been quoted as saying it had sold 450,000 CDs up to that point, this could have meant a six-figure compensation for Hildegard Publishing.

The company had already won an earlier lawsuit concerning the graphic design used on the CD's cover. Supporting materials attached to copies of the scores include that copyrighted graphic and the name of its creator, and that settlement had ordered compensation to Hildegard Publishing and required appropriate credit in future copies.

This was truly a David vs. Goliath musical struggle, with a copyright infringement suit against Angel Records/Capitol Music filed at U.S. District Court in Philadelphia.

Glickman was not allowed to tell me the amount of the highly-successful suit, creating a delicious irony. A probably very-generous compensation from Angel's souped-up tracks helped Glickman assign more composers to notate more of Hildegard's melodies, a process she continued until her death.

It doesn't take much imagination to picture the cloistered Hildegard, in her German abbey in the sky, lighting a candle and looking heavenward. Sometimes the good guys win.

Answers by Donizetti

Donizetti's *I Puritani*, conducted by Maurizio Barbacini and directed by Marc Verzatt, boasted a tenor who first hit the boards as lead singer in the rock band White Elephant. That 10-piece Chicago clone was Gregory Kunde's gig until, on a college trip with a madrigal group, he was electrified by performances of *Salome* and *Carmen* by the venerable Vienna State Opera.

His voice teacher urged him to enter some voice competitions, winning a chance at the Lyric Opera of Chicago School.

Gregory Kunde:
I was greener than Kermit, yet I understudied for Alfredo Kraus and did lots of regional opera. But since I Puritani *in Montreal seven years ago, I realized the bel canto repertoire—Bellini, Donizetti, Rossini—is all I ever want to sing. In these works, a character's emotion transcends everyday speaking, and needs more than speech.*

In bel canto, you are allowed, and expected, to interpret freely, it varies from night to night. It's not like Puccini or Wagner or Verdi, where you must sing the music exactly as written. I did a Don Pasquale *at La Scala with maestro Riccardo Muti, and at one point he urged me to come up with another musical idea for the second verse. That way, it never gets stale, and the emphasis on the words makes the dramatic singing easier.* (Academy of Music, October 9, 1995)

Marc Verzatt:
In any opera, your choices always come down to the same thing: What makes them say what they're saying? The details of the plot lead you to the stage resolutions, and the music tells me whether my ideas are right or wrong. In Elvira's mad scene, for instance, she attempts to escape reality, twice, but the sadness and poignancy in the music tells you she can't escape. If you listen, Bellini has provided all the answers. (Academy of Music, October 9, 1995)

Open Door to Music

Settlement Music School's West Philadelphia branch, opening in 1990 with 125 students, had ballooned to 500 within several years, well beyond its capacity. Miraculously, a plan to use a facility on Wynnefield Avenue took less than two years to acquire, plan and build, opening in October 1995.

I was stunned when I visited the new branch, because I had used the garden and old building it replaced for the three-model photographs I had done showing designer Maria Hart's fashions.

Along with the original branch in Queen Village, plus those in Germantown, Northeast and Jenkintown, over 7,000 students were taking advantage of ballet, adult and children's choirs, jazz improvisation and jazz ensembles, and individual instruction in piano, violin, flute and a wide range of other instruments.

It's still the largest community arts school in the country and offers instruction regardless of age, background or ability to pay, with a long list of illustrious alumni, from André Watts to Stanley Clarke.

Score!

Though the Flyers hockey team hadn't done very well during those years, they had once been one of Philly's jewels, with the Voice of the Flyers, Gene Hart, as a major reason.

Hart was a huge opera fan, and always hoped the Opera Company would use him in some colorful non-singing role. His opportunity came in November's *Die Fledermaus*, allowing him to play Ivan, a Russian valet, though his mastery in ad-libbing would not be necessary.

It turned out that show biz was in Hart's blood, considering that his father was a Budapest-born acrobat who once worked with Michael Todd. His mother was an operetta singer from Vienna, and his sister was a well-known ballroom dancer who appeared on the *Ed Sullivan Show*. He moved from Manhattan to manage the water show at Atlantic City's Steel Pier and meet his wife--who rode the famous High Diving Horse and jumped into the surf every two hours. He listened to Saturday afternoon opera broadcasts from the Met until, in 1949, he was hypnotized by his first live opera—Verdi's *Otello*.

Through the years, his Flyers itinerary allowed him to catch performances in Vancouver, Winnipeg, Chicago and San Francisco, with off-season excursions to the great houses of Vienna, Verona, Prague, London and even Bayreuth for the complete Wagner *Ring* cycle.

Gene Hart:

A couple of years ago, I played Frosch (the jailer) in a Trenton production—though it would have been a conflict if the Flyers had made the playoffs. Last month, one of the Opera Company people kiddingly said that if I only could speak Russian I could play Ivan. Well, having studied it in the Armed Forces language school, and having conversed with many Russian hockey players, I answered in Russian and got the part.

To attend the first full rehearsal, I missed his first Flyers game since 1967. In a way, it's a lark, a fun thing for an amateur, but I take it very seriously. It's a fascinating discipline that's a little frightening. I want to do my lines, look like a bear-type Cossack as well as it can be done, rather than have them seem to be just giving it away to a hockey guy. If I do my few lines, and little bits of business properly, it adds a little ingredient, but if I don't, no one will notice. (Academy of Music, November 7, 1995)

Two Amazing Women

When percussionist Evelyn Glennie, who hasn't let profound deafness keep her from commissioning and playing over 150 works, came to solo with the Philadelphia Orchestra, I went backstage the afternoon of the first performance; she was frantically running about and working with the Orchestra's percussionists to arrange the instruments. Suddenly I remembered that Emil had mentioned that she had once been out to California to work with him. I accosted her, introduced myself as a journalist who had written a preview about her, and mentioned that I was a friend of Emil's. Her eyes opened wide, and we went out to have a cup of coffee, chatting so exuberantly (with her reading my lips) that there wasn't enough to fashion into an interview.

In 2010, in Buffalo, I had a chance to hear her play the world premiere of a work by Eric Ewazen, based on prerecorded words by Robert Burns spoken by Glennie before each movement. And at a dinner afterward, had a chance to tell Emil stories and laugh heartily with this tiny dynamo, a beautiful and joyful presence inside and out.

Early in 1996, mezzo Denyce Graves returned to Philly, not this time as Carmen, but in the unexpected role of Dorabella in *Cosi fan tutte*. In previous interviews, she had often spoken of insisting on other roles to avoid being typecast, and she finally found one far away from her usual flamboyant, extroverted persona.

We had struck up a good relationship on her previous visit, and she invited me to her apartment at the Warwick. It was a curious afternoon, me with my notebook full of questions and Denyce pedaling furiously on a treadmill.

Denyce Graves:

Q: *Have you listened to the CDs of* La Vestale *(a Spontini opera she recorded with Riccardo Muti) yet?*

A: *Not yet. Listening to my own voice is like being chained up with someone throwing snakes all over me. It's the most uncomfortable feeling imaginable, it drives me insane. I have to force myself. Muti was all about serving the music. He has a sixth sense about when to give a singer time and when to move, and I really appreciated that.*

Q: *Do you mind not being the major star in the Mozart?*

A: *I mind terribly! I could be doing Delilah at Covent Garden! But there's a lot to learn in this role.*

Q: *Why is Mozart such a challenge for you?*

A: *Mozart is very exposed, it reveals all of your strongest and weakest qualities. I must listen very closely to my colleagues, because my voice is darker and heavier and needs narrowing. It's hateful vocally, way up in the upper ranges all the time. Fiordiligi (Patricia Racette) has the melody and I have the supporting line all night, providing a different kind of discipline that's important for my musical growth and career.*

Q: *What achievements make you the most proud?*

A: *When I was in St. Louis, the opera company arranged for me to sing in a prison, with full costume and a pianist. I was very frightened and almost didn't go. They brought in over a hundred prisoners with faces of stone, with armed guards all over. I told them what I did and sang arias from Carmen. At one point I asked an inmate to act as Don Jose and tie my hands with my scarf, and in one number I sat on one of the prisoners' laps. Some faces didn't change, but a lot of them asked to come up and they'd say, "That opera isn't so bad," and "Good for you, sister girl, you keep doing it." After-*

wards, one guy yelled, "If I ever get outta here, the first thing I'm going to do is hear you sing!"

Later, the warden mentioned that her audience was all murderers, most of whom were on death row—a fact I am glad I didn't know in advance. (Warwick Hotel, February 15, 1996)

That month, the Opera Company of Philadelphia staged Stravinsky's *The Rake's Progress* for the first time. The role of Anne Truelove was to be sung by Heather Dials, a resident artist of the Academy of Vocal Arts.

As if starring in a complex role wasn't pressure enough, general director Robert Driver arranged for Dials, on the day of the premiere, to receive a phone message from Elizabeth Schwarzkopf, the famed soprano who had created the role of Anne at Venice's La Fenice Theatre in 1951. It may have been just a little bit too late to adjust to the advice: "Sing it like Mozart."

It Ain't Heavy, It's My Brother's

When Paul Krzywicki, the Philadelphia Orchestra's tubist, played his brother Jan's Tuba Concerto for one of his Curtis students, the youngster asked, "What's your brother got against you?"

These two musicians, who constantly kid each other, joined forces on this piece, played by Luis Biava's Temple University Symphony Orchestra. Jan, a gifted composer who also teaches at Temple, wrote an expressive solo part as though he was writing for an easier instrument; he realized that it would be difficult to come from limited demands to a hugely demanding piece requiring flexibility and much playing in the instrument's high register.

Paul Krzywicki. Credit: Jean E. Brubaker.

Only Vaughan Williams' Tuba Concerto was as good a work in Paul's opinion, and his brother's 23-minute work—which seemed to him as if it lasted an hour—was definitely the hardest work he ever played.

You wouldn't have been able to tell in the performance, because the lines were smooth as silk and Paul gave the work a remarkable singing quality. He soon developed physical problems forcing him to step down, eliminating a chance for him to play a deserved solo with his Philadelphia Orchestra colleagues in this brilliant piece by his brother.

Three-Quarter Time

One touring colossus who needed a bigger hall, down at the Spectrum stadium, was André Rieu. I wondered—was he the pied piper of music or a shameless shlockmeister? The maestro of the three-quarter time or the schmaltz king? The reincarnation of 1860s Vienna megastar Johann Strauss Jr. or the second coming of Liberace?

The public must have decided, because while critics cringed at his enormous popularity and flamboyant style, Rieu's shows always light up the PBS telephone lines during pledge breaks.

I wanted to know the details, and he let me know in another telephone conversation.

André Rieu:

Q: *Why is this music such a big attraction in a country where 99 percent of the people have never danced a waltz?*

A: *A waltz means romance. It's one of the most touching rhythms imaginable, dancing you can feel. When you hear* The Blue Danube, *it's not just 1-2-3, 1-2-3. There are so many rhythms, so many tempi, that every night it's a different waltz. We improvise and have fun like Strauss did. It's like making love.*

Q: *How much liberty do you feel you can take with the written score?*

A: *Remember, when I am not there, the music is only white paper with black dots on it. I have a right to my own personal interpretation, as long as I am honest.*

Q: *How has great commercial success changed your goals?*

A: *I think that if you play music only for money, you should do something else. We just want to bring people to great music, and I hope someday they'll trust me enough to allow records of the standard works also.*

Q: *The only place you haven't played is Vienna. Will you eventually be invited by this conservative town to play their music?*

A: *Someday, we hope. But I'm more concerned about attracting younger audiences. More turned out on last year's American tour, more than we anticipated, sometimes dancing in the aisles.* (By phone, April 15, 1998)

Terra Ascends

Some editor had heard that my son Marc was a satellite designer at Lockheed Martin, and asked me to write about the last project to come out of the Valley Forge building where Apollo and Saturn rockets were built. Feeling proud, though quite uncomfortable writing about his project instead of music, I filed it anyway.

"After seven years of design, NASA's $750 million Terra satellite rolled out of Valley Forge and headed to Dover Air Force Base in Delaware, then driven into the enormous cargo hold of a C-5A transport to Vandenberg Air Force base in California. Originally named EOS, the 10,500-pound satellite it was named Terra, (Mother Earth), by a high school student from St. Louis in a NASA contest.

"Powered by a single large solar array, Terra's instruments, built by U.S., Canadian and Japanese companies, measure carbon dioxide, land surfaces, rainforests, clouds, ocean temperature, the effect on the earth of fires, solar radiation, thermal emission levels and a host of other data, and is now used by every country in the world."

After a summer of numerous countdowns, all aborted because of suspected problems with the Atlas rockets, Marc was still at Vandenberg nine months later, with another launch scheduled for December 19. The night before the launch, Marc took the gantry elevator to the 26th floor, opened the door to see his satellite with Terra's logo, and called me to say thanks for support though this long siege.

My family trooped to the Lockheed Martin plant to watch the delayed launch, suddenly aborted by the computer with 100 seconds to go. It looked as though he would have to return in the new year, but another satellite's launch, scheduled the next day at the same gantry, was scratched, and Terra was launched two days later.

By January, the solar array was positioned, the antenna was configured to send data back to earth, and suddenly hundreds of computer screens at Goddard Space Center in Maryland burst to life with data, and plenty of high-fives went around the control room.

Still working after 16 years, Terra sends down to earth the most conclusive data about all aspects of our planet. Its complexity allows it to be the textbook for college courses in earth science, and its website, terra.nasa.gov, is an example of what a website is capable. Even its designers never dreamed it would last 16 years; despite reluctance to politicos wedded to carbon interests, Marc—who now works for NASA--says there's talk about replacing its batteries to allow even more grim data.

Voucher for a Story

During 1998, there was a series combining a restaurant review with an interview called My Dinner With...., a takeoff on the popular film *My Dinner With André* starring Wallace Shawn and André Gregory.

It was quite a good idea, though I was hardly an expert in the culinary department. There were interviews with Jimmy Amadie, Marc Mostovoy, Peter Nero, composer Augusta Read Thomas, tenor Stuart Neill and conductor André Raphel. At the latter's dinner at Kansas City Prime, the special happened to be kobe beef steak at $145 or appetizer portion for $65. Raphel pretended he was interested, luckily only kidding, since my head was spinning imagining how that expense voucher would go over at the paper.

14. LEGENDS GONE—AND HERE

In May of 1998, Emil called to tell me that Frank Sinatra, who he had accompanied on four decades of records and tours, had died. I put together some quotes from people who had known him, and added it to the many pages of tribute the *Daily News* published.

"Frank always vocalized an hour before every performance or session," recalled Richards. "He would come in an hour early and sing vowels and scales with (guitarist) Al Viola. After that, he would sing while the arranger, Nelson Riddle or Don Costa or Billy May or whoever, would play the chart on the piano. We would play and he would listen, that was it, and we'd do the take.

"He understood that, for the musicians, the first time is always the best. It's like a live performance, it's boring to play it over and to sing it over. He always knew when the take was perfect, both vocally and musically, and say to the engineer, "Did you get it? OK, next tune."

"Count Basie trombonist Al Grey: "The Basie Band changed Frank Sinatra . . . It made him a jazz singer." (The Count Basie Band recorded with Sinatra in 1962, 1964 and 1966, and toured with him periodically, often to soldout venues.)

"Mike Smith, a Sinatra saxman: "I remember the first rehearsal we did," said Smith, who played sax in Sinatra's band from roughly 1987 to 1993 in a *JazzTimes* magazine interview. "He ran the rehearsal. He would stand in front of each guy as we were playing. He'd say "OK, I want you louder, you play softer." He knew exactly what he wanted, pretty amazing because most acts don't do that. He was very involved with the music and really knew those charts by Nelson Riddle, Billy May and Don Costa after all those years."

"Philadelphia-born David Raksin, eminent film composer of the classic "Laura," considered Sinatra's among the finest of the more than 400 different recordings (more than any other song except Hoagy Carmichael's "Stardust"). Sinatra often said in public that the song, written for the 1944 film with lyrics added later by Johnny Mercer, was his favorite ballad.

"He was simply a natural," said Raksin from his Hollywood home. "And the fact that he conducted well should come as no surprise."

In his 1969 disc with Antonio Carlos Jobim, he suggested choruses for the Brazilian legend to sing in Portuguese. Musicians on the date recalled that Sinatra gently mentioned to arranger Claus Ogerman that there were a couple of "strangers" (wrong notes) in the strings on one take. No one in the booth, or even Ogerman, had heard them—until the replay proved Sinatra correct.

Reams have been written about how George Gershwin would have transformed American music even further if he had lived as long (until 86) as his lyricist brother Ira; we must be content with a mere six "classical" pieces, the grand opera *Porgy and Bess*, and hundreds of beloved songs, mostly from shows and films.

At his centenary in September 1998, he represented the essence of America, a brash mixture of exuberant rhythmic styles, limitless optimism and sentiment that may be dated though never phony, proud of a beautiful melody and unafraid to repeat it.

Although his Russian-immigrant parents had no musical background, everything else about his life seems the quintessential American poor-boy-makes-good urban success story. Born on the Lower East Side as Jacob Gershvin, he lived in 22 different homes before the age of 19, had no piano until age 12 and was influenced by a musical melting pot of black rhythmic dance forms, Harlem piano players, Jewish cantorial music and Tin Pan Alley ditties.

He was blessed in having his brother as master wordsmith, and the perfect settings like "'S Wonderful" or "Someone to Watch Over Me" couldn't have been created by anyone but the Gershwins. Tunes are usually written to lyrics, but Ira wrote words to George's melodies, the equivalent of playing the piano upside down.

Gershwin slipped easily between the arbitrary boundaries of show and classical music. *Rhapsody in Blue*, written after a discovery that a piece of his was scheduled in three weeks, was inspired by the clickety-clack syncopation of a train ride while going to Boston for a show tryout. The famous Feb. 12, 1924, *Rhapsody* concert, beginning with that striking clarinet glissando that wouldn't be out of place for a klezmer band, astonished the Aeolian Hall audience—which included Stokowski, Heifetz, Rachmaninoff, Kreisler and Stravinsky. A New York reviewer praised the work by beginning, "Composers have treated jazz like a cat around a bowl of hot soup," an admonition that's still true, and no one has integrated jazz more idiomatically than Gershwin in his Piano Concerto in F. The free, Jazz Age times favored him, for the categorization of music wasn't as regimented as it is now.

Gershwin simply was a sheer natural to whom everything came easily, including entertaining at the piano for hours. Trips to Cuba and Paris were filtered through his senses into *Cuban Overture* and the uncanny *An American In Paris*, and even the 12-bar structure for a thousand tunes to come, "I Got Rhythm," received a concert treatment. He played tennis well and was even an expert painter and savvy art collector.

He was crushed that *Porgy and Bess* (1935) was a misunderstood flop, though he had five other successful shows all running on 45th Street at the same time. (Though Gershwin signed a Metropolitan Opera contract to write a work based on *The Dybbuk*—which he never even began—the Met didn't stage *Porgy* until 1986). Time and a public with ears and hearts have overtaken the shortsighted critics, and it has become the most famed, and most often adapted, of all American operas.

Novelist John O'Hara summed it up best—"George Gershwin died on July 11, 1937, but I don't have to believe it if I don't want to."

Selling Out Every House

In July of 1998, the top three albums on the classical chart all belong to superstar Italian tenor Andréa Bocelli. He was making his first American tour, and was going to appear at the CoreStates Center.

Robbed of his sight by a soccer injury at age 12, the Tuscan-born Bocelli studied law and sang in piano bars until fate brought him to the attention of Pavarotti and allowed study with the famed Franco Corelli. His CDs, videos and PBS specials have brought millions closer to the operatic repertoire. With six Arabian horses, a Tuscan country home and immense commercial success, Bocelli, 39, was sitting astride the musical world.

He had recently done a heavily publicized *La Bohème* on Italian television. (Some time later, Denyce Graves had told me about doing *Werther* with him in Detroit, a slightly difficult assignment because Bocelli had to be guided into stage positions.)

Gramophone magazine had punned on the term *bel canto* by referring to his style as *can belto*. Ouch! And though I wasn't a huge fan of his, and was underwhelmed by his operatic outings, I had a chance to speak with him by phone—while his two young sons played in the background—and found him a charming presence.

Andréa Bocelli:

Q: *You've said you'd never go back to pop music.*

A: *Yes, because my passion for opera comes from my earliest years, listening to discs of Gigli and Caruso. Later, when at the university, I enjoyed myself playing and singing Sinatra and Aznavour songs and—like any piano bar player—requests I couldn't refuse. But my heart was in opera. I like jazz—Erroll Garner, Bud Powell, Art Tatum—but our tradition is far from theirs.*

Q: *Do you enjoy the studio or live performance, and are audiences different from country to country?*

A: *I give my best in the studio. On the stage, I'm always worried. I have to do it, but in front of the audience it's sometimes terrible. I just try to put in my voice all of myself, every bit of knowledge, everything of my life. But audiences are the same everywhere.*

Q: *How does one deal with such enormous sudden success?*

A: *Success is beautiful but very dangerous. It's indefinable, it comes to you without any reason and can leave without any reason. It's almost obscene to have sold this many million records. What's most important is my friends, my family, what I had before success. When we eat together at home, no one speaks about my career, and I am happy about this. My parents no longer force me to practice law. Actually, in my job it's important to know the law.*

I used to get tired very easily until I learned how to hit high notes without straining. The voice is getting darker, but this happens to everybody. You just try your best. The Italians say, from nothing, you get nothing. (By phone, July 8, 1998)

In early August, I was asked to do an interview with an artist somewhat off my beat, who I knew little about. To make that even more unusual, the editor gave the assignment as a question:

What female artist had recorded the most songs (more than 1,000 in 10 languages), sold the most records (200 million) and received the most gold and platinum records (more than 300)?

When she heard silence, I was given a hint: Bob Dylan has written tunes for her, she has toured with Harry Belafonte, that her first American disc was produced by Quincy Jones and that operatic diva Maria Callas was a big fan.

Finally, I was given the answer: Greek-born balladeer Nana Mouskouri, who was about to make an American tour. Her eclectic mix of pop, rock, gospel, classical adaptations, folk and international melodies make up her song bag. In Europe she is known only by her first name, and has been a Greek representative to European Parliament and an ambassador to UNICEF. Her glasses have become such a famous trademark that they had been worn, the previous September in Los Angeles, by a congregation of drag queens celebrating the Night of 1,000 Nanas.

We spoke on the phone—after I did plenty of research.

Nana Mouskouri:

Q: *How did Quincy Jones discover you?*

A: *Quincy was in Paris, with Michel Legrand, and someone played a record of mine for them at a party. I was in Barcelona, in the middle of finals in the Mediterranean Festival, and they asked me to call back when it was over . . . You can't imagine what it was like to be a young Greek singer in 1961 and have Quincy Jones ask you to come and make records in America.*

Q: *Did you really know Maria Callas?*

A: *Oh, yes. She often came to a club in Athens where I was singing. She would request many songs. At the Conservatory, where I was studying classical voice, the teachers banned me from singing jazz. Maria told me—and I'll never forget her words—that I should become a popular singer because I loved the music, that the kind of music didn't matter.*

Q: *How do you like being the subject of 1,000 female impersonators?*

A: *It's an honor, flattering, very funny. In Europe, they love to imitate me, especially in parades. When I first started, nobody wore glasses, but I thought what was important was how I sang and not how I looked. People said it was courageous, but my glasses were protecting me.* (By phone, August 1, 1998)

Two Philly Institutions

In April, Peter Nero played *Rhapsody In Blue* in his Gershwin concert with the Phillly Pops. No surprise there—except that he did it on the Steinway Rhapsody piano, $175,000 worth of art-deco opulence (that's $2,000 per key, by the way). Fashioned from high-gloss blue-dyed veneer, and inlaid with 400 hand-cut stars made of mother-of-pearl, this instrument would have suited the work's splashy 1924 premiere. Even the music desk showed a silhouette of the New York skyline.

At the end of September, the Curtis Institute celebrated its 75th anniversary with a concert across the street in Rittenhouse Square.

The question was asked by more than one editor: just how exceptional are these young musicians, honing their difficult craft in that historic old mansion? At that time, here was the answer:

"Curtis alumni make up about a third of the "Big Five" orchestras, and that out of 700 annual applicants and nearly 600 auditions, only about 45 lucky students were accepted into the total student body of 160. The focus is on individual attention by master teachers, compared to New York's Juilliard School's 160 piano students in large classes.

"One entrant at age 7, pianist Gary Graffman, eventually became the Institute's enthusiastic director. Curtis' history of excellence began in 1924, when publishing heiress Mary Louise Curtis Bok launched her revolutionary idea with a $12 million endowment.

"Working closely with Philadelphia Orchestra conductor Leopold Stokowski and famed pianist (and first president) Josef Hofmann, their credo for Curtis Institute was "to train exceptionally gifted young musicians for careers as performing artists on the highest professional level." (I found from reading former Philadelphia Orchestra tubist Paul Krzywicki's detailed book "From Paderewski to Penderecki: The Polish Musician in Philadelphia" that Stoky, Hofmann and others considered the school a Polish one, and the Polish national anthem was actually played at the first graduation). Bok also insisted on free tuition, and that every piano, organ, conducting or composition student has a Steinway grand piano—now numbering about 90.

"Stoky had fought with the orchestra board to obtain the finest wind and brass soloists from around the world, and began their legacy based on a musical farm system. What could have been more visionary than a school with many orchestra players as teachers, and with free tuition to attract the finest young musicians in the world?

"Arguably the finest music school in the country—and perhaps the world—the Curtis Institute has produced an enormous catalog of distinguished alumni.

"Composers Samuel Barber, Leonard Bernstein, Gian-Carlo Menotti, Ned Rorem and Nino Rota; pianists Lang Lang, Yuja Wang, Murray Perehia, Yefim Bronfman, and Peter Serkin; violinists Pamela Frank, Hilary Hahn and Leila Josefowicz are only a handful of famous names from a huge roster."

15. YOU MUST LOVE WHAT YOU DO

Sitting in the proscenium box, Welsh baritone Jason Howard was looking at the empty Academy stage with a sense of profound connection. He strode onto that stage for the first time in 1992 to become one of the Pavarotti Competition winners, and was following up his performance last season as Rossini's Figaro with the role of the Count in an Opera Company production of Mozart's *The Marriage of Figaro*.

Howard became a firefighter and an enthusiastic amateur singer of traditional folk tunes and Broadway songs. A Mario Lanza record, with the first operatic arias he had ever heard, changed his life. After coming to Philadelphia on tour with his male chorus and visiting the Mario Lanza Museum in 1983, Howard told his astonished chums of his altered direction and entered Trinity College to shape the technique for a growing international career.

Howard represents the new breed of opera singer, athletic, direct and good-looking. He once entered—and won—the Sexiest Man in Wales competition just to prove that an opera singer could do it and, as the courtly Count Almaviva, he has an ideal chance to use his physical as well as his vocal abilities. We spoke while the stagehands cleared the sets after rehearsal.

Jason Howard:
Everyone perceives the Count as a cold womanizer, but he's just a product of his situation, proper for that time. At the end, he really loves his wife, who has gone from the sassy woman he fell for to a courtly woman, but he's backed his relationship into a corner. In this opera, you discover new things, universal things, every time.

Mozart packed every human emotion into these characters. Everyone can relate to their dreams, realities, sex drives and situations, and our insight into them is as deep as you want it to be. It's bottomless. (Academy of Music, November 10, 1999)

Whenever Denyce Graves came to town that meant another chance for some great quotes. This time, it was for two Grand Opera's Greatest Hits programs, fundraisers for the Opera Company.

RCA had just released her album *Prima Donna* (conducted by Maurizio Barbacini, who was also leading that gala), the first of a four-CD deal. Still, I always felt her energy and explosive spirit can hardly be captured except in person.

She was happy to speak by phone a few days before the event.

Denyce Graves:

Q: *Did singing Mozart make you fond enough of Philly to come back for the gala?*

A: *I have many, many good friends here. And, ah, Mozart—he'll strip you naked in front of everybody, tell all your secrets. I was staying at the Warwick Hotel then, remember? And one day the housekeeper, who had no idea who I was, said, "Dear, you're getting better, last week you couldn't sing those notes. You should continue."*

Q: *How do you cope with a frantic schedule?*

A: *I've decided that they really pay you for traveling, that's what really costs you. I haven't been home in months, and was there for about four hours last week to do laundry and repack. I love singing, it sustains me, but to be able to reach out to people outside the business has given me the most pleasure.* (By phone, November 21, 1999)

Two Fairy Tales

Another cancellation by mezzo-soprano Vivica Geneux created a problem for the Opera Company of Philadelphia's production of *Rossini's La Cenerentola* (*Cinderella*), though conductor Klaus Arp suggested Hungarian artist Lucia M. Schwartz. OCP's general director Driver traveled to Budapest to hear her sing in *Faust* and *Boris Godounov* with the Hungarian Opera, and knew she was right for the part.

Lucia Schwartz:

It's like a fairytale, a dream to be here in this very European-feeling city, making my first American appearance in a role I've never sung before. The part is a challenge, because this is the hardest of coloratura mezzo-soprano roles, much more than any other Rossini. Luckily I know the music, because I once sang Tisbe, one of the stepsisters, but only studied one of my arias in school. You are lucky over here to have this much rehearsal time.

In Hungary, I do about 50 performances a season, 15 operas, besides oratorios and recitals in other halls. Sometimes there are not many rehearsals, and they will often cancel an opera and announce a substitution for that night on the radio. If you are the only one who does not know the role, you only get one piano rehearsal. Once I had many friends come to town to see me in Cosi, *but the tenor cancelled and we switched to* La Traviata. (Academy of Music, February 6, 2000)

I first saw Leila Josefowicz play the violin at age 12 on Johnny Carson's *Tonight Show* and, from her earliest days at the Curtis Institute, everyone knew that the lovely young lady with the fabulous technique and deep immersion into the music was headed for stardom; she had two Philips CDs on the market before she even graduated. Her parents moved from Los Angeles, allowing her to attend Curtis to study with renowned mentors Jascha Brodsky and Jaime Laredo, and even do some modeling. She returned—while seven months pregnant—to play with Laredo and the Brandenburg Ensemble, teaming with Laredo in the Bach Double Concerto and the Mozart Sinfonia Concentante. She remained passionate about Laredo, the Mozart, the new pieces she had begun commissioning and her upcoming motherhood.

Leila Josefowicz:

That Mozart—what a miracle—an unbelievable piece with a completely different quality and character from anything else. To me, it's a perfect piece of music.

Music is completely performance-oriented. You just can't play the notes, you have to make the audience understand and feel something. For me, the greatest compliment could ever be that someone would say, "This new music spoke to me."

I'm certain that motherhood will make me a fuller musician, because all life experiences improve one's sense of music-making. It's only expression through sound, and the more experiences you have in your life, the more music can illustrate your feelings. (By phone, February 7, 2000)

Brotherly Love—And Indifference

Tributes to the legacy of William Penn continued with a choral work composed by Ezra Laderman based on the brilliant 1968 text *Brotherly Love* by University Of Pennsylvania professor Daniel Hoffman. It was commissioned by Michael Korn's Philadelphia Singers, and was delivered just before his death in 1991, but the time involved in choosing David Hayes as his successor and Laderman's heart attack delayed the project until 2000.

Hoffman's long poem is a remarkable reflection of Penn's ideal—concepts of fairness to native peoples, religious tolerance and pacifism that inspired many of the Founding Fathers' documents. As Penn becomes more mythical with the passage of time and his ideals grow forgotten, the native chiefs emerge from the shrouds of time to challenge present-day principles of success. Though many consider Philadelphia Benjamin Franklin's city, Hoffman recounted that it couldn't have been Franklin's city without Penn, calling him "the forgotten founding father, the wellspring of American democracy."

Philadelphia Orchestra bassoonist Sol Schoenbach and Romeo Cascarino were Army buddies in the 1940s, and Sol asked Romeo to write him a Bassoon Sonata when they returned. It's standard fare now in most conservatories, and the pair recorded the work for Columbia. Cascarino recalled that they went to New York early to rehearse, being scheduled to play that afternoon. When another artist was delayed, they were told to go into the studio at 10 a.m., where they read right through the piece and were out onto the street a half hour later.

Sol (who eventually became executive director of Settlement Music School after his retirement), once heard that the orchestra was willing to commission a work for the five famous principals who recorded as the Philadelphia Woodwind Quintet. Schoenbach gave Ormandy a copy of the LP with the Bassoon Sonata on it, and suggested Cascarino as the composer.

Several weeks later, Romeo received a letter from Ormandy:

Dear Mr. Cascarino:
Mr. Schoenbach has given me a copy of your Bassoon Sonata.
I haven't listened to it yet, but I'm certain that it is a fine work.
Sincerely,
Eugene Ormandy

In other words, Sol, don't you dare suggest repertoire to me.

Charmer Charles

Back in the 1970s, musicians would hang out at the apartment of bassist Miles B. Davis, a staple of the Chamber Orchestra, Opera Company and AVA orchestras. The address was 1807 Sansom Street, and their well-attended jams led Davis to begin an organization called 1807 and Friends, presenting unusual offerings of chamber music. It passed through several overseers who wanted to keep the tax-exempt status the name held, and was eventually taken over by Orchestra players Nancy Bean and Lloyd Smith. Two more Orchestra colleagues, violinist Davyd Booth and violist Pamela Fay, formed the Wister Quartet, becoming the core 1807 and Friends players, featuring many esteemed artists as guests.

On March 13, 2000, Dutoit was willing to conduct a program, with expanded instrumentation and dancers, of Martinů, Saint-Saëns and Stravinsky. That latter was the brilliant evocation of the devil's work *The Soldier's Tale*, with the late basso Julian Rodescu as narrator.

After the concert, Dutoit was given a bottle of champagne as a present, and he surprisingly asked Margie and me if we wanted to have dinner. We walked to the only restaurant nearby at the time, D'Angelo's, where a potent whiff of garlic greeted us upon entering. We sat in an empty room upstairs, and Dutoit expressed to the waiter that he couldn't eat garlic. A cook eventually came out, and promised he'd cook pasta in a brand new pot.

Very few horse players at the race track peruse the Racing Form with as much deliberation and attention to detail as Dutoit paid to the wine list, and he chose an excellent one. We had a remarkable evening with this man, whose knowledge of history, culture and the arts is second to no one I've ever met.

He mentioned that a Japanese company had asked him to write a series of programs about the cities central to musical history, Paris, London, Berlin, Vienna, and many others. When asked how it could be accessed, he smiled and admitted it was only shown on Japanese television, and never released commercially. He enthused about his love of exploring unfamiliar countries, at that time over 150, and said he was willing to go anywhere to conduct he hadn't been before.

We drove Charles to the Bellevue Stratford hotel, and were almost out of center city when we remembered the bottle of champagne, left at the restaurant. After driving back and retrieving it, I talked the concierge into giving me the number of his room, and he received it with a hearty "Merci bien!" in a white Bellevue robe.

In 2008, backstage at Saratoga, he mentioned that he had recently conducted in Kosovo, one of the last countries on earth he hadn't visited, bringing his total to over 170.

Passion On and Off the Stage

Puccini's *Tosca* is loaded with tension, and conducting while your wife is singing the lead role can't possibly make it any easier. The Opera Company's production featured the local debut of soprano Antonella Pianezzola, the spouse of their principal conductor Maurizio Barbacini.

Barbacini also had the good fortune to work with his twin brother Paolo (also a tenor and artistic director of the opera house in Reggio Emilia) and to have sung himself, including a small part in the brilliant Franco Zeffirelli movie of *La Traviata*).

Sitting next to each other like young lovers, they spoke about Tosca's character, working together and the perils of working in your home town (in his case, Verona). And—whether volatile onstage outbursts of emotion between Tosca and her lover continue at home after the performance?

Maurizio Barbacini and Antonella Pianezzola:

Barbacini: *Absolutely, the same situations of being angry or passionate comes home with us sometimes, because it is natural. When my wife is on the stage, I cannot forget her and think she is Tosca, but when the drama is unfolding with her in the big love scene, it gives me great pleasure when she is a sensation. She is a great artist and a great singer, and I am a lucky man.*

Pianezzola: *In the second act, Tosca sees the span of her whole life, trying to be a good singer, reflecting that she goes to church, gives jewels to the Madonna, helps the poor. But, in this moment, God has forgotten her and she alone must decide Cavaradossi's fate. I don't think she knows, as that aria ends, that she will kill Scarpia. She is a modern woman. She has a lover and is not married, but she is not a prostitute.*

Barbacini: *Tosca really uses all her sexuality, even towards Scarpia. He is a handsome, powerful man, and she is an artist. Antonella is a lot like Tosca, a quality that helps her in this role. Of course, because they are both singers, but also since she is a modern, sensitive and sexy woman. (Turning to his wife) I hope you don't do many things with other men but, if so, don't tell me!*

Having been a singer is a great advantage, because it's important to know what's happening with the breath, the movement of the singers. I had the opportunity to work with (the brilliant conductor) Carlos Kleiber, and he sang everything in this high tenor, and taught me to sing and realize what problems might occur for the singers.

Pianezzolla: *Yes, I remember covering Renata Scotto in Florence, and she and Renato Bruson were rehearsing* Otello. *Riccardo Muti, who was playing the score at the piano, told Bruson to sing without vibrato, and sang to give an example with a really horrible singing voice. He saw me covering my laugh with my hand, and said to me, "If I had a good voice I would sing, not conduct!"* (Academy of Music, March 20, 2000)

Getting More Serious

Whenever Peter Schickele came to town, there was always a chance for some classic laughs. He became famous for his P. D. Q. Bach concerts, having foisted on us such gems as the *Schleptet*, the *Unbegun Symphony, Pervertimento, and the operas The Civilian Barber, Oedipus Tex and The Abduction of Figaro.*

I once took my friend Bill Rodgers to see his *Hansel and Gretel and Ted and Alice*, and when the singer entered yelling words that couldn't be heard—thanks to the wolf's head he was wearing—Bill broke up with such boisterous, prolonged laughter that he literally stopped the show. Afterwards, Schickele said, "I should take that guy along as part of the act."

Schickele has some heavy credentials, having worked with Vincent Persichetti, Darius Milhaud and Roy Harris and studied at Swarthmore and Juilliard; these days, virtually all his work is "serious."

The 2000 April Fool's Day concert by the Philadelphia Orchestra featured some of this foolishness, including *Eine Kleine Nichtmusik* and the classic *Safe Sextet*. Yet there were also some of his serious works, *Bach Portrait* to texts of J. S. Bach's actual letters, usually about not getting paid, and his newly-written verse for Saint-Saens' evergreen *Carnival of the Animals*.

Peter Schickele.

Peter Schickele:
I once wrote a short, serious eight-minute piece for (the late tenor) John Ferrante, who toured with me for years, and introduced it to a very responsive and appreciative Philadelphia audience. It was performed soon after at the Brooklyn Academy, without my narration, and a bunch of people determined to find something to laugh at roared throughout the piece.

But there are advantages too. I once arranged a Joan Baez Christmas album, and was asked to score a film called Silent Running *because the producer figured out that the sound on that album had something to do with the arranger.* (By phone, March 25, 2000)

Yes, Maestro

My association with Christofer Macatsoris at the Academy of Vocal Arts, and our roles in *William Penn*, made each interview with the Maestro enlightening. It was obvious that the tuition-free AVA was a place of serious, tough, displined work, with a level of professionalism renowned throughout international operatic circles. In 2000, 140 singers auditioned, with only six making the cut.

New students soon learn the two immutable rules—always say "Si (Yes), Maestro," and never correct another singer. They also receive a full scope examination of their throats by voice expert Dr. Robert Sataloff, plus the coveted free tuition. Most have degrees in music, with ages averaging 22 or 23, with 30 the cutoff.

The institution's 65th anniversary led to another BrAVA celebration, this time featuring alumni James Morris, baritone, soprano Ruth Ann Swenson and tenor Marcello Giordani, plus revered honored guests Licia Albanese, Rose Bampton, Benita Valente and Robert Merrill, giving an opportunity to speak with Macatsoris, who had been the conservatory's music director for 22 years.

Christofer Macatsoris:
To be an opera singer means not only having a great voice, it still has to be disciplined and harnessed. A lot of physical labor goes into singing, getting over the might of a 70-piece orchestra. But it's also a study of language and how it relates to music, a study of the books or plays these operas come from, of acting and costuming. We also teach opera history, the history of great opera singers and great opera singing, for to know the present you have to know the past.

When these artists finally go out for operas, they remember working with difficulty to sing piano *and to sing this phrase marked* legato *(smoothly), and they find that nobody cares, or they don't know about it. But there are conductors who know the difference, and they're the better ones. Being here is a tiring luxury—our mission is to help these singers in discovering a sense of joy, and we have had a high record of people getting employment.* (Academy of Vocal Arts, April 2, 2000)

Two Takes, One Dream

The three Philadelphia conservatories presenting operas—the Academy of Vocal Arts, Curtis Opera Theatre and Temple University's Opera Theater—choose works more to provide performance opportunities for the available voices than for box-office revenue. (Of course, they all perform in smaller spaces than the Opera Company of Philadelphia's venue, the Academy of Music.)

One opportunity to investigate this paradox occurred in April 2000, when both Curtis and Temple did Britten's *A Midsummer Night's Dream*. This gem of a work with mortals and fairies—with audiences sometimes puzzled about who's singing—presented a challenge to both directors.

Chas Rader-Shieber:

I believe the best magic is in everyday life, something we have all experienced like falling in love, a terrifying life-passed-before-my-eyes occurrence or a transforming moment. Every kid who has donned a bathtowel and become a superhero has experienced magic, the way Shakespeare, Handel and Ingmar Bergman all show us the reason we love reality-based magic.

We're left to wonder, in the opera or the play, is it the herb making people fall madly in love, or just the circumstances? In high school it didn't take a magic herb to suddenly shift attentions and be fickle. When the magic makes Titania fall for Bottom, a character with great confidence and charm who wears an ass' head, people ask why she fell for him—just as they said that about Sophia Loren and Carlo Ponti. (Curtis Institute, April 19, 2000)

Dugg McDonough:

I remember being fascinated when sticking my head into the grand old theaters around (New York's) 42nd Street, left to decay and filled with incredible theater ghosts from years past. That led to thinking of this piece as a theatrical world, not just a generalized forest, but an old abandoned theater inhabited with the spirits of the past.

What resulted was a contemporary production with lovers from the year 2000 colliding with these theatrical spirits, with the royalty now wealthy patrons who have bought this space to renovate it back into its former glory. (Temple studios, April 20, 2000)

I loved McDonough's staging much more, perhaps in a way because it reminded me of one of my favorite films, *Vanya On 42nd Street*. Directed by Louis Malle, this shows a team of great actors getting together in an abandoned theater to do Chekhov's *Uncle Vanya*, somehow slipping from contemporary conversations into a Russian farm in a surprising osmosis. How Malle knew we would be transported through the smooth transition—and even buy it again for the second act—demonstrates the mystery of art.

Never Alive at the Curtain

"Gregg Baker came to town and was stabbed six times and decapitated. Welcome to Philadelphia, the town that hires you back." That was my lead for an interview with baritone Baker, who had portrayed the evil Baron Scarpia in *Tosca* with the Opera Company and was returning as John the Baptist in *Salomé*. In his early days, he had sung *Timbuktu* on Broadway with Eartha Kitt, was a pro football player, and here he was doing two back-to-back operas in Philly.

Gregg Baker:
I want the audience to feel the conflict between heaven and hell, the torment of a man with his commitment to God and a sudden physical attraction, both attracting and repulsing him. He's a man, not just a prophet, but when he fights the frailties of being human, he gets more fanatical, and I must do it only in face and body with a long, continuous gesture.

My experience on Broadway taught me that every day, when you go out on stage, you should go out for that person who has never seen that art form before, who has paid that $100, and you owe that person the best you can do. You can't insult anybody.

I used to ask Eartha—do you get scared? She said, "Yes, every day, and when you don't, get out of the business, because you don't have what it takes anymore." (Philadelphia hotel, April 22, 2000)

The imposing 6-foot-5, 280-pound Baker was a gentle family man with four children, whose wife Shawneen brought them from Florida to spend time with him at *Tosca* rehearsals. In one rehearsal given to school children, he came out after his evil character was killed in the second act and was given a deafening reception of hisses and boos, a response he considered a huge success at reaching them. That moment must have had special meaning to Baker, who was committed to being a football player when his own school class was taken to the Lyric Opera of Chicago for a performance of that very same *Tosca*.

Three-Quarter Time Again

André Rieu came to town again after he had finally taken his Strauss waltzes, elaborate tableaus of flowers, gowned maidens, velvet draperies and styrofoam pillars to Vienna. It had taken a while for the Viennese to warm to the Dutchman's appropriation of their three-quarter-time legend, and I had a chance to speak to him again after two Vienna sellouts.

André Rieu:
These waltzes are like life itself, not always the same, like making love. There is great joy and great sadness, gallantry and melancholy, and when you play with your heart, people sense the extreme emotions involved. Eve-

ry day is different, just as the 1-2-3 rhythm is always slightly different, even hour to hour.

If Strauss could hear, I would say, please forgive me if I do not play exactly as you would do it, but I'm using all my heart, sincerity and professionalism to play your music as well as possible. Without me, there's no music, but we recognize a responsibility to you. There is a mystery, a secret to the waltz, that I've still never been able to completely fathom. But there's more miracle in the waltz than in other musics, a combination of joy and melody—and when composed by a genius, a mirror of life. (By phone from Frankfurt, Germany, May 9, 2000)

Fangs A Lot

Just after interviewing Pennsylvania Ballet artistic director (and retired principal dancer) Roy Kaiser about the upcoming presentation of Ben Stevenson's setting of *Dracula*, dancer James Ihde (soon to become a soloist) showed me the difficulty of dancing wearing a 30-pound cape. The John Lanchbery score is drawn from Franz Liszt and has plenty of bite—as does the Count.

Kaiser was quite proud of being licensed to do this production, with its flying zombie wives, an exploding chandelier and a brooding castle with a spider-eating servant. A woman friend insisted that the Count represents the ultimate bad boy, with its combination of death, sex and personal magnetism all expressed through the beauty of dance. There are over a dozen different *Dracula* ballet stagings of the Bram Stoker story, all using different music and choreography. Kaiser, then the company's artistic director and ex-principal dancer, insisted he'd chosen the finest.

Roy Kaiser:

Stevenson is one of a handful of choreographers who can tell a story with a powerful sense of theatricality and put on a show that's a real entertainment. The lighting, flying (Flying By Foy) and scenery are more elaborate than usual, and we have a two-use license, allowing us to do it in another season.

There isn't a lot of mystery to dance, and everyone enjoys ballet after a first exposure. We all dance in our own way, and ballet is just movement refined over many years. With the richness of music, beautiful human beings in perfect physical condition expressing themselves at the height of their artistry and giving 150 percent—what more could you ask for? (Pennsylvania Ballet offices, May 29, 2000)

This story had another Philadelphia link, thanks to the Rosenbach Museum on Delancey Street (home of the original manuscript of another Irish writer, James Joyce's visionary *Ulysses*). The Rosenbach displays Stoker's notes for *Dracula* written, though not in blood, on stationery of the Bellevue Stratford Hotel, a block away from the then-38-year-old Academy of Music.

Twin Talents

For 27 years, Robert Capanna held the post of executive director at Settlement Music School, where hundreds of people of all ages and backgrounds find creative inspiration every day. Capanna also is a composer, who was about to receive a performance of a new work set to his own texts for *Songs of the Ancient Mariner*.

Robert Capanna:
When I spend any period of time, a week or two without writing, I start to feel bad, emotionally and physically. I work very hard at it, and perhaps it comes easier to some people, but without writing consistently I function much less well. I'm sympathetic to composers who are sincere, and furious at shallow music—why bother?

I got involved in writing music because it's hard to do—writing a good piece is a Zen experience, and when you think you come close to writing a good one it's highly gratifying. You just don't set out to write a masterpiece. (Settlement Music School, October 2, 2000)

At the Curtis Institute of Music, the admission levels are incredibly high, and only a fortunate few are selected annually. I discovered that there had been some musicians who had been accepted as double majors. (Lukas Foss was the only person to actually be a triple major, graduating with degrees in piano, flute, and conducting).

One musician who passed this remarkable hurdle was pianist and conductor Ignat Solzhenitsyn, father of the acclaimed Russian novelist Aleksandr Solzhenitsyn. Marc Mostovoy chose him as principal guest conductor when the organization was still called the Concerto Soloists Chamber Orchestra of Philadelphia, and he would later become the artistic director.

In October of 2000 Solzhenitsyn led the Soloists in Haydn and Mozart, and also played a chamber music concert. He left a repressive Russia at age four and has now toured there often, still vividly recalling the overwhelming impression of his first visit, in 1994, to a completely different state of affairs.

Ignat Solzhenitsyn:
For me finally to return home was more moving than I could possibly begin to describe. I played recitals and concerts with the National Symphony and Mstislav Rostropovich, 12 unforgettable days making my first acquaintance with Russian audiences.

After having it taken away from you for 20 years, of not knowing when the day would come that returning was possible, it was amazing to see signs in the Russian language, to hear Russian spoken on the street. And to visit my family and friends, and see the glorious beauty of Moscow and St. Petersburg. (By phone, October 10, 2000)

Among the musical families associated with Curtis are the father-daughter, piano/violin team of Claude and Pamela Frank, who made a brilliant recording of the ten Beethoven Violin Sonatas. Her directness and humility began at home, where her father and pianist mother Lilian Kallir exposed her to musicmaking at a very high level–virtually a prerequisite for a major career. The ebullient Pamela returned to her alma mater to perform the Dvořák Violin Concerto at the Academy, led by the institute's maestro Otto-Werner Mueller.

Pamela Frank:
I'm an equal-opportunity concerto player, I like it when other musicians have a lot of solo passages besides me, and half the time the violin takes a secondary role. I've been criticized for turning my back on the audience to watch a wind soloist, but have no interest in standing up there showing off. We weren't put on this earth to play by ourselves—if you weren't constantly reacting with great joy to what each different orchestra brings to a piece, you could be in the Anywhere, USA, orchestra.

Our instruments are just extensions of ourselves, and you can say things with your instruments you couldn't say with your mouth or eyes, becoming intimate with people without ever having to exchange words. The whole point of playing music is to share the musical experience, to be vulnerable enough to bare your heart and soul in public. If an audience doesn't feel anything, something's wrong.

I pinch myself every day that I happened to have been born into a situation with two great musicians, still my musical heroes. It took me a long time to figure out what they did for a living. They were having so much fun, it couldn't possibly be their profession. I feel very spoiled, and will never quite believe that this is what I get to do for a living, because it's what I would do anyway.

My father always reminds me what pianist Artur Schnabel used to say: "Great music is better than it can be played." You can either take that as intimidating or humbling, but humbling is a better way to live, because you always can try to make the music more beautiful. (Curtis Institute of Music, October 19, 2000)

Claude Frank, who passed away in December 2014, was one of those legendary musicians whose influence still resounds through his teaching as well as his example.

Two More Operatic Artists

The first opera production of that season, Verdi's *Rigoletto*, featured New Jersey native Christopher Robertson, a 6-foot-4 baritone who seemed height- and size-challenged for the jester's traditional small, bent-over stature. Luckily for him, director Marco Pucci-Catena, who was making his American debut, didn't insist on that obstacle to singing.

Christopher Robertson:
Pucci-Catena thinks having Rigoletto *big is better, even with a deformity. It makes him seem more dangerous, makes his relationship with (his daughter) Gilda more pitiful. And when he crumbles, it's more effective, seeing a giant tumble. For once, it's using my size to advantage, because many directors make me bend down to look smaller than the tenor.*

This is all I ever wanted to do, like an astronaut, I guess. I just belong doing this, I can't tell you how good it is, how much fun it is to work as hard. Many of my friends hate their job, and I realize how lucky I am to love what I do. (Academy of Music, October 5, 2000)

Before mezzo Stephanie Blythe—and Juan Diego Florez (a 1996 Curtis alumnus)—became huge stars at the Metropolitan Opera and almost everywhere else, they sang at the Opera Company of Philadelphia's performances of Rossini's *The Italian Girl in Algiers*. Blythe returned to Philly after doing some heavy Wagnerian roles, a real artistic transition. The daughter of a jazz musician, she admitted to listening to more Cuban and Brazilian music, Frank Sinatra and Ella Fitzgerald than opera.

Stephanie Blythe:
James Levine (artistic director of the Met) told me that when you finish a heavy-duty role, you must do some bel canto right away. It's like being marathon runner who needs to stretch before and after a race.

Isabella is my favorite of all the great Rossini heroines. It's because she's most like me! I hope I have something in common with every character I play, but Isabella, without any love duets, manipulates three men with sex, humor and intelligence. She's wily and practical, and that makes her attractive. Everything comes from strength, not weakness, and I love and believe what she says. (Academy of Music, November 4, 2000)

Villainy runs rampant in operatic plots, and some of the darkest characters in the repertory raised their rascally heads that November. There's the ruthless Don Giovanni, using his reluctant servant Leporello to conquer every woman in Seville, and the emperor Nero with his mistress Poppea, who are trying to get rid of Nero's wife Ottavia.

These scheming egos, and how they bring out the dark side of everyone around them, reveal great drama, with both works set to remarkable music. At that time, they were being interpreted by the remarkable young singers and musicians of Temple University Opera Theater (*Don Giovanni*) and Curtis Opera Theatre (Monteverdi's *Coronation of Poppea*).

Perhaps the greatness and staying power of these two operas has to do with their basic universality. They were written 229 and 373 years ago, without much change in the human essence.

Back at the Keyboard

Pianist Richard Goode had been out of action for a while with some muscle problems in his shoulders, luckily not his hands; he had been back since early in the year, and quite busy. After a 20-year absence, he had become co-director (with pianist Mitsuko Uchida) at the prestigious Marlboro Music Festival in Vermont, where he forged many of his professional allegiances. Only Uchida remains at Marlboro these days, but every year's appearance by Goode is a highlight.

Though he is renowned as a Beethoven, Bach and Mozart player, he had been playing more Chopin; in the upcoming summer of 2001, he'd be playing Chopin in Poland, where performances of their native composer's music gets Super Bowl-level attention. Like the Viennese waltz and the Brazilian samba, getting the idiomatic rhythmic feel of the mazurka has foiled many pianists.

Goode was in town for a recital with works by Bach, Chopin and Beethoven—the penultimate Beethoven Sonata, No. 31, Op. 110. That last piece, written by the totally-deaf composer, is like a white-hot struggle with the soul, a crucible of dense ideas requiring enormous concentration and the gift of revelation.

Richard Goode.

Richard Goode:
I play Bach every day, the way (the great cellist Pablo) Casals did. His music sensitizes you to voice-on-voice and harmonic relations, a basic part of every pianist's education and thinking. For a while, the early-music movement persuaded everyone that Bach disapproved of the early pianoforte, which isn't true, and that his music should only be played on harpsichord.

Years ago, at Marlboro, Rudolf Serkin told me my Bach was too romantic, a comment that remained on my mind for years. I gradually came to the realization that you have to continue to study and play the music as you feel it, to try and get to the heart of what the music is saying.

Chopin was an enigma—he insisted his students play in exact time, even used a metronome, but Berlioz said he would never conduct a concerto with Chopin playing because his playing was too wayward. I think it was probably exquisitely rhythmical, just not literal. (By phone, November 17, 2000)

16. ON THE COAST WITH EMIL RICHARDS

My pal of 58 years and I have shared a lot of great times, and his astounding life is recounted in *Wonderful World of Percussion—My Life Behind Bars*, a book I was honored to co-write.

While playing vibes with George Shearing, Emil spoke to arranger Billy May who told him that, if you're going to work, it should be where the sun was shining. In Los Angeles, it didn't take long before he was doing record sessions, including one with Frank Sinatra leading to every album and tour with Frank until the end. I still have a black-and-white, fuzzy video from Japan as Sinatra sings to an enormous outdoor crowd in 1962, with Emil playing vibes right behind him. It is still bizarre to see those Japanese mouthing Cole Porter lyrics in English.

Emil Richards, with his collection of percussion instruments.

Besides that gig, there were stints and records with Paul Horn, Stan Kenton, Lou Harrison, Harry Partch and virtually hundreds of pop artists. Eventually, through many tours and trips, Emil amassed the largest collection of percussion instruments in the world, over 650, with composers calling whenever he returned to see what he had found in the far corners of the world. There were hundreds of television shows—the wood block in *Mission Impossible*, the triangle in *M*A*S*H*, aluminum salad bowls for the apes in the original *Planet of The Apes* and gongs lowered into water for sci-fi films. For his book, we made a list of the over 2,000 movies and television shows he had played on, without even attempting the huge list of record dates—at one point 19 per week.

He once asked me to send a batch of Tibetan music, to be played while he and John Williams chose instruments for *Seven Years in Tibet* from the hundreds available at the warehouse. Naturally, in compensation, composers scored parts for other instruments, meaning Emil would get paid "doubles"—extra pay helping toward owning, storing, carting and maintenance of the instruments.

George Harrison and Emil Richards.

In 1974, he came to Philly with the *Dark Horse Tour*, playing with George Harrison, Ravi Shankar, Tom Scott, Willie Weeks and Billy Preston, and I took a few of them, including some of the Indian percussion players, to Dante and Luigi's in South Philadelphia for lunch. I learned that a tiny bit of the red pepper they dumped onto their food and into their Coke caused my mouth to be on fire for days, a result they found amusing. Emil had introduced Harrison to his wife Olivia, who once worked at A&M records where they were recording, and they all had become close friends.

Once when Ravi was at the Kimmel Center, playing with his daughter Anoushka, I went backstage with Kimmel VP Mervon Mehta, who was astonished—as I was—that Ravi remembered me. "Tom, you must come to London next week for the anniversary concert of George's passing! Emil will be there!" he said, though I couldn't make it. In the DVD of that *Concert For George*, there's an extra segment with Shankar saying that Emil also was one of the only Western musicians who ever felt the Indian rhythms and could play Indian ragas.

Emil recalled a Burt Bacharach session at A&M, where recordings were played back through gigantic speakers. One day, Bacharach went out to his car and took out the speakers from the doors, and asked the engineer to play the songs back through them. Of course, it sounded very different, with Bachrach insisting that most people would not be listening through a cutting-edge sound system, and wanted it remastered. Emil said Bacharach brought those speakers to every session.

Emil's house is like a percussion museum, with many contraptions in every room. Once a landlady who had worked with the State Department in Brazil had brought back a birimbau, and gave it to me as a present. It's a musical instrument about six feet long, like a bow with a single steel wire and a gourd resonator. I figured I finally found something Emil didn't have and, with much difficulty even in days before airport security, got it onto a plane. When he saw it, he opened the door to his garage, where four of them hung on hooks. He put the gourd against his belly, held the top of the instrument, and played a tune on it.

He did Lawrence Welk albums—without being willing to be on the TV show—and many with Elvis Presley, since the studio players were better than his band, in sessions that brought a week of high pay.

Emil was with Sinatra in one Las Vegas engagement when the singer received an opening-night telegram from Elvis Presley, the hottest act in show business, who was playing at another hotel: "Thanks, Frank, for helping me with your overflow. Elvis." Needless to say, Frank was immensely impressed by the compliment.

After spending a couple of weeks in many sessions with him in 1980, I did a long Emil profile, giving it to my cartoonist acquaintance Frank Modell, who placed it into a New Yorker editor's in-box. From long experience, I know that New Yorker rejections come back on the same small slip, though I actually received a message from the legendary William Shawn's secretary.

She said they declined to use it, but that Mr. Shawn "liked it and thought it sufficiently arcane."

The profile included Emil's recounting of the astonishing gestation of the original *Star Trek* movie.

"*Star Trek* had more sessions than any I've ever worked on, maybe *Doctor Zhivago* came close," he said. "Jerry Goldsmith came in with a score in the summer, and they called six double sessions, 36 hours' worth. After we played the main title in the rehearsal, the whole 87-piece orchestra gave Jerry a standing ovation, the only one I ever remember except for one by Alex North. They immediately cancelled the sessions, and (drummer) Larry Bunker said the music was simply too good; they didn't want gorgeous string melodies in space, they weren't sure what, but it wasn't that. If the musicians liked it that much, the public wouldn't.

"We thought this movie would be as big as *Star Wars*. Jerry called and said he was going to recompose with percussion instruments, and Shelly Manne and I played some for Jerry and Robert Wise, the director. The studio called and said they wanted all organic percussion instead of their electronics, because it sounded like a cartoon.

"I went into a studio in Santa Monica with thirty instruments and fifteen sound men in the booth. We recorded tracks with gongs, with superballs on the strings, gongs that go into water, and all kinds of sounds, and they say this will be great when the meteor goes by, vooooooooom. Meanwhile, Jerry kept writing music, and the producers kept saying no, do it over.

"Finally it's the weekend before this $40 million—big dough in 1979—movie is supposed to open nationwide the next Friday. We finish twenty minutes after midnight Saturday morning, and there are cases of champagne in the booth. The producers have Jerry in the booth and he starts to shout, "No! No! Absolutely not! Twenty-six sessions is enough!" Evidently they told him to go home and write something else, or the musicians wouldn't get the champagne. Everyone left in sympathy with Jerry, and the title everyone knows was just the last one he did.

"The next week we worked on the McDonald's promos for the movie. They had *Star Trek* music to advertise the premiums to be given away with the hamburgers, but they were afraid of competition with *Tron* and thought that the picture was going to bomb, and we had to redo it with Ronald McDonald music. That was Wednesday and Thursday, with the film opening on Friday. When the movie was a hit, they used the original music."

Of course, I included what has come to be known in the world of Hollywood callousness as the Shelly Manne story. The famous drummer gets a call from a contractor:

"Shelly, have I got a session for you! It's got all the figures and riffs you always throw in, it was written with you in mind!"

"When is it?"

"Monday."

"Too bad, I already have a date with Hank Mancini."

"But Shelly, you're the only guy who could do this job, it's the perfect showcase for you."

"Sorry, but I just can't do it. Why don't you try Joe Porcaro?"

"Well, he's at Universal that day."

"How about Larry Bunker?"

"We tried him, he's out of town."

"Well, how about....."

That article ended with another classic studio-musician story.

"A studio clarinet player dies and goes to heaven. He finds himself playing beautiful music in a fabulous orchestra, though the first piece seems very long. It goes on and on, gorgeous and tiring. Finally, he whispers to the oboe player, "When is the coda?" "Oh, that's just it," comes the reply. "There is no coda."

Soundstage Moments

Through the years, I had the chance to accompany Emil to many scoring sessions, some for many famous films.

On a California in 1994, complete with an unnerving 4.3-Richter tremor, I had a chance to hang out at the musical rehearsals for the Oscar telecast. Observing 60 legendary studio musicians led by Bill (*Rocky*) Conti eat up a diverse and complex stack of music was humbling; one take was usually sufficient for this cadre. Debbie Allen watched her dancers twirl around the cramped studios while learning the tempos, and musicians closest to the door kept an eye out for the anticipated arrivals of Dolly Parton and Janet Jackson—who never showed up.

Many chunks were taped, including the dance segment and the annual "hook music" cue, a cutoff fanfare available when an award recipient blabs too long.

There are several hundred different cues (clips of music) on the Oscar show, though some of them were taped. Some are only intros—"Sophia Loren walk on," "Sophia Loren walk off"—only a few seconds. And when Allen came with her dancers to hear the section with music from the five nominated scores, they needed to go and rehearse to music that wouldn't vary slightly if played live. Of course, music for the nominated pictures had to be rehearsed and played live whenever the winner was announced.

It was a great year for scores, with the highlights Elmer Bernstein's *The Age of Innocence*, James Newton Howard's *The Fugitive* and John Williams' *Schindler's List*.

Larry Bunker was the timpanist, and I had enjoyed him greatly when he played drums for Bill Evans. (You can see him on a YouTube video, playing behind Bill's classic "Waltz for Debby.") His parents had come to visit from Texas a while before, unfortunately coming on the day before a 5.1 earthquake the previous week, and he drove them to LAX the next morning.

During the telecast, each nominated film received a two-minute excerpt with music. On the take for *The Fugitive*, there was a long xylo solo for Emil, until he realized he didn't have enough hands for the finish. When there was a tiny rest, he suddenly handed Margie a small suspended cymbal, played the swift xylo part, ending with a small shot to the cymbal. One of the percussion guys yelled, "Hey, Margie, put in for doubles!"

The next cue was the shorter clip, the one played just when they sum up all five nominees, and it's only about fifteen seconds. Larry Bunker was unhappy, and told Conti it wasn't possible. "Bill, in the long take I had time in the middle to retune the timpani to a different key. But in this short one, they just pasted the beginning and the end together and there's no time to retune."

Conti knew Bunker was serious, and just had fun needling him a little. "What difference does it make? People are only listening on a five-inch TV speaker!" Larry persisted, and persuaded Conti to do the first few measures and come back later. Of course, at the end of the session, Conti pretended he forgot and asked everyone if they were ready to wrap. Finally, he waved to the booth and they rolled tape for Larry, only a few measures and a drum roll and boom!

To me, it was one of many examples of the legendary professionalism of these players, the best sight-readers in the world who have drifted into this arcane world of make-believe.

There were many fascinating sessions through the years. One, with actor and composer John Rubinstein, was for a TV show about Midwestern farmers called *Amber Waves*. There was a section where Emil played slapstick and Jew's-harp, while a young player did the timpani. In one section, there was a long run with a loud timpani bang on the beat. He played it a little early, a little late, early again, about six times.

Rubinstein kindly looked at his watch and gave a ten, not making a big deal out of it, and soon had a little confab with Emil, who asked the young man if he could switch with him and get in a little timpani time. It may have been this musician's trial, for all I know, and perhaps both men were trying to keep him from blowing his chance.

It reminded me of a Venice visit when no operas were scheduled at the famous La Fenice theater, before two electricians set it on fire in 1996 because they were facing some serious fines. A look inside was not possible, because the orchestra was rehearsing for a concert. They were playing the Gershwin Concerto in F, beginning with a timpani flurry and a big bang on the beat. Whoever was playing that big note missed it 11 straight times, provoking various screaming Italian epithets I'm glad I didn't understand. Years later, while the great opera house was being rebuilt, we tried to take another look, and only got a peek at that gilded interior when an exiting decorator realized that, if we were from Philadelphia, we must be friends of Riccardo Muti.

Orchestra musicians like percussionists, who don't play all the time, are given a few previous measures on their parts to help prepare for their entrances. This is a luxury not afforded the one-time film score parts for studio musicians, whose music often is marked with lots of rests.

Once, while a cue was being recorded, I noticed that Emil's xylophone part began "42 Tacet," meaning he didn't enter until measure 43. He was filling out his time sheet, and I quietly asked, "How do you know when to come in?" He looked at me in surprise, and whispered, "34, 2, 3, 4, 35, 2, 3, 4......."

Emil released one of his many CDs, *Wonderful World of Percussion*, in 1995, and I gave a copy to *Daily News* jazz guru Nels Nelson. The disc featured acoustic layers of a whole universe of percussion instruments, some more experiments in sounds than tunes, and Nels got its message enthusiastically.

"The disc is a technological *tour de force* that, in turn, had struck me dumb, evokes gales of laughter and, lastly, set me to twirling like a dervish around my normally sedate living room," said Nelson.

He mentioned one of Emil's comments: "There is validity in these old organic sounds that have existed for centuries, and I pride myself with having most of them. Of course, 'way down deep in the bush of New Guinea there may be others, but......."

That CD included the incredible rhythmic classic "Underdog Rag," named after his own publishing company; I found 15 years later that Philadelphia Orchestra percussionist Chris Deviney had the music to that amazing piece. Hint to gifted players: it's in 7/4 time.

Another session was *Star Trek 4*, taking the Enterprise crew back in time to San Francisco to save the whales from being hunted to extinction. The composer was Leonard Rosenman, who wrote a typically thick and complex score, not one a layman would hum.

I usually stayed behind Emil and his fellow percussionists, and this time Margie went into the booth, where she could watch the screen to imagine what was going on. After a while I could see director Leonard Nimoy enter the booth, and gesture if he could also sit on the couch. She would have loved to give him one of those Vulcan waves though she knew that, on the lot, you leave the stars alone. I went in after a while, followed by the producer, who said the music was crap and they should get someone else to do it. Nimoy calmly said that it was just fine, and eventually the producer left. By this time, Nimoy probably wouldn't have done the film if he didn't have enough creative control to avoid being pushed around by some producer, especially the one who had worn Jerry Goldsmith out on the first *Star Trek*.

Since the days of studios with movies shot on the back lot and full orchestras on the payroll, things have gotten much more difficult for film composers, since a few, like Jerry Goldsmith, were able to write quickly—-and therefore everyone else has to. Now, a composer doesn't begin the score until the movie is cut and the 'music editor' has figured out where the music goes. There is usually only six or eight weeks to write the music, have it scored and recorded.

Most composers like John Williams write their scores out in five staves and dictate individual parts and solos. There's still plenty of orchestration to be done by a trusted colleague, though much of it is already notated; the composer only hears the final product at the session. Emil says that one reason Williams is revered by the studio players is that, when he asks for changes during their rehearsal read-throughs, he doesn't ask for the cue to be played, assuming they'll make the adjustments for the recording. It's a matter of respect, especially since these are the best sight readers on the planet.

Before his film-scoring fame, John Williams had arranged many LPs while playing piano in the studios. Among some uncredited work was the out-of-tune piano in the film adaptation of Hemingway's *Adventures of a Young Man* and, much more familiar, the piano part in Henry Mancini's *Peter Gunn* TV music.

When John Williams came to conduct the Orchestra at the Mann, we had a most pleasant conversation. I reminded him that I was the person who had sent Emil the package of Tibetan CDs and cassettes to play for John at the instrument warehouse, helping them select instruments played in that 1997 film *Seven Years In Tibet*.

Since he has scored Steven Speilberg's films for almost forty years, I asked if that long association means he receives more time to compose. Surprisingly, he said no, he still receives the same eight weeks. The only exception was in *Close Encounters of the Third Kind*, with its long final sequence actually cut to the pre-recorded music. That score has a special place in Williams' heart, though he later said his favorite was, "Probably *E.T.*"

Once in Japan, Emil picked up an unusual metal instrument, with a different shape than he had ever seen before. He always wondered what to call it, seeing only Japanese characters on the underside. He finally showed it to a Japanese acquaintance, hoping for some kind of musically-symbolic name. The translation: "17-inch gong."

The late James Horner, of *Titanic* fame and titanic fame for it, once came to Emil's studio with a DAT recorder and recorded some instruments for sampling. That meant if Emil had a gong from some exotic country, that he had to buy, get through customs, store and maintain, Horner could sample that sound and use that instrument's timbre, playing it in any key on his synthesizer. He was asked to leave and the word got around, with some players highly annoyed. Even though Emil got rental and doubles for playing these instruments, the other musicians are sympathetic to how much expense went into acquiring them, maintaining them—and being able to play them all.

Another session we went to in 1995 was for the first *Toy Story*. I was amazed to see a gigantic orchestra, including four tubas and a couple of guys standing on chairs playing contrabass clarinets. Since this was supposed to be just a cartoon movie, I asked why it needed such a huge orchestra and Emil said, "Ask Randy." I approached composer Randy Newman, who was looking at music about three inches from his eyeglasses and standing next to a man with a Disney badge, to ask him.

"You know why?" he said, making sure the suit heard him. "Because Disney is so miserable and cheap, nobody takes the job unless they can use as many players as will fit in the studio!" The Disney guy made a serious face and walked away.

I remember this session well because I sat between Emil and Don Williams, one of John Williams' two timpani-playing brothers. Mentioning that I was from Philadelphia, Don said he was going to audition for the open timpani job in Philly, until he heard that Don Liuzzi was also in the running and figured he'd save the air fare. I remember telling this to the brilliant Liuzzi after he got the job, and he was most pleased in his humble way.

Emil and Joe Porcaro made a DVD, with some of the greatest studio players, which was a revelation. On one trip, I attended one of Emil's big-band gigs, featuring some of those heavy studio players flaming through some great charts. Near the end, an announcer gave all the musicians' names. When he said, "Emil Richards on vibes," somebody yelled, "Emil Richards IS vibes!"

Hollywood Insights

One of the strange things about soundstage sessions is that the musicians have no connection to the film at all. The players are in walled-off areas in a giant room, with a screen behind them that only the conductor can see. When film is rolled, often a black-and-white working print, a white stripe comes from the left and when it hits the right margin, the downbeat arrives.

Since the music is played in small sections, and is usually out of sequence, it's hard for the players to figure what's happening in the movie, even when they turn to find out if it's a cartoon, a Western, or a drama. I found that Emil and his wife Celeste enjoy seeing the films later, to see how the music fits. It's a little eerie to watch a film when it comes out and, at random moments, hear music that's suddenly familiar.

In 1974, Emil told me about an album he had made called *Come to the Meadow* with pianist Roger Kellaway, bassist Chuck Domanico and cellist Edgar Lustgarten, with the mellowness of the sound all derived from wood instruments. I was captivated by this record, as was my daughter Lisa, who has loved the sound of the cello ever since. Emil mentioned that Lustgarten had actually played with the NBC Symphony under Arturo Toscanini on one visit, and he introduced me to the gracious musician and his wife Kathleen, also a studio cellist, at dinner before an evening session.

Concidences that have continued to crop up in my travels, some too bizarre to even sound fictional, continually astonish me. The next morning, Emil was to pick me up on Hollywood Boulevard near the Roosevelt Hotel where I was staying. While waiting, I wandered down to Larry Edmonds' shop, famous for Hollywood memorabilia, posters, books and other fan stuff. I happened to notice, on top of a pile of 8" x 10" glossies, a great photo of the leggy Cyd Charisse in one of those killer outfits that seduced Gene

Kelly, Fred Astaire and the rest of the open-mouthed male species. I had to have it and, while just hanging around on the sidewalk, went through a browser bin of books while waiting. Way in the back behind screenplays, film history and biographies was a green-bound book with nothing on the spine. I pulled it out and it said *NBC Symphony, 1954*. Astounded, I flipped through the book and, sure enough, there was a full-page photo of young cellist Edgar Lustgarten.

When Emil came, I begged him to snag another meal with Ed and Kathleen and, as it turned out, we went to the commissary at Universal for lunch. Almost jumping with excitement, I finally showed the book to Ed, who was utterly floored. "Where did you get this?" he roared. "I never saw one of these, it was only for the board and executives." It was an unusual moment, something that could only be imagined as destined to occur.

After the afternoon session, Emil had to go and deal with transporting some of his instruments for an upcoming session, and I just went back into the commissary for a coffee. Five minutes later, a little bit down the table on the other side, walked—of all people in the world—Cyd Charisse with another woman, who were working on a *Murder, She Wrote* episode. They nodded hello, and went on with their snack, and I impulsively pulled the 8" x 10" out of its envelope and laid it on the table—pointing a little in their direction. When she finished and stood up, she noticed the photograph, and said the same thing as Edgar—"Where did you get this?" I told her I carried it around wherever I went, just in case she would appear and, luckily, she found that amusing. Posted on my bulletin board is that photo marked, "To Tom, My best, Cyd Charisse." On this chance, Jimmy the Greek would not consider giving odds.

Another wonderful musician Emil introduced to me was flutist Louise DiTullio, with whom I was familiar through an LP of sonatas played by Louise and her pianist sister Virginia. A protégé of Sheridon Stokes, the famous flutist from Alfred Newman's Fox orchestra, she has played the flute solo in over 1100 films over the last 40 years.

"I left a symphony job because I wanted the variety," said Di Tullio one day in the commissary, "but your tryout better be the best, because you only get one chance out here." Columbia Records had used the studio players as the Columbia Symphony Orchestra, and just made the Brahms Symphonies with Bruno Walter, and had decided to record the complete music of Stravinsky with the composer conducting, because he lived in Beverly Hills.

"Well, I didn't know what the session was, whether it would be a record, TV, movie or commercial job," said Di Tullio. "That morning, they tell me it's the first session with Igor Stravinsky, and we'd be doing *Petrouchka*. I had never played it, though I knew it started with a long flute solo, and there were only a few minutes to go. Talk about pressure! Stravinsky walked in and we started the rehearsal, and after a while he stopped and nodded, 'Very good.' I thought, thank you, God and Mr. Stravinsky, I still have a career." She still is the prime session flutist, a delightful woman with a charming and open personality. A recent CD of music written by many of the great composers with her in mind, *The Hollywood Flute*, was produced by my pal Jeannie Pool.

Though a few of the Stravinsky works had already been done for Columbia elsewhere, like the ballets *Orpheus* and *Apollo* with the CBC Orchestra of Canada, almost all were done by the studio players. Several musicians told me that the final session was the ballet *Le Baiser de la Fee* (*The Fairy's Kiss*) and that the first half took longer than expected. The Columbia representative came in after the afternoon break and said there were only 25 minutes left in this final session, meaning that the last half, on the second side of the LP, was completely sightread. You can hardly tell.

At a wrap event, someone mentioned how satisfying it must have been for Stravinsky to have recorded ever piece of music he had ever written. Emil heard him say that wasn't completely true: when he was writing *Les Noces*, a depiction of a Russian wedding, after WW1 in Morges, Switzerland, he wrote the first two of four tableaux for the unusual combination of two cimbaloms, harmonium and pianola, although it is usually presented in a chamber orchestra or four-piano format. Emil asked him if he'd record it if the instruments could be assembled, because he had played music on a cimbalom he kept in his living room. Eventually, Columbia scheduled a recording by the composer at SUNY in Stony Brook, New York, and it appears as an addendum on the LP.

Emil played on that recording, and Stravinsky gave him a signed photograph thanking him for his efforts in bringing the piece to life after all those years. He asked Stravinsky why he composed for that odd combination of instruments, certainly limiting performance. Stravinsky just said that those were the sounds he heard in his head. He also told Emil that he had rented each of the instruments, and learned how to play them, before composing. This was a stunner, and a story that Emil has told many students about the depth of preparation that true music-making must entail.

David Raksin

On one visit, Emil suggested I go and visit the master composer David Raksin, who had a legendary cachet in Hollywood. The composer of *Laura, The Bad and the Beautiful* (which many consider the greatest of all film themes), *Forever Amber*, and a long list of 450-plus fabled scores for film and television, welcomed me as a pal of Emil at this home. The next day we went to his favorite spot, Musso and Frank's on Hollywood Boulevard, an old-fashioned spot since the 1920s, and sat in a banquette in the booth where "he used to eat lunch with Charlie." Of course, he meant Charlie Chaplin, at that time the most famous person on earth.

David was a Philadelphian whose father played lower reeds as a sub with the Philadelphia Orchestra under Leopold Stokowski. He studied music at the University of Pennsylvania with Harl McDonald, played clarinet and had a dance band that played on riverboats, sometimes for the mob. According to David, who had more stories than anyone imaginable, he had to compose a new work as a graduation piece, and knocked out a Concertino for clarinet and strings the night before. At the performance, he threw in a long jazz improvisation as cadenza before the finale. Afterwards, the grumpy department head groused, "I've heard it played better!"

Oscar Levant heard David's arrangement of "I Got Rhythm" and showed it to George Gershwin, leading to a job scoring for Broadway shows. When Stokowski needed a gofer during the filming of *100 Men and a Girl* featuring the Philadelphia Orchestra (which stayed home) and Deanna Durbin, he took David, eventually introducing him to Charlie Chaplin—who needed someone to write the music for his *Modern Times*. Though Chaplin wanted fast music for the fabulous sequence where the Little Tramp gets caught in the gears of the assembly line, Raksin thought it would make it look like a cartoon, and suggested slow music. Chaplin fired him—until he talked it over with the wise Alfred Newman at Fox, who felt that Raksin was right. How this brash youngster had such good instincts is astounding, costing him four more firings before Chaplin trusted him enough to let him alone.

Along the way, Raksin studied with Arnold Schoenberg (there's a great photo of Chaplin, Schoenberg and Mrs. Schoenberg, and the cocky Raksin), and made an arrangement of *Circus Polka* for Stravinsky.

After years of what he called "grue and horror" flicks, a period when composers were supposed to be yes-men to know-nothing producers (David called his liaison Hinge-Head), he finally got a job at Fox, finding on Monday morning that he was fired since Alfred Hitchcock had decided there would be no music in the picture. There was a heated dialogue until Hitchcock, speaking about the film *Lifeboat*, roared, "There's no music in the Atlantic Ocean."

David Raksin.

Raksin's famous response: "Show me where there's a camera in the Atlantic Ocean, and I'll show you where there's music." Hitchcock still dismissed Raksin—eventually hiring Hugo Friedhofer to do the music.

For 1944's *Laura*, director Otto Preminger initially wanted to use Jerome Kern's "Smoke Gets in Your Eyes" or George Gershwin's "Summertime;" when they were unavailable, he insisted on Duke Ellington's "Sophisticated Lady" for the film noir *Laura*, and Raksin felt it was all wrong.

Given a Monday morning deadline to come up with an alternative, Raksin spent the weekend working without success—until he received a letter from his wife. He put it on the music stand for inspiration, not realizing she was writing from New York to ask for a divorce. He always swore that the theme for *Laura* poured out as he read the letter.

Hollywood composers are well paid for their scores, though the music is owned by the studio. In 1946, bandleader Woody Herman decided he'd like to sing the tune, and asked Raksin if he'd let the master wordsmith Johnny Mercer write some lyrics. Publishing it as a song meant enormous royalties for "Laura," recorded in more versions—vocal and jazz—than almost any other song. Cole Porter once said that "Laura" was the one song he regretted not writing.

Raksin's other scores included *The Secret Life of Walter Mitty*, *Separate Tables*, *Force of Evil* and *Suddenly*. His TV music catalog included *Wagon Train*, *Ben Casey* and *Medical Center*, as well as many more.

In later years, Raksin turned to concert music, teaching at USC, hosting a radio show about film music, and heading both the Society for the Preservation of Film Music and the Society of Composers and Lyricists.

Raksin's music was complex, brilliantly written and always perfectly matched to the screen image. He was at his best when collaborating—as with producer John Houseman, director Vincente Minnelli and actor Kirk Douglas on *The Bad and the Beautiful*—and had an unerring instinct for what worked with the visuals, a completely different skill than composing. He was one of the most fascinating, gifted and beloved figures in Hollywood for over 60 years, one of its true legends.

David once invited me to a 1989 concert at New York's Avery Fisher Hall to celebrate film music, a benefit for the Sundance Insititute. Maurice Jarre, Hanry Mancini and many more attended, and I was stunned to see the tiny George Delerue clamber upon the piano bench and immediately play his piano theme from the Francis Truffaut classic *Shoot the Piano Player*, proof to me that he had played it himself for the soundtrack.

David went up to conduct "Laura" and afterwards, as I broke for intermission and walked back down the center aisle, I found myself looking into the face of the seated Catherine Deneuve, who was used to people being struck into gasps and sweetly smiled.

Ten years later, he let me know he was going to appear at Joe's Pub in New York, where he proved his skill as a raconteur was on the same high level as his scoring.

Once, music by Morton Gould, composer and longtime president of ASCAP, was played at the Mann Music Center, and we were introduced. "Mr. Gould," I said, "I'm happy to meet you, the second most underappreciated American composer." "Who's first?" he asked. "Why, David Raksin!" Gould's reply: "Damn straight!"

Raksin had close ties to the Library of Congress, and the organization published a huge book, *Wonderful Inventions*, about the history of film, with two thin records inside featuring his music.

In 1986, he was commissioned by the Library of Congress in Washington to write a piece, *Oedipus Memnitai* (*Oedipus remembers*) for chamber orchestra and voices. A great number of famous contemporary composers attended, among them Milton Babbitt, Gunther Schuller, and many others. In facing displays in the hallway outside the theater were Raksin's original scores to *Laura* and *The Bad and the Beautiful* as well as, on the opposite wall, a loaned copy from Germany of Bach's Orchestral Suite No. 4. When Raksin came out and saw a crowd clustered around his legendary scores, he shouted, "Come on, people, get serious, that's J. S. Bach!"

Raksin was perhaps the greatest storyteller I've ever known, perhaps because he had met everyone through the glory days of Hollywood. The first time I met him he was talking on the phone to Simon Rattle, who had led the Los Angeles Chamber Orchestra early in his career. In 2009, though Rattle didn't like to do interviews, he agreed to meet with me in his hotel room, where we told David stories for an hour.

There were many, like being one of the few people who could be friends with the famously irascible Bernard Herrmann, who he called the "prince of unspecific anger." Evidently, once at a party, Herrmann had told the crowd how Raksin had no talent, and someone mentioned it to him. Raksin said that he paid no attention, because the week before Herrmann had told *The Bad and the Beautiful* producer John Houseman that Raksin was the only person with enough skill to write the score. (The brilliant Oscar-winning film about the dark side of Hollywood was originally titled *Tribute to a Bad Man*, changed by Houseman who thought it sounded too much like a Western.)

He often said, "Film composers are like embalmers. We're supposed to make an ugly corpse look good." He was right, and even Steven Spielberg has admitted that music represents half of a film's impact.

He also explained to me that many people can write music, though an instinctive sense for knowing what type of music will work in a particular sequence represents a completely different skill. In addition, he often mentioned that, even though the studio heads were complete ignoramuses about anything artistic, there was an advantage to the studio system, where everything was shot on the back lot. The fact that virtually all movies (except some Westerns) were shot on the set meant that a composer could see what a film was about, write music for it, and have the 80-piece studio orchestra play sections of it for the director. That way, by the time the film wrapped, the score had been discussed and possibly already completed.

Now virtually ever film is shot on location and, after a film has been completely edited, a composer sees it for the first time and has eight weeks to score and record it.

Raksin was very proud of a score called *The Redeemer*, though it was never released; it was based on an extended film about the final days of Jesus, made in Spain about by the Catholic Church for television. In 1959 it was decided to cut it severely to 89 minutes for foreign distribution, and the producers asked David to write a new score. In a long sequence showing Christ, carrying the cross on the way to Calvary, Raksin claimed to be influenced by Bach, writing incredibly moving music. Because of bureaucratic intrigue the film was never released in America, and he never heard the soundstage score again; it was played once by a pickup orchestra and recorded by an amateur, providing all that Raksin had to remember the project. He once gave me a copy, still played with reverence.

In June 2000, Raksin came back to Philadelphia— for the first time in 40 years—to accept a Hall of Fame award as an alumnus of Central High School. He asked if I would be his driver and guide to do some research on the memoir he was working on. It resulted in three hilarious days, visiting the three houses where he grew up: the Jewish pushcard neighborhood of Marshall Street below Girard (we discovered a book written about that very block), Natrona Street near 33rd and Columbia and on Wynnefield Avenue in Overbrook. We found that a recalled Maxfield Parrish mural had been moved from the Penn sculling building on Boathouse Row where they had played dance gigs. Those days included his delight in again encountering scrapple, visiting the Thomas Eakins paintings at the Philadelphia Museum of Art, eating at Girasole and laughing a lot, once necessitating my pulling the car over to the shoulder.

Several years before, organist Keith Chapman, who played the famous Wanamaker organ at the store in Philadelphia, had been killed in a plane crash, and Marc Mostovoy had been given his musical papers. One item was Raksin's score to a piece for organ and orchestra, *A Song After Sundown*, commissioned in 1982 for the American Guild of Organists convention in San Francisco, with Chapman as soloist. Marc knew of my friendship, and gave me the orchestral score as a keepsake. I showed it to Raksin during his visit, and he said that the parts were somehow lost after the performance, and that it would never receive another one. The music was again used as the middle movement of a work for clarinetist Eddie Daniels and a string quartet called *Swing Low, Sweet Clarinet*, played at the Santa Fe Chamber Music Festival and recorded later by another group.

The Philadelphia Youth Orchestra played every year at my son's church in Germantown, and always performing a piece for organ and orchestra. It seemed like a remote possibility, though conductor Joseph Primavera wasn't interested in it. In time, I showed the score to Kile Smith at the Fleisher Collection, who was greatly impressed by Raksin's obvious harmonic gift, though not much could be done without the parts.

Not then, anyway.

Two Giants Lost

I wrote David's obituary after his death in 2004 at the age of 92; his birthday was the day after mine. It was not surprising to learn that he had also been the president of the Composers and Lyricists Guild, and a board member of ASCAP and the Library of Congress National Film Preservation Board. But I admit to being amazed to find that, besides teaching composition at the University of Southern California, he also taught urban ecology from 1968 to 1989 in USC's School of Public Administration.

The month before, the musical world had lost the prolific composer Jerry Goldsmith and, one month after David, I had to write one more obit, this about Elmer Bernstein.

The composer of such diverse works as the jazz-based *The Man with the Golden Arm*, the tender, graceful score for *To Kill A Mockingbird*, the Western-theme standard *The Magnificent Seven* (used for years in Marlboro cigarette ads) and the epic *Ten Commandments*. Bernstein, who had studied with Aaron Copland, also authored *Sweet Smell of Success*, and *Walk on the Wild Side*; music for the comedies *Airplane*, *Trading Places* and *Ghostbusters*; and the superbly romantic 1993 *The Age of Innocence*.

Bernstein tended to work best with dramatic screen adaptations like *Birdman of Alcatraz*, *My Left Foot* and *The Rainmaker* yet also had the flexibility to compose the scary music for Michael Jackson's *Thriller* video.

Martin Scorsese, director of *The Age of Innocence*, said: "It's one thing to write music that reinforces a film, underscores it or gives it added dramatic muscle. It's entirely another to write music that graces a film, and that, for me, is Elmer's greatest gift."

Bernstein once told me, "The purpose of music in a dramatic film is to give an emotional experience, even if the audience doesn't even realize that the music is deeply affecting them." He said he never trusted the script, only the final movie, and always asked the filmmaker to describe "what we wanted the audience to feel."

In Emil's book, there's a paragraph that demonstrates Bernstein's clout:

"Elmer did not like the 'powers that be' to come on the soundstage when we were recording and bother him with musical changes. On many occasions the director or producer would stop the recording, as they do on most composers' scoring, and want to make immediate changes right on the spot. Elmer would say, "Gentlemen, you hired me to write the score, and I have written a score. Please allow me the opportunity to record the score you hired me to write, and if you don't like the finished product, you can pay me for my efforts and then I will listen to your new, or changed, opinion." It was an approach I never saw another composer take."

Preserving Film Music

Raksin suggested my getting involved with the Society for the Preservation of Film Music, mentioning that he was its current president, and put me in touch with the executive director, Jeannie Pool. That led to a host of annual conferences honoring such composers as Alex North, Ennio Morricone, John Williams, Jerry Goldsmith, Maurice Jarre and Lalo Schifrin, with Elmer Bernstein taking over the presidency years later.

The object of the Society was to discover and care for these precious original scores, placing them in college libraries and available for study. Many had been lost—for instance, when MGM was sold in 1967, the building housing all those historic scores and parts was simply burned down.

Some of these conferences featured fascinating lectures, and in one case an astonishing film called *The Covered Wagon* (1927), shot with snow, river crossings and hundreds of extras and animals, was shown with a live orchestra playing the original score.

One of the last conferences featured composer Hans Salter, a small, formal man who had studied with the Viennese School giants like Alban Berg and Franz Schreker before escaping the Nazis—as many of the great film composers did. When he arrived in Hollywood, the only job was at Universal Studios, in those days cranking out cheesy black-and-white monster pictures for the Saturday-afternoon kid crowd. Salter, who possessed enormous orchestrational skills, wrote terrifying music making these low-budget flicks with rubber monsters huge hits. In *The Mummy* and various *Wolfman* epics, his music was enormously effective. When the British company Hammer Pictures began to remake horror films in color, Universal went for broke with the final *House Of Frankenstein*, featuring the Mad Doctor, Frankenstein, the Wolfman, the Mummy and Dracula all running around inside the same house. Salter, with his feet in the Wagnerian tradition, had formal motifs for each character, and altered them throughout to give clues to the sad monster, or the menacing Wolfman, including one dodecaphonic cue called *Liquefying Brains*. Salter said that he was very fortunate, because he was the only composer in Hollywood who wasn't told what to do by producers, because he was making them a fortune. Ironically, the first picture he scored after leaving Universal was called *The Strange Death of Adolph Hitler*! He was soon able to write for less political flicks like *The Creature from the Black Lagoon* and *The Incredible Shrinking Man*.

Several of the conferences were held in New York in association with NYU's film school, with Stephen Sondheim (who had written the script and score for the thriller *The Last of Sheila*) and Japanese composer Toru Takemitsu as honorees. At an opulent American Express site, Takemitsu spoke through an interpreter about his experience at film scoring. Suddenly he became noticeably intense amidst the students, waving the interpreter away and expressing—in English— how lucky they were to have training, because there's no such opportunity in Japan, and that he had just been blessed with luck.

At one conference, the late composer Nino Rota was also honored, and his elegant daughter Nina Rota was in attendance. On the way to a luncheon at CBS, we walked to 56th Street and 8th Avenue, and I noticed a college-age hot dog vendor inspecting her large nametag and grinding his mental wheels. Just as we were about to cross, he sang the theme from *The*

Godfather and received a big smile and a wave. We asked her if it bothered her that her father, who had written five operas, symphonies, concertos and all kinds of concert music, should only be remembered for that one film, but she was very happy that he was remembered at all.

Also in attendance were offspring of famed composers Franz Waxman, Jerome Moross and Bernard Herrmann, discussing the difficulties in assembling and promoting their scores, now riding a crest of increased interest in the great era of film music.

Of course, Raksin presided, staying in New York with his friend, the musician, author and musical encyclopedia Nicolas Slonimsky, who was too ill to attend. At a dinner after the conference with Jeannie Pool, Raksin arrived with his daughter Elektra Slonimsky, whose birth had meant the end of her parents speaking only in Latin. She turned out to be hilarious and wonderfully gracious; when she and David found out it was Margie's birthday, she was serenaded by some remarkable talents.

At a New York conference in 1995, we met Kile Smith, composer and curator of Philadelphia's famous Fleisher Collection of Orchestral Music, now a close friend. Kile had discovered a misfiled score by George Antheil, the Trenton-born 'Bad Boy of Music', who had composed the score to a film about future technology for the 1940 World's Fair on Long Island. The film was stored in the Library of Congress, with the score thought lost; it was swiftly recorded, so the film could be played at the conference with its original music for the first time in almost 60 years. The Library of Congress has transferred the original film to video, perhaps spurring orchestras to play this music Smith had unearthed. Before the simplistic, oddly preachy film about the development of modern technology, Smith spoke with scholarship and drollness on its history as well as Antheil's legendary contrariness.

Pool is not only a renowned author, composer and conductor, but made a remarkable film entitled *Peggy Gilbert and her All-Girl Band*, the famous female band of the 1920s and 1930s. In 2014, she finished orchestrating an opera about stops on the Underground Railroad by African-American composer Zenobia Powell Perry called *Tawawa House*, and produced a staging by Townsend Opera in Modesto, California.

She once received a call from Paramount, with concerns about the boxes of music in the Crosby Building, needed for office space. Since Henry Mancini's widow Ginny was on the Society's board, and was a good friend of Paramount head Sherry Lansing, the Society was given permission to inspect the rooms of boxed scores. It turned out that the building was full of them, scattered all over the building with a leaky roof; volunteers assembled the scores, parts and cue sheets into special paper. After many months of work, it was thought that the scores would be distributed to libraries, though after completion Paramount decided that they would remain on the lot. Jeannie was made head of the Paramount archive with its 6,000 boxes of scores, going through the tedious task of cataloguing all their details onto computer. As will be mentioned later on, Jeannie was able to unearth the score for the first film to win an Oscar.

17. HAPPENINGS IN PHILLY

In the scramble for involvement in the new Regional Performing Arts Center (RPAC), or Kimmel Center, many of the organizations staked their claim. Of course the Philadelphia Orchestra, as well as Peter Nero and the Philly Pops, would be the main occupants of the 2,500 seat hall, eventually known as Verizon Hall.

In the small 650-seat Perelman Theater, presentations would be given by the Concerto Soloists Chamber Orchestra (soon to be the Chamber Orchestra of Philadelphia), the Philadelphia Chamber Music Society and the American Theater Arts For Youth. That latter group would give plays for children during the day on its stage, reversed on a turntable for concerts.

The Academy of Music would be the province of the Opera Company of Philadelphia and Pennsylvania Ballet, with the open dates to be booked with acts of Broadway shows.

Of course, there was great interest in having a minority ensemble in the center, with the obvious one being the celebrated African-American dance company Philadanco. My story said that, because of their tenuous financial situation and their inability to pay the high rent, a special agreement was made that the center would act for the first three years "as Philadanco's presenter, providing the theater space and advertising, and paying the company a fee to perform." With this agreement, Philadanco became the center's first official resident company.

The next day, Saturday, in a story ran in the *Philadelphia Inquirer*, the Kimmel Center's media relations director was quoted as saying, "Philadanco does not get any of the ticket fees while they perform at RPAC." That was certainly true; I had said Philadanco would receive a set payment for performing, not the ticket fees which would go to the presenter. The article said that "a *Philadelphia Daily News* story published yesterday reporting that the company would be paid by the arts center to perform was not correct."

I heard about it only because of a telephone call from the *Daily News'* editor Michael Days, who wanted to know if "our" story was accurate. Hearing from Michael, to whom my relationship had consisted of passing hellos, signalled a need to check my facts, given to me by Joan Myers Brown. In a call to the company's West Philadelphia office (on Philadanco Way), I found that she, and the troupe, were on tour in San Diego. Through someone in the hotel where they were staying, it seemed like a dead end since they were shopping at a nearby mall.

Just on a lark, I called the mall and asked that Brown be paged and, to my amazement, Brown eventually came to the phone. After expressing surprise, she listened to my concerns and asked me to fax my story, and the *Inquirer* story, to the Kinko's in the mall, after I obtained an *Inquirer* from the nearest coin machine.

A few minutes later I got a call from Joan, who I had known for years. "Tom," she said, "here's my statement. We don't pay to perform, not no way, not nohow, not never, not for free, period. They're presenting us. Does that help?"

Sure did, Joan. I called Michael, and asked him if he wanted a clarification story for Monday. "No thanks," he said, "I just wanted to make sure our story was right."

Time for Transition

Marc Mostovoy created an ensemble in 1964 called Sixteen Concerto Soloists, with each member soloing during the season, altering the name for a few years to the Concerto Soloists Chamber Orchestra. In preparing for the transition to the Kimmel Center, Mostovoy renamed the ensemble the Chamber Orchestra of Philadelphia, named Ignat Solzhenitsyn principal conductor and Jeri Lynne Johnson assistant conductor.

Founder Mostovoy, who had provided work throughout the year for the pool of musicians, thought it was time to step down from the podium. Little did Mostovoy realize that his appointments, and a new executive director, would reward his longevity with the intention of completely ousting him.

As the first season concert with Solzhenitsyn on the podium, it appeared similar to a player-manager pitching a triple-header. That described Solzhenitsyn playing, and conducting, the Bach A Major harpsichord concerto, the Haydn D Major Piano Concerto and the Mozart Piano Concerto No. 9.

Two Major Voices

It was good fortune to have met Eric Owens at the beginning of his enormous career with the Met and all over the world, yet he has remained as gracious and funny as ever. He was virtually a neighbor, from Mount Airy, who called himself the "music geek" in junior high; at 12, his life changed when he heard the powerful voices and ravishing music of opera on a Saturday afternoon Met radio broadcast.

Owens was back home to sing Sarastro in the Opera Company's production of *The Magic Flute*. He had studied oboe at Settlement Music School, jumping on Saturday afternoons from rehearsals with Joseph Primavera's Philadelphia Youth Orchestra to Settlement legend Shirley Curtiss' woodwind groups in the afternoon, as well as doing gigs around town. After winning the Philadelphia Orchestra's annual Greenfield auditions as a singer, followed by performing Mozart with them and playing oboe with Luis Biava's Temple Symphony, his singing blossomed at Temple and eventually at Curtis Institute, where he would bump into visiting musical giants in the halls.

Eric Owens.

After he had won the 1996 Placido Domingo Competition in Bordeaux, and played the assassin Sparafucile in Los Angeles Opera's controversial Bruce Beresford production of Verdi's *Rigoletto* (moving the story from Mantua to Hollywood), I asked about that show and any barriers incurred by an African-American singer.

Eric Owens:

It's always a good thing to have already done a role, to know the basic choreography, to bring things that have worked before, but to do the same production, how boring is that?

These days, I believe that only ability counts. You never know why you weren't chosen, but if there has been a case where I was discriminated against, I don't know about it. Let me give an example of opportunity—last year I sang the King of Scotland in Handel's Ariodante *at the English National Opera.*

Concerts are instant gratification, while operas require four to five weeks of rehearsal. Being on the same plateau as the orchestra, sitting in front of the cellos, is its own reward, and they're even paying me besides.

I still sometimes pinch myself and say, 'I'm really up here doing these parts. The first live opera I ever saw was in 1984, with Nelly Miracoiou in Manon. *And last year I found myself singing* Norma *at Covent Garden with Nelly. What a moment that was!* (Academy of Music, February 10, 2001)

Mezzo-soprano Rinat Shaham, now a major star, considered Philadelphia a haven fifteen years ago. She grew up in a musical family in Haifa, Israel, but resented the necessary discipline in piano studies and found an outlet in improvisation; she enrolled in a singing class when a high school drama class took too long to become formed. Chosen immediately at Curtis by its vocal department head Mikael Eliasen, she sang many roles there and returned to make her debut in the Opera Company's production of *Werther*, portraying the complex character of Charlotte, who marries the safe, acceptable Albert, though her heart throbs for the title character.

Rinat Shaham:

It takes one to know one. Like me, she has coyness, shyness and fragility, but feels real passion and love as the opera goes on. She's too weak and also too strong, preferring not to take a chance and go against tradition, rules, religion. We are all scared, passion controls us, but she pays in the end, fighting herself to be that good girl like the Oprah concept of the Mother Ship.

You should know what it is about—sex, love, passion, loss—before you sing about it. I know about desolation, and can connect on that level with the audience with emotions that are sometimes hidden. Opera is just one of the colors of the rainbow. I have to be careful with my passion, to pace myself and avoid burning out really fast, but I'd rather do that than spend 50 years singing things I don't want to sing. (Academy of Music, March 10, 2001)

It's in the Grove

One real break came with an opportunity to review the second edition of the *New Grove Dictionary of Music and Musicians*, a 29-volume, 119-pound set of 29,500 articles selling for a measly $4,850. Astonishingly, they were willing to ship me a hard copy for a review of this musical bible, realizing that only a fraction of a percent of text could possibly be absorbed before any reasonable deadline.

Within a few years, it was assumed the additional graphic and audio capabilities of the burgeoning Internet would make this set the last print version, used in my house countless times.

Later on, I was able to meet and chat again with the editor, the esteemed, charming Stanley Sadie, and vowed not to ask him if Grove felt they got their money's worth.

Gershwin's Masterpiece

The Opera Company finally staged George Gershwin's *Porgy and Bess* in April 2001, and I was allowed a large spread for a capsule background of the opera.

Gershwin had five Broadway hit shows running on the same street in 1932 when he finally agreed to adapt DuBose Heyward's novel *Porgy* into an opera. The labor-of-love project had been discussed for six years, and even Al Jolson's threats to do it in blackface on stage and screen didn't seem to concern the famed composer.

Heyward, from a once-wealthy Charleston, S.C., family, had worked with the Gullah blacks on the docks and developed a comfortable and friendly relationship with those who lived in his neighborhood. As an adult, his insights into their lives, without condescension, pity or irony, made *Porgy* a 1925 best seller because of its first honest look into this closed society.

Porgy was based on Samuel Smalls, a crippled beggar with a goat cart, who hung around Cabbage Row on Church Street, changed by Heyward to Catfish Row by the waterfront. He understood the dialect of the Gullahs, whose name was a shortening of Angola—though many had originally come from Sierra Leone.

When Heyward received a fateful letter of interest from Gershwin in March 1926, his wife Dorothy confessed that she had secretly been working on a play adaptation of *Porgy*. Gershwin saw no conflict, and the Theatre Guild immediately accepted the play, becoming a major success in 1927. Plans were made for a film starring Paul Robeson, until the producers realized it wouldn't play in the South.

After Gershwin got serious about the project in 1932, he visited Charleston several times the following year, attending black church services, weddings, funerals, and a contest of "shouting"—rhythmic patterns beaten out with hands and feet as accompaniment to spirituals—which he won. "George was probably the only white man in America who could have done it," wrote Heyward.

Though Gershwin now had a weekly radio program and producers screaming for more shows, he threw himself into his new project—with Wagner's score to *Die Meistersinger* on the music stand for guidance. Some of the numbers—"It Ain't Necessarily So," for instance—have a tinge of Yiddish theatre song about them, a twang that echoed the same universal cries he heard in South Carolina. Two years later, with Heyward writing the lyrics and his inimitable brother Ira Gershwin polishing them, *Porgy and Bess* was finished.

The Metropolitan Opera offered Gershwin $5,000 for a premiere, though the composer insisted on the Alvin Theatre, hoping for a long Broadway run. And the show's producers, afraid of being upstaged by the all-black *Four Saints In Three Acts* by Virgil Thomson and Gertrude Stein, called it a "folk opera" to avoid scaring away theater patrons.

At the Boston tryouts, the show received a 15-minute ovation, though Gershwin immediately agreed to 40 minutes of cuts. Alexander Smallens, assistant to the Philadelphia Orchestra's Leopold Stokowski, conducted; Todd Duncan, who taught at Curtis Institute from 1977 to 1990, was the Porgy, Anne Brown the Bess.

Porgy and Bess opened in New York on Oct. 10, 1935, running 124 performances. Virgil Thomson called it "crooked folklore and halfway opera," and Duke Ellington didn't like it either. It toured the country, with the show almost scuttled in Duncan's home town of Washington when he insisted—and prevailed—that blacks be allowed to sit wherever they wanted.

Gershwin played his Concerto in F with the Philadelphia Orchestra in 1936, followed by Smallens conducting a suite from *Porgy and Bess*. At that time, he said he was certain that someday his deeply-felt creation would be seen as a successful grand opera, not just a show with musical numbers. His sudden death in 1937, at only 38, stunned the musical world, and Heyward would follow three years later; they would never know future versions of their creation would become a beacon of American culture. One of the factors for its dearth of performances is the severe protective control over staging rights by the Gershwin estate.

The Houston Grand Opera's production, the first to ever play the complete work, played six weeks in Philadelphia during 1976. (Their complete recording, and a brilliant excerpt disc with William Warfield and Leontyne Price, are still available on RCA). Fifty years after its opening, and 18 months after Ira Gershwin died in his sleep, the Met finally produced *Porgy and Bess* in 1985, with both Duncan and Brown attending.

Much has been written about the racial aspects of *Porgy*. From letters, notes, and the incredible honesty within this drama and music, it's obvious that Gershwin and Heyward found enormous nobility and beauty in these characters. The denizens of Catfish Row may be poor in wealth, not in spirit. They vibrate with the closeness of family, the pride of community, with aspiration, love, weaknesses, beauty, sorrow, and overriding hope—all of the characteristics that define America.

Stanislavski-trained director Henry Miller, who had never directed *Porgy and Bess*, approached this story of the Gullah people of South Carolina with fresh eyes. His mother was a Gullah—a descendant of slaves who lived on the islands off the Charleston coast—and he says her attitude about life was mystical and her sense of Christianity pragmatic, like Sportin' Life's *It Ain't Necessarily So*.

Miller came to the production at the suggestion of Arthur Woodley, an Opera Company regular who portrayed Porgy. Though he revered Gershwin's ravishing music, he wanted to make the characters more believable than they're portrayed in most productions. In addition, he set the piece in 1911 instead of the 1920s, both to include that year's destructive hurricane and to offer historical perspective of a time when women were more dependent on men.

In a rehearsal of the second scene, where money is being raised for Robbins' funeral, Miller demonstrated his involvement even in minor characters. And when the white sheriff entered and arrests Peter at random, he's usually played as a redneck stereotype; Miller had him do it without passion, as a low-echelon functionary stuck with a thankless chore. I found his comments about this familiar classic very insightful.

Henry Miller:

I consider Bess and Crown to be very complex, physically attractive characters. In the book, Bess has a scar on her face but is sexually charismatic, and Crown is a Bunyanesque character, the type from whom women seek protection, a man cast into a macho role who plays it like a defense. He's almost a male version of Bess.

But they're not star-crossed lovers, they're like brother and sister. Bess would like to be a nice married lady with a child, but Crown knows her too well—she's like a barfly, caught in a society that casts her out.

When the chorus sings, "Oh, the train is in the station and you've gotta get on board, cause it's leavin' today...," often people get happy, jump around, dance off the stage. But since Robbins has just been taken to the funeral parlor, they wouldn't act that way—spiritual is not gospel. Ira Gershwin was saying, the train is the inevitability of life and death, of blues and joy, the tearful, spiritual joy. The chorus, a character with different sides, is singing that's how the universe works.

In many shows, Porgy's not sexual. He may be on his knees, but if we feel sorry for him, it's not interesting dramatically. He's not paralyzed. We can't make Porgy and Crown into monk and devil....

Gershwin set up the drama of the ending up brilliantly, writing a long, calm passage and a recurring boat whistle before the drama of Porgy returning. Because of that, it's perfectly believable that Porgy could take the boat, perhaps it's not just a pipe dream. We're left with hope, that Porgy may really find his Bess. (Academy of Music, April 22, 2001)

Boffo Buffo

A buffo basso usually portrays the crochety, meddlesome and usually hilarious characters who move comic-opera action along. They're sometimes done by over-the-hill singers who fake the difficult, rapid-fire runs requiring accuracy in high registers.

Not when Kevin Glavin's in town. The Pittsburgher is the embodiment of a man who was born to do what he does extremely well. He is a gregarious, larger-than-life character himself, happy with a dish of braciola at D'Angelo's, where he shows up with a long white coat and cigar to host a tableful of friends. At holiday time, he's done a Santa show with the Pittsburgh Symphony and the Buffalo Philharmonic Orchestra, savoring every moment of his good fortune.

After studies in Pittsburgh with Claudia Pinza (Ezio's daughter) and six summers in Italy, Glavin was one of the winners of the 1990 Pavarotti Competition and immediately portrayed Dulcamara in an *Elixir of Love* with Pavarotti.

He was back for another Dulcamara, the quack doctor who sells the hapless small-town bumpkin Nemorino some cheap wine that supposedly will attract the beautiful Adina.

Kevin Glavin:

I remember that first Elixir, *because they found a crack in the Academy of Music ceiling, and we moved to the Cathedral of SS. Peter and Paul. It was pouring rain, and we went on with costumes but without sets. Dulcama-*

ra is a great character, and when he sees all the girls around Nemorino, he thinks for a moment that maybe his stuff really works!

Why would Rossini, Donizetti or Mozart write these incredible virtuoso pieces if he didn't want someone to sing them well? Lots of basses can't do this role, too many high Es. I love the comedy, the great music, and being able to act and make people understand the patter. Characters have to come from a real person, otherwise it's just schtick, and you have to make the audience like them. The trick is to make the situations funny.

Opera singers have to remember that's it's not about them. If you have a gift, you're supposed to share the character with the audience and bring them in. When you do, then you know you have a good thing going. (Academy of Music, October 7, 2011)

Be Ready to Go On

So many stories have to do with cancellations, and artists who are ready to take advantage of it. André Watts has had to cancel on several occasions, giving the spotlight to many, like Lang Lang. He must still remember filling in as a teenager to replace Glenn Gould in a high-visibility 1963 televised concert, launching him into national prominence.

In 1993, a flu forced a Watts cancellation, with a few music lovers still showing up at the Academy of Music to hear his replacement, the 20-year-old Taiwan-born Meng-Chieh Liu. That night was only a month before his graduation from Curtis Institute, where he was immediately accepted into the rarefied Curtis piano faculty.

In 1996, Liu suffered a near-fatal bout with a serious viral illness. Doctors couldn't seem to find the cause for this completely debilitating virus; after several years, it miraculously vanished. Luckily, the fates had decided there was much more for this gifted musician to give us.

In 2001, Curtis graduate and renowned pianist Lee Luvisi was forced to cancel, and once again Liu was willing to be a last-minute replacement. I didn't want to miss that concert, made up completely of knuckle-busting transcriptions of Bach by Busoni, Schubert by Liszt, Strauss Jr. by Godowsky, Fritz Kreisler by Rachmaninoff and even Earl Wild's arrangement of six Gershwin songs.

This pianistic giant, usually behind the scenes and not someone you'd associate with high drama, showed that he overcame a devastating illness with an even greater artistry. Considering the astounding and complex pulses of his chosen repertoire, his final "I Got Rhythm" spoke volumes.

Good Idea, Bad Business

Around 1990, I was one of several small investors in a business that sounded promising at the time—a used classical/jazz shop that also sold new discs. Named Classical Choice, it opened first in the basement of the University of Pennsylvania's Houston Hall, in University City (in a strip which was razed for a Wharton Business School building), and finally at 21st and Walnut Streets in center city.

Business picked up and we sold CDs all over the world, with obscure labels and unknown repertory received every day. We had CD signings by violinist Pamela Frank and jazz pianist Jimmy Amadie, and began to develop a local following. One of the staff, Alan Kayser, began to bring in jazz acts at local churches. When he moved to Florida, that project was picked up by another Classical Choice employee, Mark Christman, who founded the highly successful Ars Nova Workshop in 2000 and, since then, has revitalized cutting-edge jazz in venues all over the city.

About the time we actually began to see a profit, around 2000, some other investors, evidently much wiser in business matters, suddenly needed a loss and closed the store, ending my naive business career.

One of my investor pals was *Daily News* writer Howard Gensler, who now writes the hot column *Tattle*, honoring readers with the inside story about celebrities evidently known by everyone but me. When submitting some movie pitches, he saw a piece about an Englishman who had invented the first vibrator in 1880, and threw it in as a lark. Of course, that one caught an independent producer's eye and, though someone else wrote the screenplay, Howard's idea became the hilarious film *Hysteria*, with Maggie Gyllenhaal, Rupert Everett and Hugh Dancy, and Howard visited some of the movie's filming in London.

Podium Insights

For her first podium assignment, the Chamber Orchestra's newly-named assistant conductor Jeri Lynne Johnson accompanied four soloists in the ensemble's annual competition.

Johnson had been a cum laude student and conductor at Wellesley College, studied at a University of Chicago graduate program and led summer orchestras at Aspen.

Jeri Lynne Johnson:

I didn't expect Marc Mostovoy to hire me, since I didn't go to Curtis or Juilliard. It's a major career step, like going from a Hyundai to a Mercedes, with desire and enthusiasm in these players and no more worrying about whipping an orchestra into shape.

You're taught not to trust yourself when you're younger, but you have to go with your gut, your intuition, your study, and say, that's how I think Mozart wants it to go. Some people feel there's a dichotomy between being a leader and a woman, with the extremes of trying to please everybody and being domineering and inflexible. Sometimes it's a fine line to walk. The ultimate goal is the complete synthesis between you and the orchestra and the audience, when something elemental happens, a visceral communication that transports people into that aesthetic moment. I've only been there once my-

self, during a Bach concerto in Aspen. But that's what I want. (Park bench, November 12, 2001)

In recent years, Johnson founded and serves as the music director of the Black Pearl Chamber Orchestra.

Giuseppe Verdi, savoring every nuance of his beloved Shakespeare, crafted a work of endlessly subtle complexity beneath the mirth of the comedy *Falstaff*. Paunchy Sir John's attempts to score with two ladies, and their scheme to teach him a humiliating lesson, ends with Falstaff turning to he audience and singing the stunning line, "Everything in the world is a joke!"

Falstaff's curtain is worlds away from Verdi's usual, grisly finales, and many believe that, at 80, he wrote it simply for his own enjoyment. AVA's Christofer Macatsoris dug into every nuance of the work, considered a masterpiece "by two confident, expressive geniuses"—Verdi and librettist Arrigo Boito. Though Macatsoris could conduct anywhere, AVA has always been his mission.

Christofer Macatsoris:

I was very frustrated by going out and working and not having enough rehearsals. I'm better off here, with nothing really to prove, and these 25 years of responsibility have been great. It's marvelous to see a young singer with desire come through the door, some thrashing around or screaming for direction, some overdoing it and some too shy to do enough.

I don't agree that old-time singers didn't act—maybe today there's too much movement and not enough acting. Styles change. Ten years ago, cool, reserved singing was in. Now hot singing, more passionate, is in. You see them as human beings in a drama.

Verdi was experimenting to see how fiendishly complicated he could make it, putting a 10-minute fugue at the end. But most listeners don't need to notice and are carried on a tidal wave. (Academy of Vocal Arts, November 16, 2001)

Mozart's *The Marriage of Figaro* remains a virtual catalog of human emotions, set to ravishing music. Its characters love, scheme, plot and dream with the same universal fabric of aspirations as we do today.

That's why, when designing the Curtis Opera Theatre's staging of the opera, with Rossen Milanov conducting, director Ben Levit wondered why the story wouldn't be just as relevant brought up to the present day—in a underworld family of mobsters and molls right out of *The Sopranos*. This made me wonder how he would deal with the crucial premise in the opera, servants foiling that bygone period's *droit de seigneur*—which allowed a nobleman to basically own his servants, and deflower any of them at his whimsy.

Ben Levit:

On a certain level, it's not about the underworld, about crime and violence. But it's the only kind of family social system complimentary to theirs in our time, the idea that the person over you has power and control over you, can make you do whatever he wants. I don't look at it literally, but am only thinking of something dealing with virtue and the lack of virtue. The opera is musically rich because all those great arias are plot-driven, they're all about the situation. (Curtis Institute, November 27, 2001)

It wasn't the last time this masterpiece opera was moved up in time, with the Metropolitan Opera doing just that in its 2014 production.

Chamber Interplay

Violinist Nancy Bean, at that time the Philadelphia Orchestra's assistant concertmaster, has always had her heart in chamber music. When she had a chance to play all ten of the monumental Beethoven Violin Sonatas in an extended series, it elicited a passionate yes. She plays an 1875 Henri Silvestre violin, and that glowing timbre was to be accompanied by pianist Clipper Erickson.

Nancy Bean:
These are some of the greatest pieces of music ever written, and I'm just glad to have the chance to play them. I had done seven of them through the years but, before Clipper proposed the idea, I had never thought of doing all 10 together.

"The Sonatas are all different—No. 6 has many ethereal parts, No. 10 has wonderful variations and No. 7 is dark and dramatic, Beethoven writing for himself but ripping your guts out with emotion. At the time of his first Sonata, the violin was supposed to be only an embellishment to the piano, but Beethoven soon changed that pattern. Both the piano and violin take over at times with their time to shine.

I don't like being separated from the audience, and much prefer playing in a smaller theater. It's much better to be closer, both for the audience and the players. (Her home, January 3, 2002)

Bean, also the artistic director of the chamber group 1807 and Friends and first violinist of the Wister Quartet, was true to her word. She retired from the Orchestra, as did husband/cellist/composer Lloyd Smith, to play more chamber music with two other busy Orchestra members—violinist Davyd Booth and violist Pamela Fay. Smith found another calling in composing chamber works for strings and, at last conversation, has finished his Opus 20.

Don't Even Ask

In early April 2002, I impulsively went in to see editor Zack Stalberg, whose office was bedecked with all kinds of weird souvenirs of past stories.

One was of an old *Daily News* cover I had found in my basement and donated, blazoning "Jayne Mansfield Lost At Sea," a cheesy way to get her in a bathing suit on the front page, and eventually returned in a frame.

I mentioned that I had been at the paper for 20 years at the same pay rate per story. His response: "Well, you probably were overpaid then, and are probably underpaid now, but it all evens out. Anything else?" A few years later, after I was given a raise by Debi Licklider, I couldn't help wondering how much better Zack was doing than he had been in 1982.

18. START WITH ACT ONE

Margaret Garwood began writing operas in the 1960s, when no one—especially women—was writing music with passionate melodies. Her operas *The Trojan Women* (1967), *The Nightingale and the Rose* (1974), *Rappaccini's Daughter* (1983) and the children's opera *Joringel and the Songflower* (1985) have been performed to great acclaim by small opera companies.

In between, Garwood wrote three song cycles for the Choral Arts Society and the Music Group called *Tombsongs*, *Rainsongs* and *Flowersongs*, later recorded by the Portland State University Chorus and Orchestra under Bruce Brown. (My son Marc sang with Choral Arts for two of those premieres, and Garwood's beautiful lines were the talk of the ensemble).

Garwood, called Peg by just about everyone, came from the old school of melody and tonal harmony, unheard of in those days despite the audience's love for a hummable tune. She also wrote her own libretti, and had begun work on Nathaniel Hawthorne's *The Scarlet Letter* as early as the 1970s, waiting until after *Rappaccini's Daughter* to compose it in earnest. When Act I was in progress, she was hoping to receive a performance with piano and a few singers when good luck came her way.

Margaret Garwood:

Kevin (AVA President Kevin McDowell) surprised me and said they wanted to do a full reading of the first act with orchestra and costumes. I had finished the piano score but, when I received a brochure the next day advertising it, I really had to scuffle to do the orchestration. He suggested a woodwind quartet and horn, and I asked for trombone, piano, percussion and strings, too.

Working under stress is not worth it, but sometimes a deadline can speed you on your way. The biggest nightmare for a composer is to put out a work not fully conceived, like a body with no arms and legs. I'm fortunate to have someone as gifted as Richard Raub conducting, all I could have hoped for, and now I have the inspiration to finish Acts II and III!

I originally wanted to set all of Hawthorne, but I realized The Scarlet Letter *would be my last opera, and maybe I was waiting because I was afraid to finish it. The story hit me on a strong, unconscious level. I didn't want a message opera, but it's really about the religious right, how any extremists can be vicious and tear away something beautiful. I sense that Hawthorne must have felt the same way.*

I was avant-garde back in the '60s, and after my own evolution, my music is still neo-romantic. And because there are arias and love duets, I'm out of fashion once again. But if music doesn't move you, it's not worth much.

> *Once you find the color that the opera needs, everything spins off from that. Some people think that having arias is old-fashioned, but I'm simply updating ancient conventions. That's what opera is. I'm the end of a culmination of a century—Puccini, Debussy, pop tunes and old ballads like Gershwin, Kern, Arlen. That spirit of melody permeates everything I've written. I believe that every piece is already fully created in the unconscious, and to find it you only have to listen to your own unconscious voice.* (Academy of Vocal Arts, January 7, 2002)

There was a connection to Hawthorne—his distant niece, Hallie Hawthorne Neill, a coloratura who attended one of the performances.

As mentioned before, Margaret Garwood had been married to Romeo Cascarino before Dolores, and both had that ferocious passion about melody and tonal harmony, considered old-fashioned during most of their working years.

So it was ironic that Romeo's death came the next week and, once again, it was up to me to give the sad news. Diabetes had resulted in floaters that eventually caused his blindness, and eventually reached his legs and arms over more than a decade of infirmity.

He had received two Guggenheim Fellowships in composition, the Benjamin Award for Tranquil Music and the Orpheus Award. He held an honorary doctorate from Combs College of Music, where he was head of the composition department until his retirement in 1990.

The composer worked for over 20 years on *William Penn*, an enormous outpouring of effort toward the city and its founder, whose principles of religious freedom resounded at the founding of our country a century later.

Cascarino's catalog of works was not large, heartfelt pieces rich in melody, superb orchestration, and an optimistic sense of hope and beauty. He detested the marketing necessary for performances, and his ferocious pride about his profession kept his works from becoming better known.

Cascarino grew up in a tough neighborhood and often said that, "With a name like Romeo, a guy writing classical music on the piano, I had to learn to defend myself."

He was given a near-fanatical introduction to opera by his father, Vincenzo, and friend Umberto DiGiorgio, who walked from South Philadelphia to the Met at Broad and Poplar streets to hear legends like Caruso sing.

While a student at South Philadelphia High, Cascarino became the rehearsal pianist for the school's operas, once continuing a performance of *Carmen* from memory when the lights went out. Basically self-taught, he haunted the library for books on harmony, counterpoint and orchestration.

His Norristown home was a haven for composers, singers and former students who reveled in the conversation and, in the years he was able, his famous pasta dishes.

Cascarino loved Puccini, Wagner, Ravel and other composers who wrote soaring melodies, wrapped in a cloak of orchestral richness. He felt that an artist's sole purpose was to search for and express beauty, and often remarked after hearing bloodless or academic new music, "If they could write a melody, they *would* write a melody."

After his death, it was difficult for Dolores to go to any event for a while. But we went to the premiere of that first act of *The Scarlet Letter* at Haverford School and, before it began, Christofer Macatsoris came out and dedicated the performance to Romeo, citing him as a great composer and calling his passing a great loss for the musical community. Of course, this elicited tears from Dolores and, when we went backstage afterwards, found that Chris was experiencing a 103-degree fever and had only come to Haverford to make the announcement.

More Fun with Denyce

To lighten things up, Denyce Graves was back in town to do an operatic romp, Offenbach's *La Perichole*, in a role debut. She was now a franchise, with a new CD being sold by the QVC channel, portraits in all the bus kiosks and even a new perfume line. When approached to design a line of jewelry, she remembered saying a line she had once said to me, "You don't know who you're talking to. I'm the girliest girl ever!"

I interviewed Graves in her penthouse suite at the Ritz-Carlton while she was being made up by cosmetic and hair people—-"Nobody else sees me like this!" she said. Even without makeup and perfect hair, she was most fetching.

Denise Graves:

This is the most fun I've had on an engagement. The opera is zany and loony, I was falling off the piano bench when I was learning it. Everyone dances in this show and everything seems to erupt when Dorothy (director Dorothy Danner), a human cyclone who was a dancer, starts rehearsals. She says my cut kicks aren't high enough, so I'll have to kick higher, though it's exhausting just watching all the physical activity.

This is a real stretch for me, because this time I couldn't rely on my instincts. I'm used to playing these femme fatales and, since I'm pretty tragic and always look for the melancholy and darkness in things, I've had to make it much, much lighter. And I actually live in the end this time!

I've finally arrived in my career to where producers ask what I'd like to do. It really burns me that opera singers are the artists who study the longest in this country but are just dismissed by the Grammys and award shows. We all just have to get what we do to the general public, either by TV or outreach to inner-city schoolkids. There's a reason why this material is still around—everything else falls away, but only art survives. (Ritz-Carlton hotel, January 13, 2002)

Temporary Loss

Conductor Maurizio Barbacini was in town to lead the Opera Company's *Madama Butterfly*, and I asked him to accompany me to an Orchestra concert. Roberto Abbado was conducting the Concerto for Two Pianos by Luciano Berio, with Katia and Marielle Labeque as soloists, and Ravel's *Mother Goose* Suite in the first half.

During the mechanically-led Ravel, the piece I had played in its original two-piano version for decades and loved dearly, something profound and unexplainable happened to me. At intermission, I must have wandered out of the Spruce Street doors onto the sidewalk.

Maurizio found me, and wondered why I looked strange. "Maurizio," I stammered, "it's all over. I've lost my ability to hear beauty in music." He smiled and put his hand on my shoulder.

"Tommaso," he said reassuringly, "It's not you."

Barbacini had met his wife Antonella Pianezzola, who had portrayed Tosca two seasons before, during a *Madama Butterfly*, and he considered the work his special "souvenir."

Maurizio Barbacini:

One of my joys is to discover new talent, since I really can see quality and know what a singer's life is like. It's possible to suggest and support, insist on quality, and perhaps shape careers.

I'm a very lucky man, and was able to be a singer myself in big houses. But I see many people who are willing to die for something they will never be able to realize, and I have found the courage to say to enthusiastic people, this is not a job for you. Sometimes, I meet someone 10 years later and they say, thank you, Maestro, my life has changed for the better in another field. (Academy of Music, February 24, 2002)

It was mentioned before that Barbacini had begun his career as a singer, playing Gastone in Franco Zeffirelli's opulent movie of *La Traviata*.

Years later, Barbacini took over the baton in *Traviata* (from an indisposed Placido Domingo) and happened to run into Zeffirelli backstage at the Met.

"Maurizio, are you here to sing Gastone?" asked Zeffirelli.

"No," said Barbacini. "I'm conducting!"

Classic Daily News

In early March, the Moiseyev Dance Company—on its 11th international tour—made its first appearance at the Kimmel Center. Only the *Daily News* headline writers would have come up with:

"This is no Bolshoi—but it's similar."

Two Pairs on Stage

It takes a good actress to portray the spurned Donna Elvira, who hears Don Giovanni's servant recite a whole catalog of his conquests all over Europe.

And it takes a really good actress to do a rehearsal catching her lover in the act—especially when it's her real-life husband.

Soprano Patricia Schuman had adapted to seeing David Pittsinger play Don Giovanni in steamy scenes, and came to do it in a production that updated the period.

Patricia Schuman and David Pittsinger:

Schuman: *At the first rehearsal, when he was in a decadent round bed in a silk brocade robe with two babes, that was a little strange. But when he's on stage, he's just the character, just an actor. The most important thing going is to translate the chemistry, and it helps to be wildly attracted to David. We've done other operas together as colleagues, but as soon as we get to the theater I just do my job, though the bonus is a built-in support system.*

Pittsinger: *The relation between Elvira and Don is important, because there has been the promise of marriage, and a strong attraction or bond. When you're playing it with your wife, you draw on your own experience and it's not difficult to find the depth. I let secrets I possess as a person come out and let things I hold private onto the stage. Being this honest in the moment is scary, you're living a bit of your life in front of a lot of people, but it's thrilling to do it.*

Schuman: *Sometimes it's a big surprise, but you have to give the director the benefit of the doubt, because you won't know until opening night. You have to be your own eyes, and find the foundation for the character. I remember playing Pamina in a Magic Flute in Vienna with Nikolaus Harnoncourt. Some of his tempos were very fast and some painfully slow. There was almost a riot, with booing so loud we almost couldn't continue.* (Academy of Music, March 17, 2002)

The character of Don Juan—and his compulsive need for domination, self-justification or just plain lustful conquest—has stirred the imagination of men and women, as well as playwrights and composers, for centuries.

Mozart and librettist Lorenzo Da Ponte, who titled their opera *Don Giovanni or the Rake Punished*, considered it a comic drama.

The legend of a dead man's statue, finally accepting a libertine's invitation to dinner, first emerged in print in 1630. The play, titled *El Burlador de Sevilla* (*The Trickster of Seville*), was written by a Spanish friar named Gabriel Tellez, writing under a secular pseudonym, Tirso de Molina. The nobleman and his unscrupulous pursuit of women spurred stories, plays and music by Goldoni, Dumas, Balzac, Flaubert, Byron, Pushkin, Richard Strauss and George Bernard Shaw, and he was even portrayed in a 1949 film by a dissipated Errol Flynn.

Doctoral theses have been written explaining Don Juan as without honor, deranged, a psychopath without the ability to feel guilt or shame, or a diabolical personality unable to discern right from wrong (or to fall in love).

Yet Albert Camus called him an existentialist hero, praising his desire to gratify his every wish, and Shaw saw him as a Faustian rebel, transferring the predatory characteristics to a Dona Juana, a husband-hunting female.

Mozart and Da Ponte gave us much more depth and mystery, making him more than a one-dimensional monster. They spent many evenings doing research at a cafe with Casanova; legend has it that when Casanova left Vienna for Paris to run the French lottery and stiffed them with the bar tab, they made sure that the Don's romantic attempts during the opera were always foiled.

Some women have told me they feel repulsed by him, yet admit to the same strange, lustful fascination they feel for Dracula.

Men grapple with a disrespect for his ruthlessness, though their reservations may secretly represent having to accept the rules of society—or simply the lack of opportunity.

The climax of the opera is the banquet scene, when the mocking Don is dragged down to a flaming hell by the resurrected Commendatore he murdered at the outset. (A happy ending had to be written for the more conservative Viennese audiences after the opera's premiere in Prague).

In one classic operatic tale, an overweight Don became stuck in the trap door that lowers him down to the underworld, and no amount of squirming or pulling could free the singer.

Finally, a wag in the upper gallery yelled, "Hooray, hell's full."

In April, the Opera Company's presentation of Bellini's *I Capuleti e I Montecchi* (*The Capulets and the Montagues*) featured two sopranos who would go on to enormous fame. Bellini's opera was conducted again by Barbacini, who lives in Verona where the doomed fictional lovers Romeo and Juliet supposedly lived in the 13th century. Romeo was played by Russian mezzo-soprano Anna Netrebko, who had already appeared in the Met's *War and Peace* (and has gone on to spectacular heights), and soprano Ruxana Donose, who returned many times, portrayed Giulietta.

One-Handed Artistry

After the brilliant American pianist Gary Graffman lost the use of his right hand due to a neurological affliction called focal distonia, and became president of Curtis Institute, he was still able to play some of the left-hand repertoire, like the Ravel D Major and Prokofiev Fourth Concertos.

A similar affliction also hampered Leon Fleisher, who would eventually gain use of his right hand. Both Graffman and Fleisher have requested composers to write new works for the left hand and many have, including Ned Rorem, Daron Hagen, Richard Danielpour, Luis Prado and Stanislaw Skrowaczewski; William Bolcom even wrote a puzzle-like piece for the Philadelphia Orchestra called *Gaea* that featured Graffman, then Fleisher, ending in a third movement in which both left-hand parts were played simultaneously.

19. HEROES, CARMENS, AND NUTCRACKERS

Peter Nero had planned a concert called *Voyage into Space*, featuring John Glenn as narrator. It had to wait until after four terms as U. S. Senator, finally presented in 2002 on the 40th anniversary of the famous space flight.

Nero and Glenn collaborated on the text, based on the former astronaut's memoir, to portray liftoff, the view from space and re-entry during the 20-minute multimedia piece.

He said he had a froggy throat, though you wouldn't expect stage fright from someone who has counted down for two space missions, his famed 1962 three-orbit solo and the 10-day Discovery launch in 1998 at age 77.

Glenn was an affable, very focused man, excited about performing for the first time with an orchestra, and I had a chance to ask him some questions in the Kimmel Center's green room.

John Glenn:
Q: *Have you been involved in music before?*
A: *I played trumpet in the town and college band, and sang in choral groups. My wife, Annie, earned a scholarship to Juilliard, but Pearl Harbor made that impossible. She's an accomplished organist and, during the 23 years we were on a military base, always found somewhere to play.*
Q: *Did this musical experience bring it all back for you?*
A: *Every day brings it back for me. Since 1962, it's a rare day that someone hasn't mentioned that space flight, and it is indelibly impressed on my memory anyway. I recall it daily, like the feel of heat on my back during re-entry. But I'm not one who lives in the past . . . It's another day, with something else exciting to do.*
Q: *Do you see any parallel between a conductor and a spacecraft commander?*
A: *Certainly, they both represent a team effort . . . On all these NASA missions there are thousands of people involved, with one person, like Alan Shepard or myself, who just happens to be at the point of things.*
Q: *What was it like to have Ted Williams as your wing gunner during the Korean conflict?*
A: *How did you know that? . . . He was extraordinary, and we keep in touch, though he's still recovering from a stroke.*
Q: *How do you feel when people often call you a legend?*
A: *I'm not old enough to be anybody's legend!* (Kimmel Center, April 6, 2002)

After our interview, I summoned the courage to tell him that my son worked for Lockheed Martin, had helped build the Terra spacecraft and was working on a new project, the Hubble repair mission. I also mentioned that he had been a huge inspiration in Marc's career, something that obviously moved him. He was very knowledgeable about the Hubble project, and hoped they could someday meet.

When the concert concluded, there was a VIP event in the rooftop garden atop the Perelman Theatre, and the modest Marc was reluctant to go. Glenn was at a table with Senator Vincent Fumo and various dignitaries, and we prepared to beat a hasty retreat.

Suddenly, Annie Glenn came up on the elevator, and Glenn rushed over to see her. Evidently she didn't want to stay, and as he walked back to his table I said hello and introduced Marc. Glenn grabbed his hand, and chatted about all the NASA people he knew who were also working on the Hubble project. He could not possibly have been more gracious, and was highly enthusiastic speaking to someone who helped build the complex satellites that astronauts and space projects rely on. At the time, I figured he'd rather be talking about space projects than schmoozing with politicos, who were looking over and wondering what happened to their guest of honor.

After a long while, Nero came over and someone took a photo of the four of us, still gracing a special place in Marc's living room.

Two Meaningful Beginnings

JoAnn Falletta returned to the Mann to conduct the Orchestra for two performances in July 2002. Because she had been very cordial on the phone, and intensely passionate about American composers, I went backstage and gave her a recording of Cascarino's *Pygmalion,* written as a ballet in 1957. It had been given a sight-read performance by a provincial German orchestra on an old LP, and was the only evidence I had.

She soon responded, and asked if he had written any more orchestral music. It was the start of another joyous adventure, leading to an adventure and deep friendship I couldn't have possibly foreseen.

Jimmy Amadie and his wife Lucille were introduced to me at the home of Michael Bookspan, the Philadelphia Orchestra's revered percussionist, and his wife Shirley. All I knew about Jimmy is that his hands had a painful affliction that prevented his playing; the cumulative effects of being a young boxer, practicing for many hours a day and playing as house pianist at the Red Hill Inn in New Jersey had led to many surgeries, constant pain and the loss of manual control. At one point, to illustrate a tune, he went into the living room and played a few measures before his wife Lucille ran in and stopped him, saying "Jimmy! We'll be up all night!"

He gave me a copy of his technique book, excellent for students without any prior training. I eventually had the privilege of several years of jazz study with Jimmy, who sat next to me with his hands in buckets of ice. Danny Miller from WHYY-FM had set up a DAT recorder and microphone in his living room and, some nights six or eight weeks apart, Jimmy would come down in the middle of the night and do one tune, one take. After nearly two years, his first CD, *Always with Me*, came out, and since it has been getting a little easier, there were seven more.

In October of 2011, I was astonished to see Jimmy listed as a performer at the Friday night concerts at the Museum of Art. These were often packed with people sitting at the tables and on the huge stone steps, usually with plenty of talking, serving and clinking of cutlery. I called Jimmy, who mentioned some other serious maladies all over his body as well as just his hands.

"This is something I have to do," Jimmy insisted, "no matter how much it hurts. The devil will be there, and I'm going to beat him." He took shots and acupuncture the day before, showed up at the Museum and played brilliantly with his trio—42 years since the last time he had played in public. Though the concert was being filmed professionally for WHYY, I shot some video from the side next to his beaming wife Lucille, who he acknowledged to some deafening applause.

His next dream was to play again in New York with saxman Phil Woods, which would tragically never happen. Yet Jimmy left us with that incredible Art Museum concert, the heartbeats of a life distilled into two sets.

Carmens and Tchaikovsky

It's always exciting to have *Carmen* in town, and it's even more exciting to have two Carmens. Booked three years before, mezzo Marina Domashenko had become well known and could only do five of the seven shows, with Ekaterina Semenchuk singing the other two.

Sitting between these two lovely Russian Carmens was a delight, for they expressed themselves freely (sometimes through an interpreter) with humor, intensity and passion.

Marina Domashenko and Ekaterina Semenchuk:
Q: *Do you two see Carmen differently?*

Domashenko: *To me, Carmen is like a leader of gangsters, but she has many faces, many characteristics. It's complicated to work with a frozen plan. I promise it will be original.*

Semenchuk: *I see her as a wild child, finding the truth in relationships between people. We can develop our own Carmens with peace, no war.*

Q: *Neither of you look like gypsies—Since Marina's hair is blond and Katia's is short.*

Domashenko: *You have to believe the character yourself. Once, two days before the performance, a director asked me to play Carmen with my real hair, blonde, without a wig. You cannot sing the role of a gypsy with blond hair, and the day before the premiere I colored my hair black. Now I always wear a wig.*

Q: *Do you have dreams for the future?*

Domashenko: *I haven't yet passed the line of being glad to be Carmen. It's one of the greatest roles. There are many things to do in the future—that's life.*

Semenchuk: *I'm very happy now because, back in Minsk, my dream was to be an accordion player.*

Domashenko: *I have an accordion too, from my grandfather!* (Academy of Music, November 7, 2002)

That year's go at *The Nutcracker* gave me a chance to study its history. It had taken nine years for Tchaikovsky to get around to writing the music, perhaps fearing a third ballet fiasco. His *Swan Lake* had suffered from terrible choreography and clumsy conducting, and *Sleeping Beauty* audiences were not ready for such a symphonic score.

Tchaikovsky postponed the work's composition for a visit to America, conducting at the opening of Carnegie Hall and also visiting Philadelphia, Baltimore and Niagara Falls. When he discovered the celesta in Paris on the way home, he realized that its ethereal tone was ideal for the Sugarplum Fairy music.

Afraid that his fellow Russian composers Rimsky-Korsakov and Glinka would write music for the instrument first, he immediately wrote the familiar Suite from the *Nutcracker* before finishing the final ballet. It was first played in Moscow and St. Petersburg in March 1892, nine months before the full ballet (featuring students) was premiered.

Tchaikovsky never cared for the music, calling it "far weaker than *Sleeping Beauty*," and once saying, "In spite of all the sumptuousness it did turn out to be rather boring." Sometimes composers are the poorest judges of their own work.

Perhaps he simply anticipated the fickleness of Russian audiences, because it was replaced for the next holiday's offering at St. Petersburg's Mariinsky Theater, seven weeks after the composer's death, with Humperdinck's *Hansel and Gretel*.

It didn't travel outside Russia until 1934, in London, then with sections used in Walt Disney's 1940 *Fantasia* and a 1944 adaptation in San Francisco. The first full American version was by George Balanchine for the newly created New York City Ballet in 1954, finally revised into the current 1964 show, which added innovative choreography and making the mice a little scarier.

'I want audiences to see music and hear dancing," Balanchine said about his choreography.

This mystical Russian usually spoke cryptically, often saying something clearly untrue— "I don't create or invent anything. I assemble." Before his death in 1983, he referred to himself in a Russian poet's words: "I am not a man, but a cloud in trousers."

P.D.Q. Once More

Just after Christmas, Peter Schickele had a few more pieces to make me laugh. He talked about the *Okay Chorale*, the *Pervertimento*, *Notebook for Betty Sue Bach*, the *Sonata for Viola Four Hands*, the *Fanfare for the Common Cold* and the *No-No Nonette*, threatening to play, with his New York Pick-Up Ensemble, the *Schleptet*, the *Concerto for Bassoon Versus Orchestra* and the suite from his opera, *The Civilian Barber*.

In some parts of that opera the tempo is written *Tempo di Marcia* (march tempo); P. D. Q. marked it *Tempo di Marsha* after his girlfriend. There was also a *Dance of St. Vitus*, and an *Exit of the Dragoon* marked *Tempo di on the Double*.

Orchestra 2001—And 2001

Guitarist Sharon Isbin has used her fame and considerable clout to commission many works for the guitar repertoire. With James Freeman's innovative Orchestra 2001 ensemble, she played one of those works, the 1993 *Troubadours* by John Corigliano.

Sharon Isbin:

John (Corigliano) used part of a 12th century theme by the French troubadour Beatriz de Dia, beginning and ending the piece with ghostlike evocations of these long-forgotten folk musicians. Then he asked me to stroll on and off, an idea that first sounded crazy, but became a fun challenge of playing while walking that I practiced in my living room for weeks.

The last time I played with Orchestra 2001 came 12 days after September 11, 2001 and, as a New York resident, I found it difficult to motivate myself. But I found that audiences needed and responded to a sense of humanity, of joy and transcendence. Last September 11 I was deeply honored to be asked to play at Ground Zero during the reading of the names for the family members, along with Yo-Yo Ma, Gil Shaham and the Juilliard String Quartet. There were gale-force winds and 12,000 were expected, but 24,000 showed up for an experience I'll never forget. (By phone, January 24, 2003)

Tabloid Opera

The *Daily News'* long-standing column called *Tattle*, in recent years composed by Howard Gensler, sarcastically chronicles the daily celebrity foolishness and crazy antics from Michael Jackson to Lady Gaga. One day, for an upcoming Opera Company production of Verdi's *La Traviata*, I tried to put the plot in *Tattle* terms.

"According to *Tattle*, Violetta Valery (aka Marie Duplessis or Marguerite Gautier, whatever), the frail, high-end hooker with a heart of gold, died last night after a drawn-out bout with the oh-so-fashionable consumption (shades of Garbo in Dumas' *Camille*).

"Valery's aristocratic pals say that Al Germont turned her into a one-man squeeze until their steamy five-month liaison ended in a fiery breakup.

"The way Tattle hears the story, Al's pop Georgio (the Baritone) Germont didn't want Valery's tarnished reputation to soil his family name and spoil his daughter's wedding, making her an offer she couldn't refuse—to dump his boy Al and dance the horizontal mambo with some rich Baron.

"Turned out that Al found out about Pop's ploy and reunited with her just before she went south. Ain't love grand?"

Well, if ever there was a lame story (Alexandre Dumas' play *La Dame aux Camelias*) that needed great music to disguise the plot, it's *La Traviata* (clumsily translated *The Woman Who Went Astray*).

Fortunately, Verdi produced one of his supreme masterpieces, providing gripping musical conflicts that levitate these cardboard characters into people with believable personal agendas. This most-performed opera is almost a chamber work, with the intimate moments even more powerful than the two lavish crowd scenes.

Dumas' play was the scandal of Paris, due to Valery's wearing white carnations 25 days a month—and red on the others. Verdi wanted to set it in contemporary times (1853), with the Venetian censors moving it back to 1700. Early London productions didn't even offer translations, out of consideration for "the patrons' moral well-being."

Ties with Vienna

In March, the Kimmel hosted the Vienna Philharmonic in its first Philly visit in over 30 years. The stern-faced Nikolaus Harnoncourt was on the podium, with violinist Gidon Kremer as soloist in the Berg Concerto.

The Vienna orchestra sound is unique, an old-world, burnished, sherry-and-heavy-drapes sonority, certainly the result of also playing as the Vienna State Opera orchestra. It was a different sound than any other orchestra, and perhaps simply isn't comparable. Their visit was a continuing reminder that we could hear the world's greatest interpreters at the Kimmel Center—a treat which lasted for a few years until it became financially unfeasible.

Performances of the Mozart-Da Ponte *Cosi fan tutte* (*All women behave like that*) always demonstrate that the eternal battle of the sexes hasn't changed much since its Viennese premiere in 1790.

Conductor Barbacini knew that much of the sexual tension, subtleties and delicate shadings in the Italian libretto are untranslatable into English.

Maurizio Barbacini:

Just as Italian audiences would miss something in an American opera like Samuel Barber's Vanessa, *some might not absorb all the complexity and subtleties of the story. But, if you listen closely, Mozart's music explains everything, and helps us discover the significance of every meaning.*

Mozart is the most difficult composer, requiring enormous concentration and nuances of expression, musicality and technical ability, and I'm lucky to have six good-looking singers, a real advantage in making the story more believable. (Academy of Music, March 2, 2003)

Two Asian-Born Superstars

I'd rejoiced in violinist Sarah Chang's rocketing career since meeting her at age 11 and, as a mature artist of 21, she had retained the same gracious and ebullient attitude toward music and life.

When she returned for a recital of French sonatas, along with German pianist Lars Vogt, I wondered how fame was treating her.

Sarah Chang:

Q: *Why a French program?*

A: *We wanted to do the Franck Sonata, a romantic masterpiece, then went over every sonata known to mankind. We finally chose the Saint-Saëns, a gorgeous virtuoso piece, and it just naturally happened.*

We started working on this three years ago. You have to open up a month and a half in your schedule, find a great partner, and get into a chamber music mindset. I try to avoid concertos in between, though I'll be playing one with the Vienna Philharmonic in Copenhagen soon.

Q: *How did you choose Lars Vogt as partner?*

A: *He's a soloist in his own right, and we're on the same label (EMI). With six weeks on the road and a recording, you have to like your partner, and he's great fun and interesting, a new father. I believe that the audience can feel the chemistry and emotional empathy between the performers.*

Q: *What do you do when you're not playing?*

A: *I shop like a true professional! I love going to the movies, like* Lord of the Rings, *the new James Bond. But I like to call up a few friends and get away from the backstage area and the enclosed atmosphere of airports and hotels.*

Q: *What popular music do you enjoy?*

A: *Norah Jones, she's fantastic, Marc Anthony, Alicia Keys, and Santana.*

Q: *Do you tire of people saying they heard you when you were 11?*

A: *Actually, I love it when people tell me that and the looks on people's faces when they say "My you've grown," I'm incredibly grateful to have been able to begin at a young age. People around me who saw me on album covers with frou-frou dresses now say they're too revealing, and I feel very looked after. My favorite cover is the* Fire and Ice *CD with Placido Domingo, the first one I've ever done with someone else. My mother approved the dress, my father didn't see it until after it was issued.*

Q: *What's your favorite concerto?*

A: *The Brahms, I waited until I was 18 to play it. And waited until 21 to play the Beethoven, to commit more respect, more dignity to it, and grow into it on stage. I hope when I'm 40 or 50 I can somehow begin to under-*

stand that work. But I'll be playing the Brahms soon with the Zubin Mehta and the Vienna Philharmonic, and I'll be in high heaven.

Q: *What's the hardest part of your life?*

A: *To have an intense relationship with players and friends for a few days, and then have to leave. I also wish I had more time to visit schools, to see their progress. It's very touching to me when the student tickets sell out. Or to see familiar faces, like grade school teachers in the audience.*

Q: *Does any part of your life ever get boring?*

A: *That word never enters my vocabulary! I wake up every day thankful that I'm a musician.* (By phone, March 1, 2003)

Sarah Chang.

Another Asian-born sensation, pianist Lang Lang, soon followed in recital, though his originally-scheduled program in the 650-seat Perelman Theater had to be moved to the 2,500 seat Verizon Hall. His astonishing facility, warmth and daredevil playing had made Lang an international star from Philly, and the naturally exuberant product of Curtis Institute was wildly excited about playing his first solo concert here.

Lang Lang:

I will try to play my best in my hometown. I've chosen the Brahms Six Pieces, Op. 118, the most deep music in the human soul, with feelings so complex that I understand them better every day. Then the Schubert Wanderer *Fantasy and, finally, that crazy* Islamey *(a notoriously-challenging knucklebuster) by Balakirev, that has to come last.*

In my student days, we all read the Daily News, *and I truly hope that a lot of young people will read this, come to the concert and discover that classical music is not as serious as they think. It's romantic, comfortable, exciting and very meaningful, with a beautiful soul and melodies that can make you feel differently about life. I would like to show that these pieces are the mainstream, and change what people think about this music.* (By phone, March 9, 2003)

Babes, Possible Maidens

Around 2000, soprano Rebecca Knight, 32, and mezzo Karen England, 28, were singing for tips at the plaza in front of London's Covent Garden Opera House. Knight's mother, the opera singer Gillian Knight, would occasionally come out at rehearsal break and drop a fiver into the basket.

Along came a talent scout, who booked the street performers to sing Puccini's aria *Un Bel Di* at the Football Cup finals, garnering the pair huge attention and a tough choice:

They could audition endlessly for small parts, like the roles in *The Magic Flute* they sang in a small opera house where they met five years before. Or—they could add a percussive beat to arias, and words to classical tunes from Dvořák, Beethoven and Grieg, sign a six-CD deal and rocket to the top of the crossover charts with their first, *Opera Babes*.

Guess what they chose, and guess what "classical" story suddenly appealed to an editor.

This wasn't the frontal assault of a Sarah Brightman or Michael Bolton. The *Opera Babes* sing the melodies straight without embellishment, with one singing harmony, and their hearts are obviously in the "straighter" numbers. Just as in their duets, the voices of these two fetching ladies, blended during their visit to plug their first Sony CD, *Beyond Imagination*.

Opera Babes:

Q: What happens now to your operatic aspirations?

A: To step into that level of highbrow theater, they need to see us perform. No one's going to believe that we can sing opera without a backing track and electronics, but we're prepared to be put to the test. There may be reservations about long-term careers, but this may open more doors for us in the future.

Q: *How do you feel about the name Opera Babes?*

A: *That has been the hardest thing, because it wasn't a name we would have chosen. It has created problems, because it trivializes it a bit and encourages the preconception that we couldn't sing.*

Q: *What else is in the future?*

A: *We auditioned for Simon Rattle, who was at the Royal Opera House doing (Nicholas Maw's)* Sophie's Choice. *We sang Lakmé and Figaro, and he asked us to learn the first and second Rhine maidens from Wagner's Ring.*

He'll be taking it around the world in a few years, and we'd jump into the air if we got the job! (By phone, May 18, 2003)

Arts Hotter Than Sports?

The Pew Charitable Trusts put up $2.7 million for the Performing Arts Research Coalition to study the effect on the arts. Many people, especially at the *Daily News* where the sports pages often win national awards, considered the arts a frill compared to sports—the full stadiums for the Phillies, Eagles, 76ers and Flyers.

Pew polled 4,000 people each in Cincinnati, Denver, Pittsburgh and Seattle to gain data for funders, managers, policy-makers and the media, each city sporting two, three or four professional sports teams. My take on the results:

—More people attended a live professional performing arts event in the past year than attended a professional sports event.

—There were only small percentage differences among attendees from ages 25 to 54—despite the stereotype of only old heads attending the arts.

—Ticket prices came in third as a barrier to attendance. The top two: "Prefer to spend time in other ways" and "Hard to make time to go out."

—More than nine out of 10 respondents in each community strongly agreed that the performing arts contribute to the education and development of children.

—Seven out of 10 respondents agreed that performing arts help them understand other cultures better.

By that fall, data from Austin, Boston, Minneapolis/St. Paul, Sarasota, Fla., and Washington, D.C., would be added to the study.

So what did it all mean?

Well, there might be 65,000 people at an Eagles football game nine or ten times a year. The Kimmel Center's Verizon Hall (2,500 seats) and the Perelman Theatre (650) seats are filled on many more nights, and the Academy of Music (2,900 seats) will soon be booked year-round.

The Philadelphia Orchestra plays more than 110 programs; that's 275,000 seats at near capacity. Add in the Merriam Theater, the Annenberg Center, the Wilma, Walnut Street, Forrest and Prince Theaters, the Temple University venues, a dozen theatrical productions in the region, chamber music, dance, jazz, pop, rap, folk, choruses, clubs, world music, recitals and many more.

Night after night, matinee after matinee.

All year long, bringing in more people and more ticket revenue than sports, without a major problem in ticket prices.

And since most of the venues are in Center City, the revenue generated for the adjacent restaurant and shopping establishments is enormously greater than with sports events.

And this phenomenon continues without the arts being part of most school curricula. Many people recall their high school experience of generations ago, when there were choruses, orchestras, bands, operas, dance and theater as an essential part of the school day. That's been gone for two generations though, even without it, the arts are thriving.

Even though tight school budgets won't allow for arts education, virtually every major local orchestra, opera, ballet and theatre company has an outreach program, funded by philanthropists and interested individuals to bring the arts to schools. That's the future, and it's growing.

Sports teams are vital for a major city, bringing people together when there's a shot at a pennant, a trophy or a cup.

The arts have an even greater cultural, influential and financial engine for a city, and it's always a winning season.

Jim Cotter from WRTI-FM wrote me to see if I wanted to do a "Creatively Speaking" radio piece on this, a spot that eventually won a March Of Dimes Achievement In Radio award for Best Editorial.

More radio stories ensued for a while, and I asked *Daily News* editor Michael Days if, as a freelancer, there was any conflict. He asked if I would say I was a writer for the *Daily News* and, when I said yes, he said, "Fine, advertising for us."

Loss and Uplift

On April 11, 2003, I was holding my mother's hand when she passed away in a Fort Lauderdale facility.

Someone sent a routine notice to the staff and, a few days later, I got a call from Jack Morrison, who I consider the finest newspaper writer anywhere. He suggested I put some notes down for him, even though I said she hadn't lived in Philadelphia for 40 years, and I spent a weekend writing about her. I sent my draft along to Jack, the person I most trusted to massage my words.

My sister Martha Neuringer, who lives in Oregon, called and said she was speaking at Cornell, and the only flights to Ithica came through Philadelphia, allowing a short visit. As I walked her through the airport, I bought a paper and there it was.

It began, "Ann Di Nardo, a gentle and inspiring woman who had a knack for making everyone feel like family, died died April 11. She was 89 and lived in Fort Lauderdale, Fla."

Jack's headline: "Ann Di Nardo, saw the good in others."

We both wept, and I called Jack with astonishment that he had understood her spirit completely, and hadn't changed a word.

"It didn't need anything, Tom," he said. That was truly the highest compliment I have ever received in this career.

Firebird, Denyce and Rorem's 80th

The Pennsylvania Ballet's production of Stravinsky's *The Firebird* was to be double-cast with the spectacular dancers Arantxa Ochoa and Riolama Lorenzo. Because this was to be a features-section cover story, I needed a photo of the Firebird in costume—though ballet protocol never allows costumes until the dress rehearsal. After begging artistic director Roy Kaiser, though, it was allowed for Arantxa to wear it at a rehearsal.

Arantxa Ochoa in James Kudelka's The Firebird. Credit: Paul Kolnik.

Our photographer Alejandro Alvarez, who had never been to a ballet, was stunned by Arantxa in costume—which usually happens to those capable of vision. Because the rehearsal hall had mirrors on all sides, it was nearly impossible to get a shot without background images of uncostumed dancers, and especially difficult to get Arantxa leaping. However Alex, true to his art and his indefatigable desire to get the shot, among other reasons, stayed for the whole rehearsal to make sure.

At one point the excellent rehearsal pianist Martha Koenemann stopped while choreographer James Kudelka gave suggestions to the corps. The Spanish-born Arantxa, who completely embodied the incredible grace of the Firebird, suddenly slumped and walked gracelessly toward me at the edge. "My feet hurt so much!" she whispered with her hand on my shoulder; as soon as the music started she instantly transformed into the weightless, flying Firebird.

I never have been to the ballet since without thinking about the physical toll these artists endure to make us believe in sheer beauty.

In November 2003, on a trip to Madrid, we had seen posters for Denyce Graves in *Carmen*, opening the day we were leaving. Walking past the Teatro Reale, I left a message on a scrap of hotel stationery at the backstage entrance saying "Break a leg, Denyce! Tom from Philly."

That night she called the hotel and insisted we come to the dress rehearsal and say hello afterwards. It was a spectacular performance, with opulent scenery and a huge number of people on stage, though we were yet to see the most spectacular diva performance. Afterwards, we were invited into her dressing room and, though she was most gracious, she couldn't hide her rage at the conductor, Alain Lombard.

At that moment, Lombard knocked and entered with an apprehensive look. "Now look, Alain," she raged, "I've done this role all over the world, and every conductor has kept a steady tempo. You're speeding up every number, and I have to hit the boy with the flower, go around the goat cart, spin around the women, dance with Don Jose, and all on a raked stage wearing four-inch heels—and I have to sing, too! Do you want to try it?" "Let's talk about it," said Lombard, sheepishly. "There's nothing to talk about!" said Graves. "The tempos have to be steady, no *accelerandos*, period!"

Lombard left the room, and Graves turned to us with a huge smile. "So how are you enjoying Madrid?"

She's a true performer, with a gorgeous daughter named Ella—named after Ella Fitzgerald.

Denyce Back In Philly

Graves soon returned to Philly for a concert with Patti LaBelle and Take Six, taped for PBS and called *Breaking the Rules*, reprising the gospel flavor she heard as a young girl. She had just returned from a U.S. government-sponsored cultural-ambassador visit to St. Petersburg, Russia, and Romania, and was excited about an educational project, with singers appearing in schools.

Denyce Graves:
Q: *Was gospel music part of your childhood?*
A: *It was the only music we were allowed to listen to in our house—Shirley Caesar, James Cleveland, the Mighty Clouds of Joy. What a thrill to have Shirley on my new CD (Church), I grew up with her! I was a shy, awkward kid who didn't know there was anything else until I was taken to music class one day.*

Q: *Did you always sing?*
A: *We sang at the table. When I visited a friend's house and sang, they thought I was weird. I thought it was weird not to sing! In my room, I used a hairbrush as a mike and sang to the mirror. By my sophomore year in high school, I had lost 22 friends to violence. Music was my refuge.*

Q: *What got you into opera?*
A: *A friend told me there was something I had to hear. We cut school one afternoon and went to the library to hear a record by Leontyne Price. I had no idea what it was or what she was singing about, but I knew it was*

someone who looked like me who was singing something amazing. That record changed my life.

Q: *You're really stoked about this concert with Patti LaBelle.*

A: *Yes, and there are some great dresses that you've gotta see!* (By phone, June 8, 2003)

She also told me she would appear in five hot diva outfits—a black leather gown, black strapless top and slinky pants, long satin skirt with red bustier, an elegant red gown and long blue dress ("I couldn't sing gospel in a leather dress—my mother's here!")

Later that year, Graves gave a master class at Temple University's Rock Hall. One Asian girl sang an eerily idiomatic Negro spiritual; Graves was simply floored, saying she couldn't imagine how the girl had captured that intense feeling, and couldn't possibly give any advice.

Another prim young woman in a red suit sang very well, and Graves had lots to say here. "You're singing about being jilted by a man you're madly in love with! You have to give it more passion, you're really going nuts in this aria, go for it! Use your clothes, anything!" The singer, with still a bit of stage embarrassment still in her, did it again, and this time removed her jacket. "Come on, honey, we're all friends. Let's see you go over the top!" Graves urged.

She did it again, this time singing with a near-ferocious attitude, removing her jacket as if to taunt her ex-lover and hurling it into the audience. The band of students and guests roared and cheered, and the woman's face reflected complete astonishment in having temporarily become someone else.

"You turned that girl into a woman," I said to Graves, who laughed later on. "That's all she needed," she said, "because she certainly had the voice."

A Legend and His Opera

For composer Ned Rorem's 80th birthday, his alma mater Curtis Institute gave concerts of his music for a week, including his *Miss Julie*, the first opera presented in the new Perelman Theater.

He wasn't one to duck a question, whether it's about his supreme position as master of the American art song, details from his searingly candid diaries or the process of creation.

In a phone conversation that attempted to avoid those well-documented subjects, with a trace of his justifiable prickliness, Rorem responded to inquiries he must have heard endlessly during his celebratory year.

Ned Rorem:

Q: *What are your recent commissions?*

A: *I'm writing a work for seven mallet instruments for Evelyn Glennie. I'm sort of morally against percussion and think it's ornamental at best, but I think in terms of the commission at hand. Most of what Mozart wrote was by commission.*

Q: *Many of your works involve diverse, short movements instead of long statements. Is that a disadvantage?*

A: *People worship size. Mahler and Bruckner simply go on too long. The Schubert Octet I heard last week was disgusting, it was like a fungus that never stops growing. When you hear Debussy or Ravel, they say what they want to say and then stop. That's the French style.*

Q: *Is it true that you dislike improvisation?*

A: *As an art, yes. You have to work hard to make it sound improvised like Benny Goodman's cadenzas, all worked out. Someone recently sent me a Bill Evans recording, and it sounds like a lot of doodling. (Luckily, Rorem didn't remember that I was the culprit).*

Q: *Do you feel that the tonal revival is here to stay?*

A: *For 500 years, the pendulum has swung back and forth between harmonic and contrapuntal poles. You simply must create what you believe in.*

Q: *Is crossover music our destiny?*

A: *Crossover's just a word. They said it about the music of Milhaud and Gershwin. But singers, they have it all wrong when they use different styles—just as pop singers can't sing opera.*

Q: *What do you see in the future of music?*

A: *I can't see the future any more than you can. But what's the matter with a concert with 200 people? There's a lot of mediocrity, and America still has an inferiority complex about the arts.* (By phone, November 1, 2003)

In some other interviews at the time, Rorem was even more pointed. "A song cannot have padding, opera has almost nothing but. Opera, no matter how poetic, is mainly prose; song, no matter how prosaic, is mostly poetry. Opera is more about singing than what's being sung, while song is an emanation of a text wherein the interpreter's ego vanishes. Song is a child of economy and taste, while opera is born of strength and silliness. Still, opera signifies for song-makers what theater does for novelists: possible major acclaim in a philistine world."

Rorem's music has surely not received its due, considering the amount of praise the composer has received for more than half a century.

In an interview in the *New Yorker* magazine, Rorem encapsulated the pain, disappointment and sheer impracticality of being a creative artist without bitterness: "The frustration of being nonexistent keeps us awake."

And another comment is perhaps even more poignant: "No artist wants to be understood. What an artist wants is not to be misunderstood."

Rorem's *Miss Julie*, featuring members of the Curtis Opera Theatre and the Curtis Symphony became available in a two-CD set from Albany. It also included *Aftermath*, an intense song cycle for baritone, cello, violin and piano written in response to the Sept. 11 attacks.

After that devastating day, Rorem wondered what was the point of music at all. "It soon became clear that music was the only point," he said. "Indeed, the future will judge us, as it always judges the past, by our art more than our armies—by construction rather than destruction."

20. OUR SOUNDTRACK AND GIFTED WOMEN

In the 1930s and '40s, composers from Berlin, Vienna and Budapest came to Hollywood, many to escape the Nazis, and invented symphonic film music. In the 1970s, when electronics began to take over, John Williams from Long Island brought symphonic music back.

Even Williams finds it hard to believe that many more people know the theme to *Star Wars* than know Beethoven's Fifth Symphony.

The son of a percussionist for CBS radio, Williams wrote a piano sonata at 19, studied with famed Rosina Lhevinne at Juilliard in preparation to be a concert pianist, and played in jazz clubs. Williams played the famous riff in Henry Mancini's *Peter Gunn* theme, orchestrated at Fox for such greats as Alfred Newman, Dimitri Tiomkin and Franz Waxman, and arranged for Mahalia Jackson, Doris Day and Vic Damone. He even wrote the TV music for *Lost In Space* and *Gilligan's Island*, the film music for the many disaster films and *Fiddler On The Roof* before teaming up with Steven Spielberg for *Sugarland Express* and *Jaws*.

In those 40 years of collaboration with Spielberg and George Lucas, besides *Superman*, *Schindler's List*, *the Indiana Jones*, *Jurassic Park* and *Harry Potter* films and even 14 years of conducting the *Boston Pops*, Williams has composed most of the scores we remember.

This gracious and warm presence came to conduct the Orchestra at the Mann in July of 2003 and, after telling Emil stories as usual, we got down to business.

John Williams:
Q: *How enjoyable is it to conduct after weeks of composing?*
A: *I never had a conducting career before my years with the Boston Pops, but I've grown to enjoy it more as the years have gone by. I'm very fortunate, having the opportunity to conduct the symphonies in Boston, Chicago, Cleveland, Pittsburgh—and the Philadelphia, in wonderful shape now, at a benefit in Saratoga. It's the best seat in the house.*

Q: *Does it bother you that film composers aren't respected in symphonic programming?*
A: *Most film music is, of necessity, by its nature, accompaniment. A lot of it is not conceived to stand alone, and therefore much of what we do isn't appropriate for a concert.*

The most difficult challenge is adjusting for foley (sound effects) and dialogue. But we've become addicts of visual stimulation, and with the power of cinema to reach millions of people, we're always sensitive to the dangers of easy popularization. The future of music may be more linked to film and television, but as musical purists, we consider such a notion unrealistic.

Q: *Why such a stigma, that doesn't exist in Europe?*

A: *I think prejudice against film music is stronger in the U.S. because of our American inferiority, a ghetto mentality about our composers compared to the European school. Stravinsky and Schoenberg lived in Beverly Hills and were never seduced into film music, and studios are still concerned that ivory tower high-mindedness wouldn't contribute to commercial success.*

Q: *Do you get more time to compose on a Spielberg film?*

A: *Not really. It's the same eight post-production weeks to write the material, mix, make a 10-line sketch and record. The orchestrations are conceived in the composition, and the copyists mostly are doing a stenographic job.*

Q: *Do you have a favorite?*

A: *Well . . . probably* Close Encounters (of the Third Kind).

Q: *Does it bother you when other composers blatantly steal from you?*

A: *(Laughs) I don't pay much attention.*

Q: *You used to work with Hollywood studio musicians; now you work with the London Symphony a lot. How is that?*

A: *The musicians playing now are coming from the same background, from Curtis and Juilliard, and there's not much difference anymore.* Star Wars *was done in London because it was filmed there, and because the British government gave assistance to invigorate their film industry.*

Q: *What composers most influenced you, and what do you listen to now?*

A: *Bach, Beethoven, Chopin. As a piano student, I was pretty conservative until I heard Stravinsky, Prokofiev, the modernists of the late 1940s and '50s. Maybe I'm regressing, but Haydn and Mozart appeal to me the most now.*

Q: *What would you like to be remembered for?*

A: *Anything! Few people are remembered at all, one of the great sadnesses of life. Probably* Star Wars, *but* E.T. *would mean even more.* (By phone, July 10, 2003)

At that concert, co-concertmaster William de Pasquale received a well-deserved standing ovation for his moving violin solo in the theme from *Schindler's List*. Williams told the crowd that, after seeing the rough cut of the film, he was sufficiently moved to tell director Steven Spielberg that he needed a better composer. "I know," said Spielberg, "but they're all dead!"

I felt enough good vibes from Wiliams to see him after the concert, and give him regards sent from Emil. I also told him that I had gotten an email from a reader who said Williams had stolen the theme from *Star Wars* from the transition back to the reprise of the Intermezzo from Puccini's *Manon Lescaut*.

Fortunately, Williams laughed heartily. "Frankly, I studied piano, and am not an expert in opera. If someone thinks I'm stealing, I'm glad they think I'm stealing from someone great like Puccini!"

He is a class act all the way.

Jumping ahead to August 2012, I visited Tanglewood for Williams' 80th birthday concert, attended by a packed house inside the shed and an army on the lawn. Keith Lockhart and Leonard Slatkin conducted, with cellist Yo-Yo Ma, pianist Gabriela Montero, clarinetist Anthony McGill and violinist Gil Shaham reprising the performance of Williams' piece for President Obama's inauguration. There were videos thanking the composer for his contribution to American music from the Boston Red Sox (during his *Fanfare for Fenway*) with players saying thanks, by George Lucas, Bill Clinton and even President Obama, who said that Williams had written the soundtrack to most of our lives.

James Taylor sang, and Steven Spielberg made an appearance, claiming that he had been working with the composer for half of Williams' life. He said that while filming in distant corners of the earth, people came up humming *Star Wars* or *E.T.* to him, and that "whenever I get near any body of water...well, you know."

Williams came up on the stage at the conclusion to a deafening applause, seeming overwhelmed by the reception. He deserved every bit of it.

Emil worked with Williams many times, and remembered back when he first began writing film scores and his father John Williams Sr. was the major timpanist in studio calls. John wouldn't refer to him as Dad, saying, "Can timpani play a little softer?" or "Timpani, can you hold that beat back a little?"

One year, John received a holiday card. "Dear John, Merry Christmas. Timpani."

In another season, a Mann summer concert of film music was being organized, and someone suggested a few pieces—maybe ten to fifteen minutes worth—by Ennio Morricone, the veteran Italian composer of spaghetti Westerns, *The Mission*, *Cinema Paradiso* and hundreds more. Librarian Robert Grossman found that his scores were not available for rent; the terms of playing his music meant that Morricone himself had to conduct, be flown in and put up in an excellent hotel. Needless to say, his music was not programmed.

Luciano's Farewell

After the Opera Company had ended their Pavarotti Competition, the Chamber Orchestra held another in 1996. Pavarotti expressed an interest in singing in the new hall to several of the ensemble's board members, who juggled schedules for months to arrange the event.

"Ever since our musicians had the thrill of performing with Mr. Pavarotti in 1996 for (his final) Philadelphia International Voice Competition," said Marc Mostovoy, "we hoped we would have another opportunity to work with him and provide our orchestra with great visibility." Pavarotti's friend Leone

Magiera conducted, with a Competition winner, Cynthia Lawrence, along for arias and some duets.

Pavarotti, 67 and father of a 8-month-old daughter named Alice, arrived in Philly with an entourage.

Luciano Pavarotti:

Q: *Why such generosity toward the Chamber Orchestra?*

A: *Because of the possibility of another competition. I will do it if you want it. It was always a pleasure, something pioneering that gave me an opportunity to give young singers a debut and follow them afterward. There were at least 100. And those times in this beautiful city will remain in my memory forever.*

Q: *What would it take to make another competition happen?*

A: *Money! Let's see what the city has to say.*

Q: *What singers were your inspiration?*

A: *There were many, because we imitate each other from Caruso on. When he made those records, there were no others to measure him against.*

Q: *How is your voice these days?*

A: *It is fine, but my doctor says I cannot sing if I am sick. I canceled the Met because I was sick, and was crucified, people were spitting on me. I am fine now, but if tomorrow I am not well . . . (shrug).*

At the end I will say goodbye and teach Alice to sing. I don't sing to her, I yell to her. If she is crying and I sing louder, she stops. (By phone, September 11, 2003)

The stagehands had built a dressing room with a door behind the orchestra, avoiding having the portly Pavarotti make his entrances from the wings.

I had a seat on the main floor, and Dolores Cascarino had one in the conductor's circle, behind the orchestra. (Many musiclovers insist on those seats to watch the conductor, something Maestro Sawallisch said he was never really comfortable with). We switched for the second half, and I saw that Lawrence had the music on her stand, with Pavarotti only having the words in large type. The librarian told me that some parts had all been transposed down a whole tone to allow the great tenor to reach the high notes.

Later on, I was told that food had been ordered for 6 p.m. after the rehearsal, going so smoothly that it ended early. When Pavarotti found that the caterers hadn't arrived, he emphatically said, "No food, no concert!" The promoters tried to placate him until the food finally arrived in the Kimmel Center plaza; he even insisted on a golf cart to reach the plaza, and required a new suite of large furniture in his hotel.

It wasn't one of this legend's great appearances, and he surely knew it; the audience didn't seem to care, and the affair raised plenty of money. It was to be the last time Philly would hear that magnificent voice.

Sopranos Back to Back

Many times major artists schedule their debuts in a role with second-tier companies before moving on to world's top houses like the Met, San Francisco, Paris, Vienna or La Scala.

That makes Philadelphia's Opera Company fortunate to have some of those debuts, including soprano Patricia Racette as Leonora in Verdi's *Il Trovatore*—the first opera performed in the Academy of Music back in 1957.

Between rehearsals, this lovely and passionate singer spoke about the challenges of the spotlight.

Patricia Racette:
Q: *You've said an artist has little control and great responsibility.*
A: *Yes. The audience's focus is usually on the person singing. You think of all the people who put work into that moment—the sets, costumes, direction, the conversations and collaboration that went into the interpretations, the musical side. But in that moment, the artist is carrying the ball.*

Q: *How do you go about achieving what you're known for, making your characters three-dimensional?*
A: *Acting and singing are two different skills, but they're ingeniously intertwined in opera. We have such opportunities to express text, giving us more to work with, not less. That's what I'm most proud of, fleshing out a person from personal experience, because I can't stand operas with cardboard people.*

Q: *What opened the door to opera?*
A: *I remember it absolutely clearly during the days when jazz was all I knew. I was sitting on the floor and someone played a recording of Renata Scotto singing (Puccini's)* Suor Angelica. *A whole musical world opened up to me, and I remember tearing up and hearing every color and nuance. I love her artistry, and she worked on the whole* Traviata *with me.* (Academy of Music, October 16, 2003)

For a while, the Opera Company found it economical to stage two operas concurrently on opposite days, minimizing the Academy rent. *Trovatore* was paired with *Susannah* by Carlisle Floyd, an American classic for 50 years that had achieved more than 700 performances worldwide.

Floyd, the son of a Methodist minister in South Carolina, transposed the biblical story of Susanna to a setting he knew, rural Appalachia. His music is melodic and well-scored, complete with some lovely arias, folk songs, hymn-singing and dances. His simple story involves the pretty, flirty and innocent Susannah, "nearly 19," who is persecuted by evangelical small-towners after being discovered bathing nude and enduring being seduced by a preacher.

Mary Mills portrayed Susannah, and I found that she and Racette had both received big breaks because of reigning diva Renée Fleming. Fleming recommended Mills for a 1992 *Louise* in Geneva, after the pregnant Fleming couldn't take part in the production. And, in 1998, Racette took over when Fleming bowed out of a Met *Traviata*.

Any American composer who writes an opera has to be either mad, naively hopeful or commissioned. It certainly helps to be well-regarded in more musically hip locales such as Houston, Santa Fe and San Francisco.

Susannah—a prism of human nature that was once viewed as a reaction to heartless 1950s McCarthyism and has been staged as a feminist manifesto—has lasted.

There were no political motivations for Floyd, only 28 at the time, just the intention to compose a beautiful, dramatic work. He succeeded completely, and had the ideal interpreter in the youthful Mary Mills, who absolutely could look the part.

Between rehearsals for *Susannah*, and with her 2-year-old daughter Emily at the baby sitter's, Mills took a coffeehouse break to talk about her career and her obvious affinity for the opera's title role.

Mary Mills:
Q: *How much of you is in Susannah?*
A: *Probably more than in some roles. In many ways, it's easier to focus in your acting on a character that's extremely different from you.*
Q: *What are the challenges in the role?*
A: *She is upset most of the time, pushing the limits of the voice when she's reacting to horrible things. You have to find a balance of what her range of reactions would be. She can't be freaking out all the time. And the accent—like singing "ain't." My Texas accent is much different than one from Tennessee (where the opera takes place).*
Q: *Haven't you been involved in some stage disasters?*
A: *Plenty. Once at Washington in* Carmen, *Denyce Graves threw her head back and knocked out Neil Rosenshein, and I sang Micaela's aria to him thinking he was acting. In* La Bohème *at the Met, Luis Lima cut his hand in the first act clowning, and when he took my hand to sing "Che gelida manina," it was covered with blood.*
Q: *Do you fear being role-cast?*
A: *I'm incredibly lucky to be able to stick to works I'm attracted to, and don't mind doing my bread-and-butter roles often because of such beautiful music. When you can feel the audience is moved, you react to them completely. Connecting to an audience is the best feeling in the world. That's why we do this thing called opera.* (Coffee shop, October 3, 2003)

The Opera Company decision to schedule two operas during the same time period seemed like a shrewd way to minimize the huge Academy rental fees. Yet the scheme was clearly unpopular with subscribers.

I've never been as blindsided by an issue in my career," said artistic director Robert Driver, "or taken as much grief on any topic. I never dreamed it would be such an issue, but people simply wanted a distance between their operas. Perhaps we lost more of an audience than we saved on efficient use of the Academy."

Only Play Music You Love

JoAnn Falletta returned to lead the Chamber Orchestra of Philadelphia in Dvořák's *Czech Suite* and Aaron Kernis' *Musica Celestis*, with its artistic director Ignat Solzhenitsyn performing for the first time as a Chamber Orchestra soloist with a guest conductor in Mozart's Piano Concerto No. 24.

JoAnn Falletta:

Q: *How do you choose repertory?*

A: *That's easy. I just choose pieces I love. I've always done that—if I don't believe in a work a hundred percent and can't make a case for it passionately, I don't do it. That's the way I communicate best. But sometimes you can do a piece if a soloist feels strongly about it and make a new discovery.*

Q: *How do you juggle the two orchestras in Buffalo and Virginia?*

A: *It's very stimulating, and I take different approaches to both and take what I learn from one to the other. It's a little crazy sometimes, but I can't imagine anything I'd rather be doing. No complaints from me!*

Q: *Are your choices at all determined by the quality of the players?*

A: *Yes, but only to bring out their own special character. American orchestras have developed to the point that regional orchestras are playing the way the major orchestras played years ago. I choose works for the orchestra's personality, to help their strengths and allow them to bring their special character to the piece. That's very stimulating to audiences. They can feel it.*

JoAnn Falletta. Credit: Fred Stucker.

Q: *Why are regional orchestras able to be more adventurous in programming?*

A: *Those audiences feel a much greater sense of ownership. If the orchestra commissions a work or takes a risk, they're there behind you. It's exciting to see the connection between the orchestra and the community, and it's the job of the music director to forge those ties. My object is to connect, to communicate, to convince the listener to love these works as much as I do.* (Kimmel Center, November 1, 2003)

What are the odds that two female conductors, both enthusiastic supporters of American music, would be leading a city's two major orchestras—in the same building and on the same weekend?

Any local bookie would call it maestra vs. maestra at the Kimmel Center, marking the first of two times that Falletta would be leading the Chamber Orchestra the same week that Marin Alsop was conducting the Philadelphia Orchestra.

In my column, I mentioned a strange omission of sales wisdom—of the 25 CDs then available in each conductor's catalog, not one boasted a cover portrait of these lovely dynamos.

The Reigning Queen

Soprano Renée Fleming was the reigning queen of opera, the most famous vocal artist in 2003—and still is a revered presence. Born on Valentine's Day, Fleming is an embodiment of the shift toward the dominance of American-trained singers. There were years of singing jazz in clubs, and even jazz tenor master Illinois Jacquet admitted to being stunned by Fleming's rendition of Billie Holiday's "You've Changed." Finally, there were stints at the Juilliard School and in Vienna for studies with the legendary Elisabeth Schwarzkopf and Arleen Auger.

When Fleming received an honorary doctorate from Juilliard's 98th commencement last May, she implored the students: "Challenge the idea that the arts are for a select few—teach, make more people love what you love, and help them to understand why you dedicated yourself in the first place."

Before a scheduled recital with the Orchestra of St. Luke's, I wangled an interview with her, to be held at her agent's office in New York. Dolores, a longtime voice teacher, was excited about it, and offered a bunch of inside singer questions, if we could get to it.

I had about 30 questions written in a little book, thinking we'd only cover a few. One was about her teaching methods, though she emphatically said, "I'm not qualified to teach!"

Renée Fleming

I assumed she'd be relatively formal. Sitting comfortably in a simple blouse and slacks, she treated me like an old friend; her candor and complete lack of guile were true delights. Pictures don't covey the size and deep greenness of her expressive eyes. She noticed my long list and generously said, "All right, maybe we'll need short answers! Let's go!"

Renée Fleming:
Q: *Why do you have such an affinity for Strauss?*
A: *Strauss loved the soprano voice very much, and sopranos love him. It's a matter of fit—for instance, a voice may have an Italianate sound, or French, but my voice is characterized by a Strauss or Mozart sound. His vocal writing could have been written for me, they fit perfectly. And I love the characters, too, they're very complex, real people.*
Q: *Isn't a tremendous confidence in your technique required to get to that point?*
A: *Absolutely. When young singers want to skip over the technique part and go right to the artistry, I always say—you don't understand, technique is a means to an end, it's not the end. My goal as a singer is to forget that I'm singing, and just express the emotions and meaning of the texts, to be a singing actor. I worked very hard on that for many, many years.*
Q: *When did your daughters (Amelia and Sage, then aged 10 and 7) realize that you're more than just the usual working mom?*

A: *They don't articulate it well enough for me now to be sure they do think that. I know now that they realize that what I do is relatively unusual, but more than that I'm not sure. They're proud of me, that much is clear, but they hate that it takes me away from them. I've changed my whole schedule, doing much less opera now, and more recitals and concerts. Operas just take too much time.*

Q: *Did you see singing André Previn's A Streetcar Named Desire, a televised premiere, as a risky or courageous choice?*

A: *Yes, it was a very challenging part. Even actresses think twice about taking on the role of Blanche. It's been five years, and I love the role and the piece even more now.*

Q: *Besides* Traviata, *you've recently done Rossini's* Armida, *Dvořák's* Rusalka, *Bellini's* Il Pirata *and Massenet's* Thais, *all relatively obscure works, plus* Streetcar. *Is there a reason?*

A: *I love to do new works and lesser-known pieces because it makes you free from all the comparisons. Also, let's face it, the really well-known stuff is Italian, and I don't think I have much of an Italianate sound.*

Q: *You still have performance anxiety, and do you still need a coach?*

A: *I battle it a lot, and it rears its ugly head every couple of years. Of course, the more well-known you become, the more everyone, including myself, expects. And, yes, I need outside ears, absolutely. I always work with people.*

Q: *You've said that you still have nightmares about "Dove sono" (from Mozart's* The Marriage of Figaro*).*

A: *For me, it's excruciating. You're completely exposed. I'll put that role away for a while. But if I could go back in time, I'd want to meet Mozart, a true genius.*

Q: *But you sing it so beautifully, as if we're eavesdropping on a private moment.*

A: *Do you know how long it took for it to sound that way?!* (New York office, November 29, 2003)

To this day, I wish I had had the nerve to give Miss Fleming a copy of Romeo Cascarino's beautiful song cycle, *Pathways of Love;* despite her gracious warmth and kindness, I just got cold feet. I had taped the interview for Dolores, though, a treat she greatly enjoyed.

From the train station, I went right to the paper and enthused that I had a great interview with Renée Fleming.

One editor said, "Oh, the ice skater?"

21. ABOUT EDITORS

Writers don't resent editors because they aren't good souls—it's because there are very few who make their pieces better. We're often accused of bringing biases to our work, but often the personal slant of the editor is what gets presented to the reader.

If your subject of relevance happens to be in the features (or "Arts") category, like mine, you're often dealing with editors who have utterly no awareness of, or interest in, your specialty. It has always amazed me that many features editors rarely feel they have to know—or learn—a minimal amount about the admittedly-wide spectrum of music, theater, dance, television or art, the major areas of their assignment. Yet no sports editor would last a week after admitting to no interest whatever in basketball or ice hockey.

I've had editors insist that explanation is necessary for standard terms like *a cappella*, adding in parentheses such clarification as (meaning the chorus will sing without instrumental accompaniment). The rationale is that every story should be accessible to all readers, who just might be lured into reading *something* out of their usual interest.

Take, as an example, a typical line from a recent *Daily News* baseball story: "Going for a hit-and-run, Odubel Herrera blooped a dinger just past the hot corner with a check swing on an outside splitter for another RBI." That sentence, with similar explanations inserted for the non-fan, would amount to a lengthy and incredibly cumbersome page of clumsy text. I've never had a clue what writers were talking about in hockey stories but, if I suddenly became interested in the sport, it wouldn't be that much of a hardship to look the terminology up, ask someone or, these days, email the writer.

Such choices make the assumption that the readers are basically dumb, and will take out their frustration at not understanding some crucial fact by not buying the paper. Another way of pandering to this idea is the chopping up of long sentences into little bite-size statements. Of course, a newspaper story isn't Faulkner, yet it's easy to take it personally when a fairly long, graceful sentence ends up reading like *Dick and Jane at the Seaside*. Some editors have admitted that they're aiming at a 14-year-old reading level and, having recently been shown a pile of horrendously-scrawled college applications, they could be right. And don't even attempt a semicolon, regardless of Strunk and White.

Back in *Bulletin* days, pop writer Matt Damsker would spend many hours polishing a Sunday feature story only to find that Bob Sokolsky, one of the nicest men and most arbitrary editors, had chopped it into an unrecognizable mess. Matt would seethe every weekend and on Monday mornings, after a completely innocent greeting by Sokolsky, he realized the uselessness of objecting.

One incorrect assumption is an editor's identification of his/her knowledge as typical of the average reader, and ultimately usually untrue. (There must have been at least 20 *Daily News* editors during these 33 years prior to the ever-patient and caring Laurie Conrad, most with a specific arts genre they respond to, and some with none at all.) Now that the writer's email addresses are pasted onto a story, readers feel no hesitation to question, comment, berate or occasionally praise. If they don't understand, you'll immediately find out what readers wanted to know.

The only way to feel sympathy when your copy has been 'adjusted' is to consider the task of an editor, a writer whose job it is to amend someone else's work. It must be a normal tendency to make the piece flow the way the editor would have written it. Too many times, it seems as if the perhaps-unintended intention was to bleach individuality or personal signature from the piece, as if everything is meant to read in a generic style.

Through that published email address, writers get deluges of pitches for articles. When some asked for reviews, it was evident that the pitcher hadn't even bothered to see that we didn't publish them, not that difficult to research in a town with only two daily papers. Usually the publicity for smaller groups was given to a volunteer, who had no idea what to do but who hoped to get major coverage for every little concert. I spent many hours explaining that a story on such a program would mean no coverage on their big annual gala at a high-rent venue, in essence teaching them their job.

To make things better for both of us, I prepared a one-page "How to be a public relations expert," numbered and eventually sent to 187 volunteers or organizations—until my address was cancelled. Most of it was common sense—for instance, don't sent ten pages of bios, and keep the time and ticket price a mystery; don't expect us to have to look up the time, address, phone, etc., on a website, and why not actually look at the listings to see their format, and submit them like that? Not surprisingly, it made little difference.

Once in a while, I would ask a desk editor to go to a concert, in the hopes that they would have a little more sensitivity to some of my stories, which probably represented just filler. On one occasion, I felt that a performance of *La Bohème* would offer a sure-fire introduction into what that thing was I was writing about. He left right after the opera and, when I asked him about it a few days later at the desk, anticipated a positive response. "Well, it was pretty ridiculous," he said. "They're freezing cold, so they go to a sidewalk café!"

For awhile, one editor trusted me enough to simply forward my pieces to the copy desk, making me especially careful in not betraying that respect. During those two-plus years, I received not one single question or correction from a reader but, when those golden days ended and my work was scrupulously massaged, a host of readers continually delighted in pointing out small errors and confusing sentences. A few of the gotchas were admittedly made by yours truly, though the majority had been inserted. (Your editor will usually say it was done by "The Desk," an assertion that may well be true, with the guilty party's initials lost in computer ether by the next day.) In the latter case, never respond to a reader by blaming editing for the mistake, because that breaks a basic rule of journalistic ethics—which, believe it or not, really exist. Taking the weight is why you get the big bucks. In either case, just apologize for being remiss and praise the correspondent for being shrewd enough to notice.

Another item to negotiate is whichever style book the newspaper uses, often the *New York Times* or the AP books, though the *Daily News* also uses an in-house style format. These style conventions are usually inflexible (Mr. Loaf again).

Since staff writers have the advantage of being in the office to disagree or display outrage at changes, freelancers have to accept the drawback of seeing painful alterations in print. You may be lucky and have an editor who discusses changes. Don't count on it. It is folly to think that complaining will have an ultimate effect, because the editor will either cite a style rule, claim that the original phrase was imperfect, argue that the change was made to make the copy more understandable to the general reader (i.e. the editor), blame the desk editor, assert that space was an issue or sometimes tell the truth: because they can. Besides, their concern at the moment will, understandably, always be tomorrow's paper, not yesterday's.

Still, you want to cheer when your copy is made better by *Daily News* masters like Jack Morrison, one of the great rewrite men of our generation, who lavished his alchemy to shape several of my passionate, hurriedly-written obituaries into moving narratives. Of course, there was the late Rick Selvin, still remembered for his award-winning headline after conspiracy buffs forced the exhumation of JFK's assassin: OSWALD STILL DEAD. Rick, always seen in his trademark plaid wool long-sleeved shirt, had great respect for the writer's copy and his occasional clarifications, always in the spirit of the original intention. I honored him with the compliment-intended moniker of Riccardo Selvini.

Passion in Music

I had joined many of Harold Boatrite's friends in producing a CD of his chamber music, and a few orchestral works by the Chamber Orchestra were in already the can. I asked Jeri Lynne Johnson if she would include two of Harold's works on one of her programs, with the idea of filling out a CD with his music.

Since she only had the option of choosing music for two season concerts, it was a lot to ask. Graciously, she accepted and led the Oboe Concerto and the Harpsichord Concerto—my favorite of his larger works—with dedicatee Temple Painter as soloist in January of 2004. Temple would also play the Bach F Minor harpsichord concerto in that program.

I didn't know the oboist, Geoffrey Deemer, who would turn out to be an important factor in a project yet to jell.

Considering that my first *Daily News* column was about Boatrite's 50th birthday concert, it seemed appropriate to introduce Johnson to the composer and the soloist at their house. Though Bach, Beethoven and Mozart aren't available, hearing a conductor gain valuable insights with a composer and soloist was a fascinating experience.

Jeri Lynne Johnson, Harold Boatrite and Temple Painter:

Q: *How valuable is this discussion in interpreting the music?*

Johnson: *It's invaluable for a number of reasons, because I want to be respectful to the wishes of the composer, rather than make an educated guess. I can study the style of a period, but here I have a living resource to confirm decisions and ensure that the piece is played the way it was conceived.*

Boatrite: *I've had situations where an instrumentalist simply won't do what you ask. Once, I even paid to hire another player.*

Johnson: *From my perspective, performers have become the least important part of the process, because you have the great composers on high. Without an auditory record of their wishes, their scores have an authority that most performers feel bound slavishly to obey.*

With a living composer, the score is an instruction manual for gestures and ideas and not something to be taken so literally that it inhibits spontaneity, creativity on the part of the performers.

Boatrite: *I'm not as specific in the score as a lot of composers. Some get very upset about small deviations. But if a conductor has a good idea about projecting the music, I'm more than willing to agree if it makes musical sense.*

Painter: *There's no reason in my book to be negative or rigid in music, because there's always something else to learn.*

Q: *What happens in the case of disagreement?*

Johnson: *The composer always wins in those cases; it's his piece. I'm there to interpret it and bring it to life as he conceived it.*

Painter: *(French composer François) Couperin said you must change the tempo according to the instrument, to the acoustic, the audience, the way you feel that day. Beethoven is supposed to have thrown his metronome across the room.*

Boatrite: *There's one passage where I wanted to simulate the sound of a 7-foot guitar. I couldn't have thought of that color, Temple thought of it. This is the advantage of collaboration.* (Their home, January 13, 2004)

Booking Dad, and Stepping Aside

If you were a booking agent, would it seem like an abuse of influence if you booked your father?

Mervon Mehta, who was the Kimmel Center's vice president of programming, wasn't too concerned, because his dad is Zubin Mehta, who was here with the touring Israel Philharmonic.

"No one accuses me of nepotism with this booking," Mehta said recently, laughing. "If my dad was a marginal artist, I'd have to ask the board to take a chance on him, but considering the track record of both him and the Israel Philharmonic, the good part is I don't have those fears.

"Considering that I'm often engaged for pieces requiring a narrator, you'd think it was an advantage to have a conductor as a father. To date, though, I haven't had a gig with Dad."

In January 2004, Ignat Solzhenitsyn was officially given the post of music director of the Chamber Orchestra, taking over the 39-year-old ensemble from founder Marc Mostovoy, who was to serve as senior advisor.

"I am truly proud to have been able to play a part in Ignat's growth as a conductor," said Mostovoy, "and know that he will continue to bring the highest standards of music-making to our great chamber orchestra. Meanwhile, I will intensify my work in developing innovative approaches to classical music presentation for the audiences of tomorrow."

Those approaches included a multimedia *The Four Seasons* with slides of diverse artworks and, in the ensemble's last concert, a computer projection derived from a Bach concerto and a collaboration with the Scrap Arts percussion ensemble.

Mostovoy soon discovered that, even in a changing world where everything had to be visual, that no one cared about these innovative ideas to develop audiences. It was amazing to me that, in the midst of young supposed-visionaries, this highly conservative person was the cutting-edge guy.

Choices Made for Love

For a little over two years, I had often dealt with the Kimmel Center's assistant publicity director Keisha Hutchins, who was a dream to work with. I also found she had also attended my old alma mater, Germantown Friends School, and had created a group, *Vanishing Peoples of the Earth*, singing her own material with her partner (and now husband), percussionist Doug Hirlinger.

What was even more remarkable was that, in the eighth grade, she had joined the chorus to go on a trip, eventually being inspired to sing by choir director Larry Hoenig. (My son had also been inspired by Larry, and eventually even sang next to him in the First Presbyterian Church in Germantown choir.) That led to Oberlin College, and some jobs back home in clubs, doing *Messiah* with the Philadelphia Singers and even singing in the chorus with the Denyce Graves' *Breaking the Rules* show.

I was surprised when she called to tell me she was leaving this secure post to venture into the uncharted territory of the tough music business. This struck me as an act of enormous courage, considering how much she was admired in her job.

"It was not a hasty decision," Hutchins said, "but I just turned 29, and it simply was time. I need to keep evolving, to hone in on my own style, whether tinged with folk or blues or soul, and to maintain a strong sense of who I am musically.

"Doug has encouraged me from the beginning, from when we worked in New York before I came home and took the Kimmel Center post. And we still write our songs together.

"Though I studied piano at Settlement Music School from ages 9 to 19, my mother (who died in 1999) always knew I would be a singer, and I got to sing in *Godspell* and *The Most Happy Fella*."

Hutchins is one of the few singers who enjoys having her performances picked apart to make them better.

"I have only love for the Kimmel Center," she said, "for they helped me grow as a professional and supported me at all times. If I had to practice singing in a dressing room on my lunch hour or go to a rehearsal, they understood. I always felt valued."

I've heard Keisha and her band many times, and believe she has a unique voice and writing talent, a gem playing in a rough field that grinds artists up. She was a neighbor, moving to New York to Columbia graduate school for music education and teaching, one of her many passions, and finally back to Philadelphia. On the way, she and Hirlinger have become became the parents of two girls, Clellan and Alma. Singers have been discovered—and made huge stars—with only a fraction of the presence and talent of Keisha Hutchins, and I keep hoping that quality will prevail and put her name up in lights.

Keisha Hutchins. Credit: R. Todd Miller.

One of Harold Boatrite's students, a gifted musician and choral conductor named Timothy McDonnell, founded a choral group called Schola Nova. He held a program at the Fleisher Art Memorial, featuring three pieces by Boatrite, Samuel Barber's *Agnus Dei* (a vocal setting of his famous *Adagio for Strings*), choruses from Cascarino's *William Penn* and a new *Kyrie* by my pal and fellow student Sidney Grolnic. Sitting there in that medieval-style grotto and hearing the sound of these voices and this heartfelt music, I felt deeply fortunate to be in a city that held as many amazing performers and a wealth of unique venues like the Fleisher.

Another Italian Maestro

After conducting four operas here, Italian conductor Corrado Rovaris was named the Opera Company's music director in April 2004 by its head Robert Driver. He was actually suggested to Driver by Maurizio Barbacini, who had functioned as principal guest conductor.

It turned out to be a brilliant move, because Rovaris has shaped the company's orchestra into a magnificent ensemble and given the company's productions a real gravitas. Every one of his musicians have come to admire him and his tough-love ability to get the best out of each of them toward an ideal rendering of each work.

Rovaris was born in Bergamo, a town I had gotten to know well—and where we would share an adventure later. He admitted that it took him a while to tell his organ-playing father, who was a little disappointed at such a distant move. Rovaris, his wife Anna and three-and-a-half year old daughter Marta, were preparing a permanent move to Philadelphia.

But He Kept Going

Back in the 1960s, soon after the Glenn Gould explosion, musiclovers were highly impressed by the Brazilian pianist João Carlos Martins. His performance of the impossibly percussive Piano Concerto by the Argentinian composer Alfredo Ginastera was a stunner, and his recordings of Bach replaced the sewing-machine drone of early scholars with an exuberance, romance, passion and enormous freedom that Bach would have admired.

Jay Hoffman, who was acting as his American impresario, asked if I could review a film about him, *Martins' Passion*, that was playing in the art houses. I had wondered what had happened to this artist after his meteoric rise and impressive Bach CDs.

The film recounted that Martins had inaugurated a soccer team in Central Park, where a flying stone numbed his hand and sidetracked his career. He worked in a bank in São Paolo, became director of the Stock Exchange and managed a boxer while slowly healing. After a triumphant comeback in 1984 he relapsed again, and returned to Brazil, where he started a construction company and was accused of political embezzlement—a claim that was later dismissed.

Moving to Miami after this scandal, he took injections, investigated faith healing and did therapy again until he was able to begin recording the complete works of Bach, again in Bulgaria. Things became even worse after muggers hit him with an iron rod, causing a cerebral hematoma.

Martins persisted, returning in 1991 to Carnegie Hall, though he couldn't shake hands or lift a coffee cup.

It touched me because of my knowledge of hand damage concerning Gary Graffman, Leon Fleisher and my friend Jimmy Amadie. The film showed him playing carefully, with very moving moments in scenes with his three brothers, who grew up in a house with six pianos; a visit and a duet with Dave Brubeck; and constant practice sessions on a silent keyboard.

We get the point from the first frames as a piano is nervously lifted by ropes into Martins' high-rise apartment, an emblem of the precariousness of playing. And the finale, after he plays the Brazilian national anthem at a soccer stadium with left hand and right thumb, ends with thousands of healthy hands in the air.

I found it a highly inspiring story about a man for whom loving Bach and loving life are the same thing.

Postscript to this gripping film: Though Martins could no longer play, he was about to record the Bach *Brandenburg Concertos* with the English Chamber Orchestra—as conductor.

Before Superstardom

Another huge star of today who stopped into Philly on her way to the top of the international scene was the Metropolitan Opera soprano Stephanie Blythe. She was returning to perform the title role in Offenbach's frothy comedy *The Grand Duchess of Gerolstein*, a kind of high-class Gilbert-and-Sullivan style spoof of royalty, the military and privileged pomposity in general.

The usual scheming, double-crossing and mistaken identity staples of slapstick comedy were all ideal ingredients for these singers and proven comic actors. Comic master Kevin Glavin was back with the Opera Company, and Dorothy Danner's always-kinetic directorial instincts were ideal.

Blythe, whose repertoire ranged from this goofy gem all the way to the following year's Seattle Opera's staging of Wagner's *Ring*, enjoys avoiding any typecasting.

Stephanie Blythe:
The piece isn't terribly vocally challenging for me, just a bawdy, madcap romp with convoluted plot and lots of misunderstanding. The men are breaking me up continually. In opera, the funny stuff has to be pretty well choreographed, it has to move the story forward. I've learned that when you goof around it may be funny to the performers but not always to the audience.

You can't get this high level of performance without everyone being together for five weeks as we can here. You'd be surprised at the name of very famous houses where you don't see the conductor until the last few days.

What do I listen to? Well, I love an album by Sammy Davis Jr., a very underestimated singer, made with guitarist Laurindo Almeida. (Academy of Music, April 20, 2004)

Kevin Glavin was both hilarious and accurate, as always, and spent his evenings holding court at D'Angelo's. (Just recently, in July 2013, I saw him do a brilliant *Falstaff* at Chautauqua, in English, and hoped he would someday be able to do it in Philly—of course, in Italian).

Buffalo to Carnegie Hall

Because of our growing relationship, I attended the Buffalo Philharmonic's 2004 concert at Carnegie Hall, where conductor JoAnn Falletta stirred a hard-boiled Big Apple crowd to many standing ovations, an encore and a rave in the New York Times. The May bash called Spring For Music, with $25 tickets, presented a week of regional orchestras and, because New Yorkers were used to standard repertory, the concerts were packed with unusual choices.

Falletta had inspired this orchestra to an impressive level, blurring the category of the Big Five and bringing her exuberant orchestra to new heights, and playing Alexander Zemlinsky's rare and colorful *The Mermaid*.

I wrote, "Falletta and Curtis-trained Atlanta Symphony conductor Robert Spano are shining lights on the American-born conducting scene. Next time around, perhaps Philly will have grown up enough to have an American conductor—maybe even a woman." Just wishful thinking.

In May 2013, she and the BPO returned—along with an astonishing 1550 of her hometown Buffalo supporters—to lead Reinhold Gliere's enormous *Ilya Murometz* symphony (recorded complete for Naxos). This is the advantage of having board members who are music lovers and actually attend concerts.

Despite the success of this program, Carnegie Hall announced that the 2014 Spring for Music program would be its final one.

Misha in Overdrive

I didn't have a chance to interview the brilliant dancer Mikhail Baryshnikov, though I saw him become a car.

In the theatre piece *Forbidden Christmas, or the Doctor and the Patient*, Baryshnikov's character was dumped by his fiancée for a man with a car, and simply decided to become a car himself. Seven years later, he elicited the help of a doctor to save a little girl, and the play becomes a journey through a blizzard to the girl's house—with help from an angel in red spats.

Though I would show up just to see this legend doing anything, only a dancer could have the rubber-limbed agility to actually morph into a car.

Pops on Tour

The following week, the Boston Pops Esplanade Orchestra, with Keith Lockhart conducting, made a return appearance at the Mann. Lockhart, who was also music director of the Utah Symphony, had been conducting *Tosca* with the Boston Lyric Opera.

Keith Lockhart:

Q: *Do you still enjoy touring, both last year with your Utah Symphony and with the Pops?*

A: *I find it very enjoyable for five or six weeks but might not if we did it for 30. The Boston Symphony musicians are at Tanglewood, and of these best freelancers in the Boston area, 30 of them sub with the symphony. I sincerely believe that if we played 25 weeks a year, it would be one of the top orchestras in the country.*

Q: *Why is American music so rarely played?*

A: *America's always had a musical inferiority complex. But Leroy Anderson's pieces, for instance, are every bit as expertly written as Strauss waltzes. And they were beautiful enough for (the late conductor) Carlos Kleiber to play.*

Q: *Considering how little rehearsal time is available, what was it like for you to work a month on an opera?*

A: *It was a real luxury, and every measure of* Tosca *is a brilliant meal. The Pops is another world, like being a short-order cook.* (By phone, June 19, 2004)

22. OPERATIC ADVENTURES

Since her first Philadelphia appearance, Russian superstar soprano Anna Netrebko had achieved superstar status at the Met, the Mariinsky Theater in St. Petersburg, and the major houses around the world.

She was to perform in Donizetti's comic gem *Don Pasquale*, with comic basso extraordinaire Kevin Glavin, and leap immediately into a Met production of *La Bohème* when news came that she had cancelled.

"Over the past six months, I have taken on too much work with singing and promotion, and I have paid a price for this," said Netrebko. "I am completely exhausted and need time to rest. Most importantly, I do not wish to perform for the wonderful Opera Company audience if I am not the very best I can be, since that is what all opera audiences deserve. I hope that I will be able to come to Philadelphia again soon."

That, of course, would not happen, considering her meteoric rise to the top of opera's list of major stars. American soprano Sari Gruber, a fixture on American operatic stages, replaced Netrebko.

Other famed sopranos were in town, though: Dame Kiri te Kanawa for a recital, and Renée Fleming, singing her signature *Four Last Songs* by Strauss at the Orchestra's opener.

Playing the Devil

In the world of French opera, only *Carmen* receives more stagings than Charles Gounod's *Faust*. The universal tale also has been endlessly adapted, including as the Broadway musical *Damn Yankees*.

Goethe's colossal 1808 drama inspired Gounod's graceful, melody-packed opera, performed at our Academy of Music only four years after its premiere in 1859. Met regular Richard Bernstein made his debut here, portraying the mighty Mephistopheles.

Richard Bernstein:
Q: *What happens when your ideas differ from those of the director?*
A: *My method is that, for the first two weeks, I leave my ideas at the door, let myself be a sponge and learn the interpretation. If I had a concern I'd mention it privately, not in front of the company. Basically, if it doesn't make sense, I'll make it make sense.*

Q: *You've sung both great Mozart roles for this company—Figaro and Don Giovanni. Is it true you'd like to alternate singing Don Giovanni and his sidekick Leporello some day?*

A: *Yes, Sam Ramey and Ferruccio Furlanetto did it in Salzburg once. Leporello is even harder to sing than Giovanni. It's the ultimate challenge, and I hope eventually to do it. Ramey is my idol. We still use the same vocal teacher.*

Q: Haven't you had great breaks from cancellations?

A: Yes! One was a 1998 opening night radio broadcast performance in Chicago, and Bryn Terfel, the Figaro, canceled. Zubin Mehta was conducting. Great cast—Susan Graham, Elizabeth Futral, Renée Fleming. I'll never forget that Renée came to my dressing room and said, "You're going to be great."

And he cancelled again and I got to sing with Cecilia Bartoli, a true prodigy of her art. She calls me "Figaretto," little Figaro, because Terfel is 6 (feet) 3 (inches).

Q: With all your experience, do you still have any fears?

A: Well, during these rehearsals, I wake up in the middle of the night and think, "Oh, my God, tonight's opening night!" (Academy of Music, October 4, 2004)

Back to Bergamo

Faust was soon followed by Donizetti's comic masterpiece *Don Pasquale*, with Kevin Glavin back in the title role. It gave a chance to speak with Corrado Rovaris, leading his first production since being named the Opera Company's first music director.

Rovaris, a fixture in European houses who had led four operas here in the last five seasons, was born in the beautiful northern Italian town of Bergamo, also the birthplace of Donizetti. (In fact, most of my many Bergamasco days used to begin with heavenly pastry and coffee at the Pasticceria Donizetti, now a restaurant, on the main street.)

Over bowls of pasta, I spoke with the gracious and friendly Rovaris.

Corrado Rovaris:

Q: Since you have excellent credentials in Europe, why would you want to join this company?

A: For me, it's important to finally work in a place where you have an ongoing, lasting relationship with a company. It's not just a job, much better than coming into a house for one production like a gypsy. It's refreshing to collaborate with people you can trust.

Q: Are there other advantages to being music director?

A: Your ongoing relationships with the singers and musicians are very valuable. You want to make Rossini sound like Rossini, Mozart sound like Mozart and Puccini sound like Puccini, and have the common understanding to make it happen.

Q: What are the major differences between European and American houses?

A: Rehearsal time! In Italy, for instance, we have five orchestra rehearsals, four dress rehearsals with orchestra and two general rehearsals. Here, we have only three orchestra rehearsals and two dress rehearsals.

Q: *Would you consider suggesting chamber operas in smaller halls?*
A: *Yes, certainly, why should we have to lose this large part of our repertoire? With 650 seats, perhaps in the Perelman Theater, we might try something new, but it's too big a risk for the (2,900-seat) Academy.* (Academy of Music, October 11, 2004)

This has come to pass, as the Company has presented innovative chamber operas like Osvaldo Golijov's *Ainadamar*, Kevin Puts' *Silent Night* and Thomas Adès' *Powder Her Face* and many more during the last few seasons in the Perelman Theatre.

A family friend from Bergamo, Italy, Orso Locatelli, who played in Riccardo Muti's Luigi Cherubini Orchestra in Piacenza, was a fine hornist. His brother, pianist Leonardo Locatelli, has visited me three times, playing twice in the Kimmel Center plaza and twice at my son's church; he even invited us to his wedding in June 2015, with the reception 50 miles away at a hotel on the breathtaking Lago Maggiore.

Corrado knew of these two young musicians and their father, the well-known sculptor Giò Locatelli and, of course, they knew of this famous Bergmasco through many local appearances. I asked him once if he would be willing someday to go with me to visit them at their house outside Bergamo, a virtual museum of Giò's incredible work. He agreed, and I headed to Italy, met him at the bottom of the *ascensori* below Bergamo's old town, and we had a marvelous meal with *molto animato*. Of course, they immediately went into Bergamasco, a dialect clipping the last syllable of nouns, making *La Casa del Giò* (Gio's house) sound like *Lacadjo*. Luckily, the musicians' aunt Ebe translated the conversation into French for me.

Orso eventually made it into the Maggio Musicale Fiorentino, and spent a few months practicing the horn parts in the 16 hours of Wagner's *Ring* cycle, to be led by Zubin Mehta in Valencia and Florence from 2007 to 2009. But when Mehta decided to take the Spanish horn players to Florence and didn't need the Italians, Orso decided to get out of the tough music business.

Perfect Casting

I was first royally impressed by soprano Angela Brown as Serena in *Porgy and Bess*, and marveled as she saved the day in recent Opera Company of Philadelphia seasons as a last-minute replacement in both *Ariadne auf Naxos* and *Don Carlo*.

She had learned those last two roles as a "cover "—or understudy—at the Metropolitan Opera, and they finally hired her—after three unsuccessful auditions. Her days as a cover came to an end in November 2004 when she finally went on, spurring the *New York Times* to gush, "At last, an *Aida*." She showed me a great photograph of herself, beaming outside the Met and

Angela Brown and the author.

pointing to a poster advertising herself in *Aida* with a "SOLD OUT" banner. Fortunately for the Opera Company, she already was scheduled for their performances of *Aida*. And the company's general and artistic director Robert Driver, who was directing this production, admitted to relief at having signed contracts for her appearances the following season in *A Masked Ball* and the East Coast premiere of Richard Danielpour's *Margaret Garner*, with libretto by Toni Morrison.

In between rehearsals and a dizzying media schedule, I met with the gracious and exuberant soprano.

Angela Brown:

Q: *What was it like to try for the fourth time at the Met?*

A: *I didn't have anything to lose. They couldn't hurt my feelings any more. It didn't bother me to be a cover. If you can cover, you can sing all over the world and fill in with stars. I never worried about being rich or famous, just about being good while paying dues. And I've also learned that if you're not with the conductor, you're wrong.*

Q: *When did you first consider opera?*

A: *Opera wasn't played in my home, but I remember being first enthralled when I heard Leontyne Price singing the United Negro College Fund song. Then I saw her final Met broadcast,* Aida, *in 1985. That was it for me, I felt completely at home.*

Aida has been part of me since 1992—at the Met, she needed to be born, now she can romp and play. On stage, Angela goes away, and Angie takes over! But the woman in the finale would not be me, I wouldn't have crawled into that tomb. Honey, a man's never that good! Aida could have gone back to Ethiopia, gotten married, had a couple of kids and had fond thoughts of Radames, who was beating her country's behind. But NOOOOOO . . . Right now, I'm living my dream, right where I need to be. (Academy of Music, February 5, 2005)

In opera, things often are as dramatic backstage as they are on stage. Brown had to cancel opening night because of the flu, saved by soprano Lisa Daltirus. And the tenor to sing Radames, Renzo Zulian, had the bug as well. Luckily, Academy of Vocal Arts tenor Dongwon Shin, who had covered the role for the Lyric Opera of Chicago (and who was scheduled to audition for the Opera Company the following week), took over.

The last-minute changes gave conductor Corrado Rovaris a couple of tense days, yet the stress wasn't felt by the audience, who enthusiastically hailed the impressive production—as well as the two singers who saved the day.

Exotic Journey

In the summer of 2003, I had visited the New York agent Jay Hoffman, who had put me in touch with many artists for interviews. Before I left, he gave me a copy of an opera starring one of his artists, soprano Patricia Schuman, was featured, though I didn't open it for weeks.

It was an opera written in Spanish by Daniel Catán, entitled *Florencia en el Amazones*, and it completely stunned me. In those days, I had the luxury of filling in the dead weeks with reviews of film music and new CDs, and wrote the following:

"In 1991, Mexican-born Daniel Catán's *Rappaccini's Daughter* was premiered in Mexico City, with a San Diego performance three years later. A Naxos CD of excerpts from the 1991 performance was released last year, demonstrating Catán's moving instinct for dramatic writing—especially in a mesmerizing duet.

"Catán is clear about his motivation: 'The originality of an opera need not involve the rejection of our tradition, but rather the profound assimilation of it, achieving the closest union between a text and its music.'

"This means a tonal palette, ravishing orchestration and vocal lines buoyed by the music. It also meant a 1996 opera, *Florencia en el Amazones* (*Florencia in the Amazon*), just released in an Albany double-CD live recording.

"Catán has developed even further, for this is a brilliant, exotic and compelling work.

"In the superb libretto by Marcela Fuentes-Berain, now-famous opera diva Florencia Grimaldi (portrated by Schuman) returns to her birthplace in Brazil's remote Maneus to find the love she left behind years ago. Her shipmates are a woman writing Florencia's biography (without realizing her subject is on board), a couple disillusioned with love, a ship captain and his nephew, and Riolobo, the spirit of the Amazon River, who appears in many guises.

"This metaphoric voyage of discovery involves finding love and life's meaning in unimaginable ways, and has a brilliant premise: everyone on this life voyage has a quest, and finds one completely different than what they were searching for.

"Catán, now living in Los Angeles, has found his calling with this masterpiece, an organic gem with real magic and many exquisite moments. Any opera company with access to a large orchestra could perform it, though few will have seven singers who can sing in Spanish, and gets my highest recommendation."

It actually had been a co-commission between Houston, Los Angeles and Seattle opera companies, the first Spanish-language opera to be commissioned by major United States opera houses.

It had been first done in Seattle in 1998 and, when I saw that the Seattle company was reprising the work in February 2005, I called a friend I had meant to visit and headed west.

According to Seattle Opera general director Speight Jenkins, "No production has been requested as many times of me as Catán's *Florencia en el Amazones*."

I thought the production was magnificent, simple and eloquent, and the music completely transported me. Many operatic recordings had come my way in the past 25 years though, since *William Penn*, nothing had touched my soul like Catán's music.

At intermission, I was invited into a little press room, and the public relations woman introduced me briefly to Catán, who introduced me to his stunning wife Beatriz. While I was having a coffee, the tall, very striking composer came over and said, "What was your name again?" When I told him, he said, "My son lives in London, and he collects all the press clips about my music. I remember now what you wrote about my opera. You were the only person who really understood what I was trying to achieve. Thank you! I'm very happy to meet you! Did you really come all the way from Philadelphia to hear it?"

Naturally, I was completely stunned, and amazed that he remembered something I had written years ago. He introduced me again to Beatriz, whose smile completely froze me into an oafish stammer. "She's my inspiration," he said, and all I could get out of my throat was, "It's no wonder."

Catán also wrote a comedy, followed by an opera based on the film *Il Postino*. That latter work was commissioned by the Los Angeles Opera, headed by Placido Domingo, postponed for several years because of funding. After it opened in 2010, with Domingo as Pablo Neruda, it was eventually broadcast on PBS.

Catán, the Mexican composer of Russian Sephardic Jewish descent, was working on an opera based on the classic Frank Capra film *Meet John Doe* when he died in his sleep at the age of only 62.

Catán had the courage to write in his native Spanish, restricting some companies from performing his works, especially *Florencia*. But isn't hearing operas in non-standard languages what the original concept between projected subtitles was about? How often have we heard Smetana's *The Bartered Bride* or any Russian operas (if not for the crusading Valery Gergiev?)

In December 2014, I had a chance to see it again with Jeannie Pool, while on a Los Angeles trip to visit Emil. In my dreams, I'd imagine it portrayed in Philly by the brilliant AVA-trained Ailyn Perez, who's now performing all over the world. At least we can dream.

Singing Insights

In April 2005, tenor Andréa Bocelli was the hottest artist around, having sold over 45 million CDs. His pop and sacred records had gone platinum, the operatic recordings, to my years more like tin. Audiences were still captured by his fervor, and a concert at a ballpark allowed another chance to speak to Bocelli by phone from Italy.

Andréa Bocelli:

Q: *Do negative reviews about your operatic recordings, like the* Tosca, *bother you?*

A: *Absolutely not, though I was a little disappointed at the beginning. Honestly, you can't listen to a performance when you're doing it, but I know when it's beautiful and when it's not. I'm less interested in the critics than in my own judgment. When I do something and I like it, I am very tranquil.*

Q: *Since your parents weren't musical, how did you first hear recordings of the operatic legends?*

A: *Because my mother discovered that when I heard music I stopped crying.*

Q: *What were the most important things you learned from Franco Corelli (Bocelli's inspiration, whose great career was shortened due to stage fright)?*

A: *Most important was hearing his recorded voice, because I first became a student when I was a child listening to his recordings. Sooner or later his destiny will be the same for me . . . Being on stage is a little bit like being naked, with just the voice and the intimate things you can give.* (By phone, April 3, 2005)

Christine Goerke reached major stardom at the Met through her November 2013 performances as the Dyer's Wife in Strauss' *Die Frau Ohne*

Schatten. Eight years before that, she was here with a much lighter role: Rosalinda in the Strauss classic *Die Fledermaus*.

The day after she had screamed her head off at a 10-inning Phillies win, I met with the charming soprano before rehearsal.

Christine Goerke:

Q: *How hard is it to go from drama to comedy?*

A: *It's hard when they're back to back, and I just came from doing Strauss'* Elektra. *But since I don't get to do comedy much, this is a breath of fresh air, especially since this cast has some seriously funny guys.*

Q: *Do you mean this role is easy to sing?*

A: *Vocally, it's one of the hardest things I've ever sung. In the second act, my aria needs a light coloratura, then 30 seconds later the Csardas (a Hungarian folk song) is a really a mezzo aria. If you have a light voice, you lose the bottom. A deep voice loses the top, but it's lots of fun to sing. I'm really working, but no one's gonna know! Comedy is much harder to do than operas where you just stand up and sing—we call that "park and bark!"*

Q: *What was your big opportunity?*

A: *I came into the Met young artists training program through the back door, because Glimmerglass Opera's (artistic director) Paul Kellogg recommended me to James Levine at the Met. I began singing "Come scoglio" (from Mozart's* Cosi fan tutte*) for him on that huge Met stage, and when I heard myself in that house it was a true surreal moment. I just said "Wow!" and kept on going. Even though I didn't know whether he liked me, I went outside and called everyone I knew. There can be a lot of stress, especially for those on big public view. I wouldn't want to be Renée Fleming, with your life on display, but we do it because we get to sing.* (Academy of Music, April 12, 2005)

Collaborative Advantage

Pianist Charles Abramovic is one of the most respected musicians in a city brimming with famous names. A compelling artist of remarkable versatility, Abramovic has accompanied such luminaries as violinist Sarah Chang and flutist Jeffrey Khaner on disc. A Curtis alumnus who studied with Eleanor Sokoloff and Leon Fleisher, he plays regularly with Network for New Music, Mimi Stillman's Dolce Suono and at Temple recitals, and his own *Piano Concerto* was played by Orchestra 2001. I recall a recital at the Free Library, where Abramovic played a program of obscure piano works by Tibor Serly—clearly a pianist who's an incredibly fast study, with a commitment to neglected works.

On one diverse recital, Abramovic played two world premieres: his wife Heidi Jacob's *Fantasy for Piano* and Temple professor Richard Brodhead's *Sonata Classica*, the latter commissioned by the Philadelphia Chamber Music Society.

Abramovic and Brodhead came together in a roomful of pianos to talk about the *Sonata*.

Charles Abramovic and Richard Brodhead:
Q: *How do you decide what the shape of the piece will be?*
Brodhead: *The exact shape and title didn't emerge until the middle. If you're sensitive to it, the piece's personality dictates more and more, and the will of the composer becomes less important.*

Abramovic: *There's a similar process in performance, because the piece tells you what it wants to do, almost recreating the process the composer had. One of the greatest things for a performer is that interaction when you feel what the composer wanted. In any piece, there's a certain gestation time to feel secure in doing justice to the music.*

Brodhead: *It's a great gift to be working not just with a pianist but with a composer who's married to a composer.*

Q: *How much of an advantage was it to have a colleague play it?*
Brodhead: *Since Charles can play anything, I didn't have to restrain myself technically. I can't tell you . . . the sense of security knowing that one can have a dialogue with the performer.*

The score is only a road map, and you use notation to balance directing the performance and withholding, giving freedom. I want it to be helpful, not an obstacle, always erring on the side of sparseness.

Abramovic: *No matter how thoroughly a composer notates, there's always interpretation. Surprisingly, with most of the composers I've worked with, they've asked if it can be interpreted more freely. But it's invaluable to have the composer steer you in the right direction.* (Temple University's Rock Hall, May 1, 2005)

Mentoring Legend and Dancing Lovers

I had a chance to watch legendary mezzo-soprano Marilyn Horne, a few days before a concert of American art songs, guide five marvelous young singers from AVA and Curtis in a master class.

The class was unusual for the inclusion of 17-year-old Justin Gonzales, a senior at Girard Academic Music Program in the Philadelphia school district, who sang with urgency and youthful energy. Horne showed how reining his big voice, controlling breathing patterns and shaping phrases enriched the song's beauty and made the most of his talent.

Horne, whose long and brilliant international career specialized in the *bel canto* repertoire, has remained one of the most beloved figures in opera and in the art of singing. Though it took decades to become acknowledged, Horne had provided the voice for Dorothy Dandridge in the 1954 film version of *Carmen Jones*—at age 20.

During the master class, the ebullient and deeply observant Horne stressed technique, insisting that this has to be solid before discussing expression. "After technique, beauty is most important," she urged her students. "Then, just sing!"

Horne was funny, supportive and warm to the slightly nervous singers, putting them at ease with her graciousness while insisting on details that made obvious improvements. When she demonstrated, singing half-voice while seated, she filled the room with a huge, plummy sound.

When asked how to avoid a conflict with their voice teachers' advice, Horne said, "I only give them what I know, to try to address a problem that can magnify.

"I know that singers that young can sing too much and damage their instrument. Two hours is the absolute limit for Justin, though I'm the worst one to say that," she said, roaring with laughter, "because I sang all the time from age 5 on!"

In May 2005, two principal dancers who had come from San Francisco Ballet were to partner in Pennsylvania Ballet's production of *Romeo and Juliet*. They were quite candid about their reason to change coasts, and were a delightful pair.

Zachary Hench and Julie Diana:

Q: *How did your relationship start?*

Hench: *We were on tour in Spain and, because of injuries, they asked me to learn (Stravinsky's)* Symphony in C *in two days. So it started by our working many hours together, then we danced it together in Barcelona.*

Diana: *And then went for sangria afterwards.*

Q: *How did you come to Philadelphia?*

Hench: *My family lives close by so, after a tour two years ago, we checked out the company, and Roy (artistic director Roy Kaiser) talked to me about* Swan Lake *and he really wanted Julie too, so it just worked out.*

Q: *Wasn't it difficult to leave San Francisco?*

Diana: *I was really nurtured in my 11 years, was dancing a lot, my family just moved there, the city is gorgeous, and we had an incredible apartment right on the water. But I felt it was time for a change of repertory and colleagues, just a change of inspiration. I felt very positive, with a gut instinct, and went with it.*

Hench: *I had gone to Central Pennsylvania Youth Ballet in Carlisle, and Roy had guested with my school. Once he took me to a Phillies game, and he was driving an Alfa Romeo at the time. I was 12, that was cool, and I got to see the Pennsylvania Ballet, too. And we're able to afford a house here, because in the Bay area the real estate's crazy.*

Q: *Did you know any of the company's dancers?*

Diana: *I met Arantxa (Ochoa) and Matt (Neenan) at the School of American Ballet in New York, where we both trained. And it was a joy to dance a piece choreographed by Matt this season, very organic.*

Q: *What's it like to dance a love story you're living?*

Diana: *I want to kiss him all the time. I have to pretend to be shy! We're dancing these characters, they're really us and everyone else just goes away—except we're not going to kill each other!*

Q: *Do you think the audience can tell a personal involvement?*

Diana: *Definitely. The romance, yearning, passion all carries. And this incredible music—the first day I got the chills, it's that powerful.*

Hench: *Audiences can tell reality from acting, even if you're really good, but what if you're a good actor and you really feel that way?*

Q: *Are there any disadvantages?*

Hench: *Well, you tend to be harder on each other because there's such a comfort level. With another partner, maybe you wouldn't say something about a small detail to be polite. But we'll say, "Use your back more! Get off my leg!"*

Diana: *We're still respectful to each other, but for some couples it's devastating.*

Hench: *I've seen couples screaming at each other. But we just want each other to be as good as we can be.*

Q: *Is there that much difference between companies?*

Hench: *One of the major differences is Roy, the fourth director I've had…He's still the boss, and strict, but it makes for a comfortable environment that's easy to work in.*

Diana: *Also, because of the opera in San Francisco, their ballet only performs after the first of the year. So in October, you're working on something you won't dance until April, knowing there'll be injuries and casting changes. Here, there is a chunk of concentrated rehearsal time, then you just perform it. It's so much better.*

Hench: *Technically (in San Francisco), you were juggling nine ballets at the same time in your head.*

Diana: *Basically you're a vampire, because you never see the outside of the theater. Some nights I was just glad to get through it, so I could go on the next night. Here, I can give 110 percent, so it never gets mechanical.*

Q: *How has your transition gone?*

Hench: *There's a lot of competition and plenty of egos in the ballet world. In San Francisco there are 20 principals, so you're competing all the time. We haven't encountered that here.*

Diana: *Everyone has been very welcoming and supportive, and it makes me glad to come to work. I knew nothing about Philly, but I love the season changes, the cheesesteaks, the East Coast flavor. In California, too many avocados.*

Q: *Julie, how do you keep so thin?*

Diana: *Once I hit 22 my body found its place, and I'm lucky because I eat what I want. But last night I was going for a Klondike bar and I thought, no, we're doing the balcony scene tomorrow with a lot of demanding lifts for Zack.*

Hench: *My mom always says I have to lose weight.*

Q: *What do you feel coming back from the audience?*

Diana: *Everything. I grew up and evolved in front of San Francisco audiences, but with this new audience I'm asking myself what do I want to show them about me and how will they respond? That's very exciting, to reestablish yourself, but it's also added pressure we put on ourselves. We're our own worst critics.*

Hench: *It's a thrill to feel when they're involved. The most gratifying thing is to meet someone you don't even know, who comes up and says that they were touched by our work. But that's what artists do, they please people, and that's when we are most happy. That's live art.* (Ballet studio, May 14, 2005)

At the last performance of that *Romeo and Juliet*, during their third curtain call, Hench lowered to his knee and offered a ring to Julie. The audience erupted, seeing a true love affair before their eyes—without a tragic ending.

After becoming favorites of Philadelphia audiences and reaching their retirements, the pair became ballet master and ballet mistress but, after teaching a masterclass on an Alaskan trip in 2015, decided to relocate, running the state capital's only ballet school, the Juneau Dance Theatre.

Guests, Genius and Drama

I was first aware of Bebe Neuwirth as Lilith, the neurotic sidekick to Frazier on *Cheers*, and saw her dazzle Broadway in the Tony-winning *Sweet Charity* and *Chicago*. We didn't get to see her leggy dancing ability at the Mann, for she probed the intense drama in master songs by Kurt Weill and the team of John Kander and the late Fred Ebb, with charts played by Philadelphia Orchestra.

In a phone conversation from New York, she explained that there's much more to her intentions than just standing up and singing.

Bebe Neuwirth:
Q: *How did you go about creating this show?*
A: *First of all, I don't feel comfortable just singing cold. I have absolutely no interest in that at all. For me, it's about telling the story of characters who express an emotional point of view through these songs, capturing the moment in their life leading them to sing. I see Weill's songs as coming from a beautiful heart. I'm shocked that I'm having such a good time, and it's thrilling to have that sound behind me.*

Q: *How much of a nuisance is it to be remembered by TV roles?*
A: *Sometimes I have to remind myself that several million people see you on TV, and only several thousand if you're on Broadway for two years. I have a hard time responding when someone says, "I didn't know Lilith could dance." It's just baffling to me. I've turned down an enormous number of jobs to avoid being pigeonholed as mean mother, smart bitch, or something.*

Q: *How important was family support and arts education to you?*

A: *Family support—absolutely crucial. Since art and music are used in therapy, it's obvious to me that the hearts and minds of children need to express themselves that way, and I think it's criminal to take arts from the schools. That's why performing, and theater, has great importance as a community event, not just a derivative like television, because it's the modern-day equivalent of people sitting around the fire telling stories, singing and dancing as we did thousands of years ago. That's a primal need, what human beings do.* (By phone, July 7, 2005)

Right after Neuwirth, Vanessa Williams burst into town, living her high-school yearbook words, "See you on Broadway!"

In movies like *Eraser* and *Soul Food*, with Great White Way appearances in *Kiss of the Spider Woman* and Stephen Sondheim's *Into the Woods*, and with 4 million albums sold, Williams had made her mark from Miss America days as the essence of versatility. Her schedule of television appearances, award hostings, cable television productions and singing gigs is daunting. Before her Orchestra appearance at the Mann, she had just performed in a Hollywood Bowl concert celebrating Stephen Sondheim's 75th birthday, and was about to launch the TV show *Ugly Betty*.

Vanessa Williams:

Q: *How do you deal with the pace of your schedule and place priorities on what you're offered?*

A: *When you're raising four kids you can't do everything. I go with what intrigues me, what fuels my fire. Like the Sondheim program, watching Stephen react, that concert goes in my memoirs. I'm lucky to have a great support system, and work to incorporate as much as possible.*

Q: *Could you have imagined in* Eraser *that you'd be working with a future governor?*

A: *Hardly! I've seen him since, though, and even sang at his inaugural.*

Q: *Did you have a lot of doubts that you would make it?*

A: *Well, having majored in musical theater, singing, dancing and acting every day, I approached it in a practical sense. Living near New York, I could take the train and audition, then go back and work harder if I didn't get the job. It was much more tangible being in suburban New York City and having some idea of how it all works.* (By phone, July 18, 2005)

The Secret

In October, the two piggybacked operas were Rossini's *Barber of Seville* and Verdi's *Un Ballo in maschere* (*A Masked Ball*). At our favorite espresso emporium near the Academy, conductor Corrado Rovaris spoke about the challenge.

Corrado Rovaris:

Q: *What is it like to be rehearsing two operas at once?*

A: *It's difficult because there are only 24 hours in the day. But I feel quite lucky to have a chance to play this music, and with two ideal casts.*
Q: *How important is it to have worked with the artists before?*
A: *Very! I've often worked with the leads at La Scala and here many times, and everyone cares about all of the other roles, with plenty of energy on stage. This is the secret for giving pleasure to the audience.* (Coffee shop, October 14, 2005)

Homage to Genius

Composer George Antheil once said, "Mozart fans experienced the same sensation a modern baseball audience might feel if their blindfolded hometown team beat a visiting non-blindfolded team."

On his 250th birthday, Mozart deserved a little attention. Swiss researchers attempted to learn more about his gifts by comparing DNA in a skull purported to be his, with thigh bones thought to be from his grandmother and niece. The tests were inconclusive.

Johann Chrysostom Wolfgang Amadeus Mozart was blessed with an unexplainable miracle, an innate understanding of music and the human persona that must have seemed wildly incongruous coming from an upstart who loved to clown, curse and gamble.

Any musician would agree that a composer writing a symphony in full score—and in ink, within days—is evidence that it was already fully formed in the creator's mind.

And to write music while drinking large quantities of wine, or between shots at a billiard table, is proof of another power at work. His concertos, symphonies, sacred music and chamber works have a powerful dramatic component, evident even to the most casual listener. Their structures are perfect, and the melodies always hummable, making its purity utterly daunting to budding composers. It's even more remarkable considering that, as a boy, Mozart was terrified by the sound and even the sight of a horn.

The passion is between the notes, and they can look simple to pianists or singers. The great pianist Artur Schnabel famously summed it up well: "Mozart's sonatas are too easy for beginners, too difficult for artists."

It's through his operas, like the masterpieces with librettist Lorenzo da Ponte *The Marriage of Figaro*, *Cosi fan tutte* and *Don Giovanni*, that we feel the full humanity of Mozart's music. The characters come to life through music that reveals everything about their inner thoughts, even if listeners don't understand the words.

Many know Mozart only through the play and movie *Amadeus*, a tale with only some truth as far as his impertinence and persistence is concerned. Peter Shaffer's fictional idea of his being poisoned by rival Antonio Salieri derives from an 1830 dramatic, yet satiric scene written by Alexandr Pushkin and later made into a one-act opera by Nikolai Rimsky-Korsakov.

Salieri was undoubtedly humbled by the young man's gift. It is known that he accompanied Mozart to *The Magic Flute* just weeks before Mozart's death at 35, and that he was one of the few mourners at his funeral.

Books like *The Mozart Effect* claim, with little evidence, that his music will make kids smarter. Maybe his music simply provides an unconscious awareness of the sublime.

Drama in Music, and Opera

Playwright Michael Hollinger created a fascinating piece of theater, *Opus*, as a famed string quartet struggles with the departure and replacement of one of its members. The five actors in the cast simulated the quartet playing but, since they are supposed to be world-class musicians, real world-class music was needed. The production turned to a quartet of Curtis Institute players who recorded fragments of four works—including mistakes—that were woven into the story.

The play—which eventually made its way to New York after some revisions—used Beethoven's seething op. 131 as the catalyst in the play, given its world premiere by the enterprising Arden Theater.

Hollinger, who had written a play for the Arden every two years since 1994, had been a viola major at Oberlin College though he hadn't played for 18 years until some recent chamber music sessions at Jenkintown's Settlement Music School. He had always wanted to find a musical subject for a play, and had played op. 130 at a college summer camp. He discovered that op. 131 was widely considered the Mount Everest of all string quartets—and Beethoven's favorite among the 16 he wrote, though it was not played until eight years after his death. The seven-movement, deeply probing work requires an almost spiritual rapport among the four musicians.

When the Curtis musicians played for the cast, "you could have heard a pin drop—the most stunning example of artistry imaginable," actor Greg Wood said. "Their combination sound just appears, almost like it's not coming from instruments. We watched video of them with coaches for a week, and could never have done this without them."

An instruction to the actors in *Opus* reads, "Don't fake playing music." Instead, director Terrence J. Nolen decided to have the players move only their bodies and bowing arms.

"We found that the movement of the right (bowing) arm is the essential breadth of the music, the left (fingering) hand distracting," explained Hollinger. "Not fingering meant, "Let's have full disclosure, we are not playing these, we're just dancing with the instruments." Rehearsals were like watching a park full of Chinese do tai chi—almost meditative, a bonding experience for the actors, like instrument boot camp."

There's a scene when the playing obviously comes apart, and the musicians had to deliberately go astray. "That was part of the fun," said one of the Curtis players, "and we didn't want to overdo it, since Michael was very specific in his instructions. We all saw the play on opening night, and it was clearly written (with) firsthand knowledge of playing. I thought the actors did an exceptional job of mimicking the bowing, and the way their bodies moved."

Making the replacement violist a young woman was a dramatic stroke that enhances the play's tension to its stunning conclusion. "I felt strongly about that early on," said Hollinger. "There's a general truism in the theater that rituals are powerful, especially when you break them.

"Everything in the play about musicians also holds true for theater artists, and I have immense admiration for actors creating anew every night, totally dependent on other performers, just like chamber players. It's an interesting parallel, and this has become my valentine to theater-making through another art form."

The show played off-Broadway by the Primary Stages company, where Hollinger is a faculty member, and was also made into a radio play. And it sounds pretty similar to the story in the recent film *A Late Quartet*.......

25. PREMIERE, AND PREMIER MUSICIANS

The big show in February 2006 was the opera *Margaret Garner*, written by Richard Danielpour with libretto by Toni Morrison. It had been co-produced— and already premiered—by the Detroit and Cincinnati Opera Companies, and starred favorite singers—Denyce Graves as Margaret, Gregg Baker as her husband Robert, Angela Brown as her mother Cilla and Rod Gilfry and the plantation owner. And the Opera Company of Philadelphia had the advantage of having the work mature during its performances in the other two cities.

The story: Margaret and Robert Garner and her mother, Cilla, were slaves on a Kentucky plantation owned by Edward Gaines, who probably fathered some, if not all, of Margaret's four children.

Leaving Cilla behind, the family escaped in 1856 to the free state of Ohio, where they were captured—but not before Margaret killed one of her daughters rather than return her to slavery. By some accounts, Margaret wanted to kill all the children, and herself, but was caught before she could.

In real life, Robert escaped, and Margaret was found guilty of destruction of property and sentenced to go back into slavery. Accounts differ: She was either sent to a Mississippi plantation or was on her way there when she died of typhoid at the age of 24.

Morrison altered the details of the story for dramatic effect in *Beloved*. And in the opera, there are only two children, both killed by their mother. Robert is lynched, and Margaret kills herself. Unchanged is the social furor over Margaret Garner's desperate act, and the judicial clash between Ohio's charge of murder and Kentucky's charge of destroying property.

Theater director Kenny Leon had run the Alliance Theater in Atlanta for a decade and directed Broadway productions, including *A Raisin in the Sun* on Broadway.

I had an opportunity to speak with Danielpour, director Kenny Leon and Baker during the tight rehearsals.

Richard Danielpour:

Toni Morrison and I met in the fall of 2000, and we found we were pitching each other the exact same subject. She once said she couldn't do it, and it took me 33 months instead of the 27 I estimated, and the process was full of enthusiasm and terror. It's not the composer's job to tell people what they should be feeling but to make it work as opera and theater. But this story tells what happens when we forget that we all belong to the human family.

Kenny Leon:
Q: *What did you think when you were asked to direct?*
A: *They wanted an African-American director, and they know my projects are all about diversity—that juices me. But black folks don't want to see anything dealing with slavery, because that's in the past. And white folks say, "I had nothing to do with that, can't we just move on?" That's why we have racial problems, and let stupid things get in the way of the beauty that happens between people.*

Q: *What were your ideas to avoid that happening?*
A: *I tried to avoid any material with baggage, of bales of cotton, boxes, straw hats, black men with no shirts and a man on the porch with a mint julep. We only bring in what's necessary to tell the story. And though I was worried about earning Toni's (Morrison's) trust and respect, we were on the same page about this, and during the process she gave me gentle reminders of what we agreed to in the beginning.*

Q: *What do you want people to feel?*
A: *The story is all about what happens when you take away somebody's ability to love. It puts a face on slavery and forces you into that situation to think, if you lost your mother, your husband, the future of your children, your freedom, then, as crazy as that is, taking the life of your children might be an option.*

This is not about guilt, it's more about helping us to live better, to recognize that everyone has the opportunity to be free. This isn't a slave story, it's a love story.

Baker visited Garner's actual home and plantation in Kentucky, a poignant experience he still cannot forget.

Gregg Baker:
This opera is closer to a theatrical experience than any I've ever had, because we're not locked into one angle, and are constantly discovering different ways to tell the story. For the women to give up body and soul, and still keep their strength, that's the hardest thing to understand. That's the positive point of the story, that a person can have a tremendous amount of courage, and try and keep their dignity. It's important that we get across that this is one of many human experiences, and not beat people over the head with anything.

The ultimate message is far more than just the music. It's that hope springs eternal and fosters strength, even in the worst situations. Love and hope will always prevail, and the theatrical trick is to let the audience discover how much power there is in love. (All at Academy of Music, January 28, 2006)

Sing What You Love

American soprano Sylvia McNair soared to stardom 15 years ago through major operatic appearances in Salzburg, London, Paris and at the Met. She has remained one of America's great sopranos, and appeared at the opening of the Kimmel Center's Perelman Theater in 2001.

Exactly 20 years after winning the Met's national auditions, the Ohio native decided she'd rather perform Gershwin in a cabaret setting than Handel on the operatic stage. McNair asserted her intention to devote the next 20 years to celebrating the great American songbook, with Stephen Sondheim's "Everyone Says Don't" as her personal anthem.

(She admitted in our conversation, though, that if the Philadelphia Orchestra asked her to sing Ravel's gorgeous *Shéhérazade* again, she'd be there in a moment.)

Sylvia McNair:

Q: *Why did you decide to shift from opera?*

A: *Though I had more experiences than I ever had the good sense to dream about, I don't miss the stress and the traveling away from home, always tough on the voice and on relationships. I really related to my roles, and it was fun living in the skin of a flesh-and-blood lady like Mozart's Susanna, and that life appears glamorous. But I had to study and learn to sound like an opera singer. Now I'm just singing who I am and what my voice was built to sing.*

Q: *It doesn't feel like a sacrifice?*

A: *Not at all! I always loved the American songbook, perhaps not given its due because it's not European. This is not in any way second-class music, and for me it's based on love, certainly not money. It sounds immodest, but I'm singing better than I ever have. If you don't follow your heart, you're probably not doing your best work.*

Q: *What kind of response do you feel from audiences?*

A: *Can you imagine how pleasurable it is to sing in the language that the audience speaks? There are love songs, but love goes wrong as often as it goes right. A few years ago I went through a very difficult time personally, and singing from the wound gives some lyrics a different layer of meaning. Since then, every day my prayer is to use the pain to become a better person and a better artist.* (By phone, February 6, 2006)

After this concert, I repaired to the nearby Pen and Pencil Club, the oldest press club in America, where writers, musicians, restauranteurs and associates come late and often loudly narrate opinions they've overheard. We began a conversation about the greatness of the American Popular Song, and marveled at the longevity of some of the Gershwin-Porter-Arlen classics—and Jerome Kern's "All the Things You Are," for instance, a monument of magnificent chord changes written in 1939.

A young couple groused at our talking about these old songs. "Who cares about that old-time stuff?" the damsel asked. I could only think to ask, "Name a song from the 1990s!"

After a long pause came the squeaky answer: "Achy Breaky Heart?"

I rest my case.

The truth is that, since the days of the Beatles and Stevie Wonder, songs are wrapped in presentation and video to wed them to the specific performers. Singers have to sing the classics or write their own songs; anyone can sing "I Got Rhythm" or "All The Things You Are," but it would be ludicrous to cover Michael Jackson's "Thriller," Madonna's "Like A Virgin," Tina Turner's "What's Love Got To Do With It" or anything in a Lady Gaga video, all fused to those singers—for better or worse.

Wind Blowing Good

Flutist Mimi Stillman, the youngest wind player to ever enter the Curtis Insititute, at age 12, wanted a new way to connect audiences and children to the music she loves. Her parents, Ronni Gordon and David Stillman, authors of nearly 40 French and Spanish textbooks, moved here from the Boston area and provided essential support.

At 15, her teacher Jeffrey Khaner suggested her to skeptical conductor Wolfgang Sawallisch as a Philadelphia Orchestra substitute in the Brahms Requiem. It would become a career high point and a chance to play next to her mentor. And once, after a Curtis Symphony Orchestra concert when Stillman played the famous solo in Ravel's Second Suite from *Daphnis et Chloe*, conductor André Previn said to me, "That kid was great—I should have her surgically attached!"

After graduating at 17 and obtaining her doctorate in history at Penn, she made her first album, *Mimi*, with busy pianist Charles Abramovic. And instead of taking a job with an orchestra, she founded a highly successful chamber group called Dolce Suono.

Mimi Stillman. Credit: Ronni L. Gordon.

Mimi Stillman:

Q: *Have you considered playing in an orchestra?*

A: *I really wouldn't have the flexibility to be playing recitals and doing solos. I love playing the orchestral repertoire, and sub with the (Philadelphia) Orchestra several times a year, though sometimes I couldn't because I was on the road. My approach in playing really comes from the orchestral school, from my teachers Julius Baker and Jeff (Khaner), who stressed intonation and faithfulness to the score.*

Q: *What was the idea behind* Dolce Suono*?*

A: *The intention was to provide more chamber music, to have guest composers speak about their pieces, be accessible and to break down barriers.* (Coffee shop, March 6, 2006)

Musicians who really know will tell you that hornist Adam Unsworth is a monster player. A member of the Philadelphia Orchestra (from 1998 to 2007), he's one of the few musicians who can play in the jazz and classical realms.

He had released a CD, Excerpt This, to display his impressive chops. It includes an astonishing 11-minute solo, "Halfway There," demonstrating every sound a horn could make—plus a few it didn't know it could.

Adam Unsworth:

Q: *How hard is it to switch back and forth between jazz and the orchestra?*

A: *Jazz beats your chops up, because the horn's sound is in the viola register, and you have to overblow to cut through the other instruments. You have to take it easy the next day.*

I have to warm up at least an hour, usually two hours a day, for classical music, to maintain that level of excellence. But in jazz, there are no worries, just spontaneity and looseness.

Q: *What about the CD's title*, Excerpt This*?*

A: *Well, there's a little attitude in the title, but it also refers to a priority on classical excerpts in training and, especially, in auditions. I just don't think playing a difficult passage instead of a whole work is a real qualifier for gainful employment, it's just a challenge to musicians to try to do something differently. My personal drive to create is very strong, and it's not fulfilled by the orchestra, as wonderful as that is, because our job is to recreate and be as precise as we can.*

This recording experience was like having the clouds open up, and (it) made my life incredibly positive, the most fun I've had in music. (Kimmel Center, March 9, 2006)

Unsworth meant what he said, leaving the Philadelphia Orchestra as fourth horn in 2007 to become associate professor at the University of Michigan.

Three Piano Men

Settlement Music School's mission has always been to nurture talent, not necessarily to mold professional musicians. Happily, the two have often dovetailed during the school's century-plus history, and pianist Leon Bates is one such example.

The Philadelphia-based artist has recorded several CDs, hosted the local radio program *Notes from Philadelphia* and received attention for his body-building prowess. He believes that discipline helps with pacing, fatigue and creativity.

Bates was among the Settlement 100—former students whose Settlement experience shaped their lives in exceptional ways. In preparation for its 100th anniversary in 2008, the school began selecting recipients of that honor and held annual galas. Bates spoke about his studies at the School, and privately with the influential and inspiring teacher Natalie Hinderas.

Leon Bates:
Q: *When did you begin at Settlement School?*
A: *At 12, when it was an easy walk to the Germantown branch. I had a wonderful teacher, Irene Beck, who understood my desire, instilled lessons of hard work and was like a second mother to me. Those five years, until studying at Temple with Natalie Hinderas, were pivotal to me, and having a teacher express that kind of confidence gave me a feeling of security.*
Q: *Was much of her guidance more than technique?*
A: *Oh, yes, she gave me extra lesson time at her home, gave a recital for me when I was about to leave, and let me break in her new Steinway grand. She convinced my parents to get me a grand piano instead of the spinet I practiced on. And she told me stories about the famous pianists—Rubinstein, Rachmaninoff, Serkin—and how they were not playing for packed houses when they started out.* (George Blood studio, April 13, 2006)

When Gary Graffman came from New York to the Curtis Institute at age 7, he embarked on an unimaginable journey.

Seventy years later, he can look back on his legacy as one of the greatest American pianists, despite a career curtailed by a severe limitation to his right hand, and as a renowned teacher who was also Curtis' director and, for a decade, its president. Graffman performed the most famous work in his repertoire, the brilliant and challenging Piano Concerto for the Left Hand by Ravel, as the Curtis Symphony Orchestra, led by Christoph Eschenbach, celebrated the end of Graffman's tenure as Curtis' president and director in a concert.

His successor at Curtis, Roberto Diaz, had been principal violist of the Philadelphia Orchestra, and carries on a storied tradition set by famed predecessors Josef Hofmann, Efrem Zimbalist, Rudolf Serkin and John de Lancie.

Graffman's many recordings are still prized as among the finest, though he admitted he rarely listened to them. His 1981 book, *I Really Should Be Practicing*, remains a marvelous insight into the performing life.

Gary Graffman:
Q: *What is it like to deal with a student like Lang Lang?*
A: *Well, I taught Ignat Solzhenitsyn too, and they're both gifted, though very different. Though we don't accept videos as audition material, I happened to see one of Lang before he came here, and his technique was truly frightening. Truthfully, most of their lessons didn't have anything to do with technique, because theirs is better than I had!*
Q: *What qualities are needed by Roberto (Diaz) to continue your legacy?*
A: *Some talked about having an administrator instead of a musician as president, and I was afraid that we would become a smaller version of any other conservatory. I wanted a younger musician who would be able to ask major conductors to work with us at no fee, to be a diplomat, to participate in fund raising. I've seen Roberto in action; he has all the right instincts.*
Q: *Did you always feel exhilarated when working in such an atmosphere?*
A: *Yes, dealing with the kids was unbelievable, and such nice people besides. Because the audition process is more difficult, we accept only 5 to 6 percent of applicants instead of 15 to 16, but we feel that anyone we accept would have gotten a free ride anywhere they went.*
Q: *What are you most proud of from your years as Curtis' president?*
A: *I don't think I spoiled anything! The standards remain high, and Curtis remains tuition-free. When I played with the Philadelphia Orchestra recently, I realized that half the musicians went to Curtis, and 25 percent graduated while I was here. I'm very proud of that.* (By phone, April 16, 2006)

Graffman's phone call happened to come while I was in Jefferson Hospital, where my doctor saw stress tests that he thought required immediate heart surgery. I told Graffman where I was before we chatted and, when three serious-looking surgeons showed up, I said loudly, "I can't talk to you now, I'm talking to Gary Graffman!" He roared, and said to call him later. Luckily, he has a marvelous sense of humor.

When my daughter Lisa commandeered the pictures and obtained a second opinion that urged me not to go ahead, I checked myself out. A nurse said, "Mr. Di Nardo, you're hanging by a thread." By some miracle, the thread hasn't snapped yet.

That other Graffman student, Ignat Solzhenitsyn, crafted a three-concert Chamber Orchestra marathon, leading and playing Mozart's final three miraculous Symphonies and three Piano Concertos in a career milestone.

Ignat Solzhenitsyn:

Q: *How much more difficult a challenge is it to solo as well as conduct?*

A: *Quite a lot, especially since I haven't played two of the concertos all that much. On the surface, Mozart doesn't seem very different than other composers of the time. But when we dig deeper, we realize how much more difficult it is to interpret.*

Q: *Is it possible to get to the point where there's nothing new to discover in these pieces?*

A: *It will be a dark day if that point ever comes. Mozart's music is a bottomless well. It doesn't matter how familiar the works are, there's always some new revelation.*

Q: *What's on the conductor's mind when doing these works?*

A: *There are huge perils left and right, mostly the danger of routine. You have to avoid even a single phrase sounding conventional in these miraculous works. You must know the strength and weaknesses of the players and what is realistic to achieve, knowing that there's an unattainable ideal. The public thinks we're just demonstrating it to them, but we're experienced professionals living through our own journey of discovery each time.* (By phone, April 22, 2006)

Imaginative Casting

When I met the tall, shapely and stunning mezzo Kirstin Chavez, I suddenly thought I might have mixed up the roles; she couldn't possibly convince as Cherubino, an adolescent boy, in Mozart's *The Marriage of Figaro*. Somehow, she did, and brilliantly.

Chavez has been no stranger to a few other 'trouser' roles, like Octavian in *Der Rosenkavalier* and the composer in *Ariadne auf Naxos;* the other extreme of her repertoire is a sizzling *Carmen* (sung with the New York City Opera) and a saucy Rosina in *The Barber of Seville*.

New Mexico-born Chavez grew up in Kuala Lumpur, Malaysia, blazing through the Eastman School of Music and nabbing a mantelful of awards, including the finals of the Metropolitan Opera auditions. She had recently sung at the Met in Tobias Picker's *An American Tragedy* when Susan Graham canceled, in one of those career-altering moments.

Kirstin Chavez:

Q: *How difficult—or fun—is it to transition from the intense Carmen to a giddy boy?*

A: *I try to physically mimic the way a boy would walk, hold his hands—the way I think about all my characters. Some singers in the past who did pants roles didn't make a point of acting boyish, but I find it liberating.*

Q: *How important is the costuming?*

A: *I'll find out when I try on my costume on tonight! If it squeezes the top of me, the binding changes the breathing element, especially since I'm running around, and it becomes an issue. And when Susanna disguises me in a dress, a woman playing a boy pretending to be a girl, I have to pay more attention to how he would act.*

I'm very fortunate to do this work, though I haven't had a home in a year and a half—always on the road, making it a hard life. In this business, there are no guarantees. (Her hotel, May 1, 2006)

Beast and Dragon

Denyce was back, and about to appear in New York as the campy, high-tech dragon in *Grendel*, the Elliot Goldenthal-Julie Taymor starring an astonishing Eric Owens as the monstrous beast. It had already appeared in Los Angeles, but had been delayed due to technical problems with the huge set.

Denyce Graves:

Q: *How difficult is it to perform and be a mom?*

A: *I've been fortunate, because in* Grendel *and* Margaret Garner, *we had casts that were like family, and (my daughter) Ella looked forward to seeing everyone. In* Grendel, *I'm in one 20-minute scene, and then I'm finished. I'm structuring my life differently now, carving out specific times to be busy and times to be a mother.* (By phone, July 9, 2006)

Hélène Returns, And Coincidence

The brilliant pianist Hélène Grimaud returned with her special mystique, touring with the NHK Orchestra led by Vladimir Ashkenazy. Raised in France to parents of Italian, Moroccan, Corsican and German descent, she had always been rebellious against any rigid structure, especially the Paris Conservatoire that had accepted her at age 12.

In recent years, an unusual relationship with the DG label allowed her to issue three CDs with a specific theme, illuminating the cycle of faith, death and love. The first combined works of Arvo Pärt, John Corigliano and Beethoven; the second, piano sonatas of Chopin and Rachmaninoff, and the third Robert and Clara Schumann and their friend Brahms. She would solo in the First Piano Concerto by Brahms, a composer for whom she's always had an affinity, despite his enormous pianistic challenges and her tiny hands.

This time, she actually called me from Tokyo.

Hélène Grimaud:

Q: *Is it helpful when your conductor has played—and even recorded—the Brahms himself?*

A: *I happen to enjoy that very much and have always had an affinity for conductors who are pianists. There is usually so much good musical chemistry between us, in an enabling sort of way that any talk beforehand is usually superfluous. We always move to the discussion part after rehearsal, usually to confirm and mostly talk about architecture.*

Q: *What is it about Brahms that touches you to this extent?*

A: *That's hard to define, because his music resonates within me and feels as though we're connecting. He's a classicist, yet a romantic in the most philosophical way, and encompasses a raw and transcendent aesthetic within his own universe.*

The first movement of the Brahms First seems like a requiem for Schumann's first suicide attempt. Brahms' pulsation is close to the heartbeat, fast but never too fast, his slow never too slow, just organic and fluid.

Q: *How much time do you get to spend at the Wolf Conservatory these days?*

A: *Things have changed a lot with the advent of a wonderful managing director three years ago. Since it's in good hands . . . I'm now able to focus more on music.* (By phone from Tokyo, October 9, 2006)

By that time, Grimaud's book *Wild Harmonies* had been published, and I found it fascinating. I noticed that the translator was Ellen Hinsey, a poetess living in France, who just happened to be the daughter of an old high school friend and college roommate, Norman Hinsey. Talking to Norm, he reminded me that I had actually driven little Ellen home from the hospital, and was amazed at this coincidence. I have two books of her poetry, remarkable intense and complex works, and can't pretend that I understand them all.

I told Grimaud that I knew her translator from the original French, though I hadn't seen Ellen for many years. She found this eerie, and said they had never met. Grimaud had received an unusual benefit from her publisher, who allowed her to choose her translator; after reading the first chapter of five versions, she found Ellen's translation ideal.

Steps in Time

In Philadanco's West Philadelphia studios, accolades honoring founder and director Joan Myers Brown cover every wall. If awards for persistence, determination and blind hope were given, there'd be even more.

As it is, she had to make room for another one, as Brown received the prestigious *Dance Magazine* award, with Philadanco performing a work created in her honor by Ronald K. Brown, *For Mother*.

Dance Magazine was an important resource for Brown when she founded the company in 1970, since blacks weren't accepted in many local dance schools. Hundreds of dancers owe their professional careers to her mentoring.

Many of Philadanco's excellent dancers have wider aspirations, some gravitating toward more famed companies like those of Alvin Ailey—who was introduced to dance by Brown.

Despite enormous acclaim at major venues in this country and sellouts around the world, the company had been hanging by a financial thread for all of its 36 years. Philadanco just isn't enthusiastically supported by Philadelphia's black community, a huge disappointment for Brown. Yet she remains one of the most positive and upbeat personalities imaginable—frustrated, but without a trace of bitterness.

Joan Myers Brown.

The company spends part of 40 weeks a year on the road, sometimes for 10 weeks in a row. Before a conversation with Brown, it had just done a five-week stint in Germany, and was planning a tour of Germany, Switzerland and Italy. She remembered straightening me out five years before about her arrangement with the Kimmel Center.

Joan Myers Brown:
We have about 60 pieces in our repertoire, and we commissioned about half of them. I'm proud that our 18 dancers are gainfully employed for 46 weeks a year, with paid vacation. I go on almost every tour, because I'm expected to do the TV and radio talks and just have become part of the package.

Sometimes we're on a bus for 12 hours, then I have to rehearse dancers who are 20 years old, and I'll be 75 on Christmas Day. But I don't see anyone who'd be responsible for taking over and keeping the flame, though I don't intend to die holding on to a ballet bar! When I'm home, I'm in the studio every day catching up—with no life outside of Philadanco, no socializing, no networking, and committed far into the future.

They come to me to develop, and leave when they get to be at their peak. Now Broadway is another goal, because with The Lion King *and* The Color Purple, *there are two all-black shows with lots of people working. You can work on Broadway for a while and build up a nice nest egg.*

If I had known I'd be around this long, I'd never have imagined the constant struggle for funding. We're about day-to-day survival, even with strategic planning and annual grants. No one gives you money for operating, and grants aren't available if you're in the red. There have to be projects, meaning someone else's initiative or directive that you find yourself struggling to fit into.

Racism plays a part, because if this was a predominantly white company, I wouldn't need to prove something to somebody all the time. On the other hand, though dance in Africa is part of communal life, it's still not valued as a serious art form by the African-American community. It's not a job, not work, just something for weddings and funerals. Some don't even know that Philadanco is the Philadelphia Dance Company.

We get money from a lot of people, but we only have one major black supporter, and our biggest (supporter) is a white male on Long Island. I have no 401(k) and no retirement, but I've proven I can run a company, do a financial report, and provide a world-acclaimed product. All I really wish for is more stamina—and the ability to pay my dancers more and stop worrying.

I've seen what our programs do for children, how it builds their confidence and self-esteem, and every day we see the lives we touch and change. Some days you think, "Why bother?" Then you get a kid who wants to dance, whose dream is to be in Philadanco, and I know I have to keep it going for that kid. We simply all just want to be appreciated. (Philadanco studio, October 12, 2006)

26. KEEPING A PROMISE

When the Fred J. Cooper organ was finally installed in the Kimmel Center, and many concerts were planned around it, I began to think again about David Raksin's 1984 piece *A Song After Sundown*; it had been written for the American Guild of Organists conference for Keith Chapman, soloist on the Wanamaker Organ. As mentioned before, after his tragic death the handwritten manuscript of the score and the organ part was given to me and, when showing it to David on his Philly visit, was told that the orchestral parts had been lost after the concert.

He had originally written the piece as a jazz filler for a 1961 film called *Too Late Blues*, but the music was basically drowned out by John Cassavetes' dialogue. Twenty-three years later, he adapted it again as the middle movement for a piece for clarinet and string quartet, requested by Eddie Daniels for the Santa Fe Chamber Music Festival, called *Swing Low, Sweet Clarinet;* another chamber group put out that middle movement on a CD.

A Song After Sundown is a play on words after Frederick Delius' atmospheric piece, *A Song Before Sunrise*. Raksin also wrote on the score, "I think of this piece as a kind of Blues Meditation, for those who falter at twilight."

I had told David I'd do my best to get the piece another performance but, considering that I couldn't find a conductor or an orchestra to play it, plus a venue with a pipe organ, it was a foolhardy promise.

For 16 years, I tried to get a performance of the work. The Philadelphia Youth Orchestra played an annual concert at my son's church in Germantown, but conductor Joseph Primavera wanted no part of it. I kept asking around, with less than no success.

In discussing the following year's Kimmel Center schedule with Mervon Mehta, he happened to mention looking for something to fill out a program. Our Philadelphia Singers conductor, David Hayes, also conducted the Mannes School of Music Orchestra, and they were presenting Beethoven's *Missa Solemnis* as the second half of a program.

I jumped at the chance, bringing Mervon the score and recording of the clarinet-and-strings version. He immediately saw the value of the piece and, even in hearing this reduced chamber setting, he immediately recognized it was a quality work. I had to reveal the downside: there were no parts.

Song After Sundown by David Raksin (ASCAP), holographic score.

Organ part, Song After Sundown by David Raksin (ASCAP)

Enter Kile Smith, curator of the Fleisher Collection of Orchestral Music at the Free Library of Philadelphia, who had seen the score and also agreed it was a superbly written piece. He knew a copyist in Vermont who could swiftly do the parts—for $4,500. And, amazingly, Mehta and Smith were willing to split the cost: Mehta for the performance and Smith to have the piece in the Fleisher Collection.

I sent to organ part to Michael Stairs, who was going to play the solo, and who is renowned especially for sacred music. When I wrote him to get his reactions, he said that he had been having a fabulous time at night with the Cooper organ, working out all kinds of jazz-harmony registrations that would suit the piece.

Up to that point, I hadn't even considered probably the major factor in all of this scheming—the rights to the music. I wrote to Raksin's daughter Tina who, along with his son Alex, were unaware of the Fleisher Collection, but were willing to sanction the May 2006 performance; they received a recording of the performance and a copy of the score, and the parts reside in the Collection.

Mervon and Kile gave comments to Jim Cotter at WRTI-FM, and I did a narration about the whole process for the station, used when the whole concert was broadcast later.

The moral of the story: It's better to have a beautiful work performed than to have it sit on your shelf as a souvenir—but I'm not letting go of the original.

Still—I can just hear David roaring with laughter at his piece sharing a program with Beethoven's mighty *Missa Solemnis*.

Music He Never Heard

In 1983, the studio I used for photography burned down, and I lost most of my archive of photographs. The firemen had made a hole in the roof right above my Steinway grand piano, and hadn't bothered to put the lid down. In this dark, smoky room, with no electricity and temperatures in the teens, I assumed the two inches of ice on my strings meant the end of my piano.

I had practiced the piano at lunchtime on my regular job, since it was stored in the elevator lobby on the mezzanine floor, and lifted once a year onto a stage for a children's Christmas program. When the company moved into a building without a large meeting room in 1971, I put in a bid to the purchasing department to buy the piano. After a vice-president unsuccessfully tried to use his clout to acquire it, the purchasing agent claimed he was going to make life easier for himself by selling the building's contents by the pound. He asked me how much the piano weighed, and I guessed 500 pounds. "All right, at 15 cents a pound, that's $75. Have it out of here this week." It cost more than that, $130, to hoist it up on the carriage house beam through the dutch doors on the second floor. I been fortunate enough to acquire the Steinway almost as a gift—until karma, or fate, balanced things by making me shell out thousands to make it playable.

Besides the piano and about 6,000 LP records, turned into warped Frisbees, I lost a Birdland table card on which Bill Evans had written out the "real" chord changes for "Green Dolphin Street." Another casualty was the recording of Romeo Cascarino's *William Penn*, four 10-1/2-inch reels, two for each performance.

When Romeo's diabetes caused his loss of eyesight, kidney failure and lack of feeling in his legs, he needed a lot of care and something to keep him going. I asked George Blood, who recorded the Philadelphia Orchestra at that time as well as many other ensembles throughout the city, if I could come to his studio in Chestnut Hill and have him remaster the tapes. They had a powder of soot from the fire on their edges, ruinous to a recorder's heads, but I was able to spend days rolling the tapes by hand while cleaning them with bags of cotton balls. Eventually George was able to make DATs from the four reels.

I learned a lesson about hearing memory one day, as I heard music coming from a back room where an associate was transcribing old Philadelphia Orchestra tapes to digital media. "That's Charles Munch!" I said to George, who said that they were old Ormandy tapes from the 1960s. Sure enough, it was from one of Munch's rare guest weeks when he coaxed out that unique French sound I had absorbed for four years in Boston's Symphony Hall.

Romeo had often mentioned his choice of the five scenes he thought musically best between the two performances, and we simply used those whole scenes without any patching. George also used his magic to change the acoustic from the dead Academy to something more resplendent, changing a disaster into a triumph.

At Christmas 2001, I took the CDs over to his house and, while we had our usual pasta, he sat in the living room with headphones on and listened to the whole opera. When we came in there were tears running down his face, giving me great joy. He would only have a few months more to live.

By the time JoAnn Falletta came to conduct the Chamber Orchestra of Philadelphia in 2003, she had already committed to recording his orchestral music, and Kile Smith had sent her the scores from the Fleisher Collection. I had written Klaus Heymann of Naxos in Hong Kong, who remembered articles I had written about him in his early days, and he agreed to the recording, especially trusting JoAnn, who had already made many CDs for him with her Buffalo Philharmonic. We traded suggestions for the pickup orchestra's name, and he finally suggested the Philadelphia Philharmonia.

The works included *Pygmalion*, *Portrait of Galatea*, *Prospice* and *The Acadian Land*; each was based on Greek myth or literature, and we had room for his *Blades of Grass* for English horn and strings. Dolores wanted to include two childhood piano pieces, *Meditation* and *Elegy*, painstakingly transcribed for strings in the last few months of his failing eyes.

Though *Pygmalion* had been sight-read for that old LP, and *Blades of Grass* had been played by the Chamber Orchestra and Orchestra 2001,

Romeo had never heard performances of his *Portrait of Galatea*, *Prospice* or a complete performance of *The Acadian Land*.

People knew that I had experience with raising money for CDs of chamber music by John Davison and Harold Boatrite, but they were much more modest projects and I was no fund-raising expert; no foundations were funding CDs, and any grants would be measly. So all Dolores and I had to do was raise the money.

During that run Falletta, her husband Robert, Dolores, Margie and I had dinner at Victor Café in South Philadelphia, a restaurant famous for waiters who suddenly sing arias. At one point in the dinner, Falletta took out a box and gave it to Dolores. It was a G-clef pin, and Falletta said, "When you wear it, remember, we're going to make this record, it's only a matter of when." Naturally, Dolores was reduced to exuberant tears, one of many times I would witness JoAnn bringing her enormously generous spirit to bring joy to others.

JoAnn said it could save time if I checked the scores against the individual musicians' parts: not everything, just two measures before and after each rehearsal number or letter. I visited the Fleisher Collection for several weeks and went through all the pieces as she suggested, and found only one tie between measures that needed correction. Considering that Romeo wrote out the parts by hand, this was remarkable by itself.

I figured we would use Marc Mostovoy's Chamber Orchestra as the core, and add as many people as JoAnn wanted. They had the tax-exempt status and the checks would be made out to the Cascarino Recording Fund, and mailed to my old pal Richard Shapp, who handled the finances and set the tax chits to the donors and the IRS.

One way to raise money was to make the recording available and, through George Blood, I connected with a company in Maine to make it into a 2-CD package. It was to have a booklet with all the photographs Deborah Cascarino and I had taken, the complete libretto, and an essay about Romeo and the gestation of the opera. The minimum order was for a thousand sets, but I dug deeply, and went over tiny details with the booklet designer every day for a month.

Of course, presenting the first copy to Dolores meant a lot of drama, and I treasure a photo of her holding it with elation. We made a list of all Romeo's family, friends, students, colleagues, and anyone we could think of, and offered the recording of *William Penn* for $250. To our surprise, lots of people who had attended the opera wanted the recording and were happy to give support to our new project. Others who couldn't offer that much send what they could, and checks trickled in.

Because Dolores was from Bristol, one of her dear friends hired the Bristol Theater for Dolores to sing a benefit for the project. She and baritone Thad Shirey would sing some arias in the first half and, in the second half, we planned Romeo's Bassoon Sonata, the eight songs entitled *Pathways of Love*, arias and duets from the opera and some of the choruses.

Hugh Sung.

I asked the Philadelphia Orchestra's principal bassoonist Daniel Matsukawa, who taught at Curtis, if he knew anyone who could play the Sonata, and he suggested one of his students, Andrew Miyake Cuneo. While at Curtis to speak to Andrew, I went to visit Hugh Sung, famous for playing the piano reductions of concertos for the student recitalists, and asked him if he knew of any pianists for the benefit. I played him recordings of all Romeo's music and, to my astonishment, he said he'd be honored to play the whole concert. Dolores didn't believe me when I called her with the news and, once again, had to wait for the sobbing to stop. "Hugh Sung? Is really going to play for me?" she kept asking. After the first of his eight songs at the initial rehearsal, she was quite overcome, never having heard it played as eloquently—except by her husband.

Cuneo, now principal with the St. Louis Symphony, received the standard fee, but Sung refused to take a fee for his work; we fooled him by donating to his church's fund for his work on a hymnody.

JoAnn said she had a week open in November of 2005, finally giving us a deadline. After looking over the scores, she said we needed an orchestra of 78 musicians, and the Chamber Orchestra asked their timpanist/contractor Martha Hitchins to contract the orchestra. Working out the numbers with the union head, Joseph Parente, it looked like we'd need about $75,000 for four days of sessions. As it worked out, there were three double-session days, with rehearsal in the morning and recording in the afternoon, though most of the musicians had a rehearsal for the Academy of Vocal Arts' *Don Giovanni* in the evening. There was an Opera Company performance on one night, limiting work to only one service; on that day we would rehearse and record the three short works, requiring only strings, in a morning session.

A onetime student of Romeo's and longtime friend, Frank Leone, an arranger/composer who now heads the musicians' union in Las Vegas, made a remarkable discovery: a reel-to-reel tape of Romeo playing three of the pieces in the late 1950s, from score, at the piano, complete takes. He sent a CD of *Pygmalion, Portrait of Galatea,* and *Prospice,* the latter played in a four-hand version with Margaret Garwood. Since I had heard *Pygmalion* on that old LP, the piano version made sense, but I didn't have the skill to go backwards in *Galatea* and imagine the orchestration from the piano version.

JoAnn was elated to receive the CD, realizing that the composer's tempos and dynamics were all there, a gift from beyond the grave.

Having fallen way short in funding, we sent out another letter, pleading for more funds to complete the project.

The recording venue was another problem, solved by my son Marc's volunteering his church, First Presbyterian Church in Germantown. He received approval to use the sanctuary, and asked the sextons to ensure that all the meetings and projects be moved to far corners of the large building to avoid interference with the recording.

During that period, Robert Elias had taken over as head of the Chamber Orchestra, and most of Marc Mostovoy's longtime initiatives were being replaced. As an example, whenever the Chamber Orchestra was loaned out to AVA or other groups, there was an overhead fee above the musicians' scale. Mostovoy had allowed the string players to move around, giving everyone an occasional first-chair taste. Elias held auditions and, for instance, Gloria Justen won for concertmaster. Gloria's a superb player, but some conductors, like AVA's Christofer Macatsoris, had developed longtime relationships with other players. They simply contracted the musicians they wanted themselves, and the Chamber Orchestra simply lost out on a large revenue stream; Elias, who had created the situation, soon left.

The new management didn't want Mostovoy involved in their plans, especially his ideas for multi-media that he considered the future. Halfway through our fund-raising, they negotiated for him to leave the organization he had founded in 1964, though it continued to hold our funds for a charge of ten percent.

Naxos said they'd provide the recording equipment and, on the Saturday before the sessions, a huge truck arrived at the church parking lot bearing two enormous palettes. After photographing the Rubik's Cube of electronics, the sextons helped move the board, cables, speakers, recorders, and much other equipment into a lockable space.

JoAnn was very excited that Tim Handley, a recording wizard from London she had worked with many times before, was being sent to engineer the disc. He arrived on Sunday from London with a suitcase full of microphones, and wanted immediately to see the venue. He noticed that the doors to the street weren't sealed, that a fire house was just down the street, and that the church's interior might not be an ideal acoustic, provoking understandable doubts.

We uncoiled all the cables and set up the hall, leaving Tim to install his gear in an anteroom while my son Marc and I took a truck downtown to 'borrow' about 50 music stands from a church. JoAnn and her husband Robert Alemany drove down on Sunday night, graciously willing to stay at my house two blocks from the church.

I had arranged to have caterers bring lunch to the common room on the three orchestral days, since there were no good restaurants near the church. This turned out to be a good move, because the musicians were elated to be treated to sumptuous meals. JoAnn asked cellist James Holosevsky, spokesman for the musicians, about break time, and he said 15 minutes would be fine. Per what, she asked. Oh, per the session, said Jim. I wouldn't know how significant that was until I first went to Buffalo.

The first rehearsal session started beautifully, and after a few minutes JoAnn stopped to listen to Tim's comment from the squawk box. "There's a beautiful duet between the clarinet and viola in measure 26, but the viola isn't coming through. Would you like the viola to play louder, or shall I move the microphone?" The players' faces showed surprise, realizing that Tim was reading the score, and was hearing more than they could. Another time, when the horns flubbed an entrance at rehearsal letter four, she kept going for a while until things bogged down; through the box, Handley said, "JoAnn, let's start from—let's see—four measures before letter four." I could see the relief on the horn players' faces, and this time they nailed their entrance.

JoAnn Falletta conducting Cascarino recording.

From that time on, they adapted immediately to every suggestion he and JoAnn made.

At that first break I went into the control room, concerned about what acoustic flaws Tim was dealing with. He smiled, said it was excellent, and put headphones on me to prove it. There were only a few car backfires and two fire sirens in those four days, but they all came either during rehearsals or break.

Frank Leone sat in the back with the original piano scores, ready to assist in case there was a question, and I sat up front with Dolores and Tim McDonnell, also reading the scores. Musicians kept coming up to Dolores at the breaks, saying her husband must have been an oboist/violist/horn player/ trombonist, because the parts seemed idiomatic for the instrument. This, of course, was a huge compliment to his innate musical instinct.

At one point, someone yelled, "Why do we like playing with you so much?" JoAnn smiled and said, "Because I never forget that I'm the only one here not playing an instrument!"

On Wednesday, the English horn part was played by Geoffrey Deemer, who had studied oboe with Philadelphia Orchestra's principal oboe Richard Woodhams (who he respectfully called Mr. Woodhams) at Curtis. He played beautifully, and we made sure his name appeared on the back sheet of the album; he's an outstanding musician who plays with the Chamber Orchestra, Opera Company and AVA, and often with the Philadelphia Orchestra—sitting next to Woodhams.

Cascarino recording session, November 2005. Credit: Marc DiNardo.

JoAnn's complete immersion in the music was intense and inspiring, and these players—who hadn't done much in the way of recording—played from the heart. When JoAnn suggested a wrap, though they were going to a third service, some asked if they could take their entrances again or play a section better. Before the last day, she and Tim asked if we had enough money to pay the musicians recording scale for both the morning and afternoon session, because it seemed silly not to turn on the recorders for the whole morning of the last day in case he needed some extra for patching. It wasn't much more, and everyone stayed until the last minute.

By the time we put the equipment away and returned home, JoAnn and Robert had already hit the road back to Buffalo. The next day, we loaded everything back on the palettes in roughly the same configuration as they had arrived, saw them forklifted onto a huge truck, and returned the music stands to the church downtown.

The reviews in the music magazines were highly laudatory, most of them moved by the obvious feeling in the music as well as the superb craftsmanship. Most mentioned the fact that it was a Philadelphia composer and a Philadelphia performing ensemble, but the *Philadelphia Inquirer* somehow didn't get around to reviewing it.

A few weeks later, insiders at the Chamber Orchestra told me that some didn't believe we'd ever raise that much money and, since it couldn't be returned because of IRS rules, it would have just remained in their account.

JoAnn remembered that my son Marc and I both mentioned loving Respighi's *Church Windows*, a work that, surprisingly, isn't often played. She called to say they were recording it (and other Respighi) in Buffalo, Tim Handley was coming too, and would we like to come and celebrate together? As it turned out, Tim was sent elsewhere and Thomas Z. Shepard, who had recorded many Broadway shows for Columbia, came instead. It took him two hours to adjust the microphone levels, a process Tim had done in about 15 minutes, making the players a little anxious. Under their union rules, musicians play for 40 minutes and take a mandatory 20-minute break. Since JoAnn had to finish the session in two days, lots of the musicians loitered in the halls, wanting to go back and make a good recording. JoAnn took me aside and said, "See how lucky we were in Philadelphia?" We were both upset to hear of Holosevsky's passing in June 2015; Jimmy was a marvelous cellist and a constantly-warm presence.

JoAnn has won the ASCAP award for best programming many times, and has made a point of recording music by composers, like Romeo, who deserve to be heard. Her discs include works by Behzad Ranjbaran, Jack Gallagher, Kenneth Fuchs, and many more whose works are championed by her passionate advocacy for American music. Her catalog of revelatory and diverse recordings has reached 90 CDs as conductor—and a few as guitarist.

Since that first visit, we've savored Buffalo weekends with André Watts, percussionist Evelyn Glennie, soprano Angela Brown, violinist and concertmaster Michael Ludwig, and many more. In 2012 we saw Tim again when the BPO recorded orchestral music by Duke Ellington, and two weeks later with her Virginia Symphony when she performed Mahler's gigantic Eighth Symphony both at Williamsburg and Norfolk; she immediately headed back to Buffalo for Mahler's Third and the JoAnn Falletta International Guitar Competition, making everyone realize the power of music to provide energy, dedication and generosity.

On one of those trips to Buffalo, we met Beverly Everett, conductor of the Bismarck-Mandan (ND) and Bemidji (MN) Symphony Orchestras, who had received a grant to learn from JoAnn, and met her to hear the two Mahler Eighths. In October 2014, Everett programmed *Pygmalion* in Bismarck and, of course, we traveled with Dolores to North Dakota to hear it, plus Michael Ludwig soloing in Kenneth Fuchs' gorgeous *American Rhapsody*.

During the Jamestown ceremonies in 2007, for which Jennifer Higdon had written the fanfare, JoAnn, her husband Robert and Virginia Symphony flutist Debra Wendells Cross played a glorious guitar-clarinet-flute concert in a large, packed church. Since JoAnn had conducted Virginia Symphony runout concerts the last three days, I asked them when they had time to rehearse—a question they found amusing.

Four years after our recording, JoAnn emailed me from Santiago. She was conducting the Orquestra Sinfónico de Chile, and one of the principal musicians, oboist Jeremy Kesselman, had actually played on the sessions. In JoAnn's constantly inclusive way, she had written, "Imagine, meeting someone that far away who played on our recording!" That 'our' is typical of the reasons why she is revered wherever she goes, and why our admiration and love for JoAnn is boundless.

During these whirlwind five days in Philadelphia, engineer Tim Handley told a story about a job at the Mariinsky Theater in St. Petersburg, where a video was being made of an obscure Prokofiev opera. A forest of microphones and seven cameras were set up, plus a huge orchestra, chorus, offstage band and soloists.

When ten o'clock came, conductor Valery Gergiev hadn't arrived, and about 45 minutes later someone called his agent. It seemed that he hadn't considered himself sufficiently prepared, and was having lunch in Paris. And, in Russia, if you don't play, there's no pay.

During the various waiting periods, someone showed Handley a hidden door in the royal box, leading to a long underground tunnel to a palace—and safety in case of insurrection.

Gergiev had also showed up around 8:35 for an 8 p.m. concert with the Philadelphia Orchestra one night in 1999 after spending the day in New York. Assistant conductor André Raphel got dressed and was ready to go on when he finally arrived. Such antics went on at the Met as well, until then-general manager Joseph Volpe put his foot down and, in recent years, there have been very few Gergiev no-shows.

At the 2014 Grammys, the brilliant Tim was nominated once more for recordings JoAnn made with the Buffalo Philharmonic, the Virginia Symphony, the London Symphony Orchestra and the Ulster Orchestra.

During this period, since I had about 900 extra copies of the opera CD set, I asked union president Joseph Parente about the possibility of selling them. He realized that I couldn't possibly pay recording scale from 1982, whatever that was. "If you make the Billboard charts, I'll come after you. Just go ahead," he said. He provided a letter giving permission, and I showed it to the administrator of the Philadelphia Singers, the chorus participating in the opera; he said that if it was all right with Parente, it was all right with him. Considering that they had both been paid for an unusually generous amount of rehearsal and performance scale in 1982, it didn't seem unreasonable to sell an unknown opera on a private label 24 years later, obviously not one to hit the charts.

Jay Hoffman, the New York agent who had given me that CD set of *Florencia en el Amazonas*, listened to the recording and actually offered to write a letter for me gratis extolling its merits, included in promo sets to his list of reviewers. Not surprisingly, it didn't get reviewed in Philadelphia.

Someone from Intermission, a Chestnut Hill store with a concession at the Kimmel Center, asked for some. I let them have six, with four going to the Center, absolutely the only copies sold in a retail outlet instead of through the *William Penn* website.

Several weeks later, I received a registered letter from a well-known legal firm, informing me that my CDs were being sold at Tower Records (which was emphatically not true) and that if I did not cease and desist, my property, home, bank accounts and other chunks of my persona would be seized. The impetus was from Greg Cantwell, local head of AGMA (American Guild of Musical Artists), who evidently felt the Philadelphia Singers administrator had no authority to give me the permission.

The lawyer listened to my explanation, and asked me to send my bank statements each month. Except for a flurry of sales when Henry Fogel's rave review in *Fanfare* magazine appeared, only a few drifted in. After about 18 months, I finally was told that sending this usually-unchanged paperwork was no longer necessary.

Though the chorus had been paid for extra rehearsals, in a gig 24 years previous, I guess Cantwell thought it was worth it to take a shot for more money, but to date the sheriff has not seized my home. However, if you want to hear some magnificent music, williampennopera.com is still online, along with Fogel's and other reviews.

27. MORE *DAILY NEWS* ADVENTURES

At the May 2006 week celebrating the new Kimmel Center organ, Tom Trenney played the instrument to accompany two 'silent' films, Douglas Fairbanks' *The Mark of Zorro* and Buster Keaton's masterpiece, *The General*.

Of course, there never was such a thing as a 'silent' film, because films always had a score, played live by an orchestra in the downtown palaces, with smaller-ensemble arrangements for the bigger houses and keyboard reductions for the neighborhood houses or "nabes."

Since movies were cranked out by the hundreds in those days, few films were repeated after their initial run. With the advent of sound, satirized by the late Betty Comden and Adolph Green in *Singin' in the Rain*, most original scores were forgotten, discarded except for the work of a few archivists.

That meant Trenney had to invent music to suit these films using quotes from classical works or song titles, if appropriate, but mostly improvising on a framework.

He returned just after Christmas 2006 to do three more shows: an afternoon of Laurel and Hardy, the 1928 flick *Speedy* with Harold Lloyd (and featuring Babe Ruth in a cameo) and, finally, Lon Chaney's classic *The Phantom of the Opera*. These films were new to Trenney, except for *Phantom*, a show he'd played "25 or 30 times," and helped by the fact that churches tend to play the film around Halloween.

For a church organist boasting two graduate degrees from the Eastman School, this challenge represents a very unusual moonlighting gig that gives him travel from his home in Detroit, and an exposure few classical organists receive.

Tom Trenney:
Q: *How do you approach creating the music?*
A: *I used to sketch out themes on a sheet of paper, but eventually realized that I never looked at the sheet. It always keeps evolving and changing like a living thing, perhaps carrying good ideas from a past performance, and by being careful not to get into the same monotonous keys. I've found that when you have enough technique and musical ideas, and you're open to the movements of the spirit, often something magical happens.*

Q: *Technically, how does this compare to an organ recital?*
A: *In a recital, you're walking more on eggshells. Here I feel a lot more ability to be creative in the improvisations. Playing a whole film straight through is a real endurance contest, and my goal is that an audience will forget that someone's playing and feel the music as just part of the film. Ba-*

sically, I don't take this musical experience too seriously. I don't take myself too seriously! (By phone, December 20, 2006)

Opera's a Bargain

On Christmas Day 1931, opera lovers huddled around their radios to hear the first live broadcast from New York's Metropolitan Opera. Eighty-one years and more than 1,500 afternoons later, and with more countries constantly being added to the broadcast network, Saturday afternoon's *Live from the Met* is an institution that has initiated generations into the world of opera.

In 1977, a telecast of *La Bohème* featuring Luciano Pavarotti began a series of video broadcasts on PBS, and another era began on December 30, 2006, when the Met's pared-down production of Mozart's final opera, *The Magic Flute*, beamed in high-definition clarity onto movie screens.

I went to see the next one, *I Puritani* starring Anna Netrebko, with Beverly Sills the warmup guest. When asked to go into the story, she said, "What plot?! It's just an excuse to have mad scenes in every act!" And about those mad scenes, she said, "My teacher always told me, if you feel like running all over the stage, do it! If you don't, just put your hands down and sing like hell!" That sparked announcer Margaret Juntwait's realization that she couldn't really hold Sills back, and she quickly terminated the session. Too bad, because Sills left us soon after that; she was a brilliant guest host.

Netrebko did a mad scene lying on her back on the stage with her hair falling into the orchestra pit. And, when coming off the stage, the audience was astounded to find her collared by Renée Fleming, who walked her back to the dressing room. When Fleming remarked how difficult it must be to have closeups on you beamed all over the world, Netrebko just said she was too into the role to think about it. "You want to see funny faces?" she said, turning to the camera, and squinching up her face. The audience roared, as if Netrebko could hear them.

Puritani played to one almost-full theater; a few weeks later, when Fleming sang in *Eugene Onegin*, the opera filled two theaters. Whether it was Fleming, the more familiar opera, or just the word getting around is hard to say. Fleming's escort after the first act was Susan Graham.

It was a bargain at $18 at its launch, and still offers a thrill at $25. During the 2012-13 season, the Met's "Live in HD" broadcasts drew 2,547,243 viewers in 54 countries; the following year, it was seen in 66 countries, earning $60 million, of which the Met receives about half.

Let's Change Things Again

Beginning in 2007, another format change arrived. The music writers were to do only one long paragraph about our weekly "pick," as well as all the listings, with interviews or articles "if you can sell them." When I mentioned that I didn't want to just put down the bare bones information in the listings, but give a little background, that was fine—getting more copy for the same rate is always good for editors.

December 2006 was a big month for conductor Zubin Mehta. In between accepting the Kennedy Center honors and leading the Vienna Philharmonic's famous New Year's Eve concert, he won the Israel-based Dan David award for cultural achievement, splitting $1 million with French composer Pascal Dusapin.

Nearly everyone on the planet had seen him lead the colossally popular Three Tenors concert, and his current positions as Israel Philharmonic's conductor for life and head of Florence's Maggio Musicale keep him busy. That April, he began the production of Wagner's enormous *Ring* cycle in Barcelona, Spain and the Maggio Musicale in Florence.

Yet though Mehta was the longest-tenured music director of the New York Philharmonic in its history (13 seasons), he was making his first appearance with them in four years on a tour. Since he had an open night, his son Mervon Mehta, who booked Kimmel Center events, just might have had something to do with bringing them here.

In between rehearsals, an interview on *The Charlie Rose* show, and his other phone jingling with many ticket requests for his sold-out Lincoln Center concerts, Mehta spoke by phone from Manhattan about a wide range of topics.

Zubin Mehta:

Q: *What was it like to receive the Kennedy Center honors? Did you know the Israel Philharmonic would perform?*

A: *Though I had presented the award to Leontyne Price some years back, I found it even more moving as it went along, with much more on stage than was shown on television. I was very grateful, considering I'm not American-born but have spent 30 years here making music. And the Israel players were a complete surprise—they actually were also leaving at the same time from the Tel Aviv airport, and people took me to a lounge to keep me from seeing them—real cloak-and-dagger stuff.*

Q: *How do you take on an enormous project like the* Ring*?*

A: *A performance art troupe called* La Fura Dels Baus *is collaborating on the directing, designing, lighting and everything else —the most congenial team I've every worked with. Their ideas fly around like neutrons. It begins in April, and then we will take it to Florence with another orchestra.* (Except, as stated before, the horn players).

Q: *You've been involved in many significant political events. Can music make a difference in the Middle East peace process?*

A: *We all try. With the Israel orchestra, we're taking a Palestinian pianist—an Israeli Arab—on a European tour, and we've played in Nazareth completely from our hearts for the first time, a historical event. We can't play in the West Bank, in Ramallah, but we're waiting for that status to change to allow us to go. Perhaps one concert doesn't matter, but collectively we hope we all can make a difference toward peace.* (By phone, December 4, 2006)

Right-Handed Compliment, and Flood

Though the great American pianist Leon Fleisher's hands were immobilized for nearly 40 years, he played with the Network for New Music group in December 2005. His new CD, *Two Hands,* was out, but he conducted and played Korngold's Suite for left hand and strings.

Like his fellow master pianist Gary Graffman, he went through the tragedy of losing use of his right hand. After years of hopefulness, Fleisher was able to return to the stage and, after over 30 years, returned to play a recital of Bach, Leon Kirchner, Stravinsky, and Schubert.

Born in San Francisco, Fleisher rose to early stardom after studying with Artur Schnabel, who had studied with the famous Theodor Leschetitsky, a pupil himself of Beethoven's student Carl Czerny. Along with Van Cliburn and Graffman, Fleisher was an American luminary.

We can only imagine what this giant of the keyboard could have felt in the early 1960s. Just as his recordings of the massive Brahms Piano Concertos were being considered supreme, the fingers on his right hand were successively becoming numb. Soon he could hardly write his name or wash his hands.

The focal dystonia, or involuntary muscular contractions, he had developed after years of obsessive piano practice at first seemed insurmountable. Fleisher never gave up, trying surgery, acupuncture, hypnosis, injections, aromatherapy, biofeedback and much more.

He also began teaching at Baltimore's Peabody Institute, where he inspired a generation of piano luminaries like André Watts, Yefim Bronfman, Louis Lortie, Jonathan Biss and Stewart Goodyear. He also holds some classes at Curtis Institute when possible, and also became a conductor and continued playing and expanding the left-hand repertoire along with Graffman.

Eventually, a combination of Rolfing and Botox injections brought back his ability, though not at first to the level he once had. His second, recent CD *The Journey* is a follow-up to *Two Hands,* his first release in 40 years.

A documentary short, also called *Two Hands* and dealing with Fleisher's decline and comeback, received an Academy Award nomination. It was directed by Nathaniel Kahn, a schoolmate of my children who had also been nominated in 2004 for *My Architect*, the brilliant documentary about his Philadelphia-based father, Louis Kahn.

Leon Fleisher:

Q: *How do you select the pieces you play now?*

A: *Since I have to pick and choose what I can play, I pick only pieces that I love. I realize now that in my early days I played the big works, like the Brahms B-Flat Concerto, with no idea of how difficult they were. I tell students to learn them while they're young, becoming part of their DNA and remaining less difficult whenever they're revisited.*

Q: *Did you ever think your facility would never return?*

A: *Not really. I had this ever-present sense that somehow, some way, I wasn't going to stop until something came back. I'm very proud of the fact that Gary and I created commissions for more left-hand works, by Ned Rorem, Daron Hagen, Gunther Schuller, William Bolcom, Lukas Foss and Curtis Curtis-Smith.*

Q: *Why this pattern of injury to the right hand and not the left?*

A: *You can understand this if you look at the inside of the piano with its lyre shape. The higher you get, the shorter the strings. You have to work harder with the right hand to get an equivalent volume. Also, the tune is always in the top voice, with the fourth and fifth fingers stressed the most.*

Q: *When you studied with Schnabel, did you have a sense of the tradition and legacy that went all the way to Beethoven?*

A: *I didn't relate to him in that kind of visceral sense. Everyone in those days studied with Leschetitsky and shared that lineage. But everything Schnabel did was deeply inspired and had such a sense of authenticity, shaping my understanding of music.*

Q: *Was it difficult to teach students with healthy hands?*

A: *It wasn't that I envied them or resented them, they just presented a specific new challenge. I couldn't push them off the chair and demonstrate, pushing me to adequately describe in words what I was hearing in my inner ear, this very ephemeral response. It made me a far better teacher and, if I have more value now, I attribute it to that.* (By phone, January 22, 2007)

During that concert's intermission, I noticed the Russian conductor Vladimir Jurowski, who was guesting with the Philadelphia Orchestra that week, and introduced myself. He was very impressed by the depth of Fleisher's artistry, and gave him the enormous compliment, "I haven't heard playing like that since Emil Gilels."

Since I intended to go backstage afterwards and thank Fleisher for the interview, I asked Jurowski if he would like to meet him, and he was very enthusiastic. Fleisher was very friendly to me and, after I introduced Jurowski, the conductor said he hoped they could work together someday. The pianist's expression showed a little skepticism, but I found a great joy in seeing that he and his London Philharmonic soon played a Mozart Piano Concerto with Fleisher, and traveled together on tour in the U. S. two seasons later.

My daughter Lisa had a background in movement theater, and always tries to get to Rennie Harris' dance troupe. It was doubly disappointing to submit a story about a malfunctioning sprinkler system, causing a flood that damaged the stage of the Perelman Theater. Harris' concert couldn't go on while the stage was being dried out, and the early-February concert was rescheduled to summer.

"Porgy" Returns

At a 1935 rehearsal of *Porgy and Bess*, Gershwin said, "I think the music is so marvelous, I can't believe I wrote it."

Love, betrayal and redemption—always the basic ingredients in almost every grand opera. For Gershwin, the characters in *Porgy and Bess* were people to care deeply about, and he wrapped their lives in deeply felt, penultimate American music.

At its heart, it's about love as a redemptive power, however temporary, and about the nobility and unity of a poor community.

When the Opera Company of Philadelphia restaged the opera in February 2007, it assembled possibly the opera's dream cast, all of whom were willing to give searingly personal views about Gershwin's masterpiece, and director Walter Dallas, director of Freedom Theater.

Gregg Baker (Porgy):

Gershwin gave us the blueprint and gave these characters both the music and the feelings he wanted to express. He wrote it with a lot of latitude to let the artists express themselves, knowing that generations of African-Americans would maintain its authenticity, like fine wine.

I've read about what he did and what he was feeling, trying to give an overall impression of the black community at that time. Of course, it's culturally close to what I am, yet we must assimilate it as a work of art the same way we do Verdi and Puccini. I resisted doing it early in my career, but it encompasses a lot of what I am artistically.

Angela Brown (Bess):

Finally doing Bess is exciting, because she makes me stretch my acting skills. In many roles, I'm the wife, the queen—stately, with emotions under the surface. There isn't always a lot of moving, it's "park and bark."

Bess is vulnerable, haughty and confident, a floozy when she's a little high, and her movements have to mirror all her aspects. She needs something—either happy dust or a man—and Porgy's enough to fill her. But when he's not there, she reverts back to old things. She's always on shifting sands. But I feel as though I understand her and can combine all her giant emotions in every way, like a good stew.

Karen Slack (Clara):

"Summertime" is thrilling because you get the best aria in the show—and scary because everyone knows it. These melodies are things you know, and the story is not that far from what we were.

It's another language, the Gullah dialect, and it sings, it flows.

When I was a young girl, an only child growing up in North Philadelphia, I tried to do everything differently, and my parents thought singing was just a phase. But when I saw Denyce Graves sing Carmen *with the Opera Company, I knew that was my future.*

This is the only time you get to sing with all your colleagues, with all African-American singers, who are good friends, and we always have the most fun. This is our story, about community, true Americana.

Lester Lynch, Crown:
I've probably sung Crown 150 times. It's very demanding because of the physicality of the role, the killing and a violent sexual scene. My other roles, Sharpless (Madama Butterfly) or the Count de Luna (Il Trovatore), for instance, don't require fight rehearsals, working out at the gym, brute force.

It's also a difficult role because there are lots of speaking lines and laughing over the music of the hurricane, you need to have a strong technique.

I have great respect for Gershwin, writing this at a time in American history when Caucasians were not as interested in what black folks were doing. I studied piano and played Rhapsody in Blue, and know firsthand how great he was.

Walter Dallas, director:
Q: *What's the difference between directing theater and opera?*

A: *The difference to me is protocol. I've done big musicals with many songs and spoken dialogue. Here, it's a question of who is responsible for what - who directs the supers [walk-ons], who directs the chorus, who directs the principals in the time we have together. When you get closer to opening, the maestro has to pull it together musically. And rehearsing an entrance is different, since you must adjust performers so they connect with the conductor and face front. Luckily, I've worked a lot with [choreographer] Patricia Hobbs, so we work together smoothly.*

Q: *Are you aware that you have the dream cast?*

A: *You have to be careful what you wish for. A friend of mine in New York took me to the Met some years back and I heard Angela Brown, and I said if I ever do an opera, I'd like to work with her. Then I saw* Margaret Garner *and saw Angela and Gregg (Baker), and I was stunned. And this was all before I had been offered* Porgy.

Q: *What do you say to people who have expressed reservations about the dialect?*

A: *You're asking the wrong person. I grew up in Atlanta with kids from a family who were Gullah, and was used to them switching pronouns a lot. They would say, "On me arm" or "Come go with we," and never judged this kind of Creole patois coming from Sierra Leone, Angola and Liberia. In fact, the South Carolina Gullahs have preserved folk art more than any other African-American community. Gershwin went there, listened, and captured the rhythm of the language in the music. I don't understand why anyone would be offended by it. It's like adding an extra stick of butter to the cake—you don't know why, but it tastes better.*

Q: *Do you have an overall principle to guide your decisions?*

A: *Yes: Tell the truth. I don't do anything if I can't bring anything to it. For instance, I don't connect with August Wilson's* Fences, *and I won't do it. Once I did a play that I didn't care about, for the money, and it was the worst experience of my life.*

(All interviews at Academy of Music, February 5, 2007)

Ignat Solzhenitsyn. Credit: Dario Acosta.

Pianist in Transit

Pianist/conductor Ignat Solzhenitsyn led a Vivaldi *Four Seasons*, followed the next week by playing a Beethoven Concerto with his Chamber Orchestra of Philadelphia.

In the midst of his many appearances, he had somehow found time to assist in the production of *The Solzhenitsyn Reader: New and Essential Writings, 1947-2005*, a compendium of the most powerful writings of his famed father Aleksandr, that was published the previous fall. Ignat had just burrowed out of snow in Vermont and was heading home to Philly when we spoke by phone.

Ignat Solzhenitsyn:

Q: *When traveling, do you do more recitals, conducting or playing concertos?*

A: *Probably about 40 percent guest conducting, 30 percent piano recitals and 30 percent concerti. It's relatively uncommon for a musician to have such choices, and I'm grateful to be able to pursue all these opportunities. To have a chance to perform at all those levels brings me real fulfillment.*

Q: *Did you spend much time on translations for* The Solzhenitsyn Reader?

A: *Yes, lots of time. I was mostly preoccupied with translating the poetry, and worked very closely together with the editors. Though my father's*

works had nothing to do with me, I'm very proud of what he stands for and was very happy to be involved in a small way.
Q: Do you intend to remain with the orchestra for a few more seasons?
A: I hope so, because I couldn't be happier, and I love Philadelphia. We've done a lot of good work, but there's more to accomplish together before moving on. Nothing is forever, but when it's time, I want to leave the orchestra in the best possible shape—and then hope to return as a guest.
(By phone, February 15, 2007)

That last hope ended up coming true.

Collaboration

In my earlier days, I often suggested to several organizations that they join with other disciplines in their presentations. There was great resistance, with each having a blind fear of losing audiences trickling away to the other art. Gradually, grant organizations began donating to collaborations, simply because the specific success and value of the donation could be more easily measured than granting into the operating pot.

In recent years, artistic collaborations have proliferated, with audiences for each discipline discovering the excellence of the other.

Very few organizations have had a greater history of collaboration than the Network for New Music, an organization having joined with dancers, poets, visual artists, speakers and many other disciplines, as well as commissioning, performing or presenting over 550 new works in its 25 seasons.

In 2007, their idea was to unite with Manfred Fischbeck's Group Motion Dance Company, commissioning Curtis faculty member David Ludwig's *Lamentations*. This collaboration began after Network artistic director Linda Reichert and Ludwig saw the Group Motion performance of Mozart's *Magic Flute* Overture, featuring a video component, as part of the defunct *Fresh Ink* series at the Perelman Theater. She had intended to commission Ludwig to write a work and, when Fischbeck heard the program would also include music by George Crumb, whom he had met several years before, he wanted to get involved as well.

Ludwig and Fischbeck had agreed on *Lamentations*, the five poems of biblical prophet Jeremiah, because they were looking for a topic that was contemporary yet timeless. Neither was afraid of a strong political statement, and the inspiring words seemed a perfect basis for the joint effort.

The 10 dancers had been hearing the work through computer-generated MIDI files. At the first rehearsal, they finally heard the piece scored for clarinet, double bass, harp and percussion, and led by Network's music director Jan Krzywicki, for the first time. Both Ludwig and Fischbach reveled in the possibilities they had been allowed.

Manfred Fischbeck:
David was compelled to work on the five Lamentations *because he felt they expressed our present state of war and how it was mirrored in these ancient poems, written at the total destruction of Jerusalem.*

We discussed instrumentation, and I asked for some impressionistic images . . . through our agreement, and the video component, we tried to solve the question of how you dance a thematic idea.

David Ludwig:
There were moments when tears came to my eyes, because it was both unexpected and moving to watch what Manfred had done. We had the same message in mind and were willing to adjust, we're both hearing the same story told in a different way. When you go to the dance, you need a good partner. (Both in dance studio, March 8, 2007)

28. GETTNG INTO THE ACT

About a month before revered violinist Sarah Chang was scheduled to play a recital, I was offered an idea by Marc Mostovoy, who was working on a Kimmel Center program called See Hear. His idea was that, in this day of cable and computers, some music would be better appreciated with a visual component, and it was supported by the passionate philanthropist Ted Wolf.

Marc, along with audio-video wizard Carl Weiss, were working on a performance of *Israel In Egypt*, a florid Handel oratorio that surely would have a limited audience despite its enormous musical merits. The team spent months finding paintings to illustrate the narrative of the oratorio, and the visual perspective made the experience much more vivid.

His idea was to do a three-minute video about each of Sarah's three pieces, and I would provide the still photos and written narration. She had scheduled the Beethoven *Kreutzer* Sonata, Prokofiev's Second Sonata and Richard Danielpour's *River Of Light*. I timed out three minutes of narration for the first two works, and found a wealth of photographs for them, including one with Prokofiev and David Oistrakh playing chess. It was a chance to mention that Beethoven sent the dedicated work to the famous violinist Rodolphe Kreutzer in Paris, who didn't like the looks of it and never played it.

I was hoping that there was a literary or pictorial hook for Danielpour's piece, but when I asked him he said he just liked the name. Three minutes is a lot of time to fill when you have basically nothing, and I decided to use a retrospective on Sarah's career and some photos from Danielpour's opera *Margaret Garner*. It actually worked out pretty well, I thought, and it timed out beautifully under Weiss' guidance.

It's a little daunting to hear your voice booming out into a 2,500-seat hall, making you slide down into your seat. Of course, Sarah's brilliant playing was joyful, the video didn't seem to be terribly distracting, and it actually was received very enthusiastically. I didn't realize that Carl would add just one image—a picture of Sarah playing as a tiny tyke.

Afterwards, Sarah said she really enjoyed the video, and thought the whole project was very worthwhile in bringing the audience closer to the music. But she did say, "Did you have to put that kid picture in it?" I stammered that I wasn't the culprit, but her mother said she loved it.

I received compliments from many people I knew who had attended, and who thought there should be more such presentations. Though Marc was willing to come up with the ideas, and Ted Wolf was willing to support it, the Kimmel Center didn't think it sold any more tickets, and See Hear went Blind Deaf.

High-Level Hoedown

Since we first heard the bluegrass-flavored music by the Curtis players called Time for Three, the trio's eclectic style and enthusiasm had excited a wide range of listeners. Conductor Simon Rattle called these young players "the future of music," and actor Paul Newman, after they played at his Hole In The Wall Gang Camp in Connecticut, said, "To hear these three young guys is to be thankful music was invented."

I previously mentioned the lights-out 2003 evening at the Mann, when Time for Three burst into stardom. This time, the three Curtis alumni were returning to Philly near the end of a 31-state, 120-concert marathon to appear with Peter Nero and the Philly Pops.

This Pops Hoedown concert presented a slight conflict for bassist Ranaan Meyer, since his mother, Norma, was playing in the Perelman Theater across the plaza with the ensemble Piano4. His colleagues are violinists Nicolas Kendall and Zachary De Pue. (In 2016, Zach left to remain concertmaster of the Indianapolis Symphony, and was replaced by Nikki Chooi.)

Time for Three (Ranaan Meyer, Nicolas Kendall, Zachary De Pue, 2004).
Credit: LeAnn Muller.

We caught up by phone with Meyer and De Pue the week before a concert, and they recollected hat memorable performance at the Mann.

Zachary DePue and Ranaan Meyer:
Q: *How important was that night?*
De Pue: *That was huge for us, a very surreal thing, because the night before we had gone to hear the band Phish, playing to thousands of people, and I said, "I want to do that! Someday, it's going to happen!" And the next*

night it did, and there was an amazing adrenaline rush hearing thousands of people respond to us.

Q: *How do you like to affect audiences?*

Meyer: *Last night we went to hear the Cleveland Orchestra play the Dvořák Sixth Symphony. Some of our friends were in the orchestra, and we were standing in the back dancing to it like a rock concert and being enthusiastic. An usher came over and tried to hush us down. When we come back with the Cleveland Pops, we will tell the ushers not to tell anyone to be quiet, because we want them to feel our music and do whatever is natural in response. It's a sacrilege to ask anything different from the audience.*

Q: *How do you approach the freedom in these two musical genres?*

De Pue: *When you play Brahms, it's so profound that I can take myself way too seriously. We can get stuck in our parts, doing our parts, playing our notes, and forget that it may be using folk tunes. After all, it's just music. We need to bring that same outlook and freedom in the music to communicate emotionally with the listeners.* (By phone, March 26, 2007)

Jason DePue, a Philadelphia Orchestra violinist (and brother of *Time for Three* violinist Zachary) wanted to pay homage to his cherished friends and his alma mater. Several members of the famed Guarnieri String Quartet were affiliated with Curtis Institute, inspiring many string players.

To celebrate the Quartet's members, who were retiring after 45 years together, DePue tackled one of the Everests of the repertory: the 24 Caprices by Nicolo Paganini at South Philadelphia's St. Rita of Cascia Church. With fiendish trills, double-stops, octaves, slurs and chordal effects, it presses virtuosity to the outer limits; its final 24th Caprice in A Minor became the basis of well-known variations by Rachmaninoff, Brahms, Lutoslawski and many others. DePue's skill was apparent as he played them with color and a remarkable sense of ease.

The Diva Returns

In preparation for its centenary in 2008, Settlement Music School began honoring groups of its alumni, to be eventually collected into the Settlement 100. There were plenty of luminaries to choose as an interview, though my first choice was soprano Wilhelmenia Wiggins Fernandez.

Fernandez was a longtime South Philadelphia resident, first exposed to opera at Settlement School. She eventually graduated to the prestigious Academy of Vocal Arts, and to major roles in Europe. Her Carmen, Bess and Tosca were famous, and she sang a Musetta in *La Bohème* with tenor Placido Domingo and soprano Mirella Freni in Paris.

But nothing could have prepared her for the enormous visibility gained from her role in the 1981 French film *Diva*, rocketing her to even more international fame—though she sang only one opera in her hometown.

From her home in Kentucky, she spoke about how her life was shaped by her Settlement experience.

Wilhelmenia Fernandez:
Q: *Who encouraged you to go to Settlement School?*
A: *It began at home, since my mother—who still lives in Philadelphia—is a pianist. She saw that I needed more. I began singing as early as 5, certainly at church, and it filled my life. I knew its importance early. I was always hearing my mother play the piano or organ and became very interested in reading music. In the black community there was always church, but Settlement was a source one could go to when there was no other. My teacher Tillie Barmach knew young singers and saw the farther, bigger picture. She wouldn't allow pushing the voice into the blockbusters, into an area of no return.*

This kind of guidance, or lack of it, can make or break a career at an early age. If you want longevity, you have to take care of the voice in the early years, even in the early 20s.

Q: *Do you feel slighted by not performing much opera in your hometown?*
A: *They say a prophet is never recognized in his own land. Even as a child, I knew I was not going to remain solely in Philadelphia, and my prayer was answered. I was able to perform with the Philadelphia Orchestra, led by Zubin Mehta. I don't look back on Philly with any regrets. My humble, meager beginning will always be dear in my heart.*

Q: *What happened after* Diva?
A: *It was a wonderful and fun exploration of another artistic side of myself, and I only did it because I could sing. But the film gave me an exposure that I could not have imagined, and I had to catch up with my own fame when the floodgates opened to do countless operas. My repertory simply wasn't that great, with a powerful expectation to do everything well.*

Q: *Do you still sing spirituals at the end of your recitals?*
A: *Always! This is important American music, not to be made fun of, and we can sing in a dialect just as we sing in Italian. It's not just limited to the black culture, though people who are not black are afraid of not approaching it correctly. It should not be limiting. It's part of our heritage that needs to be told.*

Q: *What are you doing now?*
A: *Since I didn't finish Juilliard, I went back to school to finish my degree and, soon, I finally graduate from the University of Kentucky. I'm not a teacher, but I coach a few students like the Wicked Witch of the West, a stickler for studying parts and having the voice paint the color. It has come almost full circle, like a flower just beginning to bud and blossom. But that first music school I had the blessings of being able to attend made me want to humble myself and follow my path, the life that was chosen for me.* (By phone, April 2, 2007)

Bali High

The throbbing sounds that stirred me on an old Mercury LP of Colin McPhee's *Tabuh-Tabuhan*, and also through works by Lou Harrison, began a fascination with Balinese music. The layered rhythms played on gamelan (roughly "hammer" in Javanese) has come to mean a band of metal xylophones, drums and gongs, though in some Balinese villages strings, flutes and even vocalists are sometimes added.

Evan Ziporyn has been carrying the Balinese torch these days *with Gamelan Galak Tika*, a group praised for creating "an exuberant blast of metal fireworks."

The multi-talented Ziporyn, a Chicago-born bass clarinetist, has toured with Paul Simon and as part of the renowned Bang on a Can All-Stars, and also performs as a soloist with Steve Reich's musicians. He's worked with a legion of Eastern and Western composers, and his compositions have been performed by many, including Yo-Yo Ma's Silk Road Project, and at arts festivals around the world.

The Philadelphia Classical Symphony's music director Karl Middleman called Ziporyn out of the blue two years ago about writing a piece, and only met him for the first time at the rehearsal. Ziporyn had brought ten percussionists from his 30-member ensemble to join Middleman's musicians for the world premiere of his Concerto for Gamelan and Strings.

We spoke with Ziporyn by phone from Boston, where this busy musician has also held a teaching post at MIT since 1990.

Evan Ziporyn:
Q: *What inspired you about the music of Bali?*

A: *I had heard the old Nonesuch recordings, and when I visited Bali in 1981, I suddenly felt all the things I had been trying to do in my own music. I heard insights into Stravinsky and Bartok, the syncopations, the ability to organize larger forms. And I found that their culture ended up being more interesting than the music itself, since most of it is a major part of religious ceremony.*

Q: *How did you approach writing your concerto?*

A: *I studied Balinese music for 10 years before I felt compelled to write, and it has become part of my own musical bloodstream and DNA, hard to separate out. For this project, I designed a whole new set of instruments that were made in Bali, built to the tuning I wanted the pitches to be. Only some of our percussion notes match the Western scale of the 16 string players, setting up a strange and compelling sonic environment. The reality of putting two cultures together is an interesting compositional challenge.*

Q: *How important were Lou Harrison and Colin McPhee to this music?*

A: *Harrison was really the guiding spirit, building gamelans and making it part of his musical universe. It was courageous, and the Balinese have taken it as an act of respect. McPhee used Western instruments to simulate gamelan sounds. By coincidence, my drum teacher had been a friend of*

McPhee's 50 years ago, and the same instruments he heard are still being played in a Balinese village. The ability to travel gives us access to musicians from Burma and Africa and Asia, making the music of the world a great luxury of our age. (By phone, April 12, 2007)

Two Great Operas

It's been mentioned that because of Christofer Macatsoris' thoroughness of preparation, and that of the Academy of Vocal Arts' other vocal coaches, a legion of stars are now in demand on the world's stages.

Back in the 1960s, Macatsoris remembers being assistant conductor for a Philadelphia Lyric Opera Company production of Massenet's *Manon* with two legends, soprano Anna Moffo and Russian tenor Nicolai Gedda. There's a church scene that requires an organ and, when the organist didn't show up, Gedda insisted that Macatsoris play the part, though he had never played organ pedals or multiple keyboards. He did his best, though Gedda screamed at him afterward and, in the process, taught him a huge lesson: always be prepared.

Macatsoris' dual goals have always been to bring out all the composer's shadings and intentions for the audience, and also to reveal to his artists a wealth of interpretive understanding essential to their professional careers.

For an AVA production of Massenet's *Manon*, the singers did a lot of research too, reading the original 1731 novel by Abbé Prévost and listening to famous old recordings.

Macatsoris' high level of preparation and detail was evident recently in his study, where he was finishing up months of marking the string bow strokes and reed articulations in the individual players' musical parts.

Christopher Macatsoris. Credit: Paul Sirochman.

Christofer Macatsoris:
Q: *Why did you choose this opera after all these years?*

A: *Our singers are very close to the ages of the characters, depicting young love and dreams that don't materialize. And we're geared to expressing intimate details in small halls, with the audience very close, instead of at the Met, for instance, where you're hundreds of feet away, with singers in their forties and up.*

We're not really an opera company, but a growing process presenting works that should be in the singers' repertoire, and they all become involved in some way. One season, for instance, (Turkish baritone) Burak Bilgili was singing at La Scala, but he came back to sing in our chorus.

Q: *What's special to you about Massenet's musical approach?*

A: *Massenet loves his heroines to be alluring and seductive, as he did with (his operas about)* Thais, Hérodiade, Cendrillon *and* La Navarraise, *and he always cast singing actresses. The theater was important when he was composing, with Victorien Sardou's plays and the great actresses like Eleonora Duse and Sarah Bernhardt.*

The original novel was seen through the eyes of Des Grieux, but Massenet shifted it to let us hear how Manon feels and how she thinks.

Q: *What challenges are there for you in conducting?*

A: *There are quick-shifting tempi, enormous mood swings and scores of delicious, small mercurial moments, all specifically marked in the score. There are many places where the rhythm goes against the words, and the downbeat is not always the strong beat. And I have to make sure not to cover the singers, to keep it clear. French music needs clarity and, for all its sweetness, it shouldn't be done in a sentimental, cloying way.*

Q: *Why do we care about Manon, who's basically selfish?*

A: *She's only a teenager, full of awe about travel, inns, jewels, clothes and luxury, and she becomes one of the great courtesans of the ages. My image is to play her like you imagine a young Leslie Caron, in* Lili. *She has no guile, she keeps going back to Des Grieux and saying she's sorry, and then she does it again. And he always forgives her because he knows she can't help herself.* (Academy of Vocal Arts, April 19, 2007)

Just after *Manon*, the Opera Company was presenting Verdi's final masterwork, *Falstaff*. Don Russell, in his Joe Sixpack column, found sympathy for Sir John Falstaff's boozy excesses. Though some may relate to Shakespeare's lecherous, obese, scheming and completely untrustworthy knight and his rascally crew of knaves, few would admit it.

Yet the intensely serious Giuseppe Verdi came out of pastoral retirement at age 79 to write his only mature comedy about Sir John. Verdi, who loved Shakespeare, had become amused by Falstaff's escapades in *Henry IV* (Parts I and II) and *The Merry Wives of Windsor*, and his demise in *Henry V*.

Perhaps it was Falstaff's lust for life and completely unapologetic revelry that appealed to Verdi, or Shakespeare's masterful use of this exuberant character.

In the finale, Verdi composed an incredibly complex fugue after Falstaff faces the audience and proclaims his view of life. "Everything in the world is a joke," he reveals, "and he who laughs last laughs best."

Considering the expectations of audiences in 1893 for a typically dramatic, Verdian death at the final curtain—and the composer's insistence that his success be measured only by box office—this was an astonishing departure, yet it instantly became a huge success at La Scala with Arturo Toscanini conducting. Because of the tumult, Verdi had to be led out through a side door of the theater, and crowds cheered for hours outside his hotel window.

Corrado Rovaris. Credit: Gabello Studios.

Conductor Corrado Rovaris, the company's music director, hails from Bergamo, Italy, a scant 55 miles from Verdi's home near Busseto. He has this composer's music in his blood, and a special appreciation for the master's farewell work.

On the day of an important Manchester-Milan soccer semifinals game, with conductor Rovaris hoping for a lopsided Milan win, we talked over lunch about the uniqueness of this rambunctious character.

Corrado Rovaris:
Q: *Why do you think* Falstaff *has a special place?*
A: *Usually opera needs arias and duets, and here you don't have that because Verdi's music describes each word and shows their connection. Other operas have action, then stop to show the situation, but here there is always action, everything is always in progress.*

It's a chamber piece, really, because to enjoy the opera you have to enjoy the text Verdi admired, without a big tune you go out singing.

Q: *Why should we care about a drunken, fat lecher? Is it because of a human desire for excess?*

A: *At the beginning you may hate his behavior, but when the third act begins you are almost on his side. It's because what he endures while trying to capture his youth is terribly sad, and that makes us relate to him. My dream is to convince people that, though told through the life of a comical character, this is a huge and important masterpiece of the history of opera.*

Q: *How do you think Verdi perceived the work?*

A: *We are in front of a man who is nearly 80 years old, who looks at jealousy, excess and love from a different perspective. He didn't want standard structure and struggled to follow all the drama and comedy in the character. There's not even an overture, because it just begins suddenly to show that it's a theater piece, as if Verdi is saying, "Let's go!"* (Restaurant, April 26, 2007)

Italian Operatic Legends

There was real sadness upon hearing about the death of Luciano Pavarotti, who had always been generous to me. Between honoring my friend Jessica Stanley, hosting me with a helpful damsel at the Four Seasons and giving me that phone interview from Germany, he had been a class act.

After his *Pagliacci* with Riccardo Muti, he had learned the challenging role of Verdi's *Don Carlo*, a huge project for a slow learner at that stage of his career. By that time, expectations were enormous and, when he cracked on two high notes at Milan's La Scala, the cognoscenti booed mightily in disapproval. In that weird world, where fanaticism is on the level of the World Cup and the Super Bowl combined, Pavarotti deeply felt that rebuke from an Italian audience.

The famed tenor once claimed that he had lost 85 pounds twice, and at one point reached a weight of 387, a number larger than the 379 performances he gave at the Metropolitan Opera. He loved kids, having three grown daughters and a more recent one, Alice. He often said, "Children are the innocent result of the stupidity of adults."

His later concerts, including a travesty at the Kimmel Center, were a disappointment. Those of us who admired his sheer bravura and enormous natural gift wished he had gone out at his peak, a Ted Williams who hit the final home run and remained a beloved icon.

Pavarotti gave opera an enormous boost, bringing the world of singing to the general public in performance and in his many telecasts with an immediacy and fervor that no one ever had before. No one's likely to do it again.

La Scala

Those words conjure an image of the world's most famous opera house, the glittering jewel of Italian vocal history in otherwise gray, gloomy Milan. Though La Scala forces have toured America with operatic productions and Verdi's Requiem, their last Philadelphia visit as a symphonic entity was in 1921, with Arturo Toscanini conducting.

Expanded into an ensemble for playing orchestral repertoire as well as opera 30 years ago by Claudio Abbado, followed by Riccardo Muti, the Orchestra Filarmonica della Scala visited with Italian conductor Riccardo Chailly at its helm.

After 16 years with Amsterdam's great Concertgebouw Orchestra, his affiliation at that time was Leipzig's famed, more flexible Gewandhaus Orchestra, considered the oldest in Europe, an ensemble that had recently visited the Kimmel Center.

For his touring program Chailly, had chosen Wagner, Respighi and an unusual, sumptuous, work: Nino Rota's suite of music from Federico Fellini's 1953 film *La Strada*.

Riccardo Chailly:

Q: *Do you need extra symphonic players to add to the opera pit orchestra?*

A: *No, because La Scala has the largest opera pit in the world. Almost 100 players can fit, much larger than even the Metropolitan Opera in New York. We have a huge orchestra of 130, with slightly different programs for our tour. And we have symphonic encores of Puccini and Verdi—and I hope the response allows us to play them!*

Q: *How close are you to Rota's music?*

A: *I once led one of his Piano Concertos, with Rota playing the solo part, and his delightful Trombone Concerto. He was a very introspective man, a master of orchestral color and an inner sense of rhythm, and I called him the Italian Prokofiev. This ballet music, mostly from* La Strada, *was commissioned by La Scala for a ballet in 1966.*

Q: *What is the political situation for the arts in Italy?*

A: *At this time, the government doesn't show enough flexibility to understand culture, surprising in a country with such a history of art. In recent years, they dropped funding for the radio orchestras in Rome, Milan and Naples, and the youth orchestra I founded, Orchestra Symphonica Giuseppe Verdi, is always on the edge of bankruptcy. I've become very spoiled in Leipzig, because the Gewandhaus includes 185 musicians, playing orchestral concerts as well as the Leipzig opera. And they also perform sacred music at Thomaskirche, where the present cantor is the 16th successor to Johann Sebastian Bach. So, for me, it's a perfect fit.* (By phone, October 8, 2007)

Philly Farewell to a Legend

You have to spin and roll your globe a bit to encounter the north island of New Zealand, where Kiri Te Kanawa was adopted as an infant by a native Maori and his Irish-born wife.

Fast forward to 1981, when Te Kanawa's singing at the wedding of Prince Charles and Princess Diana was heard by more than 600 million people, followed by the accolade of Dame Kiri the next year.

The revered soprano (who started out as a mezzo) began as a pop entertainer in New Zealand clubs, winning a song contest and a grant to study in London. Though her teacher claimed she had no singing technique, she made her way though many small parts until finding her ideal role, the Countess in Mozart's *The Marriage Of Figaro*. After that, she became one of the major names in opera, besides making pop records with André Previn, Nelson Riddle and Michel Legrand. She sang in the controversial *West Side Story* recording, led by Leonard Bernstein, and a disc of Maori songs.

It was likely that her recital would be her final one in Philly, and it included art songs, though no operatic arias. We spoke with Dame Kiri from Toronto, where she had a day off during her globetrotting journey.

Kiri te Kanawa:

Q: *Is this really your farewell tour?*

A: *Well, I'm 63 and time is running out, but there are still things to do, and I intend to keep singing in some fashion. I've taken care of my voice and still remember the advice I heard when going into Covent Garden as a young singer. Every single day the doormen, whose opinions I respected, would say, don't do like so-and-so, please don't make those same mistakes and ruin your voice.*

Q: *How proud are you of your crossover records?*

A: *They were hard work, but luckily the orchestrations were molded around me. I always adored Ella Fitzgerald, who sang very simply with such a gorgeous sound. I am very proud of singing that repertoire, because I always fancied myself being able to do it.* (By phone, October 11, 2007)

A new "Swan"

A few years before Christopher Wheeldon, resident choreographer at the New York City Ballet, was given the assignment by Pennsylvania Ballet to create a new $1 million version of the classic *Swan Lake*. He came up with a typically-innovative concept, staging the story within a ballet studio familiar through the classic Edgar Degas paintings.

Q: *Is it daunting to tackle such a classic as* Swan Lake?

A: *Not really, because I'm creating it more for the people who have neer seen* Swan Lake, *not for those who have treasured memories of some other classic production.*

Q: *Are the dancers different than they were 100 years ago?*

A: *Dancers today are technically stronger, not necessarily artistically stronger because they don't have to make up for a lack in technique. Part of what I do is to coax some of that artistry out, because I come from the very focused (London's) Royal Ballet tradition.*

Q: *Is it true you don't work any steps out before you begin?*

A: *In abstract pieces, I tend not to remotely have a clue choreographically of what I'm doing before I go into the studio, because it creates itself from what I'm feeling that day with my instincts and inspiration. Working out all the movement yourself defeats the point of creating a ballet for your dancers, because you're creating on you, not for them.*

Q: *How difficult is it to work with dancers you don't know?*

A: *I saw three shows by this company, so I knew how these dancers performed without knowing how they were in the studio. The benefit is that you don't have to spend the time getting to know how they move, how they work, whether they're creative and open to suggesting ideas themselves. That makes it more collaborative, which I prefer.*

Q: *How do you handle the three principal dancers differently?*

A: *Choreography is like tailoring, making that woman be the most beautiful woman she can be to make an audience fall in love with her. I've altered the parts for each dancer, Arantxa Ochoa, Dede Barfield, and Riolama Lorenzo, based on what they do best, but even if I set the same steps they would not be dancing the same way, and that's what's fascinating. They have to trust me, and I'm fairly successful at making people look their very best.*

Q: *How good is this company?*

A: *Nothing separates them, other than size and budget, from the best in this country. They should be touring, because they're fantastic.*

Q: *How did you derive a new focus?*

A: *To me, the Rotbart character was the weak link, a half-bird, half-man evil sorcerer who runs around flapping his wings at everyone. I wanted this character to be the root, which led me to the mysterious and sinister top-hatted figure in the background of so may Degas ballet paintings, the concept which led to both the design and the costumes.*

Q: *What bothers you the most?*

A: *Ballet is just people being physical with one another, the poetry of human contact through movements and music.*

I hate it when people say they don't go to the ballet because they don't understand what they're looking at. You're not meant to be understanding anything. You're supposed to open your mind to creating something yourself, and if you don't quite grasp something fluid, don't panic, just enjoy it. (Ballet studio, May 26, 2004)

Swan Lake was revived by the company in March 2015 and, three months later, Wheeldon won a Tony award for his choreography, and direction, of Broadway's smash hit "An American in Paris."

29. OLD AND NEW MUSIC

How would a composer write a new work for an ensemble that plays Renaissance music on 27 period instruments? That risky challenge was presented to Kile Smith by the renowned wind band Piffaro, offering him their first major commission—thanks in large measure to the innovative Philadelphia Music Project.

Smith's background in writing Lutheran liturgical anthems, as well as music for early instruments, made him a shrewd choice. To make it even more meaningful, his gifted oldest daughter Priscilla, a brilliant practitioner of the Baroque oboe, was a member of the ensemble as well. The vocal lines were handled by The Crossing, the outstanding 20-voice group led by Donald Nally.

Kile Smith. Credit: Abu Tilghman

Smith's 12-section work, *Vespers*, wrapped the hymn tunes, ancient forms and early instrument sound world in contemporary harmony. His remarkable use of the timbres in these unique instruments, and their interplay with the perfectly-pitched voices, was a revelation. Inspired by mid-1500s Reformation-era vespers and Epiphany texts, this meeting of sonic worlds 500 years apart was a brave and fascinating experiment, and an unqualified success.

Months later, the recording of *Vespers* was released and, to no one's surprise, garnered a full-page rave article in *Gramophone* magazine. It sported a color photo of the Piffaro ensemble outside, with Priscilla in the middle. The modest Smith, upon being congratulated at the international acclaim, only said, "I'm glad they used the picture with Priscilla instead of one of me!"

Priscilla (now Priscilla Herreid), also a superb singer, entered the first class of Baroque practice at Juilliard, and was soon a member of another period-instrument group, Juilliard 415—the number referring to the pitch used at that time (modern frequency is A=440). Kile's other two daughters are musicians as well: Elena (Nellie) studies cello with mentor Jeffrey Solow at Temple University, and Martina, who had been principal French horn in the Gary White-conducted Philadelphia Sinfonia (where Nellie had been principal cello), also attends Temple.

Smith, now composer-in-residence with the Helena Symphony, the Church of the Holy Trinity and Lyric Fest, is also heard on WRTI-FM as host of the contemporary music show *Now Is the Time* and co-host of *Music From the Fleisher Collection*. Kile and his singer-and-musician wife Jacqueline, who home-schooled these three remarkable musician daughters, have demonstrated the overwhelming connection between love and music.

But He Could Hear It

Mark Twain said, "A classic is something that everybody wants to have read and nobody wants to read."

Some of the musical classics of the postwar era are in that category, and none more than Pierre Boulez' *Le Marteau sans maître* (*The hammer without a master)*, the controversial 20th-century musical milestone that few have heard.

Scored for alto flute, guitar, viola, xylorimba (or xylophone), vibraphone, percussion and voice, it's not an easy piece to wrap your ears around. I remember a first hearing of Boulez's recording, sounding like completely random sounds wrapped around surrealist, mostly nonsensical poems. After five more recent run-throughs, his structural intentions still remain elusive.

The nine-movement *Marteau* was his break from strict serialism, though his complex patterns and rhythmic notation still stun audiences into a completely unique sound world. Boulez's imagination and the originality of his concept have awarded it legendary status, though its difficulty only allows performances by daring and virtuoso groups.

One such group is Orchestra 2001, who had a special reason for tackling it: the ensemble's music director James Freeman had studied with Boulez for one semester at Harvard. Freeman was struck by the depth of his analyses, once covering whole walls with arrows and notes pertaining to one or two measures of Alban Berg's opera *Wozzeck*.

James Freeman:
Boulez was very engaging, and even drank beer at the local bar with us. But I realized last week that the piece has more theater than he gives it credit for, and that it's okay that I see it differently.

I want to do it with a little more variety and flair, and a greater sense of drama, but it's frankly impossible to get a lot of it the first time. It's extremely difficult for the players, much harder than it is for me to conduct, because the tempo changes constantly, very strictly.

I remember teaching a class at Swarthmore a couple of years back and preparing a student piece that was a total mishmash of sound, a dense sweep of chaotic music. I said I couldn't hear every note in this. A student yelled, "Boulez could!"

I'm resisting being analytical about Boulez's music, terrifically important up until the '70s, when composers began to react to anything that seemed remotely cerebral. (Composer) George Crumb is fond of saying, "Boulez likes to write music so the performers are endangered." (Swarthmore College, January 21, 2008)

George Crumb discussing a score with James Freeman.

Successful Folly

Unless you have been commissioned, it's sheer folly to write an opera. *William Penn* took almost 25 years, and David DiChiera spent seven years on his *Cyrano*. As founder of Michigan Opera Theatre and Opera Pacific, and former president of Opera America—the fund-raising engine behind the creation of many new operas—he was well aware of the pitfalls.

DiChiera studied as a Fulbright scholar in Naples, Italy, and also at the University of California, Los Angeles. During that period, melodies and romantic orchestration were passé, and the academic thrust was for atonal, serial and electronic composition.

The Opera Company of Philadelphia was performing the work between the Detroit premiere and a Miami performance, giving DiChiera, who had left the orchestration to Mark Flint, the rare opportunity to make adjustments along the way to his sumptuous, romantic score, performed in early February 2008.

David DiChiera:
Back then, if you wrote in a tonal language or with a melody, you were made to feel that you were marginal. But in recent years, composers have become comfortable with all musical languages.

But we don't go through this to listen to it ourselves. Opera is for audiences, and they tell us whether they think it's serious, or sentimental, or amusing. Your instincts are valuable but, ultimately, it goes out of your hands and into those of the maestro who's recreating it. (Academy of Music Ormandy Room, February 5, 2008)

The role of Christian in *Cyrano* was tenor Stephen Costello, just out of AVA and about to become a major operatic star. A winner of the Musical Fund Society Career Advancement Award, he has sung all over Europe, and with Riccardo Muti in Salzburg; James Levine chose him to substitute on opening night at the Met, where he has performed often. He married fellow AVA graduate Ailyn Perez, is a brilliant artist who has also become an enormous star, and they made a CD of arias and duets together in 2014.

Despite his sudden though highly expected fame, Costello is an unpretentious, gracious young man from Northeast Philadelphia. A trumpet player during his years at George Washington High School, he recalls traveling to the Academy of Music stage as part of the All-Philadelphia Jazz Band.

Later, he discovered the chorus and musicals, attended the University of the Arts and auditioned for the Academy of Vocal Arts.

Stephen Costello:
My parents weren't musical, but for some reason, around the sixth grade, I wanted to play a sax. They only had a baritone sax, much too heavy to carry around, and the teacher gave me a trumpet instead, and I played it around 12 years. But I sang in chorus my last year, in South Pacific, *and auditioned at the last minute to the University of the Arts as a vocal major.*

If George Washington High School hadn't had a strong music program, I probably wouldn't be in music. I took dance and three or four different arts programs a day with other kids, just as part of life. I see young people now first learning about the arts as college undergraduates . . . it's a shame.

It's marvelous to be able to create the character and to be able to ask the composer or librettist about what they wanted. Imagine if you could ask Mozart! But this role requires serious acting as well as singing.

I still return to my voice teacher at AVA, Bill Schuman, all the time, and will for the rest of my life. When singers say they don't need coaches anymore, that's when their careers go downhill. (Academy of Music Ormandy room, February 5, 2008)

When Robert Driver became head of the Opera Company, I urged him to consider the young artists at the Academy Of Vocal Arts, Curtis and

Temple in small roles, to make them return after they achieved success. He eventually did, and after a Gounod *Romeo and Juliet*, booked three years before the pair returned as major stars, I reminded him that he couldn't afford them now.

That September after *Cyrano*, Costello and Ailyn tied the knot, and starred on the world's stages, whether together or apart; it has been a true pleasure to see their enormous success, obvious to me from their first year at AVA. Recently, in Los Angeles to visit Emil, I was thrilled to see the words Costello. Perez. *La Bohème*. LA Opera—on the side of a bus.

The pair was to sing in December of 2013 for the Philadelphia Chamber Music Society, until Costello got a gig in Vienna and the gorgeous Perez did a glorious recital alone, ending her evening with the equivalent of a hug toward the audience with *Over the Rainbow*. They both returned to perform for Opera Philadelphia's September 2014 opening season gala, though it was announced in early 2015 that their relationship has ended.

One major reason for all the interviews connected to the Opera Company of Philadelphia (now Opera Philadelphia) was their public relations wizard Tracy Galligher. Over a decade, she always created interesting angles for each show, and was savvy enough so that both papers didn't run the same story. When she announced her plans to leave town to join the staff of Lyric Opera of Chicago, so many of us realized she would be greatly missed. On a first visit to Chicago, she treated me with a glorious *Die Meistersinger* with James Morris; we returned in 2014 for Dvořák's *Rusalka* featuring Eric Owens and Mozart's *La Clemenza di Tito* with Joyce DiDonato, finding ourselves across the aisle from Opera Philadelphia's general director David Devan. In June 2014, we were overjoyed to attend her wedding to Thomas Young in Philadelphia.

Big Ears

Osvaldo Golijov's *Ainadamar* finally appeared in Philly, the first time it would be performed without its original creative team. His music overflows with an unusual blend of unexpected rhythms and completely original sonic mixtures, a throbbing collision of fresh sounds that never sound like anyone else's.

Golijov, 47, recipient of a MacArthur Fellowship—aka the "genius grant"—is the creative crucible of an enormous variety of influences. Born in La Plata, Argentina, where he absorbed Jewish liturgical and klezmer music, social and religious oppression, and Astor Piazzolla's tangos, he left at 22 for Jerusalem and later absorbed George Crumb's other-worldly palette at the University of Pennsylvania.

Ainadamar refers to the Fountain of Tears in Granada, Spain, where poet and playwright Federico Garcia Lorca was assassinated in 1936 by Franco's Fascist forces during the early days of the Spanish Civil War.

Golijov's instrumentation is powerful and unique, using Arab and flamenco guitars, throbbing percussion, congas, marimba and cajon (a xylophonic drum), as well as symphonic instruments, a flamenco singer and chorus. *Ainadamar* was written for the Boston Symphony at Tanglewood, and later revised; it was dedicated to the BSO's Anthony Fogg, a friend of Mikael Eliasen, artistic director of the Curtis Opera Theatre, which co-produced the show with Opera Philadelphia at the Perelman Theater.

At that time, Golijov was working on a film score for Francis Ford Coppola's *Tetro*, set in his native Argentina, and a super-secret project for the Met.

When I read that Golijov had declared "Music is a way in sound to map the human soul" and "I modulate cultures the way other composers modulate keys," I just had to speak with him.

Osvaldo Golijov:

Q: *How much of your percussion parts are improvised?*

A: *They can be played exactly as written, but that's not as exciting. They can use rhythmic embellishment, especially when you have players from the tradition.*

I simply do what I feel is necessary, what I feel to express what I want to express. The aim is not to startle. Composers always wrote what they heard and now, with music from all over the world available everywhere, boundaries will disappear. I don't presume to represent the future, or to be an emblem.

Q: *Do you feel courageous or apprehensive when writing something completely new?*

A: *Both are part of the process, and doubt is there all the time. But when it's written down, or the recorded document is there, it's much more clear what you intended. I've been very lucky to have worked with musicians who know my world and have projected it. Robert Spano and I are like brothers, because he understands better than I do, and is not afraid to tell me what doesn't work. If you are sure of yourself, great, but I am not. Music that I love is in that spirit of uncertainty, especially if it recalls a powerful emotion from the past. I like my music to be just like life, the transformation of grief into joy, like a collective lullaby.* (By phone, March 7, 2008)

In February of 2014, *Ainadamar* was given a full production by Opera Philadelphia at the Academy of Music, showing once again how remarkable Golijov's vision had been.

Basso Profundo

I had been floored by basso Eric Owens in his amazing title role of *Grendel* in New York and, fortunately for the Opera Company, he had been booked to sing Oroveso, the father of the title character of *Norma*, before that role increased his star power even further.

Eric Owens:

Q: *How do you like singing* bel canto *roles?*

A: *I love it, though I don't do a lot of it, because as I've grown older, my tastes have shifted to Wagner and Strauss. But it's very satisfying and keeps you honest, like medicine for the voice, the basis for everything else.*

You may be able to go on singing Puccini later in your career, but if you can't do bel canto and Mozart, then something's up, and you'd better work on it and keep it fresh.

Q: *How much did* Grendel *boost your career?*

A: *Things really started happening then! Basses usually sing the father, the king, the grandfather, all with solemn gravitas, but in this role I got to jump around, climb on things and dance. It whipped my butt, though, because there was no cover (understudy), and I actually didn't get to perform it completely until there were paying customers. My Met debut in* The Magic Flute *was a direct result, as well as (John Adams')* Doctor Atomic *in San Francisco and Chicago.*

Q: *Do you have a philosophy about acting?*

A: *Basses are not usually the center of attention. But our director, Kay Walker Castaldo, said to me one day, "This opera is about you." And everyone else too! This doesn't mean drawing focus to ourselves and not being a good colleague, but not shying away from the richness and liveliness of the character's passions. As far as Kay is concerned, that has to be true for each character to make it believable to the audience. That makes sense to me, because each of us is the hero in our own story.* (Academy of Music, March 27, 2008)

More recently, I've had the chance to hear Owens in so many different and varied roles, including the controversial Met *Ring*, and some brilliant master classes. Most recently, I was able to see him both as the water goblin in *Rusalka* and in the title role of *Porgy and Bess* for Lyric Opera of Chicago, which will feature him as Wotan in their new production of *Das Rheingold* and named him an 'unlimited community ambassador.'

Piano Man Finally Solos

Peter Nero never announced his Philly Pops programs in advance, preferring to rehearse many pieces and select the roster at the last minute. He writes many of the orchestrations, and plays his fabulous piano a little less than I always wanted. He was excited in January 2006, announcing an added Wednesday concert for the next season thanks to sellout crowds.

Peter Nero:

Q: *Are your charts written with specific players in mind?*

A: *Yes, I spend a lot of time on them because I don't want to slight any of the lead players. To make these charts work in other cities with symphony orchestras, I have to ask for freelance trumpet, sax and trombone—a reminder of how great my Philly Pops players are.*

Q: *Why don't you play more piano?*
A: *Sometimes people say I don't play enough, but when I play a lot and don't hear complaints, maybe that means they've had too much. You should always keep an audience wanting more.* (By phone, January 23, 2006)

For years I had asked him to play a solo jazz recital, and he did just that in 2002, in a joint Perelman Theater gig with Fred Hersch and Eric Reed. Even for those other two star performers, it must have been tough to follow Nero's white-hot "All the Things You Are," Jerome Kern's classic.

Nero, who had been making recordings for 48 years, still requires a daily 40-minute routine of separate-hand exercises, octave jumps with each hand and etudes by Chopin and Moszkowski. (See him warming up with the last two on YouTube by entering the words "Peter Nero.") Believe me, it takes more than exercises to acquire the skill Nero displays.

He had it when this writer first heard him play, eons ago at the Hickory House on the famed 52nd Street jazz club row in New York, and even before RCA signed him to his successful, multi-LP contract and changed his name from Bernie Nierow.

Years later, Nero finally relented, agreeing to a solo gig to benefit the Pops with bassist Michael Barnett, with the tab for the fund-raiser a hefty C-note. Though the two pianos in Verizon Hall and the one in the Perelman Theater are excellent instruments, Nero made himself feel even more comfortable by bringing his own 9-foot Steinway from home.

Peter Nero: *I'll just wing it with whatever tunes come to mind. I might ask people to give me a note - let's say four groups of five notes each, and then make up a tune and harmonize it.*

Playing solo is a stream-of-consciousness thing. The music just leads you, and you just cut loose and run amok. (By phone, April 4, 2008)

During the Orchestra's bankruptcy proceedings, Nero was relieved of his conductorship of the Philly Pops, which still survives independently under the baton of Michael Krajewski.

On one summer evening in July 2009, the unlikely piano duo of Lang Lang and Herbie Hancock met at the Mann, playing a wildly individualistic *Rhapsody In Blue* and Vaughan Williams' rarely-heard Concerto for Two Pianos. The two had met at the 2008 Grammy Awards, both awed by each other's prowess in their specific genre.

Speaking at the beginning of their tour from Copenhagen, Denmark, Lang said, "Herbie and I became good friends after the Grammys and somehow he liked me a lot. Some people thought we had great chemistry and should work together. I don't play jazz, but I have a lot of his CDs and had listened to them on my iPod when traveling. I'm really impressed by his technique and his harmonic imagination in improvisation, and always wonder how he does it. Playing with him is really a dream come true. And I believe the Philadelphia is the top orchestra in the world, totally tops, and I respect them above all others.

"I had a great chance to watch him accompany Aretha Franklin, switch harmony, react to the vocal, then go right into solo electric piano. He really plays classical music brilliantly, like the Vaughan Williams, which requires a great deal of confidence and technique.

"I've never done much improvising, but maybe I will learn a little bit from Herbie." As their tour went on, however, Lang evidently became much more adventurous in the encores.

He also poured his enthusiasm into his Lang Lang International Music Foundation, supported by the Grammys and UNICEF, with young pianists auditioning through YouTube. He invited three of them, aged eight to 10, for special mentoring, and they have already played eight-hand music on Oprah's TV show. Lang is very aware of the waves of Asian musicians in America, and especially the explosion of young Chinese pianists inspired by his enormous stardom.

"This is my most important project, because we need to care about the new generation, who will bring more young people into our classical music world. I have always had great teachers, like Mr. Graffman, guiding me through difficult situations, and these young musicians need someone who cares about them. I just became 27, and will soon reach the tenth anniversary of my career, but I recently had a letter from a 14-year-old who said, "Happy birthday, old man!"

As far as Hancock was concerned, Lang was at the top of his game.

"I had heard him at Disney Hall with the Los Angeles Philharmonic a year before the Grammys," said Hancock by phone from Essen, Germany. "I thought he was amazing, and I was dying to meet him. We talked for a while, and he seemed like a great, warm, playful person.

"Before the tour I was both delighted and frightened to death, considering that he's the consummate classical pianist. I haven't been playing classical music since I was 18, and I spent the last two months practicing three or four hours a day—that's amazing for me—to keep up with this demon. We talked about doing it for fun, for sharing our joy with the audiences. I will love the challenge of putting myself in unfamiliar situations, feeling through it and learning, until the day I die."

So did Lang loosen up during the encores at the first two concerts? "At the first concert in Montreux," said Hancock, "Lang played a Chinese folk melody. Then I improvised on top of his playing Liszt, which we hadn't rehearsed much because we wanted to go with the flow and not prepare it too tightly. I wanted to just use my ears and embrace each other musically.

"But at the second concert, in Lyon, he sang me a melody fragment offstage that I had never heard and started improvising on it. And after jumping in and improvising, I realized he was actually playing fragments from "Rhapsody In Blue." He blew me away, playing a few chords and adding some motifs on the fly. That really shocked me, and because of his smile I knew he had made that huge leap. He simply picks up anything--who knows what we'll do now?"

Afterwards, I had a chance to hang out a bit with these two fun-loving artists ijn person, and savor their deep respect for each other.

Herbie Hancock, Lang Lang, and the author

30. BAD CARTILAGE, BIG HEART

Watching ballet dancers is a mirage, an imagining that they are defying gravity and moving with superhuman grace. Though the ballerinas get most of the attention, it was impossible not to witness the remarkable prowess of James Ady, whose fluidity seemed effortless.

This dancer's remarkable artistry hid from us the intense pain of bone spurs. At the tender age of 29, principal dancer Ady was forced to retire after his performances as Franz in the comedy classic *Coppelia*. (His frequent partner Arantxa Ochoa, portraying Swanilda in this production, was five months' pregnant, though it was hardly apparent.)

Ady was in a high school for performing arts in North Carolina, and after Pennsylvania Ballet star Amy Aldridge visited the school ("She was cool and glamorous"), his goal was certain.

His departure was a real loss for the company. Dancers must accept the reality of shorter careers, often brought on by exhausted bodies and aching joints.

"A dancer into his upper 30s or even 40 is considered old," said the company's artistic director Roy Kaiser, who retired as a famed performer at 34.

Considering that the title of principal dancer isn't usually reached until the late 20s—that means a career window smaller than that of many professional athletes—and with only a fraction of the earning power.

Swan Lake, James Ady, Arantxa Ochoa. Credit: Paul Kolnik

Ady may be the only one to have noticed a deterioration in his performance skills over those last two seasons; his supreme ability always made us sense the beauty of his characterizations. His retirement was a reminder of the commitment that dancers make to their profession, and the blood, sweat, fatigue and pain they try to conceal from the audience.

Despite his star quality, Ady was known as a friendly, affable colleague. In productions of *Nutcracker*, he danced the lead Cavalier, and was willing to return in a later show that day as one of the battling mice. He was often the first to arrive at rehearsal, and was always willing to share his artistic experience with the younger dancers. Yes, he was very, very good indeed.

We sat down to talk at a Center City coffee shop, where the dancer's modest openness and good humor were much on display.

James Ady:
Dancing is the only thing I've ever been able to do, and it will be hard to leave that part of life behind. But bone spurs have worn all the cartilage away in my feet, especially the left one, with a repetitive stress injury.

Male dancers dance a lot in relevé, meaning lifting your heel off the floor and putting all your weight, even when lifting a woman, on the ball of the foot. My doctor said that if I want to walk later in life, I'd better stop dancing now . . .

I'd have tried to dance 10 more years if I could have, but this was a decision made for me, a long time coming. My technique is slipping, and I'm too proud to let that happen.

Coppelia is the first full-length ballet Arantxa and I ever did together, and she wanted to do it with me this time. Considering her pregnancy, she's sacrificing much more than I am. I'd have loved to do Romeo and Juliet with her as my last show, because doing that together at the Academy of Music was a real highlight in my career. She makes me work harder than everyone else, makes me step up my game while we can throw each other around.

I don't want to make a big deal out of having to leave, because I never thought I'd get to dance these roles. I got to kiss every one of the principal dancers in one role or another. And, a couple of years ago, I was pretty good. (Ballet studio, April 21, 2008)

Pianos and Pianists

A century ago, a piano was a fixture in nearly every American living room. The family's rented upright, spinet or grand was as essential an obligation as today's car loan, and the Philadelphia area boasted six piano manufacturers and a host of retail stores.

Piano sales peaked in the 1920s, when more than 365,000 were leased or purchased domestically every year. The Depression crushed that number to about 50,000 by 1932, and it was further diminished by the advent of television 20 years later—and, more recently, the lack of music education in most public schools.

The Mozart Effect arrived in the mid-'90s, a book emphasizing the impact of playing music on developing children's brains. Suddenly, parents wanted their kids to play instruments again, a trend that continues today.

My high school was located across the street from the Cunningham Piano Company, a prestigious local institution since 1891, though it hadn't manufactured pianos since 1941. In its heyday, Cunningham built more than 2,000 pianos in a year, most of them tall uprights (referred to as "cabinet grands") and player pianos that worked with piano rolls.

George Gershwin composed the early stages of his opera *Porgy and Bess* on a Cunningham piano near Charleston, S.C., where it still can be seen in a *Porgy* museum.

A few years ago, owners Richard Galassini and Timothy Oliver decided to take a giant leap back into manufacturing pianos. Made with parts from Italian, German, Japanese and other countries, they are assembled in Shanghai, at the factory that made the official piano at the Beijing Olympics. (A third of all pianos sold in the U. S. are made in China).

Today's new, American-made Steinway grand could easily set you back $50,000 to $60,000 or more. The first Cunningham five-foot grands cost $8,190, 5-foot-10-inch grands went for $11,800, and nine-foot concert instruments for $44,000. From another major manufacturer, a concert grand would run at least $100,000.

"Hugh Sung called and asked to see some pianos," said Galassini, "and I remembered that I had waited on him years ago when he was a youngster. He didn't remember me at all, but in trying all our pianos he eventually was impressed enough to buy a 5-foot-10-inch instrument for his home.

"We have 25 more grands coming in, and over 20 percent are already sold. We should have 200 this year, and are planning on 300 to 400 annually."

They decided that Sung should play a recital, to show off their piano and to launch a series of Cunningham-sponsored programs to establish the brand and support the local music community.

Sung and I had become friends after he played the benefit recital for Dolores, and found him an astounding pianist. He played with a Philadelphia Orchestra debut at 11, was admitted to Curtis Institute at 13, graduated in 1990 and, three years later, joined the faculty.

Holding the impressive title of Curtis' Director of Student Recitals and Instrumental Accompaniment, Sung helped schedule the popular, free Monday-Wednesday-Friday student concerts, often involving him as accompanist.

Years before a student could ever dream of playing a concerto with an orchestra, Sung's versatility supplied dozens of orchestral accompaniments, reduced to a dense piano part. To eliminate turning pages, he read music from the 6,000 scores available on his laptop, using a foot treadle to move the pages onscreen.

Sung often accompanied soloists in preliminary rehearsals for the Philadelphia Orchestra's Christoph Eschenbach, and filled in with the orchestra on celesta.

For a "visual recital," Sung played Mussorgsky's original *Pictures at an Exhibition* and Chopin's G Minor Ballade on a Cunningham concert grand.

Hugh Sung:
Q: *Why did you need a piano?*
A: *I've been playing the same Steinway since I was 5, and it had been beaten to a pulp because of my heavy technique. A piano can only take so much abuse! Though I have two instruments at Curtis, eventually mine wouldn't hold a tune for more than an hour, and the cost of repairing wasn't worth it.*

Q: *How much room is there today for new pianists?*
A: *When I first began teaching, my outlook for anyone making a career in music was pretty bleak. But in the last five or six years, the possibilities have exploded. People are launching musical businesses, tying music to technology, administration, legal matters, fund sharing for making CDs and even privatelessons.com.*

Thanks to the Internet and a wealth of new fields, there are many more opportunities to utilize music and make a difference.

Q: *Is anything more satisfying to you than guiding young talents?*
A: *Not really. At first, nurturing talent at this level was intimidating, but sharing and collaborating helps you rediscover the joys of making music. Serving and helping others brings optimism to the next generation. It's really true, the more you give.* (My home, July 16, 2008)

Sung said he loved technology, and he invited me to a seminar at a suburban music school. He set up a van full of equipment to prove his points, though he admitted it would be prohibitive for most teachers.

One student played Debussy's *Premiere Arabesque*. Sung displayed the music on a screen, as well as the amplitude of the playing recorded through a microphone. The score clearly showed that the melody was marked *mp* (*mezzo piano*), then *p* (*piano*) when repeated, with the wiggles clearly showing no diminution in volume. The girl was amazed, adjusting immediately in a repeat playing.

He also demonstrated his laptop, originally triggered to turn pages with a wired guitar pedal. Sung co-founded and perfected the two-pedal AirTurn, a wireless device that moves the music to the next page, with a pedal to go back for repeats.

AirTurn also sells a software that will allow marking the score with fingering or personal symbols in colored pencils, and saving that version as a file. In addition, they have perfected all kinds of synchronous contraptions for hand-held devices. Since most music can be downloaded free or, in the case of copyrighted recent music, relatively inexpensively, it eliminates the need for carrying music.

Sung left his post at Curtis, and AirTurn grossed over a million dollars in less than two years. For personal reasons Sung recently left AirTurn, and has continued to teach piano, this time through a website affording personal feedback called *ArtistWorks*. He also founded another weekly podcast called *My Musical Life*, featuring interviews with such notables like Gary Graffman, Aaron Rosand, David Kim, Jennifer Higdon, and launched another membership website, *A Musical Life Mastermind*, which aims to help musicians learn entreprenureal skills.

In another amazing demonstration of his ability to merge music and technology, he decided that he could teach anyone to play the piano. He arbitrarily chose Debussy's *Clair de lune*, though it does have a few tricky measures.

Sung filmed an introductory YouTube clip, and one for each measure of *Clair de lune*. In each clip there are three strips: the score, the score with fingerings and his notations, and his hands shot from above playing the notes. A player works on one measure, with explanation from Sung on the best methods, and goes on to the next one. He has had many emails from people who have never played the piano before, and only one that was problematic: a woman who didn't have a laptop had to run downstairs from her PC to her piano, then run upstairs again to get more tips before rushing down the stairs to play.

At least she didn't need a Stairmaster.

Pure Class

I had attended many events for the Crescendo Music Program, the outgrowth of the Academy of Community Music Suzuki school begun by now-retired Orchestra violinist Robert de Pasquale and his wife Ellen Fisher. In 2001, Bobby had asked André Watts to play for the 600 children, who played and sang to profoundly move the audience.

In 2008, Ellen mentioned that they had again asked André to guest at an upcoming fundraiser, and that he had hoped it could be held out of center city. André would play some solos, and Robert and his daughter Ellen would play as well. Because the First Presbyterian Church in Germantown, thanks to my son's help, had accommodated us for the Cascarino recording, I suggested they hold the affair in the church.

Everything was prepared, and the music director had his office cleaned and prepared for André to use as his dressing room. When Ellen came with Ellie and some family members, André graciously offered to change in the choristers' cloak room and give them the space.

After the first half of André's Schubert, Liszt and Chopin, ten or eleven young challenged kids moved to the edge of the stage, ready to sing their simple numbers, some with leg braces, breathing equipment, or other aids.

As in the 2001 concert, André had the music to "Twinkle, Twinkle, Little Star" in his hand backstage. I had said, "André, you just played those monster pieces without music, and you have to read "Twinkle, Twinkle?" He said, "Look at those children. There's no way I would take a chance of a memory lapse and disappointing them. They're probably the most important audience I'll ever play for." This man is a true giant, generous with his gifts here, and in many other places we don't even know about.

The night before, he had played a benefit, with the grand prize a Cunningham piano he had signed, and wouldn't take a fee for playing, accommodations, or any expenses.

Recently, Bobby de Pasquale mentioned his long history with André, having accompanied him many times, including his last August 1997 concert at Saratoga before retirement, when André played the Brahms Second Piano Concerto.

André Watts and the author. Credit: Enid Bloch.

I knew André was a connoisseur of fine wines and good cigars, and a softball-playing buddy had mentioned sneaking back some *el primo* cigars from his village in Cuba. Somehow, he got me four that I kept in a humidor, and a few months later visited JoAnn in Buffalo during the weekend that André was playing the Beethoven *Emperor* Concerto.

After the concert, we went to dinner, where I told him that all his friends in Philadelphia wanted to give him something he'd accept for his graciousness. "They're *El Presidentes!*" he cried. These are the moments my privilege has allowed which make all the hassles and difficulties irrelevant.

Astonishing Yuja

Even while she was a student at Curtis, I was stunned by the Chinese pianist Yuja Wang. A CD of Stravinsky, Brahms and Ravel, interspersed by Scarlatti sonatas, is an absolute revelation.

Graffman suggested that she audition for Charles Dutoit, who called on her to replace an ailing Martha Argerich in a Boston Symphony performance of the Tchaikovsky Concerto. After that performance, he teamed with her in London, Zurich, Los Angeles, Pittsburgh and Washington, arriving here in an astonishing Prokofiev Second Concerto with the Philadelphia Orchestra, a concert that traveled to Carnegie Hall.

"The Prokofiev Second is an enormous challenge, technically and musically, for any pianist, much more for such a young one," said Dutoit. "I felt she had the colors and the mastery to be presented in different capitals of the world, plus Carnegie Hall."

Later on, her knockout performance of the monstrously difficult Rachmaninoff Third Concerto at the Hollywood Bowl was overshadowed by the national reporting of her orange minidress.

She landed a five-CD contract with the prestigious DG label, beginning with two highly-acclaimed solo discs. She had just recorded a live DVD of the Rachmaninoff Second Concerto at a concert in Ferrara, Italy with the Mahler Chamber Orchestra under the beloved, late maestro Claudio Abbado, and was soon to play a recital in Philadelphia. I was supposed to call her after she was to arrive in Miami from Italy. Wang actually called me an hour early, saying she had gotten to her hotel earlier than anticipated, and responded to the pressure of making these one-time-only live recordings.

"It was a little nerve-wracking, because Maestro Abbado could hear everything," Wang said. "He encourages every one of these young players to listen to each other as if it's chamber music, not to just respond to what the conductor wants.

Although the diminutive Wang is known for her almost superhuman technical prowess, it's the last thing she wants to be noticed for.

"The only thing that puts me off is when people pay attention to powerful playing, instead of the music," she said. "I think if you care about physical ability, watch the Olympics! Music is what I'm doing, it's more important than the instrument itself."

Local composer Jennifer Higdon, who had just won the Pulitzer Prize for her Violin Concerto, had the good fortune to have Wang play her Piano Concerto in October with the National Symphony in Washington. The piece was originally written for Lang Lang, who sent an email turning down the premiere, perhaps because his schedule had become so frantic.

"My concerto is hard, a note-filled, 30-minute wild ride, one that would trip up a lot of pianists," said Higdon. "Yuja made it look and sound easy, an inspiring thing to hear and see. She can execute absolutely anything with her fantastic skill, and with playing that's both poetic and powerful. I believe she's one of the greatest pianists out there today."

Jennifer Higdon. Credit: Candace diCarlo.

Wang said that she had just received an email from Higdon, asking her if she'd be interested in recording the concerto if the opportunity arose. "After learning all those notes," said Wang, "I certainly hope I get to play it again!" I asked her what music she listened to, and her response was, "I don't listen to music much, but I like to see what Lady Gaga's doing!"

Graffman guided her at Curtis until 2008. "She came at age 15, and began swallowing up repertoire, a very fast learner," said Graffman. "She has a wonderful sound in hugely difficult pieces, with a convincing vision, like scenes in her mind, not just well-played notes on the paper.

"From the time she came, she wasn't dependent on anyone. Her parents couldn't get a visa, and they visited occasionally, and luckily her English was very good from the start. I suggested Spanish music, a genre she hadn't ever played, and she came in with the whole 12 pieces in Albeniz's *Iberia*. Once, after a lesson, she asked me if I had time to hear something she had also been working on—the Elliott Carter Sonata!

"Yuja moved a block and a half away from me in New York, and I see her often," Graffman said. "And I rearranged my teaching schedule to attend her concert in Philadelphia."

31. STILL RESOUNDING 70 YEARS LATER

On Easter Sunday, 1939, Marian Anderson stepped up to a battery of microphones in front of Washington, D.C.'s, Lincoln Memorial, sang *America*, and altered American history.

Wearing a mink coat and an orange-and-yellow scarf on that chilly afternoon, she changed the final phrase from "Of thee I sing" to "To thee WE sing."

This modest African-American contralto had taken the train from her South Philadelphia row house that day with her mother and sisters. Forbidden to stay at any Washington hotel due to segregation, they'd been promised lodging with former Pennsylvania Governor Gifford Pinchot.

The outdoor venue had been arranged by first lady Eleanor Roosevelt and Secretary of the Interior Harold Ickes, a Quaker, after the Daughters of the American Revolution had famously refused to allow an African-American to sing in their Constitution Hall. As a result, Roosevelt resigned from the organization, though political pressure kept her from attending the concert.

Anderson sang with her usual beauty, passion and tremendous dignity to a vast, racially integrated sea of 75,000 tearful faces on National Mall, as well as those listening on NBC radio. She performed a Donizetti aria that she had sung with the Philadelphia Orchestra, Schubert's *Ave Maria* and, after intermission, four spirituals.

The entire concert, attended by Supreme Court justices, legislators and more than 200 dignitaries, lasted less than an hour, and has inspired generations.

Though Anderson never intended to be an activist, her concert was even more of a groundbreaking event for social consciousness and racial relations than the then-unimaginable reality of a black president and first lady in the White House.

The Abraham Lincoln Bicentennial Commission, celebrating the 200th anniversary of Lincoln's birth, arranged a program on the 70th anniversary of Anderson's milestone concert. It featured the Chicago Children's Choir, the U.S. Marine Band and the *a cappella* group Sweet Honey in the Rock and, of course, Washington-born mezzo-soprano Denyce Graves. (Curiously, it wasn't picked up by any radio or television network, even C-SPAN). She would sing the exact first half of Anderson's concert, followed by "America the Beautiful," since 500 people would be naturalized at the event.

Graves was well aware of the symbolism of the upcoming event and her part in it.

Denyce Graves:

It's an awesome responsibility, although the commission's intention on honoring her legacy instead of focusing on a re-enactment takes a little of the heat from me!

One of the greatest thrills in my career was winning the 1991 Marian Anderson Award in Connecticut. I had the opportunity to meet her and chat with her, and we attended a concert together at the Charles Ives Center. She never wanted to speak about the 1939 concert, having that quiet, modest elegance without any flamboyance, and not possessing the attitude we associate with performers today.

It took great strain for her to trailblaze, but sometimes the gods draft the most unlikely. Someone had to be the first one, and I loved that it was Marian Anderson. (By phone, April 3, 2009)

Philadelphia has always been proud of Anderson's legacy, and the editors gave me room to celebrate it.

"Anderson was born in 1897 at 1833 Webster St. (now Marian Anderson Place), a modest home near 18th and Catharine streets. Her mother scrubbed floors at Wanamaker's department store, and her father sold ice and coal at the Reading Terminal.

"She sang at Union Baptist Church and recalled being humiliated at being turned down by a local music school with the words, "We don't take colored."

"The church supported her with handmade dresses and music lessons with local vocal coach Giuseppe Boghetti, who accepted her as his student after hearing her sing "Deep River."

"Anderson attended William Penn High School, though, like other black students, she was not allowed to take academic subjects, leaving before graduation to perform throughout the United States and Europe. She also sang locally and soloed with the Clef Club at the Academy of Music. She eventually returned to South Philadelphia High School for Girls, graduating in 1921 at age 24.

"Signed by impresario Sol Hurok in 1934, she eventually would be booked in important venues throughout the world, always finishing her recitals of Brahms or Schubert or Schumann with her trademark spirituals to emphasize their validity.

"In 1955, when she was well past her vocal prime, the Metropolitan Opera finally allowed her to sing her one stage role, the fortune teller Ulrica in Verdi's *A Masked Ball*.

"Her final tour, starting in 1964 at Constitution Hall and ending at Carnegie Hall in 1965, was a triumph.

"After a 20-year courtship, Anderson married Orpheus "King" Fisher in 1943 and moved to Connecticut the next year. He died in 1986; they had no children. In 1992, she moved to Oregon to live with her nephew, conductor James DePreist, and died a year later."

In 2005, a ceremony celebrating a Marian Anderson 37-cent postage stamp was held in Constitution Hall, where the DAR offered an apology and reconciliation. The singer at that occasion was Denyce Graves.

In recent years, the Marian Anderson Award has been given to such famous names as Oprah Winfrey, Harry Belafonte, Sidney Poitier, Richard Gere, Quincy Jones, Maya Angelou, Wynton Marsalis and Norman Lear. This high-ticket celebration has no connection to the Marian Anderson Historical Society, housed in a modest rowhome on South Martin Street where Anderson lived from 1924 to 1944.

The Society's caretaker Blanche Burton-Lyles has a very personal link to Anderson, since her mother was Anderson's piano accompanist at Union Baptist Church. Later, the famed contralto would have Burton-Lyles play while Anderson received guests at her home after concerts.

Anderson eventually recommended Burton-Lyles to Curtis Institute, where she studied with Isabel Vengerova and became the first African-American pianist to graduate and the first to play with the New York Philharmonic at Carnegie Hall. (In evenings, Burton-Lyles played Chopin and American popular songs at the Union League.)

Memorabilia of all kinds fill the Marian Anderson Residence/Museum, receiving more European than American guests. There's an interactive video, Anderson's old birth certificate and scrapbooks with remarkable photos, including ones of Anderson singing with Leopold Stokowski and Leonard Bernstein, performing for Finnish composer Jan Sibelius and recording with Eugene Ormandy.

Blanche Burton-Lyles:

Harry Belafonte and Gregory Peck came here when in town for the other award, and Quincy Jones insisted on receiving his award at Union Baptist. Even when Marian became famous, she came back to church and sat in the balcony, always appreciating that they had paid for her lessons.

Her final concert tour (in 1964-65) was actually sponsored by churches and sororities, especially the AKA [Alpha Kappa Alpha] that she belonged to.

Several years ago, when I purchased her birthplace on Webster Street, I discovered at the settlement that the people who had lived in that house for 40 years had no idea that Marian Anderson had been born there. (Marian Anderson Residence/Museum, April 19, 2009)

There have been other Marian Anderson Awards. Anderson started her own competition in 1941 that honored young singers for many years. In 1990, she began another competition whose first winner was the great operatic soprano Sylvia McNair, followed by Graves in 1991 and bass Eric Owens. Since 2002, that award has been given biannually by the Fairfield County (Connecticut) Community Foundation jointly with the Kennedy Center in Washington, D.C.

Perhaps no one knows more about the impact of Anderson's 1939 concert than Raymond Arsenault, author of the book *The Sound of Freedom: Marian Anderson, the Lincoln Memorial, and the Concert That Awakened America* (Bloomsbury Press). Since Arsenault was scheduled to discuss the book and Anderson's legacy at Philadelphia's Constitution Center, we met and visited the Residence/Museum together.

Raymond Arsenault:

In 1939, Lincoln wasn't yet considered the great emancipator, and the memorial wasn't sacred ground until then. Of course, Dr. King's "I Have A Dream" speech was given there in 1963, and certainly that's why President Obama insisted on that location for his pre-inaugural concert. No one thought it unusual today that Aretha Franklin sang "My Country, 'Tis Of Thee."

Anderson had faced all kinds of racism in the South. And singing at the Salzburg Festival in 1935, where Arturo Toscanini called hers "a voice such as one only hears once in a hundred years," the Nazis wouldn't even allow her name on the program. She wouldn't sing where blacks were segregated in balconies or back seats, but would allow what she called 'vertical integration,' where whites and blacks could sit on either side of the aisle.

Anderson almost canceled the Lincoln Memorial concert, never imagining she would become a civil rights icon. The concert made it evident that racial problems were of national consequence—not just a Southern problem but a stain on the national honor at a time when totalitarianism was sweeping through Europe.

Anderson was the first to enter into what was a white province—not jazz, blues, minstrelsy, vaudeville, or juke joints. Without her, we might not have heard of Leontyne Price, Jessye Norman or Denyce Graves. She confounded the stereotypes, beating them at their own game with poise, reserve and stature. (Coffee shop, April 21, 2009)

Anderson left an example of musical royalty, demonstrating the power of grace, determination and colorblindness. She once wrote:

"When I sing and see a mass of faces turned up to me, it never occurs to me that most of them are white. They are the faces of human beings. I try to look through their faces into their souls, and it is to their souls that I sing."

New Music from Everywhere

At Juilliard in the 1980s, JoAnn Falletta had met Behzad Ranjbaran, born in Tehran, Iran, and a London Symphony CD of his music arrived entitled *Persian Trilogy*. I was swept away by its power and brilliance, like *Sheherazade* on steroids: its orchestral palette was fascinating, combining a tonal, accessible sonic imagination with grand dramatic gestures illustrating 11th-century epic poetry.

Ranjbaran had also written *Songs of Eternity* for Renée Fleming, and Yo-Yo Ma had played his commissioned *Elegy*. He had been the composer-in-residence at the Orchestra's summer residency, where he premiered a piece entitled *Saratoga* and heard Joshua Bell play his Violin Concerto. I made sure to meet him at Saratoga, and he sent me a copy of Bell's performance.

As a young music student in Iran, Ranjbaran learned the Western classics though his country's folk music was banned. He practiced Prokofiev, Mendelssohn, Stravinsky and Tchaikovsky and, on the weekends, taught Persian music to children in remote villages like the one where his father had lived.

Behzad Ranjbaran and the author.

He was thrown into prison for reading banned, though legally published, poetry, and knew fellow prisoners whose political heroism sometimes resulted in torture and even execution.

In the upcoming season, Falletta was to make her first appearance leading the Curtis Symphony Orchestra. For her program, she chose *Sheherazade* as well as Ranjbaran's Violin Concerto, and asked for the gifted Elissa Lee Koljonen, wife of Curtis president Roberto Diaz, to solo. Though Diaz was not initially thrilled about the impression it might give, Falletta had worked with Koljonen as soloist with the Virginia Symphony and sincerely believed she was the perfect soloist for the work.

Koljonen learned the piece, requiring enormous interpretive and virtuoso skills, and took the train to New York to play it for Ranjbaran without accompaniment. Even brilliant musicians like Koljonen have apprehension about meeting a composer and playing a hugely challenging work for him, but Ranjbaran thought her playing was ideal.

"The Concerto lays in the hand very comfortably," said Koljonen, "without all kinds of funky fingerings, and it captured the ear of my two-year-old Sofia, who thinks it's sparkly, and my son Nico (almost three) who both listen to my practicing.

"It's very lyrical, virtuosic and everything a concerto should be. If I was asked to choose the concerto I would most love to play, it would be this one."

While studying violin and composition at Indiana University, Ranjbaran heard the 12-year-old Joshua Bell play the challenging *Zigeunerweisen*, inspiring him to compose the Violin Concerto.

Behjad Ranjbaran:

In this concerto, I wanted to contrast the modern violin to the ancient upright Iranian instrument, the kamancheh. The instrument was mostly abandoned when the modern violin came in the 19th century, but it's now being played again. The lyrical and soft passages are reminiscent of this old upright fiddle, with the strong, virtuosic passages reflective of the modern violin.

When I was young, my father said that genies and fairies came out after midnight. I remember looking toward the stars many nights to anticipate their arrival. Those impressions, that have become constant companions, are the inspiration for the concerto's second movement.

I was touched by those who selflessly gave of their lives for a better society, though I haven't yet seen the benefits of their sacrifices. In Iran, we've been engaged with modernization, a search for peace and a democracy with civility for almost 100 years. I'm hopeful that the current, Internet-driven nonviolence movement among the country's youth will foster change.

People all over the world have common concerns, the desire for their rituals and for freedom. I believe that the inner mission of music is a spiritual function in society, a common level of communication between human be-

ings. Culture is like a river—we all contribute to the flow of its inner mission, and we all become enriched. (By phone, October 20, 2009)

At one of the *Sheherazade* rehearsals, Falletta led the slow movement, "The Young Prince and the Young Princess." At one point, there's a long clarinet solo arching up and soaring down, and repeated. The young Curtis soloist played it exactly, with every note in place. Falletta said, "Remember, this is the prince singing a love song to the princess. It's all right to play with plenty of *rubato*, and give it lots of romantic feeling." The young man played it smoothly, like a long sigh, and when Falletta simply continued, he looked at his stand partner with a look that said, "Did I do that??"

All Music Was Once New

That 2009-2010 Orchestra season displayed 23 world premieres, a sign that audiences are more accepting of new works, the lifeblood of the arts pumping vibrancy into these reflections of our society.

Though it's impossible to quantify the effect of new music on attendance, virtually all performing groups noticed larger audiences when presenting premieres. These debuts typically drew younger audiences who are more open to new sounds, although savvy programmers intersperse new music with more familiar pieces to hold onto their core supporters.

New works aren't always embraced with open ears. Riccardo Muti insisted that 100 pieces have to be played to find one masterpiece, and even great works met scathing reactions at their premieres—with Rossini's *The Barber of Seville*, Stravinsky's riotous *The Rite of Spring* and Puccini's *Madama Butterfly* the most notorious fiascoes.

Even highly anticipated compositions sometimes disappoint. There have been some famous works written to open major venues, like Samuel Barber's *Antony and Cleopatra* inaugurating the Metropolitan Opera House at Lincoln Center, Leonard Bernstein's MASS that launched the Kennedy Center, and Aaron Jay Kernis' *Color Wheel* for our own Kimmel Center. None were well-received, and the Philadelphia Orchestra's six Constitutional Commissions in 1987 (one deemed unplayable by three conductors) were virtually all disliked by audiences.

The Network for New Music commissions new music through grants initiated by the performing ensemble, or by grants applied for by the composer to be performed by a specified ensemble. Some new music is a gift from the composer or is supported by a donation by a benefactor.

"We're like a research and development corporation for future repertoire," said Linda Reichert, Network's artistic director. "And one of our biggest thrills comes when a work we premiered has legs and is performed elsewhere. More groups are finding that new music is exciting and is a selling point. It's no longer scary for audience members, with a growing number of young people at concerts.

"For chamber music, our commissioning cost range is about $2,500 to $12,500, an amount we hope to increase. Fortunately, foundations like new music. Grants pay the composer, usually not our rehearsal or presentation costs, and during this economic downturn we're likely to receive about 70 percent of what we would have expected in the past. (It's now even less).

"Our advisory board is very active, and suggests works years ahead. We believe paying composers to write the masterpieces of the future is crucial, and that's what music is about. "Many people don't realize that, for a modest amount, they can easily commission a piece for an ensemble or composer for whom they feel an affinity," said composer Bernard Rands.

Network had tried many innovative approaches to reach new audiences. A collaboration with artists and galleries for some concerts was a success, and a poetry project generated interest with a whole new demographic. Piano legend Leon Fleisher conducted Network's musicians in works by Hindemith and Stravinsky.

Jan Krzywicki. Credit: Boyer College of Music/Temple University.

Jan Krzywicki, Network's conductor, is also a noted composer, and his piece for guitar, soprano and string trio was finally played in a concert by the Philadelphia Chamber Music Society. "It has taken three years from the time the work was composed at the request of the late guitarist Peter Segal, who loved a Purcell aria I eventually wove into the piece." He also wrote a brilliant work called *Concerto bucolico* at an Italian retreat, performed by the Philadelphia Classical Symphony under Karl Middleman with two first-chair Philadelphia Orchestra players, bassoonist Daniel Matsukawa and clarinetist Ricardo Morales, as supreme soloists.

In November 2014, Network opened its 30th season with a program based on the Dada-esque parlor game *Exquisite Corpse*. Augusta Read Thomas wrote the opening measures of a piece for flute, cello and piano, and 30 local composers (who would only receive the last measure written) would, in turn, add their six to eight measures. It was preceded by tiny videos by each composer, and the ultimate composition actually hung together remarkably well; it was a typically imaginative concept, and a reflection of the willingness of so many local composers to interact with the organization.

Network and many other organizations are still producing works and performing works for their own musicians, unlike the flourishing Philadelphia Chamber Music Society, a presenter of touring artists as well as local groups. Its executive director (and composer) Philip Maneval sees premieres as an encouragement and a reward to the large number of gifted composers from our area.

"Expanding the literature with new music is a huge part of our mission, and these pieces—seven local premieres and 31 works by living composers this season—generate interest, exposure, and prestige for us, said Maneval. "We've presented 35 new works since our founding, each helping to enlarge our audience.

"Some patrons have felt a special connection to an ensemble, a musician or a composer, and their sponsorship led to an original work. The idea of a tax-deductible sponsorship is a wonderful opportunity, sometimes given for an occasion, anniversary or birthday, and provides lasting recognition to a donor."

For many composers, commissions put food on the table. Others, especially those in academia, are willing to offer works for a performance by an excellent ensemble—the payback is having the music performed and often includes a recording. Many of the acclaimed Orchestra 2001's premieres, by conductor James Freeman's Swarthmore faculty colleagues and those at Penn, fall into this category, with CDs being produced as a result. And some compositions are written for an occasion. In one program Orchestra 2001 performed six new works in a celebration of Freeman's 70th birthday, adding to the 80 world premieres and 205 works performed by 125 American composers.

"From our founding 21 years ago, Orchestra 2001 has stayed on mission with a mix of local works, world premieres and local premieres," said Freeman. "It's tremendously exciting to sit down with a great composer like George Crumb, and find the real inspiration behind his music. Local premieres are very important, too, because, as any composer will tell you, the second performance is the hardest to obtain.

"We've learned some major lessons through the years. Local soloists draw better than big names and, with some exceptions, composers don't attend unless their music is being played. If you present a varied program, even with new works, attendees always find something to enjoy."

Political chaos in Moscow had increased the drama of an Orchestra 2001 tour concert in 1993, in which a Russian audience was introduced to the unique music of George Crumb. Instead of performing their program, the musicians hunkered down for two days during an insurrection and the storming of the Russian White House until calm was mostly restored and the concert was able to go on.

After 25 years of founding and leading Orchestra 2001, Freeman announced his retirement in 2014, and soon announced his intention to form a new chamber orchestra called First Editions, in which premieres will be inspired by early works by Mozart.

Latin Mass

I was asked by the Philadelphia Music Project to do a piece on Roberto Sierra's *Missa Latina*, to be performed by the Mendelssohn Club and Temple University choirs and the Chamber Orchestra of Philadelphia, all led by Alan Harler.

The Latin Mass began its evolution during the seventh century, with Guillaume de Machaut's *Messe de Notre Dame*—from around 1360—the first known example in its eventually-accepted form.

Since that time, thousands of Masses have been composed utilizing the Kyrie-Gloria-Credo-Sanctus-Agnus Dei core elements, usually to Latin texts. Perhaps the grandest of them all, Bach's B Minor Mass, was unacceptable to his Lutheran church (because of its Latin text) and not heard during his lifetime. The form evolved through Haydn, Mozart and Beethoven, though many were conceived for concert rather than liturgical purposes. In recent times, Leonard Bernstein's eclectic MASS and Osvaldo Golijov's polysourced *La Pasion Segun San Marcos* has expanded the use of popular forms, different languages and many ethnic flavors.

There was a double meaning to Roberto Sierra's *Missa Latina*—a mass to Latin texts, and one with the infusion of his Latino heritage and contemporary rhythms. A Naxos recording has allowed us to perceive his Mass as a major, highly inspired work. Whenever its rhythms emerged, their effect seemed elegantly organic and ideal to summon the power of the texts—a prayer for peace. The artists from the premiere and the recording, soprano Heidi Grant Murphy and baritone Nathaniel Webster, were his soloists.

Sierra's rhythms on claves, bongos, congas and timbales emerge organically with a sense of inevitability, never jarring and always with stunning dramatic effect; the work has enormous sweep and a fervent potency that is cumulative and intensely moving.

The Mass, subtitled *Pro Pace*, was commissioned in 2003 to celebrate two anniversaries: the 75th of the National Symphony of Washington, D. C., and the 40th of the Washington Choral Arts Society.

The prolific Sierra, the Philadelphia Orchestra's Composer in Residence for a year in the 1990s, studied in Europe with iconic composer György Ligeti and now teaches at Cornell University. He had always wanted to write a large choral piece, though not necessarily a Mass, with the commission becoming the perfect opportunity. Though a practicing Roman

Catholic, his comments that the Credo "does not limit us to membership in (one) church" seems to be reflected in that extended section's ambivalent harmony.

"I believe in one church for myself, and I'm respectful of that," said Sierra. "The Catholic Church was the only one around for a millennium and a half, the one frame of mind. Others worship with the same sincerity and goodness of heart and, though one sets music to those ancient texts, it came from my heart and soul for anyone who feels a confirmation of faith."

In his compositional palette, Sierra often uses a *Tresillo* (3/3/2) rhythm, as well as an Octatonic scale, constructed of alternating whole and half steps.

"You'll find the *Tresillo* a lot in my other pieces," explained Sierra, "and it should be at the center of expression. The body relates to this rhythm in a physical way, and the enormous variety or meters gives it a kind of dance aspect."

Alan Harler was about to leave his Temple post after 30 years, though continuing his leadership of the Mendelssohn Club for a few more. Since he toured Puerto Rico many times with the Temple and the Mendelssohn Club choirs, his friendship with Sierra went back almost three decades.

"Our visits to the Festival Casals in Puerto Rico sensitized me to the realization that there's more to Latino rhythms than just fun," said Harler. "Like all great works, the deeper one gets into the score, the more that is found. It sometimes approaches a popular idiom with translucent harmonies and Latin dance rhythms, whose forms and structure are quite complex and sophisticated."

Legacies, Finale and Champagne

Ever since the Academy of Music opened in 1857 with Verdi's *Il Trovatore*, Philadelphia has been a mecca for opera lovers. Within just a few blocks of the Academy, the home of the Opera Company of Philadelphia and the oldest opera house still in use, are two of the world's great conservatories, the Academy of Vocal Arts and Curtis Institute. The training of future stars to leap into the operatic constellation is demonstrated in their staged operatic presentations.

Less than two miles north on Broad Street, the Temple University Opera Theater had been consistently presenting two superb shows each season, with little fanfare and not much attention.

In recent years, their *Midsummer Night's Dream, Candide, Falstaff*, and brilliant double bill of *L'Enfant et les Sortileges* and *Le Rossignol* still register strongly in the memory. Many opera mavens who regularly travel to the Met in New York and Kennedy Center in Washington, D.C., never head five subway stops up Broad Street for Temple's performances.

That's their loss.

Temple's Voice and Opera Department has the huge advantage of the university's diversity and size. It can employ its choral department and, should dance or spoken parts be required, students from the theater and dance departments are enlisted. Opera students gain experience building sets and costumes. Even the art school gets in on the action—last fall, paintings by Tyler students were projected in Lee Hoiby's *A Month in the Country*.

Their spring production was Leos Janacek's jewel, *The Cunning Little Vixen*, keeping the costume and mask people busy for months.

John Douglas, in his 20th year as music director and conductor, had led companies at Chautauqua, Lake George Opera and Opera Delaware, among others.

"Repertory choices are made depending on the voices we have," explained Douglas. "Double-casting provides more opportunities for singers who need to be groomed and who are ready for major role exposure, although there are open auditions for the major roles.

"We haven't done *Vixen* in 20 years, and it fits our singers well. We treat our productions in the same conceptual way that are done in a professional company, with no less time, interest or detail. The Temple University Symphony Orchestra benefits from the experience of playing operas in the pit. This is no small feat for students, since musicians are eight feet below the stage, in the dark, often unable to hear the singers and playing music that rarely stays in tempo."

The *Vixen* was brilliantly done, and I enjoyed it more than the Opera Company production to soon follow; I've never attended a Temple opera in which I wasn't highly impressed.

So it came as an enormous shock to hear of Douglas' untimely death.

A few months later, a celebration in his honor was given at Temple's newly-refurbished Baptist Temple facility, with many who were touched by his enormous commitment. Denyce Graves and Eric Owens, among others, sang in his honor, and the rest of us sang his praises.

Hovering Legacy

Picture the great Russian pianist and composer Serge Prokofiev visiting an artist's studio in an offbeat neighborhood to hear his piano music played. In an even more unlikely scenario, imagine that musical legend deejaying other composers' works between sets.

This exact formula was followed by Prokofiev's grandson, Gabriel Prokofiev, insistent that his generation respond to classical music in more informal venues.

Some of his piano works were played in a North Philadelphia warehouse by pianist GeNIA, whose great-grandmother's brother was legendary pianist Vladimir Horowitz, and whose first teacher in Kiev was Horowitz's sister Regina. In between, Prokofiev acted as disc jockey for his mixes and percussionist Joby Burgess played a concerto banging on an array of junk.

His father, Oleg, a painter and sculptor, defected from Russia in 1972; he (and his older brother Sviatoslav) were sufficiently menaced by a draconian piano teacher that they both gave up studying. Serge Prokofiev famously said that "neither of my sons has an ounce of musicality," evidently a relief to him.

Gabriel Prokofiev wasn't pushed into music, and his grandfather's music wasn't a constant presence; he was keenly aware of his legacy, with listeners expecting, as he put it, "a genius or wizard on the keyboard."

"Now we run a London club, the Horse and Groom, upstairs from a pub. People listen with a pint in their hands and are usually impressively quiet when they hear good performers. It feels both informal and exciting, like the real world, with continuous sounds. Musicians like the idea of classical music rediscovering itself in a social setting, the way music used to be performed."

Lots of interesting ideas poured from this gracious gentleman, and we had an enjoyable day in Philly, visiting the Perelman wing of the Art Museum to see the famed, saved *The Gross Clinic* by Thomas Eakins. In July 2014, his Violin Concerto received a performance, commissioned by the BBC, during the annual Proms celebration at London's Albert Hall.

Margaret Garwood. Credit: Denise Coffey Stuart.

***Scarlet*,** **Completed**

After many years of wrestling with her music, Margaret Garwood finally completed her opera *The Scarlet Letter*, and anticipated its first performances by the Academy of Vocal Arts, Richard Raub again conducting.

Hawthorne's work about Puritan morality resonated with her, expressing the dramatic force involved in the repression of sensualism, which always leads to perversion. Curiously, Garwood can trace her ancestry back to Mayflower days and to Miles Standish—she finds this amusing yet without significance.

Garwood's composing method is slow, and she agonizes over each note.

"I'm afraid of commissions, because composers always have to stop before it's finished. The trouble with music today is too many premature births, works not given their proper time. Composing is a slow process and can't be rushed."

Garwood's works are masterful, and the years she put into each one gives every line, and every phase, a meaning not possible with a commission deadline. She left us in May 2015, knowing after the ravishingly-scored *Scarlet* that she would never begin another opera.

Champagne Earned

Michel Legrand brought his trio to the Keswick Theater in Glenside, and afterwards, along with WRTI's Jill Pasternak and her daughter Amy, we greeted Legrand, who said he was writing, composing and directing his fourth French film. Of course, he told a few Emil stories from their many scores done together.

After a New Jersey concert, I had the opportunity to speak with local sax legend Larry McKenna about Legrand. "Years ago, he played the Latin Casino," said McKenna," and the contractor asked if I wanted to play the gig, with a solo part in a piece called "Gossiping." I asked the musician who had played it on Michel's last visit if he had the music, and found that it was a monstrously hard solo. I practiced and woodshedded for days and, at the rehearsal, Legrand played it at the normal fast tempo, not at a practice tempo, and I did my best. Afterwards, Michel said, 'You are the greatest sightreader in the world! Let's have some champagne afterwards!' Of course, I didn't tell him that I wasn't sightreading."

After months of investigation, *Daily News* reporters Barbara Laker and Wendy Ruderman did a ten-month expose series about rogue cops called "Tainted Justice." Their tireless work won them a Pulitzer Prize, and they followed up with a book, *Busted*; in a huge disappointment four years later, prosecutors decided not to pursue the case. On a more positive note, the

Daily *News'* staffers, sportswriters and front-page scribes constantly win national awards, the latter for their extraordinary, often-priceless headlines.

37. THE END... SORT OF

One day in late March 2011 I received a call from features editor Debi Licklider. It seems that the new editor Larry Platt, who had come from *Philadelphia Magazine*, had decided that the coverage of music was no longer of value to *Daily News* readers. That meant yours truly, jazz writer Shawn Brady, club writer Sara Sherr and hip-hop writer James Johnson were unnecessary. This came as a blow, mostly because of the concept that no one cared, because it certainly wasn't to save a lot of money.

For years, my editor Laurie Conrad had been amazingly open-minded and trusting with my suggestions for stories and, of course, had worked tirelessly to deliver a competitive features section. When suddenly limited with a tiny freelance budget and less pages, her hands were tied, and it must have been frustrating to her as well.

Luckily, they were willing to fill out the month, meaning that I was able to do my final Pick of the Week for something with a lot of personal meaning: Luis Biava's conducting of the Temple University Orchestra and Chorus in the overwhelming Requiem of Giuseppe Verdi. Biava had asked Eric Owens, who had once played oboe for him in the Temple Orchestra, to sing, and Owens helped acquire the other three soloists.

It was not surprising, though highly disappointing. I needed something to lift my spirits, and something arrived.

Dolores had been contacted by one of Romeo's European relatives, asking if she knew about a huge celebration being held in Saumur, France, about its influence on William Penn during his stay there. Evidently Penn had flunked out of Oxford, and was a military recruit, but his father Admiral Penn (for whom Pennsylvania is named) sent him to Saumur for life seasoning, without realizing it had become a center of pacifist thinking. Of course, what his son learned changed his life and, considering what things would be like if he hadn't come here and established religious freedom, it changed America too.

She planned a segment at the William Penn conference and, after two weeks of bumming around Cinqueterre and southern France, I met her in Saumur. We were whisked to an enormous estate, complete with stables, orchards, gardens and an immense castle, where we represented Philadelphia for a few days and attended a William Penn naming ceremony in a park.

Upon returning, it was time for the now-colossal Opening Tap for Philly Beer Week, when Mayor Nutter took the Hammer that has travelled the streets all day to open the first keg.

Don Russell, who had started the whole concept of Philly Beer week, had heard about the flash-mob concerts the Opera Company had given at the Reading Terminal and at Macy's, and wanted one for Beer Week. Luckily Alan Harler, leader of the Mendelssohn Club and just retiring from Temple choirs, thought it was a great idea. I thought the "Drinking Song" from *The Student Prince* would be ideal, and Alan found that about forty of his chorus were willing to sing it, scattered throughout the Visitors' Center at a specific time to a recorded intro—and get a comp ticket to the festivities. Thanks to viral meningitis picked up on my return flight, I missed it, but Don said it was a big success.

After making Philly the national beer capital and creating the wildly successful (and profitable) Beer Week, the group's board decided they didn't want to pay Don, proving once again the uselessness of boards.

Head to the Coast

After getting used to being finally unemployed, after sometimes having had five or six simultaneous jobs, there was only one essential thing to do to wrap this whole experience: go and visit Emil in a world of wizards, new and old friends.

Luckily, Jeannie Pool, working in the Paramount Music Department, had sold the money people on doing the score to the first movie to win the Academy Award, the 1929 silent *Wings*. Director William Wellman, a WWI pilot, asked actors and fliers to do some astounding daredevil stunts that would never be sanctioned today, and there are some breathtaking moments—and a cameo by the young Gary Cooper.

Only the piano score had been found, and she oversaw its orchestration by Dominic Hausse. There were some pop songs of the time woven into the score, five of them still in copyright but, since Paramount was not about to pay any royalties, Hausse had to substitute similar melodies.

In the 1920s, movies were being cranked out in much greater numbers than we can imagine today. After a film wound down through the neighborhood houses it was basically useless, and most were melted down because of the value of the silver nitrate in the emulsion. We're fortunate that film societies have tracked down any of these films, and many masterpieces made after the arrival of sound in 1929 have turned to dust in cans housing film vaults.

Another major consequence of sound was, of course, the flood of hundreds of out-of-work musicians in all the major cities.

Peter Boyer had already conducted one session with midi (electronic) parts and nine solo players, including flutist Louise Di Tullio. The day I visited the studio, Jeannie was recording the strings (only violins and violas—supposedly electronic celli and basses sound close enough to acoustic instruments that money can be saved). That night, brass would come in and the strings would finish the next day.

Boyer had also done orchestrations for some films written by the brilliant film composer Michael Giacchino, who I was to meet with Emil the next day. Though there were years of work still to be done to catalogue the Paramount archive, Jeannie was laid off as soon as *Wings* was released on DVD—though she wrote the voluminous and intricately detailed liner notes for the sound recording CD. After orchestrating and presenting the opera *Tawawa House* by Zenobia Powell Perry, she produced a Naxos CD of Perry's keyboard music by pianists Josephine Gandiolfi, Deanne Tucker and LaDoris Hazzard Cordell, and is finishing a book about famous 1920s-30s female bandleader Babe Egan and her Hollywood Redheads.

Just as I was wrapping up this book, Jeannie informed me that David Raksin's book *The Bad and the Beautiful: My Life in a Golden Age of Film Music* was finally available, but only until now in a Kindle edition. Raksin knew everyone in three generations of music, and he was a true raconteur, full of delicious Hollywood stories through 70 years of Hollywood history. Let's hope it's issued in every possible format, guaranteed to be a classic.

The next morning, at Warners, Emil and I wandered around the lot to the large scoring stage, where there was to be a double session. "Warners was going to knock this building down," said Emil, "and Clint Eastwood insisted they not only keep it, but redo it with state-of-the-art equipment. It's the only stage on the huge lot. If they need another they have to go to Sony, Universal, or some other stage, a consideration that would never have been dreamed of ten years ago.

"Clint is the only director who always comes to the scoring sessions. He always comes in and calls me "Dayg," (short for Dago)." The sign out front proudly says "Eastwood Scoring Stage," housing a space that can fit a nearly-symphonic orchestra.

The youthful-looking Giacchino now has the clout to have a real orchestra instead of working like many composers on synthesizers, because in superhero, apocalyptic, zombie and monster films nobody really cares as long as there are sound effects. In July 2014, Giacchino came to Philadelphia and introduced his score before a Mann showing of *Star Trek-Into Darkness*—a South Jersey musician who showed a photo with a Phillies hat and said beforehand he'd never dreamed he'd hear his music played by the Philadelphia Orchestra. Thomas Newman conducted for the packed house.

In a long *New Yorker* interview by Alex Ross about Giacchino's work in the television series *Lost*, Giacchino had lauded Emil's improvisational work and insisted that Ross visit him at his home. This typically gracious gesture meant a long investigation of Emil's percussion collection and insights into the art of playing many instruments, and knowing when to use each one effectively.

Because it was a Christmas movie, everyone had been asked to wear red, and many came in with moose antlers, holiday shirts and other paraphernalia. Orchestrator Tim Simonic conducted, with Giacchino listening in the recording booth. Because everyone was sightreading, with headphones clicking each beat, only Simonic's big gestures could be seen, and big lights showed the number of the measure and the beat corresponding to the music—measure 65/2, 3, 4. With a set of headphones, you could hear the cues—two measures, eight clicks, and boom. The playing by these superb musicians was astonishingly tight, and sometimes they did a slight retake

Emil Richards, still playing at his peak. Credit: Rob Shanahan.

only to please the recording engineers. "Gail (Levant), on that harp part, measure 57 to 64, could you play your left hand an octave higher?"

"If we've been playing all day and I make a mistake," said Emil, "I say I messed up. Everyone moans, but it's what you have to do because they'll find it in the final mix. Each one of us has done it, sometimes the horns have sore lips, but we're pros and it must be right, no matter what."

The following year, Emil would soon work with Giacchino on big-budget movies *Tomorrowland* and *Jurassic World*.

Considering the time pressures on such work, the musicians are amazingly laid-back, playing with an easy grace. In fact, I don't think any musicians are as low-key as percussionists—all the ones I've met out there and in Philadelphia are calm and serene in manner, surprising considering that their playing is completely revealed.

Emil introduced me to his friend Michael Lyle, who gave me a tour through the Universal Studio lot. There was a huge fire on the lot about five years ago and, after the insurance money arrived, Steven Spielberg and some other biggies decided to build some sets on that area. It was incredible to drive through city streets, little towns, Western prairies, a modern glass-front office building and many other sets that are now constantly used. The construction, detail and even window lettering were immaculate, built by an army of artisans whose skills at artifice continue to be ever-more specific.

Michael showed me the set where the Conan O'Brien show was filmed after Jay Leno moved temporarily from the Tonight show to ten o'clock. The building was renovated for a cost of $25 million, but the show only ran seven months until Leno returned to *Tonight*. A NBC news show was planned to go into the space until it was decided that it would remain at NBC Burbank. Lyle took me to the large canvas covering the opening and peeled it back to show me what remained: four concrete walls and a dirt floor.

That night, Emil played a concert with pianist David Garfield, a guitarist playing with them the first time called Ernest Tibbs, and drummer Joe Porcaro, who Emil had known since he was eight years old in Hartford, Connecticut. For the first tune, he said, "We're going to play "Misty," but let's do it as a waltz!" He pulled the ¾ time bit again on them with "Take the A Train" in a later set, the kind of thing normal to players on this exalted level.

Joe's three sons began as the highly successful pop group Toto, and I had the chance to meet one, composer Steve Porcaro. In his backyard studio loaded with keyboards and complex electronics, Steve gave me a great story for the paper about how television scores are written under great pressure, in that case music to a hospital show called *Gideon's Crossing*.

The next day, Lyle took me to the Foley stage at Universal. Virtually every sound in a film (except explosions) is added on a Foley stage because it's too impractical to record sounds on location. The stage is equipped with flooring of wood, carpet, concrete, sand, linoleum and more; huge shelves of shoes; a pit for smashing glass; another water pool; and a vast array of noisemaking objects and devices. The final Foley track shares the soundtrack with dialogue and music, to be mixed later.

Lyle showed me a two-minute excerpt from the beginning of a *House* episode, when three men chase another through alleys, up ladders, over roofs and through buildings, with pipes falling, steps clanking, windows breaking, and four sets of loud footsteps. It took an immense amount of work just to duplicate all the exact sounds necessary for what seems like a short piece of film, but it's what they do every day. I don't think I'll ever watch a film again without being aware of the sounds these Foley masters have created.

A Summer Gig and Connecting Friends

Since things were lean at the paper, I visited the Chautauqua Foundation one July evening day when JoAnn Falletta was guest-conducting their orchestra. Thanks to her sponsorship, they have invited me for three years as guest reviewer for their crack orchestra—with opera and ballet evenings in between. Though he wasn't conducting the weeks I was there, Rossen Milanov, who had been an associate conductor for many years with the Philadelphia Orchestra, and stepped down as music director of New Jersey's Symphony in C, was named Chautauqua's music director in October 2014.

We had become friends with the Philadelphia Orchestra's marvelous principal clarinetist Ricardo Morales, his wife (and Orchestra violinist) Amy Oshiro-Morales and their delightful daughter Victoria. In late 2012, JoAnn Falletta asked for Ricardo's email address, with a hope that he would come and play the Mozart Concerto with the Buffalo Philharmonic. Of course we went up for the performances in October 2013 and, just before the concert in Ricardo's dressing room, he asked me for my opinion of his two clarinets, both with basset extensions. He was concerned that his usual clarinet had two keys in the low register that weren't sealing properly. He played a few notes on it, and then played some more on an instrument that had been made for him, called the MoBa, which I preferred.

He said, "All right, I'll use the MoBa, but I haven't played it in two years! Besides, the keys for the low notes on the basset extension are placed opposite from my usual clarinet but, if you think it sounds better, let's go with it!" I was stunned that he would play with this level of risk, but it sounded fabulous as usual.

On that journey, JoAnn asked Ricardo if he would play it with the BPO on their February 2014 tour of Florida, and we were able to share his performance again, this time in West Palm Beach with a follow-up dinner at the Breakers.

When the Buffalo Philharmonic's release of the Mozart with Ricardo was released, JoAnn sent me a copy with a note saying, "All thanks to you!" Of course, that wasn't true, but it's just JoAnn's way of making everyone feel included. Her genuine generosity of spirit and respect for her musicians has resulted in orchestras who support her, and play, with a unique passion.

Ricardo Morales and JoAnn Falletta in Buffalo.

40. POST SCRIPTS

Though I had been bounced, I eventually was allowed to submit weekly listings to the *Daily News* gratis and, after a few months, Gar Joseph, soon to retire, approved a small fee. Lauren McCutcheon had to patiently field these weekly listings, and those from other contributors, and sum them up in the midst of many other chores.

One story a new features editor allowed was the launch of Play On, Philly! at St. Francis de Sales church in West Philadelphia, based on Venezuela's *El Sistema* plan, the idea that had made a star out of Gustavo Dudamel. The guiding forces were Carole Haas Gravagno who, as an ex-teacher who had grown up in that now-diverse neighborhood, cared deeply that kids have music in their lives at an early age, and Stanford Thompson, who had graduated from Curtis. By the time the story was written, that features editor had already been fired. Another one I got away with was about Philadelphia Sinfonia's highly successful Kimmel Center concert, conducted by Gary White, who would later team up again with Keystone State Boychoir for the second time at Marc's church to celebrate Peace Day Philly.

By 2013, things had picked up a little for the paper, and it began a new Saturday weekend edition, featuring a full-page five- or six-question interview. The first was with the Orchestra's new music director Yannick Nézet-Séguin and, though I had spoken with him twice before, their public relations people wanted me to email them the questions, evidently choosing the best ones and providing responses by email, a totally unacceptable process.

Back when I had relative carte blanche to do stories, many about the Orchestra, I was thoroughly covering the same beat as the competition which had two full-time staffers. Stories would often appear in the *Inquirer* and someone would call from the *News* to ask why we didn't have it; of course, unless it was something monumental, they weren't interested in running it a day late anyway. Granted, the *Inquirer* did weekly reviews and required more care and feeding. But though a level playing field was always promised, the release would arrive the next day or at 11 p.m., making me wonder if, as a p.r. person, I'd rather get ink in both daily papers than one.

I always made it very clear to these contacts that, even if I groveled and pleaded importance for the story to run a day late, it was unlikely because these were entities in competition with each other. "How short-sighted of them!" was the common response. The usual explanation was that it must have been leaked but, after finding out from other reporters that the release had been given the morning before, the story always changed to "Well, they have a larger circulation!" The worst part of not writing stories was the emphatic end of complimentary tickets; the best part was the elimination of groveling.

But after Yannick came more of those full-page interviews, as diverse as I could imagine. I had a chance to speak with Pennsylvania Ballet's brilliant ballerina Amy Aldridge, Wanamaker organist Peter Richard Conte, Philadanco founder Joan Myers Brown, pianist/conductor Ignat Solzhenitsyn and the newly-named Pennsylvania Ballet artistic director (and legendary dancer) Angel Corella. Bass Eric Owens, here to sing King Philip II in Verdi's *Don Carlo*, followed, as well as the astonishing, now-retired ballerina Arantxa Ochoa, who took over as head of the Ballet's school to train the youngsters for the annual production of *The Nutcracker,* and Opera Philadelphia's general director/president David Devan, speaking about showing operas for free in HD on Independence Mall. Here are their insights:

Amy Aldridge:
Q: *When did you realize that dancing was your career?*
A: *I used to swim competitively until I was 12, and was interested in both equally. But swimming made my back and neck so broad that I had to make the choice. Everything in my gut said it was the right one, though I'm still very competitive whenever I get in the pool.*

Amy Aldridge. Credit: Alexander Izalaev.

Q: *What don't audiences realize about what you do?*
A: *They only see the beautiful and think we're just floating around, but to get to that place takes so much pain. They don't realize how challenging it can be on your mind, as well as your body. It's hard not to feel flawed as a*

person when you're not always perfect. We're human beings, not machines, and how you fix it, how you save it on the spot without notice, that's the magic, that's the work of a true artist.

In a high-energy ballet, it's hard to go home and be a normal person. I just stare at the wall, because it took all the energy out of me. If there's a lot of dancing en pointe, sometimes I can't even put my street shoes on, and my toes hurt so much I can't stand the sheets touching them. For this show, I'm taking a lot of Epsom salt baths.

Q: How aware of the audience are you when you're dancing?

A: *I don't see them at all. It's just a big, black sea. In* Slaughter on Tenth Avenue, *which I have danced three times, there's a fun moment where you point to someone in the front row, but other than that, I don't see anybody. If I focus on someone, I lose my own focus.*

Q: How do you hold all those steps in your head, and your feet?

A: *I never get lost when there's music to relate to, I'm a pretty musical dancer who usually gets a rhythm for all the steps. In some harder ballets you have to count all the time instead of listening to the music—10, 12, 8, you keep counting, but it can get distracting. Counting over and over keeps me up at night.*

Q: Because of all the times you're lifted, do you have to be concerned about what you eat?

A: *Each dancer is different. I don't eat red meat, but I don't deprive myself of anything I like, just eat healthy and have a little chocolate every day. My one thing I will never give up is Doritos. I could make a meal of snacks.*

Sometimes a dancer is asked to put on a little weight, or lose some, depending on the role. It's only a very small amount, but an athletic build may need to be a bit softer, more feminine, or vice versa.

Q: How do you look back at your career?

A: *I've been dancing in Philadelphia for 20 years, more than half of my life, giving a huge part of myself to the city and have received a lot back. I would never never give anything less than my absolute best.* (Ballet studio, October 8, 2013)

Peter Richard Conte:

Q: *How do you manage such a daunting holiday schedule, playing the Wanamaker organ at Macy's, the Longwood Gardens organ and the one at St. Clemens Church?*

A: *I wonder myself somedays, and need a color-coded calendar. But there are three assistants at Macy's and staff organists at the hourly sing-alongs at Longwood. Just switching gears between the two consoles takes years of experience.*

Q: *Do you have much to do with Macy's famous Christmas Light Show?*

A: *The show is prerecorded, with an organ solo just after the show. If I'm playing a recital after the show that day, I can push a button on the con-*

sole and play the ending live. Crowds go crazy hearing that sound from all around them instead of from speakers, like a giant hug.

Q; *How do you think the organ recitals help business?*

A: *Shoppers might have come in to buy a pair of shoes and, transfixed by this sound that moves them, stop and buy something else. Wanamaker loved music, and Leopold Stokowski and the Philadelphia Orchestra often came and played works with the organ for 10,000 people.*

Q: *How much tradition do you feel, being The Grand Court Organist?*

A: *It's an enormous honor, and it will be 25 years next September—though some assistants have been there even longer. People come from all over the world to hear the Wanamaker Organ. It takes years to master it and still scares me after 10 days away from it. We refer to it as "Baby," but it's huge, with six manuals, the pedal keyboard and 28,500 pipes. It's simply part of Philadelphia history.*

Q: *How supportive has Macy's been to the huge maintenance needs?*

A: *Phenomenally—they completely get the historical role as an international musical icon. After all, the organ is built into the structure.*

When I began here, the organ was in terrible shape, 15 percent playable. Now there are two full-time and two part-time maintenance staff, led by Curt Mangel, and they have brought it back from near death to the best shape of its life, 100 percent playable. By the way, we actually function under the Macy's Parade Studio, the people who run the New York Thanksgiving Day parade.

Q: *How do you select other organists for yours for your radio show with Jill Pasternak?*

A: *Besides longtime assistants, some come from the organ camp that Macy's sponsors, and the radio shows are another venue to let some of these young talents be heard. It's an important opportunity, because organists are generally hidden behind a curtain, and rarely recognized. Luckily, I like being incognito.* (Restaurant, November 20, 2013)

In October 2014, Conte soloed in Joseph Jongen's wild Symphonie Concertante with the Philadelphia Orchestra at the Kimmel Center. Written in 1926 for the Orchestra and the Wanamaker organ, the premiere was cancelled, but those same forces finally played the piece within Macy's vast atrium space in 2008.

Joan Myers Brown:
Q: *How did you start, and how important is dance to the community?*

A: *The 4-H Club taught music and dance at my elementary school, and I joined the ballet club at West Philadelphia High School. I was a flower who wanted to be the princess! But the arts are no longer accessible, and kids are missing out on something very valuable in their lives. The arts and dance affect the children that they touch, and they learn perseverance and self-esteem, not just the guts and glory of jumping around the stage in a costume.*

They see Dancing with the Stars, *with people doing tricks, and don't realize there's a craft that must be learned. To learn to dance on your toes requires pain and suffering, thanks to the court of Louis XIV, but ballet training is essential to any dancer.*

Q: *How do you get commissioned works?*

A: *Early on, we were given works, but the costs are much more now. One piece costs more in remounting fees than we paid to create it. And unless you use music in the public domain, it's easier to have someone write an original composition than to pay the royalties. Music by some composers costs $350 each time, the choreographer only got $35.*

Q: *Who does most of the training these days, and what's the structure?*

A: *I have had the same teachers for 20 or 30 years, but I do it if someone can't show up. Our school is for-profit, with 600 kids and maybe 60 full or partial scholarships, which pays the company's space rent. The company is non-profit, we only charge for the summer intensive courses. And there's a second company which does runout shows, we load them in a bus and they dance for free. Once the school was the source for the company's dancers, but grants insist auditions must be open to everybody.*

Q: *Do you get much support from the black community?*

A: *No, but they don't support the Freedom Theater, the African-American Museum, Bushfire Theater, Point Breeze, even churches. Out of 600 kids in my school, 50 will come to our concert. I ask them, how do you want to do ballet and not come and see ballet?*

Q: *Where does your support come from?*

A: *Mostly from foundations in New York, because they're more interested in the artistic product. If it wasn't for them, there would be no Philadanco. There's very little from the major foundations in Philadelphia, because they want you to have a corporate infrastructure, CEO, CFO and board, and we don't have the room or the money to put in all the people they want me to hire. But I don't think we have anything to prove any more.*

We've performed all over the world, first dance company in several countries, in Europe for five weeks, a three week residency at Long Island University, and just sold out nine shows at the Joyce Theater in New York. But we can't sell out four shows in Philly.

Q: *Don't you still great satisfaction in mentoring so many young people?*

A: *Yes, there's more work for black dancers now, like* The Lion King *and* The Color Purple *on Broadway, two went to Ailey last year, and we have been doing the* James Brown Project *at the Apollo Theater. City Councilperson Blondell Reynolds-Brown was one of my dancers, and Mayor Nutter's wife Lisa danced in my school.*

It's like a finishing school—I can't tell you how many young women have told me that if they hadn't gone to dancing school, they wouldn't have succeeded in life. They gained from the training and the involvement, working as a group, learning endurance, perseverance. It's what gives me the energy to continue.

Q: Is it hard to encourage men to dance?
A: Hip-hop has opened the door for more men, who didn't start dancing until they were in their teens because of peer pressure. They have to be very strong. One young man waited until the death of his mother, who frowned on men dancing, to be sent to a summer program and eventually made it into a major company.

Q: What about the future of the company?
A: Well, it's like an old tree, and acorns are falling and growing up all around it. There isn't anyone who wants to pick up the responsibility, so I keep going—I don't have dance, dance has me. The company will be 45 years old, and the school 55 in the 2014-15 season.

I don't want to die on the ballet bar, but on the beach looking like an alligator pocketbook. (Philadanco studio, April 1, 2014)

Ignat Solzhenitsyn:
Q: How much of your schedule is conducting, playing solo recitals and performing concertos, and how comfortable is it for to switch from the keyboard to the podium?
A: These days, it's about 60 percent conducting, 30 percent piano recitals and 10 percent concerti. It's very comfortable, like second nature now, though the preparation can never be compromised, and the problems of scheduling are ever-present. Learning how to say no is essential to avoid overcommitting.

Q: When you come back to Philly, what are your musts?
A: It's such a constantly vibrant place, and there are always new restaurants to try. Of course, Parc is now an institution, just across the street from Curtis. And I always try to make time to see the Phillies in that wonderful park with the skyline, as well as the Eagles, sharing all the passion of Philly fans.

Q: In your travels, how often do people ask about your father Alexandr Solzhenitsyn) and his revelatory writing?
A: Very often, and I find it amazing how many people across the world have told me how life-changing his works are. It was a function of the profoundly difficult and shattering experiences that he went through in his life, and he had to address those issues and tell the truth about the camps and the evil of man, even in his fiction.

Q: You left Russia at age 4. What changes have you recently seen there since your first visit back in 1994?
A: When I went back then, Russia was at its low point in power, prestige, wealth and confidence. Despite many problems, the most positive aspect now is the rise of the middle class that has risen out of nowhere, which will demand stability and responsive government, and a desire for leisure and culture, things which don't seem so important during periods of survival. And the success of the Sochi Games seems good for the world.

Q: Does it become easier with experience for you to make your first appearance with an orchestra?

A: *It's easier, but the responsibility gets greater and becomes more difficult because of expectations, both theirs and yours. The great pianist Artur Schnabel, whose student Maria Curcio was one of my teachers, famously said that great music is better than it can ever be performed. Without that awesome sense of an unbridgeable gulf between the possible and the ideal, why go into music to dream small dreams? Facing impossible challenges is what keeps us going.* (Coffee shop, March 9, 2014)

(The Russian situation became tense just after our interview and, since Solzhenitsn was in Moscow, he answered another question later.)

Q: *How do you see the current situation in the Ukraine and Crimea?*

A: *Though the actual, very volatile situation on the ground in the Ukraine is definitely tense and very serious, I expect it to be resolved in the short term without major escalation or more bloodshed.*

I believe western Ukraine will be fine. But, to me, the real long-term problem concerns the residents of eastern and southern Ukraine, where millions of people consider themselves Russians or are oriented toward Russia. The key to watch is whether their point of view is respected. (By phone from Moscow, March 14, 2014)

Angel Corella:

Q: *Why did you choose Pennsylvania Ballet?*

A: *They decided to choose me, after a process of 35 candidates. I have had a connection because my sister danced here, and I came down often on weekends. It's the company I have seen the most, and is the right size to manage, to have responsibility for. I couldn't have been received with a more positive welcome. But, believe me, being a director is not as easy as it looks.*

Q: *Will we get to see you dance?*

A: *Well, at our gala on October 2, I pulled Amy Aldridge out of the audience and we did a swing dance. I'm doing my last dancing in Spain on January 4 (2015), but wasn't planning on doing any here. The dancers need to know that I'm not taking space from them. Eventually, your body can't retain any more, and transition is a way to staying connected, sharing, encouraging. If I have to, I might maybe as a showcase, but I don't say no, I don't say yes.*

Q: *Is it true that you have photographic memory about all the steps in a ballet?*

A: *It's a curse, I'm going through them all the time constantly. In bed I can't get them out of my head and it's hard to go to sleep. I've always learned the steps for every single person, it's impossible for me to forget. I did the Balanchine piece a long time ago in London, and still remember every step.*

Q: *Will you schedule more premieres, or more standard major works, and will you do any choreography?*

A: *I want to balance the full-length pieces like* Romeo and Juliet, Swan Lake *and* Don Quixote, *with new, edgy choreography. And we have Mat-*

thew Neenan, who knows the dancers intimately, as choreographer-in-residence, and I hope to extend his contract. I did some pieces in Spain with music by Electric Light Orchestra and some swing, but I'm not going to make the dancers suffer.

Q: *What were your first memories of America?*

A: *I loved movies, especially Gene Kelly. He did what is our aim, to make the audience feel like they're dancing with you. The way to do this is to make each dancer feel as though they have something unique, and your job is to bring it out of them. You know what you can do, but you have to gain their trust to find how much they are willing to achieve.*

Q: *What are your impressions of Philadelphia?*

A: *Have been mostly in the studio and trying to find a place to live since I arrived, but I love the feel of the city, big but not overwhelming. I'm overwhelmed by all the murals, which include the society and make them feel like they're part of the mural, like what we're trying to do. I haven't gone to any Spanish restaurants—want something different than home in Madrid!* (Ballet studio, September 24, 2014)

Eric Owens:

Q: *What is it like to portray King Philip, who senses his son Carlo is in love with the Queen?*

A: *He spends the opera suspecting it, not knowing, and maybe he doesn't really want to know. Every tiny thing makes him suspect even more, and the frustration of not knowing drives him crazy. It really helps to have such a cohesion and comfort level about this production, because of working with singers I've known for years.*

Q: *Why did you choose this role to sing?*

A: *This is a role I've been wanting to do, and loved it even before I wanted to be a singer. It's arguably Verdi's best opera and, for me, the brass ring of bass roles, dramatically as well as musically. I'm so grateful that Opera Philadelphia wanted to do it with me. This is my home town company, which is doing amazing things, an example of what an opera company can do.*

Q: *The bass is usually the heavy, or authority figure. Wouldn't you enjoy some lighter roles?*

A: *Yes, because I'm usually either the father, clergy guy, priest, devil or bad guy. But I also did some comic Rossini roles, two with Larry Brownlee, who will be here soon playing Charlie Parker. I'd love to do Bottom in Midsummer Night's Dream, or maybe Falstaff some day.*

I'm having a career that I'm so grateful for, it's all gravy now. I'm open to any and everything, there's nothing else I'm dying to do. My career has been a long, steady climb—like Bolero, that starts quietly and builds to a crescendo.

Q: *How difficult was it to debut in (Washington Opera's) Flying Dutchman and come right into singing another new role?*

A: *It's was a pretty intense experience, and there's another after this!* Dutchman *is the Wagner that's most like Verdi, a little more like organized yelling. But singing Verdi is such a joy, a different set of physical demands, relentless, like doing a hundred situps. The other day in rehearsal, I had to stop for a moment because the music was so very beautiful that I was simply overwhelmed.*

Q: *How important are your outreach activities and master classes?*

A: *I enjoy it more than getting up on stage! In masterclasses, I learn more than they do, seeing the insanity of singing well and understanding about muscles. It helps you to define what you're talking about, when you have to explain with simplicity.*

There are some basics—if you're not with the ensemble and not in tune, it's wrong! And I encourage them to search their soul, because this life, this lifestyle, is not for everybody, maybe not matching a person's ambitions. I hate it when schools take the tuition when a person probably shouldn't be there.

Q: *What are your musts when you're here, and what are your best memories of Philly?*

A: *Of course, I go to Mount Airy to see my Mom and family, but still haven't made it to the Barnes Museum. For restaurants, I enjoy the Devon Seafood Grill and Vernick, a farm-to-table spot on Walnut Street.*

I've sung with orchestras in Berlin, Chicago, Boston, the BBC, but whenever I sing with the Philadelphia Orchestra I'm like a little kid, I still get nervous. When I was at Central High, some of us interviewed Maestro Muti for the Daily News. (Curtis Institute, April 14, 2015)

Arantxa Ochoa:

Q: *Did you audition and choose the* Nutcracker *children?*

A: *Not this year, as in past years. Sandra Jennings came this year from the Balanchine Trust, and she chose 103 from the 157 in our school. The rehearsing is done by Sandra and two former company dancers—John Martin, who teaches at the school and does the angels and battle scene, and Jessica Gattinella, who coaches Marie, the prince and the party scene.*

Q: *What kind of commitment does it require?*

A: *The children come after school from six to eight-thirty, and Saturdays and Sundays. Some do their homework in the car on their way home. They may have to get special permission from school to get here earlier the week before we open, and they have to be brought to all performances. This is a huge commitment for the parents as well, but nothing can describe the joy that they will receive.*

Q: *How do the children respond to rehearsal?*

A: *Some have seen the show since they were babies. They come to rehearsal eager to learn and be pushed, and they love interacting with the company's dancers and bonding in the dressing rooms. All those little girls who had watched the show, and dreamed of being part of it, are now fulfilling their dream.*

Q: *Do you hope they'll all go on to be dancers?*

A: *I tell them from the beginning, this is the best thing that can happen to you, it's not like going to work, it's your life, become whatever you want to do. But if you don't give 100% every day, don't waste your time. You want them to respect you, not be afraid of you, but you have to learn how much to push and how much to nurture. You have to need to dance, not just want to dance.*

Q: *Do things ever go wrong?*

A: *Yes, sometimes they become nervous when they finally see that Academy stage, and then in the dress rehearsal with orchestra and students in the audience. We tell the kids with hoops what to do if they drop them, the eight kids how to get out from under Mother Ginger's skirt without stepping on it, and the angels how to avoid tripping on their dresses.*

Q: *How does the school work?*

A: *We accept everyone from age five to eight, then by audition for professional levels from eight to 18. When they're ready, some will become part of the second company, which dances with the company and does outreach programs, and we help some find positions in a major company.*

Q: *Don't you miss dancing?*

A: *I never thought I'd say it, but no! Now I get to share everything in my experience with these children. They are like little jewels, and we must teach them to dance with their soul, because ballet is so much more than just steps, and to present themselves through their unique personality. Our job is to find it, like a little flame, to help them through life. This is the best reward, to have a kid think, she taught me how to be somebody special.*

Whatever they do in life, they need to learn hard work, discipline, passion. My dream is to find a way for these children to perform in public besides the Nutcracker. (Pennsylvania Ballet studio, April 5, 2015)

Incredibly, her last line was cut by an editor who thought it was too self-serving. But, thanks to parents and several donors, Ochoa's dream came true the following June, when kids from all levels stunned an Annenberg Center audience with amazing precision and commitment after an introduction by Angel Corella. Two shows were necessary in 2016, featuring all 150 students, with the show likely to become an urgently-antipated annual event.

David Devan:

Q: *Besides Opera on the Mall, what community outreach does the company do, and how important is it?*

A: *We think the term 'outreach' looks down at the public, and don't think of our projects outside the standard venues as a separate thing. Our goal is to present a civic footprint, like our pop-up performances at the Reading Terminal or Macy's we call Random Acts of Culture. We want people to be part of it on their own terms.*

As far as our "Sounds Of Learning" program, we have exposed over 150,000 school-age kids by busing them to dress rehearsals. We have teaching artists in the schools, and are working on producing a whole Hip H'opera based on 150 poems of hip-hop artists.

Q: *How do you balance the spirit of innovation against the reality of necessary ticket sales?*

A: *Our subscribers can elect the shows outside of the Academy and the Perelman. We need to be a multi-channel opera company, to create a range of experiences so people can curate what's interesting to them.*

Innovation has taken a bad rap in classical music. Though our chamber operas and Aurora series have been very progressive, and we expected a small number or subscribers to choose them, they all sold out. We had to add two performances to "ANDY-A Popera," and were amazed how many subscribers were there. And half of the attendees had never been to our Academy shows.

Q: *How much has the company's national image benefited from its recent innovative programming?*

A: *Considerably!* There have been four pieces in the New York Times, also Opera News, and the blogosphere has blown up, generating a huge interest beyond Philadelphia. Here, we've reached 3,000 new households every year.

Another reason is that we have the largest new works practice in America, through our residency and commissioning program. We have three composers-in-residence, and six commissions in development.

Q: *Will it help in bringing more major stars to Philly?*

A: *Many are waiting to be here but, since Europe books earlier than in the U. S., we're contracting as far out as 2020. We've become known as a place where artists can be excited about their work, because our object is to find the right project for the right artist in career-defining opportunities.*

Many artists have, as their condition, that (music director) Corrado Rovaris would be conducting, and they know our orchestra has improved immeasurably. By the way, Corrado and I recently signed contracts through 2020.

Q: *Is it more advantageous to do several smaller shows than to add more performances of the Academy of Music repertory operas?*

A: *We think it's better to be sold out with five performances and have resources left to develop another project. People now at their living room sofa have such a broader range of aesthetics that we need to respond in a way that's responsible to our living art. Restless, innovative attitude is an American way, especially here in the original American city.*

Q: *How does Opera on the Mall pay off?*

A: *We spend $250,000 for the project, with the best HD screens on the east coast, $90,000 alone for surround sound. There are six cameras in the Academy, with directors working on it for 10 days ahead of the show. By the way, 15,000 people had signed up for the original date (postponed because of rain). If none of them ever come to the Academy, I'm okay with that.*

My job, our mission, is to provide opera to this community. The message is that culture is alive and well. Opera has done that--Lady Gaga didn't do it, we did! (Academy of Music, October 8, 2015)

Though Annenberg and Pew Foundation grants have become virtually nil, with many worthy performing organization scrambling for the few small funding sources available, the financial situation for the arts seems grim in 2015. Even the professional Philadelphia Singers was forced to end its run after 43 years at the end of the 2014-15 season, and no amount of reports about the civic importance of the arts, for prestige or financial reasons, has had much impact.

But not all prospects are bleak. The Philadelphia Chamber Music Society, which brings in the world's great musicians and singers for an amazing $25, continues its run of 60 performances a year. The 2015-16 season honored founder Tony Checchia, whose love for music has brought international artists, 60 world premieres and countless new devotees to his packed season of 60 concerts, often costing triple that in New York the next night.

Besides operas presented by Opera Philadelphia, Temple University Opera Theater and Curtis Opera Theatre, the collaboration between Curtis and Opera Philadelphia has resulted in many chamber operas, some too specialized for the large Academy of Music but ideal for the smaller Perelman. In recent years, they've presented *Ainadamar, Wozzeck, Antony and Cleopatra, The Cunning Little Vixen, Elegy for Young Lovers, Owen Wingrave, Dialogues of the Carmelites* and *Ariadne auf Naxos*. Opera Philadelphia has also strayed from the standard repertoire as well, scheduling *Svabda—A Wedding, ANDY: A Popera, A Coffin In Egypt, Silent Night, Oscar* and *Yardbird*, based on the life of Charlie Parker, with hot star Lawrence Brownlee in the title role and the stunning Angela Brown playing his mother Addie.

Those two stars were brilliant in *Yardbird*, the company's first world premiere since its first season 40 years before. The project began when conductor Corrado Rovaris (who had played jazz piano in a ritzy Sardinian summer resort) heard saxophonist/composer Daniel Schnyder in Switzerland, and envisioned an opera featuring Brownlee, who had performed in Philadelphia on his way up the ladder to vast stardom.

Schnyder played with a percussionist who suggested his sister Bridgette A. Wimberly, an award-winning poet and playwright, as librettist. Her first play had the incredible good fortune to star the late Ruby Dee, and after she encouraged breast cancer survivors in her native Cleveland to write short plays about their experience, the renowned Dee actually came and played the roles.

"My mother's twin brother was an alto saxophonist," said Wimberly, "and my grandmother felt that when he became a heroin user, it was Charlie Parker's fault! But my research about Parker moved me to the core, and I realized how much of his life was shaped by women."

Her idea was perfect: after Parker died at the home of Nica (his patroness, the Baroness Pannonica de Koenigswarter), his body was not identified for several days. In the opera, he returns to Birdland, the club named for him which had thrown him out, to compose the orchestral work he had always dreamed of writing. Addie (Brown electrified the stage), three wives, Nica, Dizzy Gillespie and lurking drugs all visit him and foil his composition, giving him insight into this brilliant, tragic, troubled existence. Brownlee sang a few bebop riffs that actually came from Parker's tunes, and a mesmerizing aria to his horn, simply owning the role that Schnyder wrote for him perfectly.

"It's not a jazz opera," said Schnyder, who scored the one-act opera for 15 players. "It's made for classical singers and musicians, challenging and unusually hard because it's about a virtuoso. Charlie studied Stravinsky and could memorize scores, hearing orchestral colors without losing the rhythm, and always dreaming of composing for large orchestra, but he still changed the world of music."

The five performances in the 650-seat Perelman Theater were completely sold out, but the show was reprised in April 2016 at New York's legendary 1500-seat Apollo Theatre, where Parker played his last concert.

Schnyder kindly gave me a CD of his music for saxophone, plus trombone and piano, written as score for the famous 1926 F. W. Murnau film of *Faust*. This music envelops the listener in an eerie, moving and completely captivating world, amazing for only three instruments. It must be ideal for this masterpiece of German expressionism, and Schnyder was excited that it will be played live with a screening of the film in 2016 at a Washington, D. C. venue.

At intermission of a Philly Pops concert in October 2015, old friend Michael Ludwig married violinist Rachael Mathey, with Mayor Michael Nutter officiating. Since Michael had stepped down as concertmaster with JoAnn Falletta's Buffalo Philharmonic to solo all over the country, he and Rachael have also played the Pops' first two violin chairs.

He also reinstated the Roxborough Symphony as conductor, with its first concert featuring the two in the Bach Two-Violin Concerto; it was a special moment, considering that he had often played with his father Irving Ludwig, a longtime Philadelphia Orchestra violinist, but never in public until this chance to perform the work with his wife.

The ensemble is one of so many area orchestras, includeing those in Ambler (led by WRTI-FM host Jack Moore), Lansdowne, Kennett, Main Line (Don Liuzzi conducting), Lower Merion (Mark Gigliotti leading), and many more too numerous to list. Of course, besides the Philadelphia Orchestra, outstanding performances are also given by the Curtis Symphony, the Temple Symphony, and Symphony in C.

Yes, Philly has become a great orchestra town, but don't forget the excitement generated by the student orchestras, like the many Temple ensembles, the three factions of Gary White's Philadelphia Sinfonia, the Philadelphia Youth Orchestra led by Louis Scaglione, the All City Orchestra with Joseph Conyers on the podium and Play On, Philly! There's an intensity to hearing these young players, and fun in knowing that their lives are strikingly changed by this experience. It's dearly hoped that Play On, Philly! can serve as a template for any school which can raise the cost of after-school coaches and, perhaps some day in my fantasy future, music and the arts will once again be an essential part of every school curriculum.

In February of 2016, we finally were able to celebrate Jennifer Higdon's opera *Cold Mountain*, adapted slightly from its Santa Fe run for five performances presented by Opera Philadelphia. The show featured the superb soprano Isabel Leonard (who soon returned to do a duet recital with the amazing guitarist Sharon Isbin) and tenor Jay Hunter Morris. Baritone Nathan Gunn had to withdraw for personal reasons but, fortunately, Jarrett Ott, who had covered the work in Santa Fe, saved the day. Powerful and provocative, its imaginative staging was complimented by the splendid score led by the brilliant maestro Corrado Rovaris. It was a true joy to share these hometown shows with a beaming Higdon on the Academy stage, and to feel the overwhelming reaction from an audience who has experienced her steps on a remarkable journey of creativity. Three months later in London, *Cold Mountain* won the Best World Premiere award at the International Opera Awards.

In one remarkably hopeful sign, especially for Curtis Institute and the imaginative leadership of its president Roberto Diaz, his outgoing board chair Nina Baroness von Maltzahn blessed the conservatory with an astounding $55 million over five years, about the amount Gerry and Marguerite Lenfest had given the famed school. It makes us think there is money for the funding-strapped arts—somewhere.

My *Daily News* email address had run after my stories for 15 years but no one had mentioned that, during the freelance purge, someone should have told me to relinquish my byline email address. Hundreds of my contacts over 30 years were there, but one day my access suddenly stopped. I asked a tech person if I could have it back temporarily to forward a new address to my legion of contacts, but she could only restore about the last 30. This seemed an ominous milestone, and perhaps time to sum up the last four decades.

Throughout all these years, I have been immensely fortunate to have dealt with some outstanding public relations people, whose patience and generosity, even when I wasn't giving them much ink, made the stresses bearable and often joyful. The list includes Tracy Galligher Young, succeeded by ball-playing buddy Frank Luzi at Opera Philadelphia; Jennifer Kallend at Curtis Institute; Lisa Miller (who recently stepped down) at Network for New Music, a host of folks at Pennsylvania Ballet and everyone at the Philadelphia Chamber Music Society.

After long and contentious legal dealings about ownership of the papers, it was finally resolved on a positive note though, only four days later, co-owner Lewis Katz died in a plane crash, leaving philanthropist H. F. (Gerry) Lenfest holding the bag and owning the paper, a role he evidently hadn't envisioned. A new publisher in October 2015 announced that 17 of the *Daily*

News editorial staff of 60—including many dedicated writers who have become good friends—and only 12 members of the *Inquirer* (from between 150 to 200) would lose their jobs a few weeks before Christmas.

In January 2016, Lenfest transferred the struggling papers to a newly formed Institute for Journalism in New Media, giving $20 million to endow the entity. The Philadelphia Media Network, which publishes both papers, becomes a self-governing for-profit company which is owned by the Institute. This arrangement will allow the non-profit Institute to accept charitable donations to "support specific journalism projects" without compromising its editorial policy or being involved in any conflicts of interest. Soon after, newsrooms of both papers, with very different personalities, were merged into the same office.

Weeks after the news teams of both papers were merged into the same space, I was assigned a piece by the Inquirer about the Philly Pops, which eventually ran in the *Daily News*. Another story about a gala concert, celebrating Anthony Checchia's 30 years of leading the Philadelphia Chamber Music Society, finally did run in the Inquirer. Ten years ago this consorting with the competition would have been considered treasonous, but film reviews and other stories now appear in both papers: the difficult and constantly-changing reality of this important business, competing in the swamp of bloggers and 24-hour news bloviators, means a new and necessary flexibility.

It's hard to know what will happen in the newspaper biz, but the way things are going future arts stories will need to appeal to a celebrity-sated readership meaning—in my field—there will probably be very few indeed.

CODA

Forty years of dealing with the disinterested and indifferent has still had an enlightening side, those adventures with remarkable artists willing to express he heartfelt meaning of their missions. So many of them wanted to speak about the mystery of performance, and seemed to be glad to get away from the usual obligatory questions and speak about why, how and what they do.

This journey has given me an enormous respect for the courage and incredible determination of these musicians, composers, singers, dancers and other creators, who pursue the role they believe destined to follow.

I once asked a dancer, who was changing shoes on bloody feet, why she underwent such a daily ordeal, low pay, only a year-to-year contract and a relatively short career. Her answer: "If we didn't love this more than anything else in life, it wouldn't be possible."

I can't pretend that was my motivation, but these performers have consistently shown me the formula for a fulfilling life.

INDEX

100 Men and a Girl, film, 188
1807 and Friends, 164, 205
1807 Sansom Street, Philadelphia, 164
1940 World's Fair, 194
200 Motels, album, 28
2001: A Space Odyssey, film, 108
23rd Street Café, 3
33rd Street, Philadelphia, 191
42nd Street, NY, 168
52nd Street, NY, 18, 320
88 Charing Cross Road, book, 93
AAA Diagnostic Clinic, 77
Aaron, Henry, 84
Abbado, Claudio, 309, 329
Abbado, Roberto, 209
Abbott, Julia, 5
Abraham Lincoln Bicentennial Commission, 332
Abramovic, Charles, 256-257, 268; *Piano Concerto*, 256
Abruzzo, Italy, xx
Academy Awards (Oscars), 108, 109, 190, 194, 294, 346
Academy Awards telecast, 181-182
Academy of Community Music, Suzuk school. 114, 327
Academy of Music, 36, 38, 52, 54, 57, 58, 60, 63, 70, 89, 103, 111,115, 122, 123, 128, 129, 170, 195, 201, 202, 222, 233, 249, 316, 318, 324, 332, 341, 360, 361, 362
Academy of St. Martin-in-the-Fields, 92, 132
Academy of Vocal Arts (AVA), 55, 57, 63, 71, 75, 78, 110, 133, 134, 143, 144, 151, 164, 167, 168, 204, 207, 253, 255, 257, 284, 286, 303, 306, 316, 317, 341, 344
"Achy Breaky Heart," song, 267
Adams, John, *Doctor Atomic*, 319
Adams, Joy, 5
Addams, Charles, 94
Adès, Thomas, *Powder Her Face*, 251
Adirondack Scenic, 57, 60, 69
Adventures of a Young Man, film, 184
Ady, James, 323-324
African-Americans, 78, 105, 116, 125, 127, 194, 195, 226, 276, 296, 331, 333
African-American Museum, Philadelphia, 355
Age of Innocence, The, film, 181, 192
Ailey, Alvin, 274, 355
Airplane, film, 192

AirTurn, 326-327
Alaska, 260
Albanese, Licia, 55, 143, 167
Albany, record label, xxi, 227, 253
Albéniz, Isaac, *Iberia*, 330
Albert Hall, London, 89, 343
Aldridge, Amy, 323, 352-353, 357
Alemany, Robert, 285
Alexander Nevsky, film, 50
Alfano, Franco, 110
Alhambra, Spain, 82
Alice in Wonderland, book, 95
"All Blues," song, 44
"All Shook Up," song, 30
"All the Things You Are," song, 267, 268, 320
All City Orchestra, 363
Allen, Debbie, 181
Allen, Steve, 80
Alliance Theater, Atlanta, 265
Allison, Mose, 36
All-Philadelphia Jazz Band, 316
Almeida, Laurindo, 38, 247
Alpha Kappa Alpha (AKA), 334
Alsop, Marin, 236
Alvarez, Alejandro, 224
Alvin Theater, New York, 199
Amadeus, film, 262
Amadie, Jimmy, 154, 203, 214-215, 246
Amadie, Lucille, 214, 215
Amara, Lucine, 85
Amber Waves, TV film, 182
Ambler Symphony, 363
"America the Beautiful," song, 332
"America," song, 126
American Express, 193
American Guild of Musical Artists (AGMA), 289
American Guild of Organists, 191, 277
American In Paris, An, Broadway show, 312
American Music Theater Festival, 99
American Popular Song, The, book, 26
American Society of Composers, Authors, and Publishers (ASCAP), 2, 43, 190, 192, 287
American Theater Arts For Youth, 195
Ampex, tape machine, xxi
Amram, David, *Twelfth Night*, 132
Amsterdam, 92, 310
Anderson, Ernestine, 45
Anderson, Leroy, 15, 248
Anderson, Marian, 25, 105, 125-128, 331-334
André, Maurice, 91
Angel/EMI, record label, 84-85, 145-147, 219

369

Angelou, Maya, 333
Angola, 199, 297
Animals Animals Animals, book, 94
Anka, Paul, 18
Ann Onymous, 15
Annenberg Center, Philadelphia, 9, 139, 222, 360
Anonymous 4, 146
Antheil, George, 138, 194, 262
Anthony, Mark, 219
Apollo rocket, 153
Apollo Theater, NY, 355
Appalachia, 233
Applause magazine, 50, 73
Arcadia Theater, Philadelphia, 14
Arden Theater, 263
Arf 'N' Annie, comic strip, 3
Argentina, 245, 317
Argento, Dominick, *Postcard from Morocco*, 132
Argerich, Martha, 329
Aristotle, 138
"Arkansas Traveler," song, 123
Arlen, Harold, 208, 268
Armed Forces language school, 149
Arp, Klaus, 162
Ars Nova Workshop, 203
Arsenault, Raymond, 334
Art in Cartooning, The, book, 94
Art Nouveau Jewelry, 49
ArtistsWorks, 327
Aruba, 69
ASCAP—See American Society of Composers, Authors, and Publishers
Ashburn, Richie, 84
Ashkenazy, Vladimir, 31, 273
Aspen, CO, 203-204
Associated Press (AP) Stylebook, 241
Astaire, Fred, 23, 186
Athens Conservatory, 158
Athens, Greece, 158
Atlanta Symphony, 247
Atlanta, GA, 144, 265, 297
Atlantic City Jazz Festival, 29
Atlantic City, NJ, 3, 89, 126, 149
Atlas rockets, 153
Au chien qui fume, restaurant, Paris, 93
Auden, W. H., 137
Auger, Arleen, 236
Austin, TX, 222
Avery Fisher Hall, NY, 189
Aznavour, Charles, 30, 157
B. Dalton bookstore, 49
Babbitt, Milton, 190
Bach Portrait, 166
Bach, Johann Sebastian, 10, 15, 38, 74, 79, 80, 81, 88, 99, 100, 112, 166, 174, 190, 191, 202, 204, 230, 242, 243, 245, 246, 294, 310; *Brandenburg Concertos*, 79, 92, 246; Chorales, xx; Concerto for two violins, 133, 163, 363; *Harpsichord Concerto in A Major*, 196; *Harpsichord Concerto in D Minor*, 46; *Harpsichord Concerto in F Minor*, 241; *Flute Sonatas*, 37; *Mass in B Minor*, 15, 79, 93, 340; *Orchestral Suite No. 4*, 190
Bach, P. D. Q. (Peter Schickele), 8, 166, 217; *Abduction of Figaro, The*, 166; *Civilian Barber, The;* 166; 216; *Concerto for Bassoon Versus Orchestra*, 216; *Dance of St. Vitus*, 217; *Eine Kleine Nichtmusic*, 166; *Exit of the Dragoon*, 217; *Fanfare for the Common Cold*, 216; *Hansel and Gretel and Ted and Alice*, 166; *No-No Nonette*, 216; *Notebook for Betty Sue Bach*, 216; *Oedipus Tex*, 166; *Okay Chorale*, 216; *Pervertimento*, 166, 216; *Safe Sextet*, 166; *Schleptet*, 166, 216; *Sonata for Viola Four Hands*, 216; *Unbegun Symphony*, 166
Bacharach, Burt, 179
Bad and the Beautiful, The, film, 187, 189
Bad and the Beautiful, The, film score 187, 190
Bad and the Beautiful, The: My Life In a Golden Age of Film Music (David Raksin), book, 347
Badura-Skoda, Paul, 91
Baez, Joan, 36, 167
Baker, Gregg, 169, 265, 266, 296, 297
Baker, Janet, 31
Baker, Julius, 269
Baker, Shawneen, 170
Balakierev, Mily, *Islamey*, 220
Balanchine, George, 216,
Balanchine Trust, 359, 357
Bali, 5, 305, 306
Balinese music, 305
Baltimore, MD, 216, 294
Baltsa, Agnes, 120
Balzac, Honore de, 211
Bampton, Rose, 123, 143, 167
Bancroft, Anne, 94
Band Box Theater, Germantown, Philadelphia, 14
Band Wagon, The, film, 23
Bang on a Can All-Stars, 305
Barab, Seymour, *The Toy Shop*, 71
Barbacini, Maurizio, 147, 161, 165-166, 209, 211, 218-219, 245
Barbacini, Paolo, 165
Barbarino, Vinnie, 21

Barber, Samuel, 159; *Adagio for Strings,* 245; *Agnus Dei,* 245; *Antony and Cleopatra,* 337
Barber, Skip, 2
Barbirolli, Sir John, 131
Barbosa-Lima, Carlos, 25
Barcelona, Spain, 158, 258, 293
Barfield, Dede, 312
Barmach, Tillie, 304
Barnes Museum, 359
Barnett, Michael, 32p
Barney Miller, TV show, 48
Barnum, P. T., 95
Barnum's Museum, 95
Baroque horn, 51
Baroque oboe, 313
Baroque trumpet, 91
Barrett, Sweet Emma, 9
Bartók, Béla, 43, 48, 109; *Violin Concertos,* 104
Bartoli, Cecilia, 250
Bartolini, Lando, 144
Baryshnikov, Mikhail, 247-248
Basie, Count, 36, 155
Bassey, Shirley, 22
Bates, Leon, 269-270
Battle, Kathleen, 132
Baumann, Hermann, 51-52
Bayreuth, Germany, 149
Bazell, Marciam, 110
BBC Symphony, London, 359
Bean, Nancy, 164, 205
Beatles, 268
Beatriz de Dia, 217
Beauty and the Beast, film, 139
Beck, Barbara, 74
Beck, Irene, 270
Beecham, Sir Thomas, 84, 137
Beethoven, Ludwig van, 79, 91, 100,113, 114, 131, 137, 140, 174, 205, 221, 230, 242, 273, 294, 295, 301, 340; *Fidelio,* 123; *Missa Solemnis,* 15, 277, 280; *Piano Concertos,* 105, 298; *Piano Concerto No. 1,* 27; *Piano Concerto No, 4,* 91; *Piano Concerto No. 5 ("Emperor"),* 116, 328; *Piano Sonatas,* 91, 112, 116; *Piano Sonata No. 31,* 174; *String Quartet, Op. 131,* 263-264; *Symphonies,* 84; *Symphony No. 3,* 33; *Symphony No. 4,* 22; *Symphony No. 5,* 52, 229; *Violin Sonatas,* 172, 205; *Violin Sonata No. 9 ("Kreutzer"),* 301; *Violin Concerto,* 219
Beijing Olympics, 325
Belafonte, Harry, 158, 333
Belfast, Ireland, 76
Bell, Joshua, 335, 336
Bellevue Stratford Hotel, 44, 165, 170
Bellini, Vincenzo, 148; *I Capuleti e I Montecchi,* 211; *Norma,* 13, 197, 318; *Il Pirata,* 238
Belzer, Richard, 16
Bemidji Symphony Orchestra (MN), 288
Ben Casey, TV show, 189
Beneath the Valley of the Dolls, film, 50
Beneath the Valley of the Ultra-Vixens, film, 50
Benjamin Award for Tranquil Music, 208
Bennett, Tony, 9
Benny Hill, TV show, 39
Bentonville, AR, 60
Beresford, Bruce, 197
Berg, Alban, 139, 193; *Lulu,* 58, *Violin Concerto,* 218; *Wozzeck,* 314
Bergamo, Italy, 245, 250, 251, 308
Bergman, Ingmar, 168
Berio, Luciano, *Concerto for Two Pianos,* 209-210
Berlin, Germany, 111, 164, 229, 359
Berlin, Irving, 45, 114
Berlioz, Hector, 2, 174
Bernhardt, Sarah, 307
Bernstein, Elmer, 181, 192
Bernstein, Leonard, 23, 104, 159, 311, 333; *Candide,* 132; *Mass,* 337, 340; *Trouble in Tahiti,* 31
Bernstein, Richard, 249-250
Betsy Ross House, Philadelphia,
Bevan, Kevin, 73
Beverly Hills, CA, 24, 45, 186, 230
Beyond Imagination, s, 221
Biava, Luis, 151, 196, 345
Big Red, RCA mobile recording studio, 88
Bijou Café, Philadelphia, 30, 35, 41
Bilgili, Burak, 307
Billboard, 145, 289
Biltmore Estate, NC, 97
Bing, Rudolf, 132
Birdland, 41, 281, 363
Birdman of Alcatraz, film, 192
Birimbau, 179
Birmingham, UK, 133
Bismarck, ND, 288
Bismarck-Mandan Symphony Orchestra (ND), 288
Biss, Jonathan, 294
Bistro St. Tropez, restaurant, 8
Bizet, Georges, 137; *Carmen,* 15, 80, 120-121, 147, 150, 208, 215-216, 224, 234, 249, 272, 296, 303; *Flower Song from Carmen,* 122; *Jeux d'Enfants,* xx; *Pearl Fishers, The,* 122
Bjorling, Jussi, 85
Black Mass, film, 13-14

Black Pearl Chamber Orchestra, 204
Blackwell, Otis, 30
Blake, Joseph, 116
Blegen, Judith, 88
Blob, The, film, 87
Blood, George, 281-282
Bloomsbury Press, 334
"Blue In Green," song, 43
Blythe, Stephanie, 173, 246-247
BMI, 43
Boathouse Row, Philadelphia, 191
Boatrite, Harold, xx, 12, 52, 73-74, 140, 241-242, 245, 282; *Harpsichord Concerto*, 241; *Oboe Concerto*, 241; *Piano Sonata*, 12
Bocelli, Andréa, 157-158, 255
Boghetti, Giuseppe, 126, 332
Bogusz, Edward, 54
Boito, Arrigo, 101, 204
Bolcom, William, 295; *Gaea*, 212
Bolling, Claude, *Suite for Flute and Jazz Piano*, 145
Bolshoi Ballet, 210
Bolton, Michael, 221
Bond, James, 22, 219
Bond, Jimmy, xx
Bono, Sonny, 28
Bookspan, Michael, 214
Bookspan, Shirley, 214
Boone, Debby, 145
Boone, Pat, 145
Booth, Davyd, 164
Bordeaux, France, 197
Borden, Judy, 111
Borge, Victor, 18
"Born Free," song, 145
Boskovsky, Willi, 48
Boston, MA, 12, 21, 53, 63, 156, 199, 222, 229, 248, 268, 305, 359
Boston Lyric Opera, 248
Boston Pops Esplanade Orchestra, 248
Boston Pops, 229
Boston Red Sox, 231
Boston Symphony Hall, 281
Boston Symphony Orchestra, 2, 104, 105, 318, 329
Botox, 294
Boulez, Pierre, 28, 314, 315
Boulez, Pierre, *Le Marteau sans maître*, 314
Bourbon Street, New Orleans, 9
Boyer, Peter, 346
Brady, Shawn, 345
Brahms, Johannes, xx, 43, 48, 74, 114, 137, 273-274, 303, 329, 333; *Clarinet Quintet*, 91; *A German Requiem*, 2, 96,
102, 26; *Piano Concertos*, 29; *Piano Concerto No. 1*, 273-274; *Piano Concerto No. 2*, 294, 328; *Six Pieces, Op. 118*, 220; *Symphonies*, 84, 186; *Symphony No. 1*, 92; *Symphony No. 2*, 22; *Violin Concerto*, 219-220
Brain Candy, column, 75, 96
"Brain Waves," song, 46
Brandenburg Ensemble, 163
Braun, Helen, 57, 59
BrAVA Philadelphia, 143, 167
Brazil, 37, 101, 135, 155, 179, 245, 246, 254
Brazil Stock Exchange, 245
Brazil, State Department, 179
Brazilian music, 173
Brazilian samba, 174
Breakers, The, Hotel, 350
Breaking the Rules, show, 225, 243
Breen, John, 57
Breslin, Herbert, 128
Brice, Percy, xx
Brightman, Sarah, 221
Brillhart, Jeffrey, 71
Brissie, Lou, 83
Bristol, PA, 282
British government, 230
Britten, Benjamin, *Midsummer Night's Dream, A*, 168; *Owen Wingrave*, 362
Broad Street, Philadelphia, 2, 36, 125, 341
Broadway, NY, 10, 11, 17, 23, 161, 169, 188, 195, 198, 199, 245, 260, 261, 264, 265, 276, 287, 312, 355
Brock, Lou, 84
Brodhead, Richard, 256-257; *Sonata Classica*, 256
Brodsky, Jascha, 163
Bronfman, Yefim, 159, 294
Bronx, NY, 113
Brookmeyer, Bobby, 26
Broomall, PA, 77
Brotherly Love, poem, 163
Brown, Angela, 251-253, 265, 287, 296, 297, 363
Brown, Anne, 199
Brown, Bruce, 207
Brown, Elaine, 2
Brown, Iona, 132-133
Brown, Joan Myers, 195, 274-276, 352, 354-356
Brown, Les, 91
Brown, Ray, 48
Brown, Ronald K., 274
Brownlee, Lawrence, 358, 362, 363
Brubeck, Dave, 15, 246
Bruckner, Anton, 227
Bruson, Renato, 166

Bryn Mawr, PA, 123, 134
Brynner, Yul, 10
Buchwald, Art, 50
Buck the Bartender, sports column, 7, 82
Budapest, Hungary, 149, 162, 229
Buffalo Bill (Cody), 24
Buffalo Philharmonic Orchestra, 103, 201, 235, 247, 281, 289, 350, 363
Buffalo, NY, 150, 247, 285, 287, 288, 328
Bulgaria, 131, 246
Bull, John, 19
Bunch, John, 26
Bunker, Larry, 180, 181, 182
Burgess, Joby, 342
Burlador de Sevilla, El (The Trickster of Seville), play, 211
Burma, 306
Burns, Robert, 150
Burnt Weeny Sandwich, album, 28
Burton, Gary, 15
Burton-Lyles, Blanche, 333-334
Bushfire Theater, 116, 355
Bushman, Sam, 77
Businger, Toni, 57, 59, 63, 69
Busoni, Ferruccio, 112, 202
Busseto, Italy, 308
Busted, book, 344
Byron, Lord George Gordon, 211
Cabbage Row, Charleston, 199
Caesar, Shirley, 17, 225
Caesar, Sid, 11
Café Society, 46
Cage, John, 116, 137
Cain, Jackie, 22
Calder, Alexander, 70
Caldwell, Sarah, 15
Callahan, John, 57-61, 63, 69
Callas, Maria, 158
Cambria Records, 347
Camden Courier-Post, 31
Camille, film, 217
Camus, Alfred, 211
Canada, 18, 114, 153, 187
Cantwell, Greg, 289
Capanna, Robert, 171; *Songs of the Ancient Mariner*, 171
Cape Town, Africa, 79
Capobianco, Tito, 78
Capra, Frank, 255
Cardiff, Col. Hugh, 24
Cardiff, Wales, 22
Carlisle, PA, 258
Carmen Jones, film, 257
Carnegie Hall, NY, 45, 127, 216, 246, 247, 329, 333
Caron, Leslie, 307
Caronia, Tony, 84

Carr, Vikki, 15
Carreras, Jose, 145
Carson, Johnny, 18
Carter, Elliott, *Piano Sonata*, 330
Cartoonists Guild, 94
Caruso, Enrico, 157, 232
Casals, Pablo, 101, 174
Cascarino, Deborah, 62, 282
Cascarino, Dolores Ferraro, xx, 31, 54, 55, 57, 58, 61, 102, 208, 209, 232, 236, 238, 281-283, 286, 288, 325, 345
Cascarino, Romeo, xxi, 31, 53-55, 57-58, 60, 62-63, 163-164, 208-209, 214, 238, 245, 281-282, 284, 287, 327, 345; *The Acadian Land*, The, 281, 282; *Bassoon Sonata*, 163-164, 282; *Blades of Grass*, 281; *Meditation and Elegy*, 281; *Pathways of Love*, 238, 282; *Prayer for Philadelphia*, 53, 71; *Portrait of Galatea*, 281, 282, 284; *Prospice*, 281, 282, 284; *Pygmalion*, 281, 284, 288; *William Penn*, xxi, 53, 55-71, 78, 88, 133, 134, 167, 208, 245, 254, 281-282, 289, 315
Cascarino, Vincenzo, 208
Casoli, xx
Cassavetes, John, 277
Castaldo, Joseph, 9; *Lachrymosa*, 9; *Viola Concerto*, 9
Castaldo, Kay Walker, 61, 319
Castelnuovo-Tedesco, Mario, 81
Castles in Spain, album, 21
Catán, Beatriz, 254
Catan, Daniel, 253-255; *Florencia en el Amazones*, 253-255; *Il Postino*, 254; *Meet John Doe*, 255; *Rappacini's Daughter*, 253
Catfish Row, Charleston, 199, 200
Cathedral of Sts. Peter and Paul, 103, 201
Catholic Church, 14, 146, 191, 340-341
CBS, 104, 193, 229
Central City Opera Orchestra, CO, 142
Central High School, Philadelphia, 191, 359
Central Park, New York, 22, 46, 123
Central Pennsylvania Youth Ballet, Carlisle, PA, 258
Century Four, 54, 62
Cerf, Bennett, 96
Chailly, Riccardo, 310
Chalifoux, Alice, 105
Chamber Orchestra of Philadelphia, 51, 63, 92, 123, 172, 196, 235, 281, 340
Chaney, Lon, 291
Chang, Sarah, 219-220, 256, 301
Chant, album, 145
Chaplin, Charles, 36, 187-188

Chapman, Keith, 191, 277
Charisse, Cyd, 17, 23, 185-186
Charles Ives Center, 332
Charles, Ray, 15
Charleston, SC, 199-200, 325
Charlie Rose show, 293
Charlie's Angels, TV show, 48
Charpentier, Gustave, *Louise, 233*
Chausson, Ernest, 140
Chautauqua Institution, 247, 342, 349
Chavez, Kirstin, 272-273
Checchia, Anthony, 13, 103, 362, 365
Cheek, John, 57, 60, 88
Cheers, TV show, 260
"Chega de Saudade," song, 15
Chekhov, Anton, 168
Cherry Hill Hospital, 16
Cherubini, Luigi, 138
Chestnut Hill, Philadelphia, 281, 289
Cheyenne Autumn, film, 108
Chicago, IL, 147, 149, 250, 305, 329
Chicago Children's Choir, 332
Chicago Lyric Opera School, 148
Chicago Lyric Opera, 169, 317, 319
Chicago Sun-Times, 50, 95
Chicago Symphony Orchestra, 32, 229, 359
Chicago, show, 260
Chilcott, Robert, 87
Chittum, Donald, 344
China, 263, 325
Chooi, Nikki, 302
Chopin, Frederic, 27, 100, 174, 230, 320, 328, 333; *Ballades,* 124, 326; *Scherzo in B-Flat Minor*, 101; *Sonata for Piano*, 273
Choral Arts Society, 60, 102, 207
Christman, Mark, 203
"Christmas Song, The," 45
Church of the Holy Trinity, Philadelphia, 103, 314
Church of the Savior, Wayne, PA, 87
Church Street, Charleston, 199
Church, CD, 225
Cincinnati, OH, 91, 222
Cincinnati Opera, 265
Cincinnati Symphony, 6, 12
Cinema Paradiso, film, 231
Cinqueterre, Italy, 345
City Council, Philadelphia, 3, 39, 77, 355
City Hall, Philadelphia, 53, 70, 77, 134
City Office of Arts and Culture, Philadelphia, 70
Civil War, 347
Clancy Brothers, 77
Clancy, Bobby, 78
Clapton, Eric, 25

Clark, Dick, 16
Clarke, Stanley, 148
Clash, band, 59
Classical Choice, 202-203
Clemente, Roberto, 84
Cleopatra, film, 108
Cleveland, OH, 362
Cleveland Institute of Music, 105
Cleveland Orchestra, 229, 303
Cleveland Plain Dealer, 95
Cleveland Pops, 303
Cleveland, James, 17, 225
Cliburn, Van, 25, 294
Clinton, Bill, 123-124, 231
Clinton, Hillary, 124
Clooney, Rosemary, 9
Close Encounters of the Third Kind, film, 184, 230
Cobb, Jimmy, 43
Cobb, Ty, 84
Cochrane, Mickey, 83
Cocteau, Jean, 139
Cody, WY, 24
Cole, Nat, 41, 45
Coleman, Cy, 22-23
Coles, Honi, 26
Color Purple, The, show, 276, 355
Coltrane, John, 21
Columbia Avenue, Philadelphia, 191
Columbia Records, 8, 9, 21, 37, 43, 99,163, 186, 187, 287
Columbia Symphony Orchestra, 186
Columbia University, 34, 244
Columbus Circle, New York, 23
Combs College of Music, 55, 57, 59, 60, 70, 102, 208
Comden, Betty, 10, 22-23, 291
Coming to America, film, 50
Comissiona, Sergiu, 14
"Comme d'habitude," song, 18
Composers and Lyricists Guild, 192
Concert for George, DVD, 179
Concertgebouw, Amsterdam, 92
Concertgebouw Orchestra, 92, 310
Concerto Soloists Chamber Orchestra of Philadelphia, 19, 51, 73, 75, 87, 88, 89, 91, 116, 123, 132, 134, 141, 171, 195, 196
Condon, Eddie, 97
Confidence Man, The, play, 13
Confucius, 139
Congressional Gold Medal, 125
Connecticut, 302, 332-334, 349
Conrad Middle School, DE, 134
Conrad, Laurie, 240, 345
Constitution Center, Philadelphia, 334
Constitution Hall, Washington, DC, 126,

331, 333
Constitutional Commissions, 337
Conte, Peter Richard, 352, 353-354
Conti, Bill, 181-182
Conversation Hall, City Hall, Philadelphia, 70, 134
Conyers, Joseph, 363
Cook, Barbara, 52
Cooke, Peggy, 54
Cooke, Todd, 54, 63
Cooper, Gary, 24, 346
Copenhagen, Denmark, 219, 320
Copland, Aaron, 48, 139, 192
Copley Square, Boston, xx
Coppelia, ballet, 323-324
Coppola, Francis Ford, 318
Cordell, LaDoris Hazzard, 347
Corella, Angel, 352, 357-58, 360
Corelli, Franco, 2, 144, 157
CoreStates Bank, 141
CoreStates Center, 157
Corigliano, John, 273; *Troubadours*, 27
Corio, Ann, 17
Cornell University, 223, 340
Cortot, Alfred, 113
Costa, Bice, 101
Costa, Don, 155
Costello, Marilyn, 105
Costello, Stephen, 316-317
Cotter, Jim, 71, 223, 280
Count Basie band, 36, 155
Couperin, François, 242
Courage of Flies, The, play, 116
Covent Garden opera house, London, 150, 197, 221, 331
Covered Wagon, The, film, 193
Cranston, Lamont, 3
"Creatively Speaking," 71, 223
Creature from the Black Lagoon, The, film, 193
Creole dialect, 297
Crescendo Music Program, 115, 327
Creston, Paul (Giuseppe Guttoveggio), 114
Crimea, 357
Crochet & Co., 93-94
Crosby Building, Paramount Pictures, 194
Crosby, David, 29
Cross, Debra Wendells, 288
Crossing, The, 313
Crownover, David, 55-56
Crumb, George, 299, 315, 317, 339
Crystal Bridges Museum of Modern Art, 60
Cuba, 156, 328
Cuban music, 173
cummings, e. e., 88
Cuneo, Andréw Miyake, 283

Cunningham Piano Company, 325-326
Cunningham pianos, 325-326
Cunningham, Merce, 109
Curcio, Maria, 357
Curtis Institute of Music, 13, 27, 76, 78, 101, 113, 124, 151, 159, 162, 171, 172, 173, 196, 198, 199, 202, 203, 211, 220, 226, 230, 256, 257, 263, 268, 270, 299, 302, 303, 317, 325, 326, 327, 329, 330, 333, 351, 356, 364
Curtis Opera Theatre, 124, 168, 173, 204, 227, 286, 294, 318, 341
Curtis Symphony Orchestra, 124, 227, 270, 271, 283, 336-337, 363
Curtis-Smith, Curtis, 295
Curtiss, Shirley, 196
Czerny, Carl, 100, 294
D'Angelo's, restaurant, 164, 201, 247
D'Indy, Vincent, 97
Da Ponte, Lorenzo, 211, 211, 218, 262
Dallas, Walter, 296-298
Daltirus, Lisa, 253
Dalto, Diane, 71
Dame aux Camelias, The, play, 218
Damn Yankees, show, 249
Damone, Vlc, 229
Damrosch, Walter, 138
Damsker, Matt, 8, 239
Dan David award, 293
Dance Magazine, 274
Dancing with The Stars, TV show, 355
Dancy, Hugh, 203
Dandridge, Dorothy, 257
Danielpour, Richard, 211, 265, 301; *Margaret Garner*, 252, 265; *River of Light*, 301
Daniels, Eddie, 277
Dankworth, Alec, 31
Dankworth, Jacqui, 31
Dankworth, Johnny, 9, 15, 31, 46
Danner, Dorothy, 209, 246
Dante and Luigi's, restaurant, 179
Dark Horse tour, 179
Darrenkamp, John, xxi
Daughters of the American Revolution, 126, 331
Davidsbund Chamber Players, 124
Davis, Dale, 38
Davis, Miles B., 164
Davis, Miles, 12, 21, 43, 97
Davis, Sammy, Jr., 247
Davison, John, xx, 282; *Bagpipe Concerto*, 19; *Mass*, xxi
Day, Doris, 229
Days, Michael, 19995, 223
De Falla, Manuel, 81

De Lancie, John, 270
De Los Angeles, Victoria, 85
De Molina, Tirso, 211
De Pasquale, Ellen, 327
De Pasquale, Joseph, 9
De Pasquale, Robert, 114, 328
De Pasquale, William, 230
De Pue, Jason, 303
De Pue, Zachary, 76, 302
De Rosa, Vincent, 48
De Schauensee, Max, 1, 7, 15, 19
De Tomasi, Beppe, 122
De Wolf, Rose, 76
Debussy, Claude, 2, 46, 97, 100, 208, 227; *Clair de lune*, 327; *La Mer*, 124; *Pelleas et Melisande*; *Preludes*, 112; *Premiere Arabesque*, 326
Deemer, Geoffrey, 241, 286
"Deep River," song, 332
Degas, Edgar, 311-312
Deibler, Sean, 60, 102
Delancey Street, Philadelphia, 91, 170
DeLarrocha, Alicia, 36
Delerue, George, 189
Delibes, Leo, *Lakme*, 221
Delius, Frederick, 45, 46, 137; *A Song Before Sunrise*, 277; *Upon Hearing the Cuckoo in Spring*, 45, 46
Delius Trust, 46
Deliverance Baptist Church, 84
Dello Joio, Norman, *Air Power*, 140
DeMaio, Don, 2, 3
Deneuve, Catherine, 189
Denmark, 127, 320
Dentella, Ebe, 251
Denver, CO, 222
Denver, John, 37
Depp, Johnny, 14
DePreist, James, 127-128
Detroit, MI, 63, 70, 95, 157, 265, 291, 315
Detroit Free Press, 95
Detroit Sting Quartet, 96
Devan, David, 318, 352, 360-362
Devon Seafood Grill, 359
Diaz, Roberto, 364
Dictionary of the English Language, 137
DiDonato, Joyce, 317
DiNardo, Marc, 29, 60, 153, 207, 213-214, 284, 287, 351
Dirty Frank's bar, xx
Disney Hall, Los Angeles, 321
Domanico, Chuck, 185
Domingo, Placido, 120, 210, 219, 254, 303
Donose, Ruxana, 211
Doran, Richard, 55, 57
Dortmund, Germany, 128, 130

Douglas, John, 342
Douglas, Kirk, 189
Dover Air Force Base, DE, 153
Down Beat magazine, 21
Dracula, 141, 193, 211
Dracula, ballet, 170-171
Dracula, book, 170
Draper, Tom, 31
Drexel University, 27, 53, 102
Driver, Robert, 70, 119, 128, 135, 151, 162, 234, 245, 252, 317
Drummer, newspaper, 2-3, 74
Duchamp, Marcel, 117
Duchin, Peter, 123
Dudamel, Gustavo, 351
Duffy, John, 107, 139
Duffy's Tavern, radio show, 137
Dumas, Alexandre, 97, 211, 217, 218,
Duncan, Todd, 199
Durante, Jimmy, 28, 145
Durbin, Deanna, 188
Dusapin, Pascal, 293
Duse, Eleonora, 307
Dussek, Jan, 140
Dutoit, Charles, 75, 164-165, 329
Dvořák, Antonin, 221; *Czech Suite*, 235; *Rusalka*, 238, 319; *Symphony No. 6*, 303; *Symphony No. 8*, 95; *Violin Concerto*, 172
Dybbuk, The, 156
Dylan, Bob, 158
E. T., film, 184, 230, 231
Eakins, Thomas, 191
Eakins, Thomas, *The Gross Clinic*, 60, 343
Early Jazz, book, 112
"Easter Parade," song, 45
Eastman School of Music, 272, 291
Eastwood, Clint, 347
Ebb, Fred, 266
Ebert, Roger, 50
Eckstine, Billy, 25
Edison, Harry (Sweets), 26
Edison, Thomas, 24
Editors, 1, 3, 7, 8, 13, 14, 16, 31, 33, 34, 49, 51, 52, 63, 73, 75, 77, 94, 95, 114, 128, 130, 153, 158, 159, 179, 198, 212, 221, 223, 238, 239-240, 293, 298, 345, 351, 351, 360, 363
Edmonds, Larry, 185
Ed Sullivan Show, 149
Egan, Babe, 347
El Sistema music program, 351
Eleanor Roosevelt Human Rights Award, 125
ELECTRICity, newspaper, 3
Electric Light Orchestra, 358

Elias, Robert, 284
Eliasen, Mikael, 198, 318
Elliman, Yvonne, 25
Ellington, Duke, 189, 199, 288
Elliott, Jack, 48-49
Elliott, Sam, 24
Elman, Mischa, 96
Elstree Studios, England, 31
EMI, record label, 84-85, 145, 219
Emmy award, 107
England, Karen, 221
English Chamber Orchestra, 246
English National Opera, 197
Ennis, Del, 83
EOS satellite, 153
Eraser, film, 261
Erickson, Clipper, 205
Erlanger Theater, Philadelphia, 10, 11
Erotic Memoirs of a Male Chauvinist Pig, film, 13
Eschenbach, Christoph, 15, 270, 326
Essen, Germany, 321
Europe, 126, 129, 130, 144, 146, 158, 162, 210, 230, 250, 267, 293, 303, 310, 316, 332, 333, 334, 340, 345, 355, 361
European Parliament, 158
Evans, Bill, 5, 21, 41-42, 43, 44, 45, 181, 227, 281
Evans, Gil, 43
Everett, Beverly, 288
Everett, Rupert, 203
Everitt, Margaret Anne, 54
"Everyone Says Don't," song, 267
Ewazen, Eric, 150
Excerpt This, album, 269
Exquisite Corpse, 338
Fain, Ferris, 83
Fairbanks, Douglas, 291
Fairfield Community Foundation, CT, 334
Fairmont Hotel, Philadelphia, 44
Fairmont Hotel, San Francisco, 45
Fairmount Park, Philadelphia, 127
Falana, Lola, 34
Falletta, JoAnn, 214, 235-236, 247, 281-287, 328, 335, 349, 350, 363
Fanfare for Fenway, 231
Fanfare magazine, 289
Fantasia, film, 216
Farlow, Tal, 41
Farrell, Eileen,26
Fauré, Gabriel, 38; *Pie Jesu* from *Requiem*, 87
Faust (Goethe), 50, 211
Faust legend, 23
Faust (Murnau film), 363
Fay, Pamela, 164, 205

Feather on the Breath of God, A, album, 146
Fellini, Federico, 310
Felton, James, 5, 8, 27, 34
Feltsman, Vladimir, 112
Fences, play, 298
Ferguson, Allyn, 48
Ferguson, Maynard, 15
Fernandez, Wilhelmenia Wiggins, 75, 303-304
Ferrante, John, 167
Festival Casals, Puerto Rico, 341
Fiddler on The Roof, film, 229
Fields, W. C., 95
Fifth Amendment, band, 38
Filipova, Elena, 131
Finck, David, 145
Finland, 127, 333
Finn, Robert, 95
Fire and Ice, CD, 219
First Baptist Church, 60
First Editions, 340
First Pennsylvania Bank, 141
First Presbyterian Church in Germantown, Philadelphia, 243, 277, 284, 327
Fischbeck, Manfred, 299-300
Fischer, Edwin, 113
Fisher, Eddie, 44
Fisher, Ellen, 114, 327
Fisher, Orpheus "King," 333
Fisher, Richard, 3
Fitzgerald, Ella, 29, 173, 225, 311
Fitzwater Street, Philadelphia, 126
"Flamenco Sketches," song, 44
Flash-mob concerts, 345
Flaubert, Gustave, 211
Fleisher Art Memorial, 245
Fleisher Collection of Orchestral Music, 13, 124, 191, 194, 280, 281, 282, 314
Fleisher, Leon, 211-212, 246, 256, 294-295, 338
Fleming, Renée, 233, 234, 236-238, 249, 250, 256, 292, 335
Flint, Mark, 315
Flintstone, Fred, 145
Florence, Italy, 166, 251, 293
Florez, Juan Diego, 173
Florida, 44, 63, 170, 203, 350
Floyd, Carlisle, *Susannah*, 233-234
Flying By Foy, 170
Flynn, Errol, 211
Focal distonia, 211, 294
Fogel, Henry, 289
Fogg, Anthony, 318
Foley stage, 349
Fonda, Jane, 24
Football Cup, 221

For Mother, ballet, 274
Forbidden Christmas, or The Doctor and the Patient, show, 247
Force of Evil, film, 189
Ford Theater, Detroit, MI, 95
Forever Amber, film, 187
Forman, Nessa, 34
Forrest Theater, 103, 222
Forrester, Maureen, 88
Fort Lauderdale, FL, 223
Foss, Lukas, 48, 172, 295
Foundation for New Music, 48
Founding Fathers, 163
Fountain of Tears, Granada, Spain, 317
Four Saints in Three Acts, opera, 199
Four Seasons Hotel, Philadelphia, 309
Fournet, Jean, 92
Fox orchestra, 186
Fox studio, 188, 229
Fox, Virgil, 15
Foxx, Jimmie, 83
France, 321
Franck, César, 2; *Violin Sonata*, 219
Franco, Francisco, 317
François, Claude, 18
Frank, Claude, 172
Frank, Jeannette Selig, 115
Frank, Pamela, 159, 172-173, 203
Frankie Bradley's, restaurant, 11
Franklin, Aretha, 36, 321, 334
Franklin, Benjamin, 163
Franklin, Joseph, 139
Frazier, Cie, 9
Freak Out, album, 28
Fred J. Cooper organ, 277
Free Library of Philadelphia, 13, 124, 256, 280
Freedom Theater, Philadelphia, 296, 355
Freeman, James, 217, 314-315, 339-340
Freiburg, Germany, 143
French lottery, 211
Freni, Mirella, 303
Fresh Ink series, 299
Friedhofer, Hugo, 189
Friends of Alec Wilder, 26
From Here To Eternity, film, 9
From Paderewski to Penderecki: The Polish Musician in Philadelphia, book, 159
Fuchs, Kenneth, 287; *American Rhapsody*, 288
Fuentes-Berain, Marcela, 254
Fugitive, The, film, 181
Fulbright Scholarship, 315
Fumo, Senator Vincent, 71, 128, 214
Fun with Dick and Jane, film, 24
Furlanetto, Ferruccio, 249
Furman, Slapsy Maxey (Max), 17
Fusaro, Carla, 122
Futral, Elizabeth, 250
Gable, Clark, 24
Gage, Ruthanne, 59
Gaines, Edward, 265
Galassini, Richard, 325
Gallagher, Jack, 287
Galway, James, 91, 145
Gamble, Oscar, 82
Gamelan Galak Tika, 305
Gandolfi, Josephine, 347
Garbo, Greta, 217
Gardner, Ed, 137
Garfield, David, 349
Garland, Judy, 44
Garner, Errol, 15, 41, 157
Garner, Cilla, 157
Garner, Margaret, 265
Garner, Robert, 265
Garrison, John, 88
Garwood, Margaret, 31, 80-81, 102-103, 208-209, 284, 343; *Flowersongs*, 208; *Joringel and the Songflower*, 208; *The Nightingale and the Rose*, 31, 208; *Rainsongs*, 208; *Rappaccini's Daughter*, 80-81, 102, 208; *Scarlet Letter, The*, 208, 209, 343-344; *Tombsongs*, 102, 208; *Trojan Women, The*, 208
Gate 5, record label, 99
Gattinella, Jessica, 359
Gedda, Nicolai, 306
Gehrig, Lou, 83
General, The, film, 291
Geneux, Vivica, 162
Geneva, Switzerland, 233
GeNIA, 342
Gensler, Howard, 203, 217
George II, 121
George V hotel, Paris, 93
George Washington High School, Philadelphia, 316
Gere, Richard, 333
Gergiev, Valery, 255, 288
Germantown Friends School, 2, 7, 243
Germantown, Philadelphia, 11, 14, 105, 121, 148, 191, 270, 277, 284, 327
Germany, 50, 51, 92, 105, 111, 124, 128, 130, 140, 146, 147, 190, 214, 219, 273, 275, 309, 321, 325, 363
Gershwin estate, 200
Gershwin, George, 75, 97, 141, 155-157, 159, 187, 198-200, 202, 208, 227, 267, 325; *An American in Paris*, 156, *Cuban Overture*, 156, "*I Got Rhythm*" *Variations*, 156, 182, 200; *Porgy and*

Bess, 156, 198-200, 296-298, 319, 325; *Rhapsody in Blue*, 156, 159, 297, 320-321; "Summertime," 189
Gershwin, Ira, 52, 103, 138, 156, 200, 201
Gerstley, Henry, 55, 60
Getz, Stan, 26, 29, 89
Gewandhaus Orchestra, 310
Ghost, film, 109
Ghostbusters, film, 192
Giacchino, Michael, 346-347
Giargiari Voice Competition, 75
Gideon's Crossing, TV show, 349
Gieseking, Walter, 84
Gigli, Beniamino, 157
Gigliotti, Mark, 363
Gilbert and Sullivan, 246
Gilels, Emil, 295
Gilfry, Rod, 265
Gillespie, Dizzy, 25, 26, 29, 45, 48, 363
Gilligan's Island, TV show, 229
Gilroy, Jim (Rainbow), 62
Gimbels department store, 9
Ginastera, Alfredo, *Piano Concerto*, 245
Giordani, Marcello, 167
Giordano, Umberto, *Andréa Chenier*, 144
Girard Academic Music Program (GAMP), xx, 133, 257
Girard Avenue, Philadelphia, 191
Girard College, Philadelphia, 141
Girasole, restaurant, 122, 191
Girls High School, 105
Giulini, Carlo Maria, 32
Glass, Philip, 88, 139-140; *Beauty and the Beast*, 139; *Koyaanisquatsi*, 139; *T. S. E.*, 139
Glavin, Kevin, 201-202, 246, 247, 249, 250
Glen Campbell, 15
Glenmede Trust, 56
Glenn, Annie, 213-214
Glenn, John, 213-214
Glennie, Dame Evelyn, 149-150, 226, 287
Glenn Miller's Air Force Band, 89
Glickman, Sylvia, 146-147
Gliere, Reinhold, *Symphony No, 3, Ilya Murometz*, 147
Glimmerglass Opera, 256
Glinka, Mikhail, 216
"God Bless America," song, 28, 45
Goddard Space Center, 153
Godfather, The, film, 194
Godowsky, Leopold, 202
Godspell, show, 244
Goerke, Christine, 255-256
Goethe, Johann Wolfgang von, 50, 249
Goldenthal, Elliot, 273
Goldfinger, film, 22

Goldoni, Carlo, 211
Goldsmith, Jerry, 108, 180, 183, 192, 193
Goldstein, Stan, 31, 32
Goldwyn, Ron, 73
Golijov, Osvaldo, 251, 317-318; *Ainadamar*, 251, 317-318; *La Pasion Segun San Marcos*, 340
Gonzales, Justin, 257
Goode, Richard, 101, 112-113, 174
Goodman, Benny, 45, 47, 227
Goody, Sam, 3
Goodyear, Stewart, 294
Gordon, Ricky Ian, *A Coffin in Egypt*, 362
Gordon, Ronni, 268
Gore, Al, 123
Gore, Tipper, 123
Gorme, Eydie, 48
"Gospel Train," spiritual, 126
"Gossiping," song, 344
Gothic Voices, 146
Gould, Glenn, 202, 245
Gould, Morton, 190
Gounod, Charles, *Faust*, 2, 249, *Romeo and Juliet*, 317, *Soldier's Chorus* from *Faust*, 2
Goya, Francisco, 95
Gozzi, Carlo, *Turandot, Princess of China*, 111
Grabey, Jerry, 15
Graffman, Gary, 124, 159, 211-212, 246, 270-271, 294, 321, 327, 329, 330
Graham, Billy, 78
Graham, Martha, 109
Graham, Susan, 250, 292
Grainger, Percy, 45
Grammy awards, 209, 289, 320, 321
Gramophone, magazine, 131, 139, 157, 313
Granada, Spain, 82, 318
Granados, Enrique, 140
Grand Canyon, 125
Grappelly, Stephane, 41, 47
Graves, Denyce, 120-121, 150-151, 157, 161-162, 209, 224-226, 234, 243, 265, 273, 296, 332, 333, 334, 342
"Great Balls Of Fire," song, 30
"Green Dolphin Street," song, 41, 281
Green, Adolph, 10, 11, 22-24
Green, Mayor Bill, 55, 57, 63, 291,
Greenfield auditions, 196
Gregory, André, 153
Grendel, opera, 273, 319
Grendel's Lair, 39
Grey, Al, 155
Grieg, Edvard, 21; *March of the Dwarfs*, 2
Grierson, Ralph, 103
Griffith, Nanci, 123

Grimaud, Hélène, 273-274
Grisman, David, 47
Grolnic, Sidney, 12-13; *Kyrie*, 245; *Rhapsody*, 12
Gross Clinic, The, 60, 343
Grossman, Robert, 231
Ground Zero, 217
Group Motion Dance Company, 299
Grove Dictionary of American Music, 96
Grove Dictionary of Music, 51, 96, 114
Grove Dictionary of Opera, 114
Grove, Dick, 48
Grove, Lefty, 83
Gruber, Sari, 249
Guarneri String Quartet, 303
Guggenheim Fellowship, 208
Guimarães, Leila, 128
Guinn, John, 95
Gullah dialect, 199, 296, 297
Gullah people, 199, 200
Gunn, Nathan, 364

Guttoveggio, Giuseppe (Paul Creston), 114
Gwynn, Peggy, 53
Gyllenhaal, Maggie, 203
Gypsy, show, 11
Haas Gravagno, Carole, 134, 351
Haas, Dorothy, 54-56, 58, 63, 69, 70, 134
Haas, Dr. F. Otto, 54, 134
Hagen, Daron, 211, 295
Hahn, Hilary, 159
Haifa, Israel, 197
Haines, Howard, 102
"Halfway There," 269
Hamletto, 19
Hammer, Beer Week, 345
Hammer Pictures, 183
Hancock, Herbie, 320-321
Handel, George Frederic, 88, 123, 137, 168; *Ariodante*, 103, 197; *Hallelujah* chorus, 121; *Israel in Egypt*, 301; *Messiah*, 122, 243; *Roman Vespers*, 88-89
Handley, Tim, 285-289
Hanff, Hélène, 93
Hardy, Oliver, 291
Harlem, New York, 156
Harler, Alan, 340-341, 346
Harnoncourt, Nikolaus, 211, 218
Harrer, Maggie, 109-110
Harris, Rennie, 295
Harris, Roy, 140, 166
Harrisburg, PA, 77
Harrison, Don, 34
Harrison, George, 179
Harrison, Lou, 178

Harrison, Olivia, 179
Harry Potter, film, 229
Hart, Gene, 149
Hart, Maria, 97, 148
Hartford, CT, xx, 349
Harvard University, 314
Hasselblad, camera, 14, 62, 89
Hausse, Dominic, 346
Haverford College, xx
Haverford School, 209
Hawthorne, Nathaniel, 80-81, 207-208, 344
Haydn, Franz Joseph, 15, 114, 140, 171, 230, 340; *Horn Concerto in D*, 51; *Piano Concerto in D*, 196
Hayes, David, 163, 277
Hayes, Roland, 126
Hazard, Robert and the Heroes, 75
Heifetz, Jascha, 156
Helena Symphony, 314
Hemingway, Ernest, 184
Henry IV, play, 307
Henry V, play, 307
Henze, Hans Werner, 139; *Elegy for Young Lovers*, 362
Hepburn, Audrey, 104
Herbig, Gunther, 95
Hench, Zachary, 258-260
Heritage: Civilization for the Jews, 107
Herman, Woody, 45, 91, 189
Herreid, Priscilla Smith, 313-314
Herrera, Odubel, 239
Herrmann, Bernard, 190, 194; *Psycho*, 92
Hersch, Fred, 320
Heymann, Klaus, 130-131, 281
Heyward, Dorothy, 199
Heyward, DuBose, 198-200
Hickory House, New York, 320
Higdon, Jennifer, 327, 329-330; *Cold Mountain*, 364; *Concerto 4-3*, 77; *Piano Concerto*, 329; *Fanfare for Jamestown*, 287; *Violin Concerto*, 329
High Diving Horse, 149
Hildegard Chamber Players, 146
Hildegard Publishing Company, 147
Hildegard von Bingen, 145-147
Hildegarde, 46
Hilton Hotel, Dortmund, Germany, 128-129
Hindemith, Paul, 338
Hinderas, Natalie, 270
Hines, Earl, 25
Hines, Gregory, 48
Hinsey, Dorothy, xx
Hinsey, Ellen, 274
Hinsey, Norman, xx
Hip H-opera, 361

380

Hirlinger, Alma, 244
Hirlinger, Clellan, 244
Hirlinger, Doug, 243, 244
Hitchcock, Alfred, 188-189
Hitchins, Martha, 283
Hobbs, Patricia, 297
Hoenig, Larry, 243
Hoersch, Ray, 13-14
Hoffman, Daniel, 163
Hoffman, Jay, 245, 253, 289
Hofmann, Josef, 159, 270
Hoiby, Lee, *A Month in the Country*, 342
Hole In The Wall Gang Camp, 302
Holiday in Rome, album, 21
Holiday, Billie, 236
Hollinger, Michael, 263-264
Hollywood Boulevard, Los Angeles, 187
Hollywood Bowl, 261, 329
Hollywood Flute, The, CD, 187
Hollywood Golden Classics, album, 145
Hollywood Hotel, film, 45
Hollywood, xx, 28, 37, 46, 48, 80, 108, 139, 141, 155, 180, 185. 187, 189, 190, 193, 197, 229, 230, 347
Holosevsky, James, 285, 287
Honegger, Arthur, 97
Hong Kong, 281
Hope, Bob, 17
Hopkins, Anthony, 94
Hopkins, Linda, 11
Horn, Paul, 178
Horne, Marilyn, 15, 119, 257-258
Horner, James, 184
Horowitz, Regina, 342
Horowitz, Vladimir, 35, 342
Horse and Groom club, London, 343
Horszowski, Mieczyslaw, 27, 100-102, 113
Hotel Dorchester, London, 32
House of Frankenstein, film, 193
House, TV show, 349
Houseman, John, 189, 190
Houston Grand Opera, xxi, 141, 200, 234, 254
Houston Hall, University of Pennsylvania, 202
How to Enjoy Your Bagpipe, 19
How to Succeed in Business Without Really Trying, show, 44
How to Write Your Own Gilbert and Sullivan Opera, 19, 89
Howard, Jason, 161
Humperdinck, Engelbert, *Hansel and Gretel*, 133, 216
Hubble spacecraft, 214
Humphrey, Percy, 9-10
Humphrey, Willie, 9
Hungary, 138, 162, 256
Hunt, J. Ray, 76
Huntingdon Avenue, Boston, 12
Hurok, Sol, 333
Hutchins, Keisha, 243-244
Hysteria, film, 203
"I Got Rhythm," song, 156, 188, 202, 268
"I Have A Dream" speech, 334
I Love Paris, album, 21
I Really Should Be Practicing, book, 271
"I've Got Your Number," song, 11
Ibert, Jacques, 38, 81
Ickes, Harold, 331
Ihde, James, 170
Il Gallo Nero, restaurant, 122
Imperial Court, Japan, 125
In Darkest Africa, 19
Incredible Shrinking Man, The, film, 193
Independence Mall, 352
India, 100, 141, 179
Indian Treaty, 53
Indiana Jones, films, 135, 229
Indiana University, 336
Indianapolis Symphony, 77, 302
Institute for Journalism in New Media, 365
Intermission, 289
International Opera Awards, 364
International Tribune, 93
Internet, 198, 326, 336
Into the Woods, show, 261
Iovino, Franco, 122
Iran, 335-336
Iron Curtain, 130
Irving Street, West Philadelphia, xx
Isbin, Sharon, 217, 364
Israel, 112, 197, 293
Israel Philharmonic, 242-243, 293
Istomin, Eugene, 101
"It Ain't Necessarily So," song, 199, 200
It Wasn't All Velvet, book, 45
"It's Legitimate!," song, 10
Ithica, NY, 223
Ives, Charles, 15, 332
Jackson, Janet, 145, 181
Jackson, Mahalia, 229, 268
Jackson, Michael, 192, 217
Jackson, Millie, 52
Jackson, Milt (Bags), 29
Jacob, Heidi, *Fantasy for Piano*, 256
Jacquet, Illinois, 15, 236
Jaffe, Allan, 9-10
Jaffe, Ben, 10
"Jalousie," song, 47
James Brown Project at the Apollo Theater, 355
Janacek, *The Cunning Little Vixen*, 54, 342
Japan, 104, 114, 153, 164, 177, 184, 193,

Jarin, Kenneth, 123
Jarre, Maurice, 189, 193
Jaws, film, 229
JazzTimes, magazine, 155
Jefferson Hospital, 271
Jenkins, Speight, 254
Jennings, Sandra, 359
Jerusalem, Israel, 300, 317
Jesus Christ Superstar, show, 25
Jewish cantorial music, 156, 317
JFK Stadium, 59
Jimmy the Greek, 186
JoAnn Falletta International Guitar Competition, 288
Jobim, Antonio Carlos, 15, 155
Jochum. Eugen, 92
Joe Sixpack, 77, 307
Johns, Jasper, 117
Johnson, James, 345
Johnson, Jeri Lynne, 196, 203-204, 241-242
Johnson, Samuel, 34, 137
Jolson, Al, 22, 44, 198
Jones, James Earl, 50
Jones, Jo, 26

Jones, Margie, 29, 47, 56, 69, 93, 164, 182, 183, 194, 282
Jones, Norah, 219
Jones, Quincy, 158, 333
Jones, Tom, 28
Jongen, Joseph, *Symphonie Concertante*, 354
Joplin, Scott, 12, 114
Josefowicz, Leila, 159, 162-163
Journey, The, CD, 294
Joyce Theater, NY, 355
Joyce, James, 170
Judiciary Square, Washington, DC, 123
Juilliard 415, Baroque group, 314
Juilliard School of Music, 13, 78, 97, 104, 166, 203, 213, 229, 230, 236, 304, 314, 335
Juilliard String Quartet, 217
Juneau Dance Theatre, 260
Juntwait, Margaret, 292
Jurassic Park, films, 229
Jurassic World, film, 348
Jurowski, Vladimir, 295
Justin, Gloria, 284
Kahn, Louis, 294
Kahn, Nathaniel, 294
Kaiser, Roy, 170, 224, 258, 323
Kallend, Jennifer, 364
Kallir, Lillian, 172
Kalodner, John David, 8

Kamancheh, Persian instrument, 336
Kander, John, 260
Kansas City Prime, 154
Kaplan, Gabriel, 21
Kardon Institute, 115-116
Karlowicz, Mieczyslaw, 140
Karpov, Anatoly, 91
Kassia, 146
Katz, Harry Jay, 3, 11
Katz, Lewis, 364
Kayser, Alan, 203
Keaton, Buster, 36, 291
Kellaway, Roger, 185
Kellogg, Paul, 256
Kelly, Ed, 62
Kelly, Gene, xix, 9, 23, 185-186, 358
Kendall, Nicolas, 76, 302
Kennedy Center honors, 293
Kennedy Center, Washington, DC, 334, 337, 341
Kennedy, John F., 138
Kennett Symphony, 363
Kenton, Stan, 91, 178
Kentucky, 265, 266, 303
Kern, Jerome, 114, 145, 189, 208, 267, 320
Kernis, Aaron, Color Wheel, 337; Musica Celestis, 235
Kesselman, Jeremy, 288
Keswick Theater, Glenside, 344
Keys, Alicia, 219
Keystone State Boychoir, 351
Khan, Chaka, 145
Khaner, Jeffrey, 256, 268, 269
Kiev, Ukraine, 342
Kim. David, 327
Kind of Blue, album, 43-44
King and I, The, show, 10
King, Dr. Martin Luther, 334
King, Pee Wee, 123
King's Singers, 87
Kirchner, Leon, 294
Kiss of the Spider Woman, show, 261
Kitt, Eartha, 169
Klauber, Bruce, 3, 39
Kleiber, Carlos, 166, 248
Klein, Richard, 38
Knight, Rebecca, 221
Knight-Ridder, 95
Kodaly, Zoltan, 139
Koenemann, Martha, 224
Kohler, William, 54-55
Kohn, Blanche Wolf, 115
Koljonen, Elissa Lee, 336
Konitz, Lee, 39
Konstanty, Jim, 83
Kool Jazz Festival, 26, 89

Korn, Michael, 54, 61, 79-80, 87, 88, 103, 163
Korngold, Erich Wolfgang, *Suite for left hand and strings,* 294
Kosovo, 165
Krajewski, Michael, 320
Kral, Roy, 22, 26
Kraus, Alfredo, 148
Kreisler, Fritz, 156, 202
Kremer, Gidon, 218
Kreutzer, Rodolphe, 301
Krumpholtz, Johann Baptist, 140
Krupa, Gene, 5, 45
Krzywicki, Jan, 151-152, 299, 338; *Tuba Concerto,* 151-152, *Concerto bucolico,* 338; *In Evening's Shadow,* 338
Krzywicki, Paul, 151-152, 159
Kuala Lumpur, Malaysia, 272
Kubalek, Antonin, 114
Kubrick, Stanley, 108
Kuerti, Anton, 101
Kunde, Gregory, 147-148
"La Bohème," song, 30
La Casa del Giò, Bergamo, Italy, 251
La Fenice opera house, Venice, 151, 182
La Fura Dels Baus, art troupe, 293
La Plata, Argentina, 318
La Scala opera house, Milan, 110, 122, 130, 144, 148, 233, 262, 307, 308, 309, 310
LaBelle, Patti, 11, 225-226
Labeque, Katia, 210
Labeque, Marielle, 210
Laderman, Ezra, 163
Lady from Philadelphia, The, 25, 125
Lady Gaga, 217-268, 330, 362
Lahr, Bert, 48
Laila Wallace/Reader's Digest Foundation, 107
Laine, Cleo, 9, 15, 31-32
Lake George Opera, 342
Laker, Barbara, 344
Lanchbery, John, 170
Landon, H. C. Robbins, 89
Lang Concert Hall, Swarthmore College, 88
Lang, Lang, 159, 202, 230-221, 271, 320-321, 329
Lang Lang International Music Foundation, 321
Lansing, Sherry, 194
Lansdowne Symphony, 363
Lanza, Mario, 161
Laredo, Jaime, 163
Larkins, Ellis, 26
Las Vegas, NV, 179, 284
Last Of Sheila, film, 193

Late Quartet, A, film, 264
Latin Casino, NJ, 16, 34, 79, 344
Laura, film score, 187, 189, 190
"Laura," song, 155, 189
Laurel, Stan, 291
Law and Order, TV show, 16
Lawrence, Carol, 71
Lawrence, Cynthia, 232
Lawrence, Steve, 48
Lawrenceville, NJ, 16
Lear, Norman, 333
Led Zeppelin, 125
Legrand Jazz, album, 21
Legrand, Christiane, 87
Legrand, Michel, 21, 41, 87, 158, 311, 344
Legrand, Raymond, 21
Leipzig, Germany, 310
Lekeu, Guillaume, 140
Lenfest, H. F., "Gerry," 364, 365
Lenfest, Marguerite, 364
Lenni-Lenape Indians, 53
Leon. Kenny, 265-266
Leonard, Isabel, 364
Leonard piano, 2
Leoncavallo, Ruggero, *Pagliacci,* 122, 309
Leone, Frank, 284, 286
Leonhardt, Gustav, 92
Leschetitsky, Theodor, 100, 294
Levant, Gail, 348
Levant, Oscar, 188
Levine, James, 50, 89, 105, 132, 173, 256, 316
Levit, Ben, 204-205
Lhevinne, Rosina, 229
Liberace, 96, 152
Liberia, 297
Library of Congress, 190, 194
Library of Congress National Film Preservation Board, 192
Licad, Cecile, 101
Licklider, Debi, 206, 345
Life, magazine, 104
Lifeboat, film, 188
Ligeti, György, 340, *Lux Aeterna,* 108
"Like a Virgin," song, 268
Lili, film, 307
Lima, Luis, 121, 234
Lime Rock racetrack, 2
Lin, Jenny C. C. (Chia Ching), 116
Lincoln Center, New York, 293, 337
Lincoln High School, Philadelphia, 35
Lincoln Memorial, 125-126, 331, 334
Lincoln, Abraham, 94, 332
Lindbergh, Charles, 126
Lindsay, Bob, 7
Lion King, The, show, 276, 355
Lipkin, Seymour, 101

Liszt, Franz, 11, 48, 170, 202, 321, 328
Little Me, show, 11
Liu, Meng-Chieh, 202
Liuzzi, Don, 185, 363
Live From the Met, 292
Lloyd Webber, Andrew, 24
Lloyd, Harold, 291
Locatelli, Giò, 251
Locatelli, Leonardo, 251
Locatelli, Orso, 251
Lockhart, Keith, 231, 248
Lockheed Martin, 153, 213
Locust Rendezvous, bar, 62
Lofton, David Antony, 144
Lombard, Alain, 225
London Philharmonic, 295
London Symphony Orchestra, 114, 230, 335
London, England, 6, 9, 18, 25, 31, 53, 89, 114, 121, 124, 132, 149, 164, 179, 203, 216, 218, 221, 254, 267, 285, 311, 329, 343, 357
"Lonely Teardrops," song, 16
Long Island, New York, 194, 229, 276
Long Island University, 355
Longwood Gardens, 353
Lorca, Federico Garcia, 317
Lord of the Rings, film, 219
Loren, Sophia, 168, 181
Lorenz, Lee, 94
Lorenzo, Riolama, 224, 312
Lortie, Louis, 294
Los Angeles, CA, 48, 120, 158, 162, 177, 254, 255, 273, 315, 317, 329
Los Angeles Chamber Orchestra, 190
Los Angeles Opera, 120 197, 254, 255
Los Angeles Philharmonic, 29, 321
Lost In Space, TV show, 229
Louis XIV, 355
"Love Me Tender," song, 30
Lower East Side, New York, 156
Lower Merion Symphony, 363
Lucas, George, 229, 231
Luciano Pavarotti International Voice Competition, 54, 119, 121, 122, 128, 129, 130, 161, 231
Ludwig, David, 299-300 *Lamentations*, 299-300
Ludwig, Michael, 288, 363
Ludwig, Rachael Mathey, 363
Luigi Cherubini Orchestra, 251
"Lullaby of Birdland," song, 11
Lully, Jean-Baptiste, 140
Lumpy Gravy, album, 29
"Lush Life," song, 89
Lustgarten, Edgar, 185-186
Lustgarten, Kathleen, 185-186
Lutoslawski, Witold, 303
Luvisi, Lee, 202
Luzi, Frank, 364
Lyle, Michael, 348-349
Lynch, Lester, 297
Lynch, Maureen, 57
Lyon, France, 321
Lyric Fest, 314
Lyric Opera of Chicago, 148, 170, 253, 317, 319
*M*A*S*H*, TV show, 178
Ma, Yo-Yo, 123, 217, 231, 305, 335
Mabel Pew Myrin Trust, 88
MacArthur Fellowship, 317
Macatsoris, Christofer, 57, 60, 61, 78, 143, 144, 167, 204, 209, 284, 306-307
Machaut, Guillaume de, *Messe de Notre Dame*, 340
Mack, Connie, 83
Macy's, 345, 353-354, 360
Macy's Parade Studio, 354
Madonna, 93, 145, 268
Madrid, Spain, 224-225, 358
Maggio Musicale, Florence, Italy, 251, 293
Magiera, Leone, 119, 231-232
Magnificent Seven, The, film, 192
Magritte, Rene, 145
Mahler Chamber Orchestra, 329
Mahler, Gustav, 138, 140, 227; *Symphony No. 3*, 15, 288; *Symphony No. 6*, 125; *Symphony No. 8*, 288; *Symphony No. 9*, 133
Main Line Symphony, 363
Main Point, Bryn Mawr, 36
Maine, 282
Makem, Tommy, 77
Makris, Cynthia, 143
Malle, Louis, 168
Man With The Golden Arm, The, film, 192
Mancini, Ginny, 194
Mancini, Henry, 48, 180, 184, 189, 194, 229
Maneus, Brazil, 254
Maneval, Philip, 339
Mangel, Curt, 354
Manhattan Transfer, 16
Manhattan, NY, 93, 112, 126, 149, 293
Mann Center for the Performing Arts (Mann Music Center until 1998), 15, 25, 74, 75, 76, 89, 127, 184, 190, 214, 229, 231, 248, 260, 261, 302, 320, 347
Mann, Herbie, 21
Manne, Shelly, 180
Mannes College of Music, 41, 277
Mansfield, Jayne, 205
Mantua, Italy, 197

Maori songs, 311
Marabella, Angelo, 122
Marabella's, restaurant, 122
Marc, Alessandra, 111
Marceau, Marcel, 16
Marcello, Benedetto, 92
March of Dimes Achievement in Radio, 223
Marian Anderson Award, 332
Marian Anderson Award in Philadelphia, 333
Marian Anderson Day, 127
Marian Anderson Historical Residence and Museum,
Marian Anderson Historical Society, 333
Marian Anderson Library, U. of Pennsylvania, 25
Marian Anderson Place, 332
Marian Anderson postage stamp, 333
Marian Anderson Sickle Cell Anemia Care and Research Center, 125
Mariinsky Theater, St. Petersburg, 216, 249, 288
Mario Lanza Competition, 144
Mario Lanza Museum, 161
Mark of Zorro, The, film, 291
Marlboro Music Festival, Vermont, 13, 103, 105, 174
Marlborough racetrack, 2
Marriner, Molly, 94
Marriner, Neville, 92, 93, 132
Marschner, Heinrich, *Der Vampyr*, 141
Marsalis, Wynton, 333
Marsh, Robert, 95
Marshall Street, Philadelphia, 191
Martin, John,
Martin Street, Philadelphia, 333
Martin, Tony, 17
Martins, João Carlos, 245-246
Martins' Passion, film, 245
Martinů, Bohuslav, 48, 164
Marx Brothers, 36
Marx, Chico, 44
Maryland, 153
Mascagni, Pietro, 138; *Cavalleria Rusticana*, 18
Massachusetts Insitute of Technology (MIT), 305; Massenet, Jules, 307; *Cendrillon*, 307; *Hérodiade*, 307; *La Navarraise*, 307; *Manon*, 306-307; *Thais*, 238, 307, *Werther*, 157, 198
Mathis, Edith, 92
Matsukawa, Daniel, 283, 338
Maw, Nicholas, *Sophie's Choice*, 221
May, Billy, 155, 177
Mays, Willie, 83
McAnany, Tony, 145

McBride, Christian, xx
McCarthyism, 234
McCarver, Tim, 82
McCutcheon, Lauren, 351
McDonald, Harl, 187
McDonald's, 180
McDonnell, Timothy, 245, 286
McDonough, Dugg, 166
McDowell, Kevin, 207
McFerrin, Bobby, 127
McFerrin, Robert, 127
McGill, Anthony, 231
McKenna, Larry, 344
McKibbon, Al, xx
McKinney, Frank, 97
McKinney, Jack, 76
McLaine, Shirley, 11, 16
McLaughlin, William, 55, 63
McMillan, Sir Ernest, 18
McNair, Sylvia, 145, 267, 334
McPartland, Marian, 26
McPhee, Colin, 305-306; *Tabuh-Tabuhan*, 305
McQueen, Steve, 87
McRae, Carmen, 45
"Me and Mrs. Jones," song, 28
Meat Loaf, 52, 241
Medical Center, TV show, 189
Mediterranean Festival, 158
"Meet Me in No Special Place," song, 36
Meet the Composer Foundation, 107, 139
Mehta, Mervon, 179, 242, 277, 280, 293
Mehta, Zubin, 29, 104, 220, 242, 250, 251, 293, 304
Mel Tormé and Friends, 45
Melville, Herman, 13
Mencken, H. L., 138
Mendelssohn Club of Philadelphia, 141, 340-341, 346
Mendelssohn, Fanny, 146
Mendelssohn, Felix, 27, 133, 140, 146, 335
Mendelssohn, unpubished Piano Concerto, 27
Mennin (Mennini), Peter, 114
Menotti, Gian-Carlo, 139, 159
Menuhin, Hepzibah, 47
Menuhin, Yehudi, 47
Mercer, Johnny, 155, 189
Mercer, Mabel, 26
Mercury, record label, 305
Merriam Theater, 36, 103, 222,
Merrill, Robert, 85, 143, 167
Merry Wives of Windsor, The, play, 307
Met, Philadelphia, 208
Metropolitan Museum of Art, New York, 113

Metropolitan Opera auditions, 111, 272
Metropolitan Opera, 1, 50, 57, 58, 63, 103, 123, 125, 127, 132, 149, 156, 173, 174, 196, 199, 200, 205, 210, 211, 232, 233, 234, 246, 249, 252, 253, 255, 256, 267, 272, 288, 292, 297, 307, 309, 310, 316, 318, 319, 320, 333, 337, 341
Metropolitan Opera orchestra, 12
Mexico City, 253
Meyer, Norma, 302
Meyer, Ranaan, 76, 302-303
Meyer, Russ, 50
Meyerbeer, Giacomo, 92
MGM, 193
Miami, FL, 104, 246, 315, 329
Michelangeli, Arturo Benedetti, 84
Michigan Opera Theatre, 315
Middle East, 145, 293
Middleman, Karl, 305, 338
Midler, Bette, 11
Midori, 104
Migenes-Johnson, Julia, 58
Mighty Clouds of Joy, The, 17, 225
Milan, Italy, 100, 110, 122, 308, 309, 310
Milanov, Rossen, 204, 349
Miles Ahead, album, 43
Milhaud, Darius, 166, 227
Miller, Ann, 17
Miller, Danny, 214
Miller, Henry, 200-201
Miller, Lisa, 364
Miller, Mitch, 9
Million-Dollar Infield, 82
Mills Brothers, 48
Mills, Mary, 233-234
Milnes, Sherrill, 57, 143
Milstein, Nathan, 137
Milton Keynes, England, 31
Mimi, album, 268
Minneapolis/St. Paul, MN, 222
Minnelli, Vincente, 189
Miracoiou, Nelly, 197
Misfits, The, film, 108
Miss America, 261
Mission Impossible, TV show, 178
Mission, The, film, 231
"Misty," song,
Mitchell, Charles, 7
Mitchell, Danlee, 99-100
Modell, Frank, 179
Modern Jazz Quartet, 29
Modern Times, film, 188
Modesto, CA, 194
Moffo, Anna, 306
Moiseyev Dance Company, 210
Montclair, NJ, 22

Montero, Gabriela, 231
Monteverdi, Claudio, *Coronation of Poppea, The*, 173
Montoya, Carlos, 32
Montreal, Canada, 148
Montreal Opera, 134
Montreaux, Switzerland, 321
Monty Python, TV show, 109
Moore, Jack, 363
Moore, Melba, 36
Morales, Ricardo, 338, 350
Morales, Victoria, 338
Moran, Robert, 141; *Dracula Diary, 141; Requiem, 141*
Morges, Switzerland, 187
Moross, Jerome, 194
Morricone, Ennio, 193, 231
Morris Arboretum, 55, 134
Morris, James, 57, 167, 317
Morrison, Jack, 73, 75, 223, 241
Morris, Jay Hunter, 364
Morrison, Toni, 252, 265-266
Moscow, Russia, 171, 216, 339, 357
Most Happy Fella, The, show, 244
Mostovoy, Marc, 38, 51, 54, 55, 60, 70, 75, 89-90, 92, 116, 123, 134, 154, 171, 191, 196, 203, 231, 243, 282, 284, 301
Moszkowski, Moritz, 320
Mothers of Invention, 28, 145
Mount Airy, Philadelphia, 45, 196, 359
Mouskouri, Nana, 158
Movies on Tape, book, 49
Mozart Effect, The, book, 263, 325
Mozart on the Square, 116
Mozart, Wolfgang Amadeus, 8, 15, 25, 27, 48, 90, 91, 100, 112, 114, 116, 123, 140, 150, 151, 161, 162, 171, 174, 196, 202, 203, 211-211, 227, 230, 237, 238, 242, 250, 262-263, 267, 271, 272, 316, 319, 340; *La Clemenza de Tito*, 318; *Clarinet Concerto*, 91, 350; *Clarinet Quintet*, 92; "Come Scoglio," 256; *Cosi fan tutte*, 218, 256; 262; *Don Giovanni*, 110, 173, 211-211; 262, 283; "Dove sono," 38; *Horn Concerto No. 2*, 51; *Magic Flute, The*, 109, 135, 196, 292, 299, 319; *Marriage of Figaro, The*, 161, 204-205, 238, 262, 272-273, 311; *Piano Concertos*, 46, 295; *Piano Concerto No. 9*, 90, 196; *Piano Concerto No. 15*, 116; *Piano Concerto No. 24*, 235; *Rondo*, 51; *Sinfonia Concertante*, 163
Mueller, Otto-Werner, 172
Mühlfeld, Richard, 91

Muller, Edoardo, 119
Mulligan, Gerry, 26, 45, 89
Mummers parade, 74,
Mummy, The, film, 193
Munch, Charles, 2, 281
Munsel, Patrice, 143
Murder, She Wrote, TV series, 186
"Murmuring Zephyr," song, 105
Murnau, F. W., 363
Murphy, Eddie, 50
Murphy, Heidi Grant, 340
Musial, Stan, 83
Music from The Fleisher Collection, radio show, 314
Music Group, 207
Music Man, The, show, 52
Musical Fund Society Career Advancement Award, 316
"Muskrat Ramble," song, 10
Musso and Frank's, LA, 187
Mussorgsky, Modeste, *Boris Godounov*, 162; *Pictures at an Exhibition*, 326
Muti, Cristina, 93
Muti, Riccardo, 36, 84, 93, 95, 107, 122, 144, 148, 150, 166, 182, 251, 309, 310, 316, 337, 359
My Architect, documentary film, 294
"My Country, 'Tis Of Thee," 334
My Dinner With André, film, 153
My Left Foot, film, 192
"My Man's Gone Now," song, 25
My Musical Life, 327
My Musical Life Mastermind, 327
"My Soul Is Anchored in the Lord," spiritual, 126
"My Time Is Your Time," song, 44
"My Way," song, 18
Naidoff, Stephanie, 71
Nally, Donald, 313
Naples, Italy, 310, 315
Napoleon, 138
NASA, 153, 213, 214
Nash, Graham, 29
National Building Museum, Washington, DC, 123
National Mall, DC, 331
National Register of Historic Places, 141
National Symphony, Washington, DC, 105, 172, 329, 340
Natrona Street, Philadelphia, 191
Naxos Records, 130-131, 247, 253, 281, 284, 340, 347
Nazareth, Israel, 293
Nazis, 193, 229, 334
NBC, 331, 349
NBC Burbank Studios, 349
NBC Studio 8-H, 48

NBC Symphony, 185-186
Neenan, Matt, 258, 358
Negro spirituals, 78, 125, 199, 304, 331, 333
Neill, Hallie Hawthorne, 208
Neill, Stuart, 144, 154
Nelson, Nels, 39, 63, 74, 114, 183
Nemeth, Jane, 128
Nero, Peter, 46, 71, 80, 87, 154, 159, 195, 213-214, 302, 319-320
Netherlands Bach Ensemble, 93
Netrebko, Anna, 211, 249, 292
Network for New Music, 256, 294, 299, 337-339, 363
Neuringer, Martha, 223
Neuwirth, Bebe, 260-261
New American Orchestra, The, 48
New England Conservatory, 12
New Grove Dictionary of Music and Musicians, 114, 198
New Guinea, 91, 183
New Jersey, 16, 22, 173, 214, 344, 349
New Locust Theater, Philadelphia, 23, 30
New Mexico, 74, 272
New Orleans, Louisiana, 9-10, 12
New Paltz, NY, 112
New School, 89
New World Symphony, 104
New York City Ballet, 216, 311
New York Mets, 107
New York Philharmonic, 104, 126, 293, 333
New York Pick-Up Ensemble, 216
New York State Council on the Arts, 107
New York Times stylebook, 52, 241
New York Times, 15, 52, 241, 247, 252, 361
New Yorker magazine, 17, 63, 94, 179, 227, 347
Newman, Alfred, 186, 187, 229
Newman, David, 347
Newman, Paul, 302
Newman, Randy, 184
Newman, Thomas, 347
Newton Howard, James, 181
Nézet-Séguin, Yannick, 351-352
NHK Orchestra, 273
Niagara Falls, NY, 216
Nice, France, 89
Nicholson, Jack, 16
Nierow, Bernie, 320
Night of 1,000 Nanas, 158
Nilsson, Birgit, 89, 111
Nimoy, Leonard, 183
Nixon, Marni, 38
Nolen, Terrence J. 263
Nonesuch Records, 27, 100, 101, 305

Norfolk, VA, 288
Norman, Jessye, 334
Norristown, PA, 208
North Carolina, 97, 323
North Dakota, 288
North Philadelphia, 296, 342
North, Alex, 108-109, 180, 193
North, Harry, 108-109
Northeast Philadelphia, 148, 316
Norvo, Red, 47-48
Norway, 10, 51
"Notes From Philadelphia," radio show, 270
"Now Is The Time," radio show, Nugent, Ted, 17, 37
Nutter, Lisa, 355
Nutter, Mayor Michael, 77, 345
NYU film school, 193
O'Brien, Conan, 349
O'Connor, Donald, 23
O'Dowd, Joey, 75
O'Hara, John, 157
Obama, President Barack, 231, 334
Oberlin College, 243, 263
Ochoa, Arantxa, 224, 258, 312, 323, 324, 352, 359-360
Odgon, John, 27, 31
Off-Broadway, 264
Offenbach, Jacques, *Ba-Ta-Clan*, 15; *Grand Duchess of Gerolstein*, 246-247; *La Perichole*, 209; *Tales of Hoffman*, 122
Ogden, food vendor, 77
Ogerman, Claus, 155
Ohio, 265, 267
Oistrakh, David, 301
"Ol' Man River," song, 89
Oliver, Timothy, 325
Omaha, NE, 24
On the Set, book, 49
On the Twentieth Century, show, 22
Opening Tap, 345
Operaman, 132
Opera Babes, 221
Opera Company of Philadelphia Competition, 122
Opera Delaware, 342
Opera Ebony, 59, 78
Opera News, 361
Opera on the Mall, 360-361
Opera Pacific, 315
Opera Philadelphia (previously Opera Company of Philadelphia), 54, 58, 60, 62, 70, 75, 80, 103, 110, 119, 121, 128, 129, 131, 134, 135, 143, 149, 151, 161, 162, 164, 165, 168, 169, 173, 195, 196, 198, 200, 209, 211, 217, 231, 233-235, 245, 246, 249-253, 265, 272, 283, 286, 296-298, 307, 315-316, 317, 318, 319, 341, 342, 345, 352, 358, 360-361, 364
Opera Quiz, 1
Opus, play, 263-264
Orchestra 2001, 105, 217, 256, 281, 314-315, 339-340
Orchestra Filarmonica della Scala, 310
Orchestra of St. Luke's, 236
Orchestra Symphonica Giuseppe Verdi, 310
Orchestra, The (later The New American Orchestra), 48
Oregon, 31, 63, 122, 223, 333
Orlando, Danielle, 119
Ormandy, Eugene, 2, 164, 281, 333
Ormandy Room, Academy of Music, 35
Orphans of the Opera, play, 13
Orpheus Award, 208
Orquestra Sinfónico de Chile, 288
Osaka, Japan, 104
Osborne, Donny, 45
Oscars, *see* Academy Awards
Oshiro-Morales, Amy, 350
Other Side of the Rainbow, book, 44
Ott, Jarrett, 364
Ouija board, 5
"Over The Rainbow," song, 317
Overbrook, Philadelphia, 191
Owens, Eric, 196-197, 273, 317, 318-319, 334, 342, 345, 352, 358-359
Oxford University, 345
PA Public Utililty Commission, 77
Pachelbel, Johann, 123
Packard Building, Philadelphia, 141
Paganini, Niccolo, *24 Caprices*, 104, 303
Painter, Temple, xx, 12, 88, 241-242
Paisiello, Giovanni, *Barber of Seville, The* 71
Palestine, 293
Palestra, 8
Palumbo, Frank, 44
Palumbo, Kippie, 44
Palumbo's, 44
Panama Street, Philadelphia, 55
Panassié, Hugues, 97
Pannonica de Koenigswarter, Baroness Kathleen (Nica), 363
Pantano, Andy, 35
Paoli, PA, 87
Papua, New Guinea, 91
Paradise Theater, Detroit, MI, 95
Paramount Archive, 194-194, 346
Paramount Pictures, 50, 194, 346
Parc, restaurant, 356
Parente, Joseph, 283, 289
Paris Conservatoire, 21, 273

Paris, France, 21, 32, 81, 93, 97, 156, 158, 164, 211, 216, 218, 233, 267, 288, 301, 303
Parker, Charlie, 89, 358, 362-363
Parker, Lisa DiNardo, 37, 44, 59, 63, 71, 185, 271, 295
Parker, Ruth, 56-57
Parrish, Maxfield, 191
Pärt, Arvo, 273
Partch, Harry, 178; *Revelation in the Courthouse Park*, 99-100
Parton, Dolly, 181
Party with Comden and Green, A, show, 23
Pascal, Blaise, 82
Pasternak, Amy, 344, 354
Pasternak, Jill, 344
Pasticceria Donizetti, Bergamo, Italy, 250
Paul, Billy, 28
Pavarotti Competition, *see* Luciano Pavarotti International Voice Competition
Pavarotti, Alice, 232
Pavarotti, Luciano, xix, 25, 32, 35, 103, 110, 119, 121, 122, 127, 128-130, 144, 157, 161, 201, 231-232, 92, 309
Pawley, John, 49
PBS, 50, 73, 107, 152, 157, 225, 255, 292
Peabody Institute, Baltimore, 294
Peace Day Philly, 351
"Peacocks, The," song, 29
Pearl Harbor, 107, 213
Peck, Gregory, 333
Peggy Gilbert and Her All-Girl Band, film, 194
Peiffer, Bernard, 11
Pen and Pencil Club, 73, 267
Pen and Pencil softball team, 76
Penn, Admiral William, 345
Penn, Gulielma, 53-55
Penn, William, 53-54, 345; *Prayer for Philadelphia*, 53
Pennsylvania Academy of Fine Arts
Pennsylvania Ballet, 170, 195, 224, 258, 311, 323, 352, 357, 364
Pennsylvania Composers Forum, 124
Pennsylvania Opera Theater, 80, 109, 132
People Paper, 74
Peraza, Armando, xx
Perehia, Murray, 101, 159,
Perelman Building, Philadelphia Museum of Art, 343361, 362, 363
Perelman Theater, Kimmel Center, 195, 214, 220, 222, 226, 251, 267, 295, 299, 302, 318, 320, 321
Perez, Ailyn, 255, 316, 317
Perlman, Itzhak, 41, 145,
Perry, Zenobia Powell, *Piano works*, 347;

Tawawa House, 194, 347
Persian music, 335
Persichetti, Vincent, 13, 87-88, 97, 166; *Flower Songs*, 87; *Symphony No. 5*, 32; *Symphonies*, 114; *Sybil, The*, 132
Pesco Sansonesco, Abruzzo, Italy, xx
Peter Gunn, TV show, 184, 229
Peterson, Oscar, 145
Petri, Michala, 38
Pew Charitable Trusts, 222
Pew Foundation, 56, 63, 107, 222, 362
Phantom of the Opera, The, film, 291
Philadanco, 195, 274-276, 352, 354-356
Philadanco Way, Philadelphia, 195
Philadelphia 76ers, 222
Philadelphia Athletics (A's), 83
Philadelphia Board of Education, 105
Philadelphia Chamber Music Society, 103, 195, 317, 338, 339, 362, 364, 365
Philadelphia Civic Center, 62, 70-71
Philadelphia Classical Symphony, 305, 338
Philadelphia College of Art, 99
Philadelphia Daily News, 8, 34, 39, 52, 63, 70, 73, 74, 75, 76, 77, 82, 95, 113, 116, 128, 155, 183, 195, 203, 205, 210, 212, 217, 220, 222, 223, 239, 240, 241, 242, 340, 351, 359, 364, 365
Philadelphia Daily News headline writers, 344
Philadelphia Daily News softball team, 75-76
Philadelphia Dance Company, *see* Philadanco
Philadelphia Eagles, 222, 356
Philadelphia Evening Bulletin, 1, 5, 6, 7, 8, 14, 15, 16, 23, 31, 33, 38, 52, 54, 59, 73, 74, 80, 239
Philadelphia Flyers, 28, 149, 222
Philadelphia Grand Opera Company, 2
Philadelphia Inquirer, 15, 19, 33, 52, 63, 73, 74, 195, 287, 351, 365
Philadelphia Lyric Opera Company, 2
Philadelphia, magazine, 13, 345
Philadelphia Media Network, 365
Philadelphia Museum of Art, 60, 116, 191, 215
Philadelphia Music Alliance Walk of Fame, 125
Philadelphia Music Project, 107, 116, 313, 340
Philadelphia Musical Academy, 105
Philadelphia Orchestra Constitutional Commissions, 337
Philadelphia Orchestra Greenfield auditions, 196

Philadelphia Orchestra, 2, 8, 9, 13, 15, 25, 26, 33, 37, 81, 82, 62, 75, 76, 77, 84, 89, 90, 92, 93, 103, 105, 114, 133, 142, 149, 151, 152, 159, 163, 164, 166, 183, 184, 187, 188, 195, 196, 199, 200, 205, 210, 212, 214, 222, 229, 236, 249, 260, 261, 268, 269, 269, 270, 271, 281, 283, 286, 288, 295, 302, 303, 304, 321, 325, 326, 327, 329, 331, 335, 337, 338, 340, 347, 349, 350, 351, 354, 359, 363
Philadelphia Philharmonia, 281
Philadelphia Phillies, 82, 222, 256, 258, 347, 356,
Philadelphia Singers, 54, 60, 63, 79, 80, 87, 88, 163, 243, 277, 289, 362
Philadelphia Sinfonia, 314, 354, 363
Philadelphia Woodwind Quintet, 8, 26, 164
Philadelphia Youth Orchestra, 141, 191, 196, 277, 363
Philips Records, 21, 84, 162
Phillips, Edna, 105
Philly Beer Week, 77, 345, 346
Philly Pops, 46, 71, 80, 87, 91, 159, 195, 302, 319-320, 364
Phish, band, 302
Phoenixville, PA, 87
Phonolog, 43
Piacenza, Italy, 251
Pianezzola, Antonella, 165-166, 210
Piano4, 302
Piazzolla, Astor, 317
Picasso, Pablo, *Guernica*, 109
Piccadilly, London, 89
Picker, Tobias, *An American Tragedy*, 272
Piffaro, 313
Pilot, Ann Hobson, 104-105
Pinchot, Governor Gifford, 331
Pink Floyd, 47, 93
Pinza, Claudia, 201
Pinza, Ezio, 211
Piston (Pistone), Walter, 114; *Fantasy*, 105
Pittsburgh, PA, 201, 222
Pittsburgh Symphony, 14, 15, 45, 201, 229, 329
Pittsinger, David, 211
Pizzetti, Ildebrando, 101
Placido Domingo Competition, 197
Playboy, 94
Play On, Philly!, 351, 364
Planet of The Apes, film, 178
Platt, Larry, 345
Point Breeze, Philadelphia, 355
Poitier, Sidney, 333
Poitrine, Belle, 11

Poland, 6, 174
Polish National Anthem, 159
Politics, Aristotle, 138
Polo Lounge, Beverly Hills, CA, 24
Ponce, Manuel, 81
Ponchielli, *La Gioconda,* 19
Ponti, Carlo, 168
Pool, Jeannie, 187, 192, 194, 255, 346-347
Pope Pius X, 27, 101
Poplar Street, Philadelphia, 208
Porcaro, Joe, 181, 185, 349
Porcaro, Steve, 349
Porgy, book and play, 198-199
Port of History Museum, 62, 63
Porter, Andrew, 63
Porter, Cole, 38, 97, 177, 189, 267
Portland, OR, 31, 122
Portland Opera Chorus, 122
Portland State University Chorus, 208
Portland State University Orchestra, 208
Poulenc, Francis, *Dialogues of the Carmelites*, 362
Powell, Bud, 41, 46, 157
Powelton Village, Philadelphia, xxi
Prado, Luis, 211
Prague, Czechoslovakia, 110, 149, 211
Prayer for Philadelphia, 53
Preminger, Otto, 189
Preservation Hall Jazz Band, 9-10
Presidential Medal of Freedom, 125
Presley, Elvis, 99, 179
Preston, Billy, 179
Previn, André, 22, 31, 124, 145, 268, 311; *A Streetcar Named Desire*, 238
Prévost, Abbé, 306
Price, Leontyne, 25, 200, 225, 252, 293, 334
Prima Donna, album, 161
Primary Stages company, 264
Primavera Fund, 142
Primavera, Joseph, 142, 191, 277
Prince Albert, 146
Prince Charles, 311
Prince of Philadelphia, The, 89
Prince Theater, 222
Princess Diana, 311
Prizzi's Honor, film, 108
Prokofiev, Gabriel, 342-343, *Violin Concerto,* 343
Prokofiev, Oleg, 342
Prokofiev, Sergei, 112, 140, 230, 288, 301, 310, 335, 342; *Piano Concerto No. 2,* 329; *Piano Concerto No. 4,* 211; *Romeo and Juliet*, 258; *War and Peace,* 211; *Violin Sonata No. 2,* 301
Prokofiev, Sviatoslav, 342

Proms, 343
Pucci-Catena, Marco, 172
Puccini, Giacomo, 25, 148, 208, 231, 250, 296, 310, 319; *La Bohème*, 84, 121, 122-123, 128, 144, 157, 234, 240, 249, 292, 303, 317; *Gianni Schicchi*, 108; *Il Tabarro*, 71; *Il Trittico*, 71, *Madama Butterfly*, 13, 209, 297, 337; *Manon Lescaut*, 230; *Suor Angelica*, 233; *Tosca*, 132, 134-135, 165, 169, 210, 248, 255, 303; *Turandot*, 110-112
Puccini arias, "Che gelida manina," 234; "Nessun dorma," 25, 110; "Recondita armonia," 25; "Un bel di," 221
Puerto Rico, 341
Pulitzer Prize, 329, 344
Purcell, *Dido and Aeneas*, 75
Pushkin, Aleksandr, 131, 211, 262
Puts, Kevin, *Silent Night*, 251
Quakers, 53, 61, 331
Queen Elizabeth II, 89
Queen Victoria, 146
Queen Village, Philadelphia, 148
Quintette of the Hot Club of Paris, 57
QVC, 209
Racette, Patricia, 150, 233-234
Rachmaninoff, Sergei, 156, 202, 270; *Piano Concerto No. 2*, 329; *Piano Concerto No. 3*, 116, 329; *Piano Concerto No. 4*, 84; *Piano Sonatas*, 27, 273; *Rhapsody on a Theme of Paganini*, 303; *Vocalise*, 38
Rader-Shieber, Chas, 168
Radocchia, Emilio, xx
Raim, Cynthia, 7, 12, 101
Rainmaker, The, film, 192
Raisin in the Sun, A, play, 265
Raksin, Alex, 280
Raksin, David, 155, 187-191, 192, 194, 347; *Circus Polka* (Stravinsky), 188; *Concertino for clarinet and strings*, 188; *Oedipus Memnitai*, 190; *Redeemer, The*, 191; *A Song After Sundown*, 191, 277-280; *Swing Low, Sweet Clarinet*, 191, 277
Raksin, Tina, 280
Ramallah, Palestine, 293
Ramey, Samuel, 249-250
Rampal, Jean-Pierre, 91, 92, 101, 145
Rands, Bernard, 338
Ranjbaran, Behzad, 287, 335-337; *Elegy*, 335; *Persian Trilogy*, 335; *Saratoga*, 335; *Songs of Eternity*, 335; *Violin Concerto*, 335-337
Raphel, André, 154, 288
Rattle, Simon, 33, 190, 221, 302

Raub, Richard, 144, 207, 344
Ravel, Maurice, xx, 2, 100, 208, 227, 329; *Bolero*, 13, 358; *Daphnis et Chloe*, 2, 268; *Introduction and Allegro*, 105; *L'Enfant et les Sortilèges*, 93, 341; *Mother Goose Suite*, xx, 210; *Piano Concerto in G*, 84; *Piano Concerto in D*, 211, 270; *Sheherazade*, 267
RCA 44BX microphone, xxi
RCA Records, 88, 141, 161, 200, 320
Reading Terminal Market, 38, 55, 332, 345, 360
Red Back Book, The, album, 12
Red, White and Cole, 38
Redeemer, The, film score, 191
Reed, Eric, 320
Reger, Max, 96
Reggio Emilia, Italy, 165
Regional Performing Arts Center (RPAC), 195
Reich, Steve, 88, 305
Reichert, Linda, 299, 337
Reinhardt, Django, 47
Reinhardt, Max, 111
Renaissance music, 146, 313-314
Rendell, Ed, 70, 128
Rendell, Mrs. Edward (Midge), 70
Respighi, Ottorino, 310; *Church Windows*, 287
"Return to Sender," song, 30
Revaux, Jacques, 18
Reynolds-Brown, Blondell, 355
Rich, Buddy, 5, 15, 26
Richards, Celeste, 185
Richards, Emil, xx, 155, 177-187, 346-349
Richter, Sviatoslav, 112
Ricordi, Giulio, 110
Riddle, Nelson, 9, 155, 311
Rieu, André, 152, 169-170
Rifkin, Joshua, 79
Rimsky-Korsakov, Nicolai, *Sheherazade*, 335, 336-337
Ripley's (club), 47
Rittenhouse Square, Philadelphia, 56, 70, 101, 159
Ritz-Carlton hotel, 209
Rizzo, Frank, 3
Roach, Max, 41, 46
Roberts, Robin, 83
Robertson, Christopher, 172
Robeson, Paul, 199
Robin Hood Dell, 15, 17, 25, 127,
Robinson, Big Jim, 9
Rock and Roll Revue, 16
Rock Hall, Temple University, 226
Rodescu, Julian, 164
Rodgers, Bill, 8, 166

Rodrigo, Joaquin, *Concierto de Aranjuez*, 25
Rogers, W. P., 127
Rolfing, 294
Romberg, Sigmund, "Drinking Song" from *The Student Prince*, 346
Rome, Italy, 88, 310
Romeo and Juliet, ballet, 258-260, 357
Ronald McDonald, 180
Rooney, Mickey, 17
Roosevelt Hotel, Los Angeles, 84
Roosevelt, Eleanor, 126, 331
Root, Frank, 13
Rorem, Ned, 96, 124, 138, 139, 159, 226-228; *Miss Julie*, 226-227; *Piano Concerto No. 4*, 124, 211
Rosand, Aaron, 327
Rose Tattoo, The, play and film, 108
Rose, Nelson, 11
Rosenbach Museum, 170
Rosenman, Leonard, 183
Rosenshein, Neil, 234
Ross, Alex, 347
Ross, Katherine, 24
Rossini, Giacchino, 78, 148, 202, 250, 358; *Armida*, 238; *Barber of Seville, The*, 71, 161, 261, 337; *La Cenerentola*, 162; *Italian Girl in Algiers, The*, 173-174
Rostropovich, Mstislav, 171
Rósza, Miklós, 138
Rota, Nina, 193-194
Rota, Nino, 159, 193 *La Strada*, 310
Roussel, Albert, 81, 101; *Evocations*, 93
Rovaris, Anna, 245
Rovaris, Corrado, 245, 250-251, 253, 261-262, 308-309, 361, 364
Rovaris, Marta, 245
Rowles, Jimmy, 29
Royal Ballet, London, 312
Royal College of Music, London, 18
Royal Opera House, London, 221
Rubinstein, Arthur, 32, 270
Rubinstein, John, 32, 182
Ruderman, Wendy, 344
Ruggles, Carl, 103
Running Press, 49
Runyon, Damon, 75
Russell, Anna, 18-19, 89
Russell, Don, 77, 345-346
Russia, 78, 79, 112, 46, 149, 156, 168, 171, 187, 215, 216, 225, 249, 255, 288, 295, 339-340, 342, 356-357
Ruth, Babe, 291
Sadie, Stanley, 95, 198
Saint-Saëns, Camille, 27, 100, 164; *Carnival of the Animals*, 166; *Piano Concerto No. 2*, 32; *Samson and Delilah*, 150; *Violin Sonata*, 219
Salieri, Antonio, 262-263
Salter, Hans, 193
Salzburg, Austria, 127, 249, 267, 316
Salzburg Festival, 334
San Diego, CA, 99, 195, 253
San Francisco, CA, 18, 45, 105, 183, 191, 216, 294
San Francisco Ballet, 258, 259-260
San Francisco Chronicle, 33
San Francisco Opera, 120, 121, 149, 233, 234, 319
San Francisco Symphony, 103
Santa Fe Chamber Music Festival, 191, 277
Santa Fe Opera, 103, 234, 364
Santa Monica, CA, 180
Santana, 59, 219
Santiago, Chile, 288
São Paolo, Brazil, 135, 245
Sarasota, FL, 222
Saratoga Festival, 229, 328, 335
Saratoga, NY, 165
Sardinia, 362
Sardou, Victorien, 307
Sargent, Sir Malcolm, 89
Sargis, Alexander, 5
Sataloff, Dr. Joseph, 49
Sataloff, Dr. Robert, 49, 60, 167
Saturday Night Live, TV show, 132
Saturen, David, 127
Saturn rocket, 153
Saumur, France, 345
Sawallisch, Wolfgang, 103, 232, 268
Scaglione, Louis, 363
Scarlatti, Domenico, *Piano Sonatas*, 329
Schenk, Otto, 50-51
Schickele, Peter, 8, 88, 166-167, 216-217
Schifrin, Lalo, 48, 193
Schiller, Friedrich von, *Turandot, Prinzessin von China*, play, 111-112
Schindler's List, film, 181, 229, 230
Schmidt, John, 57
Schnabel, Artur, 113, 172, 262, 294-295, 357
Schneider, Helen, 30
Schnyder, Daniel, *Charlie Parker's Yardbird*, 362-363
Schoenbach, Sol, 55, 58, 63, 70, 163-164
Schoenberg, Arnold, 114, 140, 188, 230; *Pierrot Lunaire*, 9
Schola Nova, 245
School of American Ballet, 258
Schreker, Franz, 193
Schubert, Franz, 91, 138, 140, 202, 294, 328, 333; *Ave Maria*, 126, 331; *Octet*,

227; Songs, 78; *Waltzes,* 91; *Wanderer Fantasy,* 220
Schuller, Gunther, 12, 190, 295; *Horn Concerto,* 12
Schuman, Bill, 316
Schuman, Patricia, 211, 253-254
Schumann, Clara, 273
Schumann, Robert, 1, 27, 91, 100, 112, 114, 273, 274, 333
Schwartz, Ed, 39
Schwartz, Lucia M., 162
Schwarzkopf, Elisabeth, 151, 236
Scivias (Know the Ways), book, 146
Scorsese, Martin, 192
Scott, Tom, 179
Scotto, Renata, 166, 233
Scrap Arts percussion ensemble, 243
Scriabin, Alexander, *Etude,* 11
Scuncio, Marc, 35
Seattle Opera, 246, 254
Seattle, WA, 222
Sebastian, John, 37
Sebastian (Sebastiani) John, 37
Secret Life of Walter Mitty, film, 189
Secret Service, 123
See Hear, Kimmel Center series, 301
Seerey, Pat, 83
Segal, David, 141-142
Segal, George, 24
Segal, Peter, 338
Segal, Rachel, 142
Segovia, Andrés, 32, 35, 35-36, 81-82, 91
Selvin, Rick, 75, 76, 94, 96, 241
Semenchuk, Ekaterina, 215-216
Separate Tables, film, 189
Septee, Moe, 35
Sequentia, 146
Serkin, Peter, 101, 159
Serkin, Rudolf, 113, 174, 270
Serly, Tibor, 256
Sesame Street, 13
Settlement 100, 270, 303
Settlement Music School, 89, 115, 144, 148, 164, 171, 196, 244, 263, 270, 303-304
Seven Years in Tibet, film, 178, 184
Shaffer, Peter, 262
Shaham, Gil, 217, 231
Shaham, Rinat, 197-198
Shakespeare, William, 8, 9, 168, 204, 307, 308; *Merchant of Venice, The,* 102
Shank, Bud, 48
Shankar, Anoushka, 179
Shankar, Ravi, 179
Shannon Airport, Ireland, 78
Shapp, Richard, 282
Shaw, George Bernard, 96, 211

Shaw, Robert, 15
Shawmont Middle School, Philadelphia, 134
Shawn, Wallace, 153
Shawn, William, 179-180
"She's Having My Baby," song, 18
Shearing, Ellie, 46
Shearing, George, xx, 11, 15, 41, 45, 46, 80, 177
Shepard, Alan, 213
Shepard, Thomas Z., 287
Sherr, Sara, 345
Shibe Park, 2, 82-84
Shin, Dongon, 253
Shipley School, Bryn Mawr, PA, 134
Shirley-Quirk, John, 57
Shoot the Piano Player, film, 189
Show Boat, club, 41
Shropshire, England, 83
Shubert (now Merriam) Theater, 36
Sibelius, Jan, 90, 96127, 333
Sierra Leone, 199, 297
Sierra, Roberto, *Missa Latina: Pro Pace,* 340-341
Silent Running, film, 167
Silk Road Project, 305
Sills, Beverly, 15, 292
Silvers, Phil, 10
Silverstein, Barbara, 109, 132
Silvestre, Henri, violin, 205
Simmons, Al, 83
Simon, Paul, 47, 305
Simonic, Tim, 347
Simpson, Joy, 78-79
Simpson, Marietta, 79
Sims, Sylvia, 46
Sims, Zoot, 26, 45
Sinatra, Frank, 8-9, 18, 89, 155, 157, 173, 177, 179
"Sing, Sing, Sing," song, 45
Singer, Lou, 46
Singer, Samuel, 15, 19
Singin' in The Rain, film, 23, 291
Singing City, 2, 53, 71
Singing Simpson Family, 78
Sitting Bull, 24
Sixteen Concerto Soloists, 196
Skip Barber Racing Schools, 2
Skrowaczewski, Stanislaw, 211-212
Slack, Karen, 296-297
Slatkin, Leonard, 15, 231
Slaughter on Tenth Avenue, ballet, 353
Slonimsky, Elektra, 194
Slonimsky, Nicolas, 194
Smallens, Alexander, 199, 200
Smalls, Samuel, 199
Smetana, Bedrich, *Bartered Bride, The,*

Smith, Bessie, 1
Smith, Elena (Nellie), 314
Smith, Ellen, 116
Smith, Grace, 105
Smith, Jacqueline, 314
Smith, Kate, 28
Smith, Kile, 13, 124-125, 191, 194, 280, 281; *Hymn and Fugue No. 2*, 124; *Vespers*, 313-314
Smith, Lloyd, 164, 205
Smith, Martina, 314
Smith, Mike, 155
Smith, Priscilla, 314
Smith, Sue, 115-116
"Smoke Gets in Your Eyes," song, 189
Snoopy, 104
Snyder, Tom, 24
Society for the Preservation of Film Music, 92, 189
Society of Composers and Lyricists, 189, 192-194
Sokoloff, Eleanor, 256
Sokoloff, Vladimir, 13
Sokolovic, Ana, *Svabda (A Wedding)*,
Sokolsky, Bob, 9, 14, 21, 34, 239
Solow, Jeffrey, 304
Solzhenitsyn Reader: New and Essential Writings, The, 298
Solzhenitsyn, Aleksandr, 170, 298, 356
Solzhenitsyn, Ignat, 171, 196, 235, 243, 271-272, 298-299, 352, 356-357
"Someone To Watch Over Me," song, 156
"Sometimes I Feel Like A Motherless Child," spiritual, 79
Sondheim, Stephen, 193, 261, 267
Sony, record label, 43-44, 104, 221
Sony Studios, 347
"Sophisticated Lady," song, 189
Sopranos, The, TV show, 204
Soul Food, film, 261
Sound of Freedom, The: Marian Anderson, the Lincoln Memorial, and the Concert That Awakened America, book, 334
South Broad Street, Philadelphia, 2, 125,
South Carolina, 199-200, 233, 297
South Pacific, show,
South Philadelphia, 44, 179, 208, 282, 303, 331
South Philadelphia High School for Girls, 105, 127, 333
South Street, Philadelphia, 39, 47
Souther, David, 145
Southwark, Philadelphia, 115
Soviero, Diana, 134-135
Spain, 191, 258, 318, 358
Spanish Civil War, 80, 317
Spano, Robert, 247, 318
Spartacus, film, 108
Spectrum, 28, 37, 128, 130, 152
Speedy, film, 291
Spielberg, Steven, 184, 190, 229, 230, 231, 348
Spikol, Art, 13
Spirituals, 78, 125199, 304, 331, 333
Spoleto Festival, Charleston, SC, 103
Spontini, Gaspare, *La Vestale*, 150
Spring for Music, 247
Spruce Street, Philadelphia, 62, 143, 210
St. Christopher's Hospital for Children, 125
St. Clements Church, 353
St. Francis de Sales church, 351
St. Louis, MO, 12, 150, 153
St, Louis Symphony, 283
St. Paul, MN, 222
St. Paul Chamber Orchestra, 89
St. Peter Street, New Orleans, 9-10
St. Petersburg, Russia, 171, 216, 225, 249, 288
St. Rita of Cascia Church, Philadelphia, 303
Stacy, Jess, 45
Stadler, Anton, 92
Stairmaster, 327
Stairs, Michael, 88, 280,
Stalberg, Zack, 75, 128, 212, 205-206
Standish, Miles, 344
Stanislavski method, 200
Stanley, Jessica, 3, 22, 23, 32, 35-36, 49, 63, 94, 309
Star Trek, film, 111, 180, 183
Star Trek 4, film, 183
Star Trek-Into Darkness, film, 347
Star Wars, film, 114,180, 229, 230, 231
Starr, Val, 134
State University of New York, New Paltz, 112
Steel Pier, Atlantic City, 149
Steiger, Rod, 16
Stein, Gertrude, 199
Steinway piano, xx, 117, 159, 270, 280, 320, 325, 326
Steinway Rhapsody piano, 159
Stern, Isaac, 97
Stevens, Connie, 17
Stevens, David, 93
Stevenson, Ben, 170
Stewart, Slam, 48
Still, William Grant, *Ennenga*, 105
Stillman, David, 268
Stillman, Mimi, 256, 268-269
Stoker, Bram, 170

Stokes, Leo (Leopold Stokowski), 89
Stokes, Sheridan, 186
Stokowski, Leopold, 6, 89, 156, 187, 188, 199, 333, 354
Stolzman, Richard, 91
Stony Brook, NY, 187
Storyville Club, Boston, xx
Stout, Gordon, 26
Strange Death of Adolf Hitler, The, film, 193
Stratas, Teresa, 58
Strauss, Johann, Jr., 91, 152, 170; *Die Fledermaus,* 202, 256; *On The Beautiful Blue Danube,* 108, 152; *Waltzes,* 48, 170, 248
Strauss, Richard, 138, 143, 211-211, 237, 319; *Ariadne auf Naxos,* 251, 272; *Also Sprach Zarathustra,* 108; *Der Rosenkavalier,* 272; *Die Frau ohne Schatten,* 255-256; *Ein Heldenleben,* 12; *Elektra,* 256; *Four Last Songs,* 249; *Salomé,* 143
Stravinsky, Igor, 43, 81, 89, 137, 138, 156, 186, 230, 294, 305, 329, 335, 338, 363; *Apollo,* 187; *Circus Polka,* 187; *The Fairy's Kiss, The,* 187; *Firebird, The,* 224; *Les Noces,* 187; *Orpheus,* 187; *Petrouchka,* 186; *Rake's Progress, The,* 151; *Rite of Spring, The,* 101, 337; *Le Rossignol,* 341; *Soldier's Tale, The,* 164; *Symphony in C,* 259; *Symphony of Psalms,* 102; *Three Movements from Petrouchka,* 32
Strawbridge & Clothier department store, 71
Street, Mayor John, 70
Streetcar Named Desire, A, play and film, 108
Strunk (William, Jr.) and White (E. B.), *The Elements of Style,* 239
Studio 8-H, RCA, 48
Style books, 52, 241
Suddenly, film, 189
Sugar Babies, show, 17
Sugarland Express, film, 229
Sullivan, Margaret, 127
"Summertime," song, 189, 296
Sundance Institute, 189
Sung, Hugh, 283, 325-327
Super Bowl, 174, 309
Superman, film, 229
Suzuki method, 114-115, 327
Swan Lake, ballet, 216, 258, 311-312, 357
Swarowsky, Hans, 90
Swarthmore College, 88, 166, 315, 339
Sweden, 2
Swedish Ballet, 97

Sweelinck, Jan, 92
Sweet Charity, show, 260
Sweet Honey in the Rock, 332
Sweet Smell of Success, film, 192
Swenson, Ruth Ann, 167
Swenson, Swen, 11
Swingle Singers, 87
Switzerland, 187, 275, 321, 362
"'S Wonderful," song, 156
Sybil of the Rhine, 146
Symphony Hall, Boston, 2,
Symphony Hall, Detroit, MI, 95
Symphony in C, Camden, New Jersey, 349, 363
Szeryng, Henryk, 132
Szigeti, Joseph, 101
Tabuteau, Marcel, 90
"Tainted Justice," 344
Taiwan, 116, 202
Take Six, 123, 225
"Take The A Train," song, 349
Take The Music Home, column, 117
Takemitsu, Toru, 193
Takiff, Jonathan, 74, 114
Tanglewood Festival, 104, 231, 248, 318
Tattle, Daily News column, 203, 217
Tatum, Art, 80, 157
Tawawa House, opera, 194, 347
Taylor, James, 231
Taymor, Julie, 273
Tchaikovsky, Peter, 15, 138, 216, 335; *Eugene Onegin,* 131; *Nutcracker, The,* 216, 324, 352, 359-360; *Piano Concerto No. 1,* 25, 329; *Sleeping Beauty,* 216; *Swan Lake,* 216, 258, 359
Tcherepnin, Alexander, *Harmonica Concerto,* 37
Te Kanawa, Dame Kiri, 145, 249, 311
Teacher, Buzz, 49
Teacher, Larry, 49
Teatro Royale, Madrid, 225
Tebaldi, Renata, 2
Tehran, Iran, 335
Tellez, Gabriel, 211
Temple University, 15, 78, 89, 151, 196, 222, 226, 256, 270, 314, 317, 341, 363
Temple University Baptist Temple, 342
Temple University Choirs, 340, 341, 345, 346
Temple University Music Festival, Ambler, 14
Temple University Opera Theater, 15, 168, 173, 341, 362
Temple University Symphony Orchestra, 151, 196, 342, 345, 363

Ten Commandments, The, film, 192
Tennessee, 234
"Tennessee Waltz," song, 123
Tenniel, John, 95
Terfel, Bryn, 250
Terra satellite, 153
Tetro, film, 318
Texas, 24, 181, 234
Theater Guild, 199
Theatre de Champs-Élysées, Paris, 101
Thessalonika, Greece, 146
Thibault, Gilles, 18
Thicke, David, 8
Thielmans, Jean (Toots), xx, 41
This Was Burlesque, show, 17
Thomas Jefferson Chorus, 60
Thomas, Augusta Read, 154, 338
Thomaskirche, Leipzig, 310
Thompson, Bill, 18
Thompson, Martin, 122-123
Thompson, Randall, 138
Thompson, Stanford, 351
Thomson, Virgil, 199
Three Tenors, 145, 293
"Thriller," song and video, 192, 268
Thyhsen, John, 60
Tibbs, Ernest, 349
Tibet, 146
Tibetan music, 178, 184
Tiger Bay, Cardiff, Wales, 22
Tilson Thomas, Michael, 103-104;
  From the Diary of Anne Frank, 104
Timbuktu, show, 169
Time for Three, 76, 302-303
Tin Pan Alley, 156
Tiomkin, Dimitri, 229
Tircuit, Hewell, 33; *Percussion Concerto*, 33
Titanic, film, 184
To Kill A Mockingbird, film, 192
Toch, Ernst, 48
Todd, Michael, 149
Tokyo, Japan, 273
Tomato, record label, 100
Tomorrowland, film, 348
Tonight Show, The, 18, 80, 104, 162, 349
Tony award, 312
Too Late Blues, film, 277
Torme, Mel, 26, 44-46,
Toronto, Canada, 19, 58, 311
Torroba, Federico Moreno, 81
Toscanini, Arturo, 12, 101, 110, 123, 127, 185, 308310, 344
Toto, band, 349
Towarnicky, Carol, 73-74
Tower Records, 47, 289
Tower Theater, Philadelphia, 29

Town Hall, New York, 126
Townsend Opera, 194
Toy Story, film, 184
Trading Places, film, 192
Trafalgar Square, London, 132
Tramp Abroad, A, book, 138
"Trampin'," spiritual, 126
Travolta, John, 21
Treaty Elm, 69
Trenney, Tom, 291-292
Trenton, NJ, 149, 194
Tribute to a Bad Man, 190
Trinity College, UK, 161
Trivial Pursuit, 39
Troc (Trocadero) Theater, 17, 132
Tron (film), 180
Troyanos, Tatiana, 103
Truffaut, Francois, 189
Truman, Harry, 96
Truman, Margaret, 96
Tucker, Deanne, 347
Turkey, 146, 307
Turin Conservatory, 110
Turina, Joaquin, 81
Turner, Tina, 268
Twain, Mark, 138, 314
"Twinkle, Twinkle, Little Star," 328
Two Hands, CD and documentary, 294
Tyler School of Art, Temple University, 342
U. S. District Court, Philadelphia, 147
U. S. Marine Band, 332
Uchida, Mitsuko, 174
Ugly Betty, TV show, 261
Ukraine, 357
Ulster Orchestra, 289
Ulysses, book, 170
"Unchained Melody," song, 109
Uncle Vanya, play, 168
"Underdog Rag," song, 183
Underground Railroad, 347
UNICEF, 104, 158, 321
Union Baptist Church, Philadelphia, 126, 332, 333
Union League, 333
United Negro College Fund, 252
Universal Studios, 17, 181, 186, 193, 347-349
University City, Philadelphia, 202
University of California, Los Angeles, 315
University of California, San Diego, 99
University of Chicago, 203
University of Illinois, 99
University of Kentucky, 304
University of Michigan, 269
University of Pennsylvania, 163, 187, 202, 317

University of Southern California (USC), 192
University of Southern California School of Public Administration, 192
University of the Arts, Philadelphia, 99, 103, 316
Unsworth, Adam, 269
USS Arizona Memorial, 107
Uzan, Bernard, 134-135
Valencia, Spain, 251
Valente, Benita, 13, 88, 103, 167
Vallee, Rudy, 44
Valley Forge Music Fair, 16, 81
Valley Forge, PA, 121, 153
Vancouver, Canada, 149
Vandenberg Air Force Base, CA, 153
Vanishing Peoples of the Earth, band, 243
Vanya on 42nd Street, film, 168
Variety, 63, 128
Vaughan Williams, Ralph, 18; *Serenade to Music*, 102; *Tuba Concerto*, 151; *Two-Piano Concerto*, 320-321
Vaughan, Sarah, 15, 48
Velvet Fog, The, 44
Veney, Ruby, 29
Venezuela, 351
Vengerova, Isabel, 333
Venice, Italy, 151, 182, 218
Venuti, Joe, 47
Verdi, Giuseppe, 25, 78, 101, 107, 139, 148, 203, 218, 296, 307-09, 359; *Aida*, 78, 107; *Un Ballo in maschere*, 127, 261, 333; *Don Carlo*, 130, 309, 351, 358-359; *Falstaff*, 78, 101, 203, 307-309, 341; *La Forza del Destino*, 78; *Un Giorno di Regno*, 78; *Luisa Miller*, 103; *Otello*, 101, 149; *Requiem*, 310, 345; *Rigoletto*, 172, 197; *La Traviata*, 217-218, 238; *Il Trovatore*, 78, 233, 341
Verdi arias: "Celeste Aida," 25; "La donna è mobile," 132.
Verizon Hall, Kimmel Center, 195, 220, 222, 320
Vermont, 103, 105, 174, 280, 298
Vernick, restaurant, 359
Verona, Italy, 149, 165, 211
VerPlanck, Marlene, 26
Verzatt, Marc, 147-148
Veterans Stadium, Philadelphia, 77, 82
Vetrone, Bob, 7-8, 82
Vetrone, Boop, 8
Victor Café, Philadelphia, 282
Vienna, Austria, 27, 51, 91, 100, 110, 149, 152, 164, 169, 180, 211, 211, 218, 229, 238
Vienna Philharmonic, 48, 218, 219-220, 293
Vienna State Opera, 121, 147, 218, 233, 317
Vienna Woods, 91
Viennese School, 90, 193
Viennese waltz, 48, 152, 170, 174
Vietnam, 3, 24
Villa-Lobos, Heitor, 37, 81, 100; *Etudes*, 38; *Harmonica Concerto*, 37; *Preludes*, 38
Viola, Al, 155
Virginia, 126,
Virginia Symphony, 235, 288, 289, 336
Virginian, The, TV show, 44
Vision, album, 145-147
Vivaldi, Antonio, 123; *Four Seasons, The*, 298; *Two-Violin Concerto*, 133
Vogt, Lars, 219
Voice of the Flyers, 149
Volmoller, Karl, 111
Von Bingen, Hildegard, 145-147
Von Bulow, Hans, 138
Von Maltzahn, Nina Baroness, 364
Voyage Into Space, concert, 213
Wagner, Richard, 89, 96, 138, 148, 173, 193, 208, 310, 319, 359; *Die Flegende Hollander*, 358-359; *Die Gotterdamerung*, 28; *Die Meistersinger*, 199, 317; *Parsifal*, 138; *Das Rheingold*, 319; *Ring* cycle, 18, 50, 149, 221, 246, 251, 293, 319
Wagon Train, TV show, 189
Wales, 22, 161
Walk of Fame, 125
Walk on the Wild Side, film, 192
Walker, Kay *see* Kay Walker Castaldo
Walker, Nancy, 10
Wall of Fame, Academy of Music basement, 62
Waller, Fats, 1
Walnut Street, Philadelphia, 203, 359
Walnut Street Theater, Philadelphia, 11, 55, 71, 89, 134, 222
Walsh, Hugh, 57, 58, 60, 62
Walter, Bruno, 186
Walton family, 60
Walton, William, *Façade*, 9
"Waltz for Debby," song, 181
Wanamaker Organ, 191, 277, 352, 353, 354
Wanamaker's department store, Philadelphia, 332
Wang, Yuja, 159, 329-330
Ward, Robert, *The Crucible*, 132
Warfield, William, 200
Warner Bros., 5
Warner Studio, 347

Warwick Hotel, Philadelphia, 150, 162
Warwick, Dionne, 15
Washington Choral Arts Society, 340
Washington Opera, 234
Washington Post, 96
Washington, DC, 126, 190, 199, 222, 329, 331, 332, 334
Watkins Glen racetrack, 2
Watts, André, 36, 148, 202, 287, 294, 327-328
Wavendon Allmusic Plan, 31
Waverly Street, Philadelphia, xx,
Waxman, Franz, 92, 194, 229
Waxman, John, 92
Wayne, John, 24
Weasels Ripped My Flesh, album, 28
Webern, Anton, 114, 140
Webster Street, Philadelphia, 126, 332, 334
Webster, Ben, 21
Webster, Daniel, 19, 63
Webster, Nathaniel, 340
Weeks, Willie, 179
Weill, Kurt, 138, 260; *Das Kleine Mahagonny*, 15
Wein, George, xx
Weiner, Ed, 8
Weiss, Carl, 301
Welch, Raquel, 16
Welcome Back, Kotter, TV show, 21
Welcome Park, Philadelphia, 55, 134
Welk, Lawrence, 179
Wellesley College, 203
Wellman, William, 346
Wells, Robert, 45
Westchester, NY, 22
West Palm Beach, FL, 350
West Philadelphia High School, 354
West Philadelphia, xx, 25, 29, 46, 47, 116, 148, 195, 274, 351
West Side Story recording, 311
West Side Story, show, 11
West, Benjamin, 53, 69
Westerns, 24-25, 185, 190, 192, 231
Wharton Business School, 203
What a Way to Go, film, 11, 23
"What's Love Got To Do With It," song, 268
Wheeldon, Christopher, 311-312
"White Christmas," song, 45
White, E. B., 239
White Elephant, band, 147
White House, 104, 125, 138, 332
White, Gary, 314, 351, 363
Whiteman, Paul, 47
Whitman, Walt, 137
Who, band, 59

Who's Afraid of Virginia Woolf, play and film, 108
"Whole Lotta Shakin' Goin' On," song, 30
WHYY, 214, 215
Wilbur, Roy, 133-134
Wild Harmonies, book, 274
Wild Times, TV film, 24
Wild, Earl, 202
Wilder, Alec, 5, 8, 9, 46; *Sextet for Marimba and Woodwind Quartet*, 26; *Suite for* Horn and String Quartet, 26; Woodwind Quartet No. 13, 26; *Woodwind Quintets*, 8
Wilder, Joe, 26
William Penn, 53, 54, 163, 345
William Penn High School, 332
William Penn Opera Committee, 55
William Penn, opera, xxi, 53, 55-71, 78, 88, 133, 134, 167, 208, 245, 254, 281-282, 289, 315
Williams, Beverly, 31
Williams, Don, 185
Williams, John (guitarist), 31
Williams, John, *On Willows and Birches*, 105; 105, 178, 181, 183-184, 185, 193, 229-231
Williams, John, Sr., 231
Williams, Ted, 83, 213, 309
Williams, Vanessa, 261
Williamsburg, VA, 288
Wills, Maury, 84
Wilma Theater, 222
Wilson, August, 298
Wilson, Colin, 138
Wilson, Gahan, 94-95; *Gahan Wilson's America*, 94
Wilson, Jackie, 16, 79
Wilson, Teddy, 45
Wimberly, Bridgette A., 362
Winfrey, Oprah, 198, 321, 333
Wings, film, 125
Winnipeg, Canada, 149
Wise, Robert, 180
Wister Quartet, 164, 205,
Wister, Mrs. Ethel ("Peppi"), 63, 69
Wolf Conservatory, 274
Wolf, Ted, 301
Wolfman, The, film, 193
Wonder, Stevie, 268
Wonderful Inventions, book, 190
Wonderful World of Percussion—My Life Behind Bars, book, xx, 10, 177
Wonderful World of Percussion, CD, 183
Wood, Greg, 263
Woodhams, Richard, 286
Woodley, Arthur, 200
Woods, Phil, 26, 215

World Cup, 309
WRTI-FM, 71, 223, 280, 314, 344
Wynnefield Avenue, Philadelphia, 148, 191
Wynnefield, Philadelphia, 89
Wynnewood, PA, 146
Yale University, 122
Yannopoulous, Dino, 55, 57-59, 61, 71
Yeaworth, Irwin, 87
Yepes, Narciso, 38
Yiddish theatre, 199
"You've Changed," song, 236
Young, Thomas, 318
Young, Tracy Galligher, 317, 364
Youngman, Henny, 36
"Your Molecular Structure," song, 36
YouTube, 117, 181, 320, 327
Zappa, Ahmet, 28
Zappa, Diva Muffin, 28
Zappa, Dweezil, 28
Zappa, Frank, 28-29, 104
Zappa, Moon Unit, 28
Zavislan, Tamara, 115
Zeffirelli, Franco, 165, 210
Zemlinsky, Alexander, *The Mermaid*, 247
Zimbalist, Efrem, 270
Zimbalist, Mary Louise Curtis Bok, 159
Ziporyn, Evan, 305-306; *Concerto for Gamelan and Strings*, 305
Zulian, Renzo, 253
Zurich, Switzerland, 329

ABOUT THE AUTHOR

Tom Di Nardo is a Philadelphia journalist who has written on the performing arts for the *Philadelphia Evening Bulletin* and, since 1982, for the *Philadelphia Daily News*. He has also written articles on classical music, opera, ballet, dance and jazz for many local and national publications.

His other recent books are *Listening to Musicians: Forty Years of the Philadelphia Orchestra* and *Wonderful World of Percussion: My Life Behind Bars*, the biography of legendary Hollywood percussionist Emil Richards.